T0360404

Evolving Patterns in
Global Trade and Finance

World Scientific Studies in International Economics
(ISSN: 1793-3641)

Series Editor   Robert M. Stern, *University of Michigan and University of California-Berkeley, USA*

Editorial Board   Vinod K. Aggarwal, *University of California-Berkeley, USA*
Alan Deardorff, *University of Michigan, USA*
Paul De Grauwe, *London School of Economics, UK*
Barry Eichengreen, *University of California-Berkeley, USA*
Mitsuhiro Fukao, *Keio University, Tokyo, Japan*
Robert L. Howse, *New York University, USA*
Keith E. Maskus, *University of Colorado, USA*
Arvind Panagariya, *Columbia University, USA*

Vol. 31   Exchange Rates and Global Financial Policies
by Paul De Grauwe (London School of Economics, UK)

Vol. 32   Asian Free Trade Agreements and WTO Compatibility:
Goods, Services, Trade Facilitation and Economic Cooperation
by Shintaro Hamanaka (Asian Development Bank, Philippines)

Vol. 33   Economics and Politics of Trade Policy
by Douglas R Nelson (Tulane University, USA)

Vol. 34   Applied Trade Policy Modeling in 16 Countries: Insights and Impacts
from World Bank CGE Based Projects
by David G Tarr (Consultant and Former Lead Economist, The World Bank, USA)

Vol. 35   The Floating World: Issues in International Trade Theory
by Wilfred J Ethier (University of Pennsylvania, USA)

Vol. 36   Trade Policy in Asia: Higher Education and Media Services
*edited by Christopher Findlay (University of Adelaide, Australia),
Hildegunn Kyvik Nordas (Organisation for Economic Co-operation and
Development, France) & Gloria Pasadilla (APEC Secretariat, Singapore)*

Vol. 37   The Path of World Trade Law in the 21st Century
by Steve Charnovitz (The George Washington University, USA)

Vol. 38   International Trade, Distribution and Development: Empirical Studies of
Trade Policies
by Paul Brenton (The World Bank, USA)

Vol. 39   Evolving Patterns in Global Trade and Finance
by Sven W Arndt (Claremont McKenna College, USA)

The complete list of the published volumes in the series can be found at
http://www.worldscientific.com/series/wssie

39 World Scientific
Studies in
International
Economics

Evolving Patterns in
Global Trade and Finance

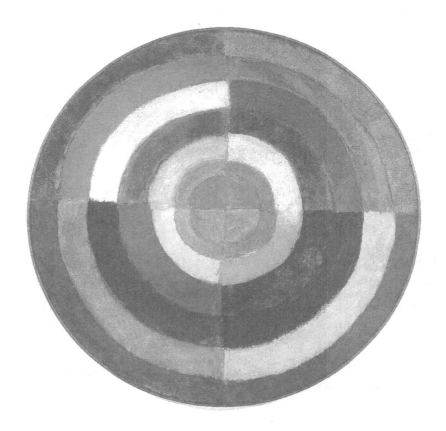

Sven W. Arndt
Claremont McKenna College, USA

 **World Scientific**

NEW JERSEY · LONDON · SINGAPORE · BEIJING · SHANGHAI · HONG KONG · TAIPEI · CHENNAI

Published by

World Scientific Publishing Co. Pte. Ltd.

5 Toh Tuck Link, Singapore 596224

USA office: 27 Warren Street, Suite 401-402, Hackensack, NJ 07601

UK office: 57 Shelton Street, Covent Garden, London WC2H 9HE

Library of Congress Cataloging-in-Publication Data
Arndt, Sven W.
    Evolving patterns in global trade and finance / Sven W. Arndt (Claremont McKenna College, USA).
        pages cm. -- (World scientific studies in international economics ; 39)
        ISBN 978-9814603409 (hardcover : alk. paper)
    1. International trade. 2. International finance. 3. International economic relations. I. Title.
HF1379.A786 2014
    382--dc23

                                        2014010696

British Library Cataloguing-in-Publication Data
A catalogue record for this book is available from the British Library.

Cover image credit: Robert Delaunay, "Premier Disque" (1913). Uploaded by Coldcreation to
Wikipedia (http://en.wikipedia.org/wiki/User:Coldcreation).

Copyright © 2015 by World Scientific Publishing Co. Pte. Ltd.

*All rights reserved. This book, or parts thereof, may not be reproduced in any form or by any means,
electronic or mechanical, including photocopying, recording or any information storage and retrieval
system now known or to be invented, without written permission from the publisher.*

For photocopying of material in this volume, please pay a copying fee through the Copyright Clearance
Center, Inc., 222 Rosewood Drive, Danvers, MA 01923, USA. In this case permission to photocopy
is not required from the publisher.

In-house Editor: Chye Shu Wen

Typeset by Stallion Press
Email: enquiries@stallionpress.com

Printed in Singapore

About the Author

Sven W. Arndt (Ph.D., University of California, Berkeley) is the Charles M. Stone Professor of Money, Credit, and Trade at Claremont McKenna College (CMC). He has also taught regular courses at Claremont Graduate University. He served as Director of the Lowe Institute of Political Economy at CMC. He has held positions on the faculties of the University of California in Los Angeles and Santa Cruz and as visiting professor at Stanford University; the Bologna Center of the Johns Hopkins School for Advanced International Studies; the Institute for Advanced Studies in Vienna; the Universities of Mannheim and Konstanz in Germany; and the Chinese University of Hong Kong.

He has served as Director of the Office of International Monetary Research, U.S. Department of the Treasury; visiting scholar, Board of Governors of the Federal Reserve System; trade project director at the American Enterprise Institute; and research scholar with the U.S.-ASEAN Trade Initiative.

He has served as President of the North American Economics and Finance Association and of the International Trade & Finance Association, and as Managing Editor of the *North American Journal of Economics and Finance*. He is a Distinguished Fellow of the International Banking, Economics and Finance Association.

He has authored and co-edited several books, including *The Political Economy of* Austria; *Fragmentation: New Production Patterns in the World Economy*; and *Real-Financial Linkages Among Open Economies*. He has published articles in a variety of professional journals, including the *American Economic Review*, *Econometrica*, the *Economic Journal*, the *Journal of Political Economy*, the *Journal of Economic Asymmetries*, and the *North American Journal of Economics and Finance*.

His current research interests include cross-border production networks and trade patterns; exchange-rate regimes; and global imbalances and financial instability.

Table of Contents

About the Author   v

Preface   xi

Acknowledgments   xiii

Introduction and Overview   1

Part I: Beyond the Standard Trade Model   13

1. Free Trade and Its Alternatives   15
   The Oxford Handbook on International Commercial Policy

2. On Discriminatory vs. Non-Preferential Tariff Policies   49
   The Economic Journal

3. Customs Union and the Theory of Tariffs   59
   The American Economic Review

4. Domestic Distortions and Trade Policy   71
   Oxford Economic Papers

Part II: Fragmentation and Cross-Border
   Production Networks   81

5. Fragmentation   83
   The Princeton Encyclopedia of the World Economy

6. Super-Specialization and the Gains from Trade 91
   Contemporary Economic Policy

7. Global Production Networks and Regional Integration 97
   Empirical Methods in International Trade: Essays in Honor
   of Mordechai Kreinin

8. Production Networks in an Economically Integrated Region 111
   ASEAN Economic Bulletin

9. Trade Diversion and Production Sharing 123
   The Journal of Economic Asymmetries

10. Production Networks, Exchange Rates and Macroeconomic
    Stability 137
    The Global Economics of a Changing Environment

11. Trade, Production Networks and the Exchange Rate 149
    The Journal of Economic Asymmetries

12. Intra-industry Trade and the Open Economy 179
    Korea and the World Economy

13. Fragmentation, Imperfect Competition and Heterogeneous Firms 197

Part III: Macro Policy Challenges in Open Economies 205

14. Policy Choices in an Open Economy: Some
    Dynamic Considerations 207
    Journal of Political Economy

15. Joint Balance: Capital Mobility and the Monetary System
    of a Currency Area 227
    The Economics of Common Currencies

16. International Short Term Capital Movements: A Distributed
    Lag Model of Speculation in Foreign Exchange 241
    Econometrica

17. Regional Currency Arrangements in North America 253
   Bank of Greece, Economic Research Department — Special Studies Division, Working Paper No. 40

18. Adjustment in an Open Economy with Two Exchange-Rate Regimes 275
   The Journal of Economic Asymmetries

19. Stabilization Policy in an Economy with Two Exchange Rate Regimes 287
   Global Economy Journal

20. Policy Challenges in a Dual Exchange Rate Regime 301
   Korea and the World Economy

21. The "Great Moderation" in a Dual Exchange Rate Regime 317
   Global Economy Journal

Index 329

Preface

This volume is part of a World Scientific series in International Economics, edited by eminent scholar, teacher and policy advisor Robert M. Stern of the University of Michigan. The studies in this series include works on the theory, empirical investigation and evaluation of international economic policies and institutions. In addition to trade issues, topics cover international macro, money and finance, as well as international legal and political economy. Monographs and edited volumes make up the core of the series.

The focus of the present volume is on the meaning and implications of evolving and emerging patterns in international trade and finance. The included papers explore major topics, such as preferential economic and monetary integration, cross-border production fragmentation and vertical intra-industry trade, and macroeconomic adjustment in economies with orthodox and hybrid exchange-rate regimes. In the realm of preference areas, evolution has taken the form of both "deepening" and enlargement. The resulting increase in complexity raises new challenges at both structural and policy levels. Cross-border fragmentation of production is a relatively new, but rapidly growing phenomenon. The papers on fragmentation develop the essential theoretical foundations for assessing the implications of what is popularly known as "off-shoring" and they do so at the level of both industries and heterogeneous firms. In the macro domain, policy opportunities and conflicts at national, regional and global levels are examined. In the U.S., for example, the mixed nature of its current exchange rate regime undermines the country's policy autonomy and helps create conditions for global financial instability.

An important objective throughout this volume is to ascertain how well economic theorists and policy makers are dealing, or have dealt, with these challenges.

Acknowledgments

I am greatly indebted to Bob Stern for conceiving this project and for his guidance and encouragement and to Zvi G. Ruder, Senior Executive Publisher, for his generous support. At World Scientific, Agnes Ng provided important editorial guidance at the beginning, while Shu-Wen Chye has been a patient and extraordinarily helpful editor for most of the project. Special thanks must also be conveyed to Jimmy Low, the artist who designed the modernist and minimalist cover for this book. At the Claremont Colleges Libraries, Allegra Swift, Sue Hwang and Luis Arias of the Record Center have provided valuable assistance in accessing papers and obtaining permission to reprint them. At Claremont McKenna College (CMC), thanks go to the Financial Economics Institute for research support, to Terri van Eaton for administrative assistance, and to Soyeon (Nikki) Yea and Yijing (Artemis) Shen for research assistance.

Beyond those who were directly involved in the project, many individuals have over the years provided inspiration and encouragement for the research that led to the papers included in this volume. I appreciate the support of key mentors Harry Johnson and Bob Mundell, and of long-time colleagues Max Corden, Alan Deardorff, Ron Jones, Anne Krueger, Tom Willett, Mike Plummer and Hans-Juergen Vosgerau.

A number of institutions and organizations have provided valuable experiences on the practical, non-academic side of trade policy and related issues. My stint as Director of the Office of International Monetary Research at the U.S. Department of the Treasury and my participation in the trade policy research project at the American Enterprise Institute were particularly rewarding. Among its many initiatives, the Institute organized an annual World Forum in Beaver Creek, Colorado, hosted by former President Gerald Ford and attended by ex-leaders such as Valery Giscard-D'Estaing, Helmut Schmidt, James Callahan and Malcolm Fraser, as well as policy makers and advisors like Alan Greenspan, Henry Kissinger and Paul Volcker, together with approximately 50 CEOs from major U.S. and foreign corporations. For those events, which predate the annual World Economic Forum in Davos, I had the privilege of preparing trade policy briefing papers for the participants and in the process learned much about the interests and motivations of politicians and business leaders. Their perspectives often contrasted sharply with those of the Nobel Laureates and other leading economists who, for over three decades, attended the Claremont-Bologna Monetary Conferences. Among them were Paul Samuelson, Robert Solow, James Tobin, Franco Modigliani, James Meade, Roy Harrod, Milton Friedman, Robert Mundell, Lionel Robbins, Richard Cooper, Max Corden, Jeffrey Frankel and Ronald McKinnon.

I came to CMC in 1990, where I had the good fortune of directing the Lowe Institute of Political Economy for a decade and a half and where the fragmentation research project was conceived and where most of the papers in Part II were written. I benefitted greatly during those years from working with an excellent staff led by Terri van Eaton and Kelly Spetnagel and senior research assistants Disha Zaidi and Maria Tzintzarova. My long-time colleague in the Institute, Senior Economist Alex Huemer, made important contributions toward training student researchers in statistical methods, large-scale data management and econometric analysis. He played a key and indispensable role in the production of the Claremont Policy Briefs, which were published jointly with Thomas Willett's Claremont Institute for Economic Policy Studies. Last, but not least, Alex was my co-author and strong contributor in the preparation of the paper that is reprinted in Chapter 11. The quality of the econometrics in that paper is a testament to his skills.

Of course, the most important debt of gratitude goes to individuals who made no direct contribution to the project, but without whose support and encourage-ment — exemplified by patience, tolerance, and a stoic resignation to the foibles of fate — this flight of fancy would not have left the ground: my wife Linda, my daughter Nicole and my precocious grandchildren Will, Paige and Justine.

Finally and more formally, I wish to express my appreciation to the many copyright holders who have graciously granted permission to reprint the papers in this volume. They are listed in order of the chapters in which the papers appear.

Chapter 1: "Free Trade and Its Alternatives" in M.E. Kreinin and M.G. Plummer (eds.), *The Oxford Handbook on International Commercial Policy* (Oxford: Oxford University Press, 2012). Reprinted with permission of Oxford University Press.

Chapter 2: "On Discriminatory vs. Non-Preferential Tariff Policies," *The Economic Journal*, Vol. 78, No. 312 (December 1968). Reprinted with permission of John Wiley and Sons.

Chapter 3: "Customs Union and the Theory of Tariffs," *The American Economic Review*, Vol. 59, No. 1 (March 1969). Reprinted with permission of the American Economic Association.

Chapter 4: "Domestic Distortions and Trade Policy," *Oxford Economic Papers*, Vol. 23, No. 1 (March 1971). Reprinted with permission of Oxford University Press.

Chapter 5: "Fragmentation," in *The Princeton Encyclopedia of the World Economy*, edited by K.A. Reinert and R.S. Rajan (Princeton University Press, 2009). Reprinted with permission of Princeton University Press.

Chapter 6: "Super-Specialization and the Gains from Trade," *Contemporary Economic Policy*, Vol. 16, No. 4 (October 1998). Reprinted with permission of John Wiley and Sons.

Chapter 7: "Global production networks and regional integration" in M. G. Plummer (ed.), *Empirical Methods in International Trade: Essays in Honor of Mordechai Kreinin* (Northampton, MA: Edward Elgar Publishing Ltd, 2004). Reprinted with permission of Edward Elgar Publishing Ltd.

Chapter 8: "Production Networks in an Economically Integrated Region," *ASEAN Economic Bulletin*, Vol. 18, No. 1 (April 2001), pp. 24–34. Reproduced here with the kind permission of the publisher, Institute of Southeast Asian Studies, Singapore <http://bookshop.iseas.edu.sg>

Chapter 9: "Trade Diversion and Production Sharing," *The Journal of Economic Asymmetries*, Vol. 1, No. 1 (May 2004). Reprinted with permission of Athenian Forum Press.

Chapter 10: "Production Networks, Exchange Rates, and Macroeconomic Stability" in J. A. Brox and N. C. Balthas (eds.), *The Global Economics of a Changing Environment* (Waterloo, Canada: North Waterloo Academic Press, 2009). Reprinted with permission of J.A. Brox and N.C. Balthas.

Chapter 11: "Trade, Production Networks and the Exchange Rate," *The Journal of Economic Asymmetries*, Vol. 4, No. 1 (with A. Huemer, June 2007). Reprinted with permission of Athenian Forum Press.

Chapter 12: "Intra-industry Trade and the Open Economy," *Korea and the World Economy*, Vol. 11, No. 3 (December 2010). Reprinted with permission of the Association of Korean Economic Studies.

Chapter 14: "Policy Choices in an Open Economy: Some Dynamic Considerations," *Journal of Political Economy*, Vol. 81, No. 4 (July–August, 1973). Reprinted with permission of University of Chicago Press.

Chapter 15: "Joint Balance: Capital Mobility and the Monetary System of a Currency Area" in H.G. Johnson and A.K. Swoboda (eds.), *The Economics of Common Currencies* (London: George Allen and Unwin, 1973). Reissued by Routledge (New York, NY, 2013). Reprinted with permission of Taylor and Francis Group.

Chapter 16: "International Short-Term Capital Movements: A Distributed Lag Model of Speculation in Foreign Exchange," *Econometrica*, Vol. 36, No. 1 (January 1968). Reprinted with permission of the Econometric Society.

Chapter 17: "Regional Currency Arrangements in North America," (Bank of Greece, Economic Research Department — Special Studies Division, Working Paper No. 40 (May 2006). Reprinted with permission of the Bank of Greece.

Chapter 18: "Adjustment in an Open Economy with Two Exchange-Rate Regimes," *The Journal of Economic Asymmetries*, Vol. 8, No.2 (December 2011). Reprinted with permission of Athenian Forum Press.

Chapter 19: "Stabilization Policy in an Economy with Two Exchange Rate Regimes," *Global Economy Journal*, Vol. 12, No. 2 (June 2012). Reprinted with permission of de Gruyter. (Original version available at www.reference-global.com.)

Chapter 20: "Policy Challenges in a Dual Exchange Rate Regime," *Korea and the World Economy*, Vol. 13, No. 2 (August 2012). Reprinted with permission of the Association of Korean Economic Studies.

Chapter 21: "The 'Great Moderation' in a Dual Exchange Rate Regime," *Global Economy Journal*, Vol. 12, No. 4 (November 2012). Reprinted with permission of de Gruyter. (Original version available at www.reference-global.com.)

Introduction and Overview

There have been far-reaching changes in international trade and finance during the past half-century. Not only has the share of trade in the GDP of most countries expanded with the reduction of tariffs, transportation costs, and assorted other barriers, but significant innovations in communications technologies have facilitated the growth of economic and financial linkages among countries. These developments have also opened the door to cross-border production sharing and global production networks. Changes of such magnitude and import inevitably raise challenges not only for policy makers, but for economic theorists and model builders. The papers assembled in this volume explore the implications of these changes and assess the quality of the policy response.

Traditionally, international trade has been viewed as occurring among dissimilar economies and as being largely *inter-industry* in nature. The first decades after World War II (WWII), however, saw increasingly rapid growth in *horizontal intra-industry* trade, particularly among the advanced countries of the Atlantic region. Inter-industry trade takes place among dissimilar economies, with different factor endowments and technological know-how, so that countries' exports and imports tend to come from different industries. In contrast, horizontal intra-industry trade occurs among similar economies and is characterized by exports and imports of end products belonging to the same industry, but containing different varieties of a product. In more recent times, *vertical intra-industry* trade between advanced and emerging economies has captured an increasing share of the trade of many nations. This type of trade, characterized by imports (exports) of components and exports (imports) of final products belonging to the same industry has gone hand-in-hand with the growth of cross-border production networks.

The emergence of cross-border production sharing is in itself an important example of the evolving nature of international specialization and trade. At the end of WWII, goods trade was dominated by end products, which could readily be described as "Made in Country X or Y." Manufacturing companies produced

1

their goods from start to finish in domestic facilities, sold most of them in the home market, and exported the rest. This pattern began to change with the arrival in Europe of regional preference areas — the European Economic Community (EEC) and the European Free Trade Area (EFTA). As American exporters lost competitiveness, they responded with "tariff jumping" direct investment to establish production facilities in Europe. In the new environment, U.S. exports fell, but U.S. foreign sales and revenues rose. The era of the multinational enterprise (MNE) had begun.

When trade and finance undergo major transformations, important challenges arise for economic theorists and policy makers alike. In the case of trade in goods and services, the emergence of horizontal intra-industry trade made it clear that the traditional inter-industry analytical framework and its modern representation in the Ricardo model and in the Heckscher–Ohlin factor-proportions framework might soon lose relevance. In addition, assumptions that all goods were tradable and homogeneous, that competition was perfect, and that markets were efficient and undistorted, reinforced questions about the suitability of these approaches.

Concerns like these spurred the development of the so-called "new" trade theories of the 1970s and 1980s, where trade is assumed to take place among similar economies and where imperfect competition, scale economies and product differentiation are the rule. In more recent times, however, the H-O factor-proportions model has enjoyed a resurgence of relevance with the rapid growth of vertical intra-industry trade, in which dissimilarities rooted in factor endowments and factor intensities, as well as technical know-how, give rise to specialization at the "intra-product" level where trade in components and intermediate products is an important element in total trade.

The two approaches together provided economists with a much richer tool set for analyzing the trade patterns they were observing in the real world. Vertical intra-industry specialization and trade work particularly well between advanced and emerging economies, that is, between dissimilar economies. As a number of papers in Part II show, the factor proportions model provides critical insights into the nature and welfare effects of cross-border production sharing. While that is a significant contribution in its own right, it leaves untouched the aforementioned assumptions of homogeneous products, perfect competition and constant returns to scale, which clearly do not fit the realities of the modern world. A feature of this new reality, which has attracted the attention of theorists, is the prevalence of heterogeneous responses to trade opportunities among the firms in a given industry.

As Chapter 13 shows, elements of the "new" trade theories and of the factor-proportions model may be combined to explain variations in the approach among heterogeneous firms to cross-border production sharing. The new theories provide the basic structure of imperfect competition, scale economies and product differentiation, while the notion of factor endowment dissimilarities is reinterpreted as differences in firm characteristics. Within this framework, the principles explaining industry behavior in the Heckscher–Ohlin context of industries or countries can be shown to explain the behavior of modern heterogeneous multinational firms as well.

At the macro level, the changes have been no less dramatic. In the first two decades after WWII, the Bretton Woods adjustable-peg exchange-rate regime was the rule. In the aftermath of the collapse of that system in the early 1970s, there has been no such uniformity of purpose. After a period of floating rates in the 1970s, Western European nations joined in the European Monetary System, which was largely modeled on Bretton Woods. Early this century, a subset of those nations began operating the European Monetary Union (EMU) with the euro as its common currency. Within a decade of its inception, that system fell into turmoil facilitated by the global financial crisis and abetted by a variety of ill-advised macroeconomic policies.

Over the decades, these fluctuations in global exchange-rate arrangements were accompanied by an ongoing debate over the relative merits of fixed and floating rates. A key element in these discussions concerned the effectiveness of macroeconomic stabilization policies. The papers in Part III consider various aspects of this issue from national, regional and global perspectives. Of particular interest in this context, are the implications for the United States of its hybrid or mixed exchange-rate regime in which the dollar floats against the euro and most other currencies, while being fixed to the yuan by unilateral intervention of the Chinese authorities. This arrangement is shown to have serious consequences for U.S. economic stability and policy autonomy and for global economic and financial stability.

Part I: Trade Policy in a Changing Economic Environment

Chapter 1 provides a systematic and comprehensive review of the adjustments that have taken place in theoretical modeling as observed patterns of trade have evolved. The discussion is organized in terms of the relative merits of three trade regimes — free trade, non-discriminatory protectionism, and preferential trade agreements. The analysis begins with a world that satisfies the relatively ideal conditions of the H-O model and then draws on insights from the "new" trade theories to consider the implications of barriers to competition that are "too big to ignore." Chapters 2 and 3 explore issues which often receive limited treatment in the standard literature on preferential trade liberalization, including the effects of country size and of the number of countries entering as well as remaining outside the agreement. It is shown that raising the complexity of the arrangement brings terms-of-trade effects to the fore; it increases the policy options but also the likelihood of policy conflicts and beggar-thy-neighbor practices.

Chapter 4 focuses on the welfare effects of domestic distortions in a country with three sectors, one of which produces non-tradables. Although the assumption that all goods produced in a country are tradable has an impressive history in the trade literature, in most countries significant numbers of industries produce non-tradable goods and services only and are thus protected ("sheltered") from foreign competition. The discussion and findings in this chapter, as well as in Part III, suggest that the consequences of developments in those sectors for the economy overall are also too important to ignore.[1]

Part II: Fragmentation and Cross-Border Production Networks

In the course of economic globalization, national goods, services, and financial markets have become increasingly interconnected and interdependent. Trade in goods and services has gradually taken an ever larger share of GDP and trade in financial instruments has captured a rising share of national financial transactions. In recent years, globalization has moved beyond trade toward greater integration of production, as production sharing and production networks have made rapid advances. Moreover, while cross-border "fragmentation" of production occurred initially mainly in the manufacturing sector, it has in recent years spread to trade in services as well.

The papers in Part II focus on various aspects of cross-border production integration. When production of a product or a service is spread across countries, with each taking responsibility for the component or production phase in which it has comparative advantage, specialization and trade have moved from the intra-industry level to the intra-product level. As noted above, this type of trade and the foreign investment flows associated with it belong to the vertical intra-industry variety. In view of the importance of dissimilarities across countries, this pattern of trade and global production is highly amenable to analysis by means of the Ricardo model and especially the factor-proportions model.

Chapter 5 provides a succinct definition of fragmentation, reprinted from the Princeton Encyclopedia of the World Economy.[2] Following this introduction, Chapter 6 presents an initial general equilibrium assessment of the effects of fragmentation on employment, output, factor returns, and welfare in a country's import-competing sector. This is done for both large and small countries in the context of a free-trade regime. In this case, two countries with different factor endowments (or technologies in a Ricardian context) are both producing a certain product, but one of them is the exporter and the other the importer, implying incomplete specialization between them.

When production sharing is introduced, specialization is extended to the *intra*-product level, with each country outsourcing the component which is intensive in its scarce factor. Production sharing enables both countries to reduce costs, thereby improving competitiveness and the ability to raise output and employment in the industry. When the countries are small, these rearrangements of production have no effect on world prices. When they are large, the rise in their combined output causes world prices to fall, with positive welfare effects for the importer of the product and negative effects for the exporting partner.

In advanced, high-wage countries, workers typically worry that trade with low-wage countries will undermine competitiveness, reduce earnings and diminish living standards. The surprising finding is that workers' earnings rise not only in the outsourcing industry but, under conditions of reasonable degrees of inter-industry labor mobility, in other industries in the economy. Also counterintuitively, employment and output in the labor-intensive, outsourcing import industry rise. Yet, the intuition is simple and reflects what is known about the division of labor and the way factories, offices and sports teams may improve the quality of their performance by matching tasks with the talents and abilities of individuals.

In Chapter 7, the effects of production sharing in general equilibrium in a world of MFN protectionism are compared to its effects in the context of preferential trade liberalization (PTAs). In the former, production sharing may raise or lower welfare, depending on the relative magnitudes of the distortion created by the tariff and of the efficiency gain from fragmentation. At the root of the problem is the fact that both the tariff and fragmentation push specialization in the "wrong" direction.

In the context of PTAs, on the other hand, production sharing is capable of changing an arrangement that would by itself be trade-diverting into a trade-creating one. In other words, deeper integration via production sharing may convert an inadvisable preferential trade project into a feasible one. It is important to note again that fragmentation strengthens competitiveness in the industry in which it occurs, causing output and employment in that industry to rise. In the model at hand, it unequivocally raises national welfare under free trade and in free trade areas, but may raise or lower welfare in an MFN trade policy regime.

The discussion in Chapter 7 next employs a three-country partial equilibrium framework to show how two countries, both of whom have comparative disadvantage at the product level in relation to a third country, but have comparative advantage in different components and production stages, can convert a net trade-diverting PTA into a welfare-improving one by specializing in the components in which each possesses comparative advantage.[3] The chapter also looks at the implications of production sharing for the sensitivity of the trade balance to exchange-rate movements and finally it examines the effects of vertical intra-industry FDI flows associated with the implementation of production sharing.

Chapter 8 explores cross-border production sharing as the possible basis for policy cooperation in a system committed to "open regionalism." The Association of Southeast Asian Nations (ASEAN) countries have strong incentives to prefer this approach to regional trade liberalization in order to avoid overt discrimination against important extra-regional trading partners. Furthermore and in view of the importance to Asian nations generally of export-led growth, production sharing in the export sector is a major tool for export promotion. It is shown that production sharing in the export sector with partner countries can be welfare-enhancing even where a conventional free trade area would be welfare-reducing.

Further in this chapter, the discussion of fragmentation in the import sector compares the effects of a large tariff in place on a low world price with a small tariff on a higher world price, assuming that the two policies result in the same tariff-inclusive domestic price. Under these circumstances, introduction of production sharing raises welfare in the latter but not in the former. Although fragmentation raises efficiency in both cases, it also causes resources to be shifted into the uncompetitive sector, which is once again a shift of specialization in the "wrong" direction. In the small-tariff case, the benefits of fragmentation are able to more than offset the distortion due to the tariff; but the distortion introduced by the high tariff is too large a distortion to be offset by the gains from production sharing.

Chapter 9 employs a two-country general equilibrium model to consider the effects of rules of origin. Specifically, when two countries with offshore sourcing of components from third countries form a PTA and one of the countries enforces domestic-content restrictions, welfare is shown to decline in both. Earlier papers in this part have focused on production sharing in import as well as export sectors. This chapter also considers the implications for external trade when cross-border component sourcing occurs in a country's non-tradables sectors, as may be increasingly seen among service industries. An immediate consequence is a partial loss of protection from foreign influences and thus a partial loss of "shelter" from foreign competition. As before, however, foreign sourcing lowers costs and raises output.

Although the main focus of the papers in this part is on the microeconomics of fragmentation and production sharing, the phenomenon is not without consequences of a more macroeconomic character. Chapter 10 introduces production sharing into a standard open-economy macro model. A key feature of this extension is that exports now appear as arguments in the import-demand function and imports appear in the export function. This creates a direct link between exports and imports, in addition to the indirect linkages in the standard model through changes in domestic production. Further, domestic and foreign GDP now appear together on both sides of the trade balance equation. An important objective of the chapter is to determine the extent to which fragmentation alters the sensitivity of the trade balance to variations in exchange rates.

Moreover, a rise of the share of network trade in a country's total trade alters the economy's responses to domestic macro policies and to foreign shocks and disturbances. Furthermore, network trade has the same effect on the slope of the balance-of-payments (BOP) function as capital mobility and thus generates the same changes in policy effectiveness as changes in capital mobility. It is important to note, however, that these consequences apply to the non-network parts of the economy. At the same time the impacts of both monetary and fiscal policies on the network-linked sectors of the economy are weakened.

Chapter 11 explores empirically some of the issues raised in the previous chapter. The focus is on bilateral trade between the United States and Mexico, where network trade is particularly important in passenger vehicle manufacturing and in sectors like textiles and apparel, electronics and processed foods. The main concern of the paper is the effect of network trade on the sensitivity of the trade balance to movements in the dollar/peso exchange rate. This concern extends to the sensitivity of the trade balance to relative inflation and the real bilateral exchange rate and finally to the sensitivity of the trade balance to movements in bilateral GDPs. In all cases, the sensitivity of the trade balance to movements in the exchange rate declines and the magnitude of this change is found to be significant.

The empirical model is a quarterly model covering imports and exports in the years 1989–2002. Since the period includes preparation for and implementation of the North American Free Trade Agreement (NAFTA), the possible consequences of that event for trade patterns are controlled for. The evidence suggests that the customary relationship between the peso-dollar exchange rate and the U.S.– Mexico bilateral trade balance fades as the share of network trade in total trade rises. The evidence shows further that the explanatory power of Mexico's GDP in that country's auto-sector import equation declines, while that of U.S. GDP in the same equation rises.

Chapter 12 explores the implications of the findings in the preceding two chapters for the power of monetary and fiscal policies under both fixed and floating rates. It embeds the trade balance equation developed in Chapter 10 in a standard open-economy macro model and shows that the effect of network trade on macro adjustment depends on whether the direct link runs from exports to imports or the other way around. The chapter also shows that the presence of network trade alters the meaning and importance of exchange-rate pass-through, as well as the manner in which international shocks and disturbances are transmitted from country to country.

The chapters in this part have thus far followed the traditional trade literature in focusing the analysis at the level of industries or sectors. This is particularly appropriate when industry structure is assumed to be one of perfect competition. However, as the "new" trade theories reviewed in Chapter 1 argue, when the degree of competition is less than perfect, the nature and extent of competition among firms cannot be ignored. Those trade theories have provided the basis in recent years for the growth and development of a literature on the role of heterogeneity among large firms. Specifically, the challenge has been to explain the considerations that determine whether a firm enters trade or not.

Some contributors to that literature have asserted that the traditional models used in various ways in the preceding chapters are incapable of explaining the observed behavior of heterogeneous firms. This concern is a response to new empirical evidence suggesting that responsiveness to trade opportunities varies across firms, but the theory does not address the issue of fragmentation. As noted earlier, Chapter 13 develops an argument showing how the conceptual framework for analysis of fragmentation and cross-border production sharing at the level of industries and sectors can be adapted to the study of fragmentation at the level of heterogeneous firms. In this approach, endowment differences among countries in the factor-proportions model are replaced by differences in firm characteristics that result in differences in production costs. Overall, the findings and conclusions at the industry level hold in this case as well, suggesting that critics' claims to the contrary may be exaggerated.

Part III: Macro Policy Challenges in Open Economies

In Part III, the focus shifts to exchange-rates and macro policy in open economies, with concerns about the choice of exchange-rate regimes and the effectiveness of macro stabilization policies high on the list. In the early years of the modern, post-war era, the literature was pre-occupied with policy challenges at the national level. However, as globalization has intensified and countries have become more interdependent, issues of policy interaction and policy conflicts have grown in importance. "Beggar-thy-neighbor" policies, which represent a well-known threat to stability in the context of trade policy, are raising increasingly complex challenges at the macro level.

Conflicts may arise as a result of direct and deliberate efforts by countries to "improve" their competitiveness through exchange-rate manipulation, but they may also be the unintended result of spillover effects associated with purely "domestic" policies. The global financial crisis and recession of the early 21st century are vivid and daunting examples of the new reality.

The subject of Chapter 14 is part of the internal-external balance literature and deals with questions of the assignment of policy instruments to policy targets. In the older literature, which includes Swan (1955), Fleming (1962), Mundell (1962) and goes back to Tinbergen (1952), the optimal solution in a world of two instruments and two targets tended to be a one-on-one assignment for the entire length of the adjustment process. This chapter explores the implications of adjustment speeds that vary across markets, making it feasible to assign more than one instrument to a single target for an interval of time, after which one or both instruments are redirected to the other target. If financial markets adjust faster than goods and services markets and if adjustment in the latter markets depends on signals from the financial sector, then directing both instruments to the financial/monetary part of the economy first may be a superior strategy. This chapter also explores the effects on adjustment and stability when equity capital flows are added to the traditional interest-sensitive debt flows of the standard model.

Chapter 15 examines policy conflicts within a currency area or monetary union. The principal concern is with beggar-thy-neighbor effects within the union created by fiscal policy initiatives in individual countries. In the framework of this paper, countries not only possess excessive fiscal policy autonomy, but enjoy significant monetary policy autonomy as well. Thus, the model's specific assumptions do not fully match those of conditions in the Eurozone during the recent sovereign debt crises, but the issues involved are nevertheless related to Europe's financial stability problems. Concerns include the optimum permissible degree of national policy autonomy and the need for mechanisms to protect the monetary union from beggar-thy-neighbor policies of the few.

Chapter 16 addresses the perennial problem of expectations, capital flows, and exchange rate determination in open economies. The specific case is Canada during the 1950s, when the country operated a floating-rate regime in the midst of the Bretton Woods adjustable-peg system. The chapter develops a theoretical model in which agents think in terms of a "normal" range of values within which they expect the exchange rate to move over time. Short-term departures of the rate away from "normality" then have two effects. They give rise to adjustment in the rate expected in the near term, accompanied by expected reversion toward normality over time. These adjustments and revisions of expectations in turn influence the pattern of capital flows. Empirically, the chapter estimates an equation that incorporates the foregoing expectations process, but takes into account as well capital flows that may be driven by considerations not directly related to these types of expectations.

Chapter 17 returns to the theme of deeper integration, but in this instance the discussion revolves around the pros and cons of monetary integration in the NAFTA. The chapter starts with an assessment of the extent to which existing conditions in the NAFTA satisfy traditional optimum currency area (OCA) criteria.[4] It suggests that in spite of substantial capital and labor mobility in the region, adjustment based on factor movements may nevertheless be an inefficient substitute for exchange-rate realignments, especially in the short and medium runs. On the other hand, the earlier finding that cross-border production sharing and vertical intra-industry trade tend to reduce the sensitivity of the trade balance to exchange-rate movements, weakens the case for floating rates as the preferable adjustment vehicle.

The last four chapters address problems stemming from the *de facto* U.S. exchange-rate regime. While the official (*de jure*) regime continues to be the "independent float," the actual regime is a dual-rate system in which the dollar floats against the majority of currencies, including the euro, but in which it is also pegged unilaterally to the Chinese yuan, that is, to the currency of a large country. The phenomenon of countries fixing to the dollar is not new as such, but the nations who have done so in the past have tended to be relatively small and thus their actions had no materially significant implications for U.S. policy makers.

Chapter 18 develops a short-run sticky-price version of the standard open-economy macro model in order to compare the effectiveness of U.S. monetary and fiscal policies in a *de jure* regime with that in the dual-rate system. It concludes that Chinese intervention has the power to undermine the effectiveness of U.S. monetary policy. Although much of U.S. trade occurs under floating rates, China's intervention generates outcomes that look more like those of a regime of fully fixed rates.

Chapter 19 tests the longer-run, flex-price version of the model and shows that the results of the previous chapter continue to hold, except that the specifics of the adjustment process are altered. These alterations are not unexpected, because they arise mainly as the countervailing effects of price adjustments. The chapter then proceeds to examine the international transmission of macro shocks and argues that China's strong economic performance and ability to supply vast arrays of products to the world at relatively stable prices lulled U.S. monetary authorities into believing that they had conquered the price/output trade-off. In the era of the "great moderation," they were able to push expansionary policies without fomenting inflationary pressures in ways that would not have been possible under more "normal" conditions.

Chapter 20 introduces a non-tradables sector into the flex-price version of the model and, together with specific assumptions about expectations formation, focuses on the fact that the "great moderation" was limited to tradables prices, while non-tradables prices experienced significant inflation. The consequent real appreciation of the dollar added to competitive pressures faced by U.S. manufacturing industries. U.S. tradables industries saw competitive pressures rise not only from price stability in China, but from inflation in non-tradables prices. Sheltered from foreign competition, non-tradables industries were free to raise factor prices in order to attract labor and capital from tradables producers and to pass the higher factor costs through to higher prices. This suggests that competition from domestic sources may have been a contributing cause of the observed decline in U.S. manufacturing.

This theme also dominates the discussion in Chapter 21.[5] There, the notion that the Fed's tendency to view the housing bubble as simple asset-price inflation with no significant implications for the real economy is seen as a major policy error. The Fed should have been more careful to distinguish between inflation in the value of existing real estate and inflation in construction and the cost of new housing. Inflation in the former may legitimately be interpreted as an asset price bubble, but inflation in the latter should have been taken as real-sector inflation with significant effects on relative prices and real exchange rates and thus with serious implications for the real economy.

Endnotes

1. In Part III, the implications of a large non-tradables sector are examined in the last two chapters.
2. See also Deardorff (2006).
3. Chapter 9 pursues this issue further.
4. For a succinct statement of the traditional criteria for an optimum currency area (OCA), see Tower and Willett (1976).
5. This chapter is based on my presidential address to the International Trade and Finance Association in Pisa in May 2012.

References

Deardorff, A.V. (2006), *Terms of Trade: Glossary of International Economics* (London: World Scientific).

Fleming, J.M. (1962), "Domestic Financial Policies Under Fixed and Floating Exchange Rates," IMF Staff Papers, 9, (March), pp. 369–380.

Mundell, R.A. (1962), "The Appropriate Use of Monetary and Fiscal Policy under Fixed Exchange Rates," IMF Staff Papers, 9 (March) pp. 70–79.

Swan, T.W. (1955), "Long-Run Problems of the Balance of Payments," in Arndt, H.W. and M.W. Corden (eds.), *The Australian Economy: A Volume of Readings* (Melbourne: Cheshire Press, 1963). Reprinted in R.E. Caves and H.G. Johnson (eds.), *Readings in International Economics* (London: Allen and Unwin, 1968).

Tinbergen, J. (1962), *On the Theory of Economic Policy* (Amsterdam: North Holland).

Tower, E. and Willett, T.D. (1976), "The Theory of Optimum Currency Areas and Exchange Rate Flexibility," Princeton University: Special Papers in International Finance, 11.

Part I

Beyond the Standard Trade Model

Chapter 1

Free Trade and Its Alternatives*

Sven W. Arndt

Abstract

Free trade as the widely preferred policy regime has enjoyed a very long and largely successful run. In recent years, however, political support for it has cooled substantially, especially
in the arena of multilateral trade negotiations. Its wide acceptance was in part nurtured by
memories of the devastating protectionism of the interwar years. Interestingly, the strongest
and most unequivocal intellectual support for it comes from a model whose assumptions
are more than a little at odds with modern reality. The case for free trade becomes more
ambiguous under circumstances involving product differentiation and intra-industry trade,
economies of scale, imperfect competition, and externalities.

Nevertheless, while introduction of greater realism weakens the universality of the case
for free trade; it does not add up to an argument for protectionism. When markets are free,
it can readily be shown that trade should also be free. In the years since World War II, trade
barriers have been reduced significantly, while many markets have become less free, with
greater concentration of economic power and rising volumes of transactions that do not take
place in markets at all. This is particularly true in the financial services industries. Hence,
the alternatives to free trade are not just simply a return to protection, but strengthening
competition in markets that are encumbered by public and private distortions.

JEL Classification: F11, F12, F15

Keywords: Free trade; Protection; Market distortions

1. Introduction

The era of free or freer trade is now well over half a century old. Trade in goods,
as well as services is significantly less encumbered than at the end of World War
II and most of the world's economies are more open and more fully integrated into
the global system than ever before. World trade has grown more rapidly than world
production and many traded goods and services have become internationalized as
cross-border production networks have multiplied. Even non-tradables are feeling

---

*I am indebted to Nik Miller, Nanako Yano and Saumya Lohia for valuable research assistance and
to Max Kreinin for helpful advice and guidance.

the winds of foreign competition, as some of their parts and constituent activities and tasks have become tradable.

The belief that free trade is superior to its alternatives has enjoyed wide and robust support in many parts of the world and has served as the guiding principle for the series of multilateral trade negotiations that began shortly after the war, but are currently stalled in the Doha Round. Yet much of the theoretical case for free trade is based on a model which assumes an economic world in which markets are perfectly competitive and free of distortions and populated by firms that are small and not too-big-to-fail. There are no externalities or scale economies in this world; all goods and services are tradable, trade is always balanced and economic growth just happens.

This view of the world is more than a little at odds with reality. While reduction of trade barriers and opening of national economies have brought fresh winds of competition, market structures in many parts of the world have evolved in the opposite direction, with fewer firms and more concentration of economic power, with capture of economic policy by private interests in a variety of instances, and with non-trivial information asymmetries and assorted externalities. There may be grounds for arguing that freeing markets from the trade restrictions that remain may be less urgent than freeing markets from the welter of other distortions and barriers to efficient utilization of the world's productive resources.

This chapter begins by reviewing the basic case for free trade in terms of the workhorse factor-proportions model. The conclusions of this "benchmark" model are then stress-tested by removing each of the key assumptions in turn. Not surprisingly, the case for free trade becomes less airtight, as a variety of specific market situations arises in which trade-based barriers such as tariffs or non-trade interventions such as production and other subsidies can produce superior welfare outcomes. But these theoretical findings of superiority do not necessarily translate into interventionist policy prescriptions, because in many cases the costs associated with practical implementation may exceed the expected benefits.

2. The Benchmark Model

The benchmark model assumes perfect competition in all markets, constant returns to scale and no externalities or market distortions of any kind. It focuses on "comparative advantage" based on differences across countries in resource endowments and across industries in factor intensities. Countries are assumed to be differentially endowed with the main factors of production — land, labor (skilled and unskilled) and capital — and technologies are assumed to differ across products ensuring that the factors will be combined in different proportions at given relative factor prices.

The essential conclusion of this model is that the economic welfare of each country is best served when it focuses on producing goods and services that make intensive use of the factor or factors of production with which it is relatively well-endowed. Each will then produce more than it consumes of goods and services in which it has *comparative advantage*, while producing less than it consumes of goods in which it has comparative disadvantage. Each exports its excess production of the former, while importing the latter in order to bridge the shortfall of domestic production relative to consumption. It is within these conditions that the welfare results of free and restricted trade are compared.

The small country in partial equilibrium

There are two widely used approaches to the analysis of economic welfare in this context. One, the so-called partial-equilibrium approach, focuses on the market for a single good or service, while the other — the general-equilibrium approach — considers economy-wide effects. In both cases, the welfare results depend on whether a country is small or large *vis-à-vis* the rest of the world, where smallness means that the country has no influence on the world price of any product.

On the import side, the partial-equilibrium version of the small-country case is depicted in Figure 1. The smallness assumption ensures that the country faces a horizontal world supply curve, S_x^w, and given world price P_x^w. At that price,

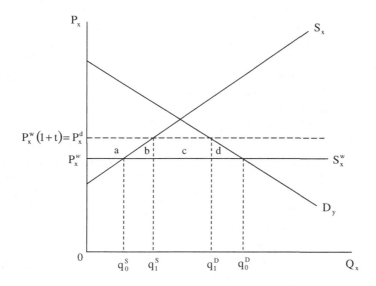

Figure 1.

domestic production is at q_0^S, domestic consumption is at q_0^D, and imports of $q_0^S q_0^D$ cover the gap between domestic demand and supply. Imposition of an import tariff works like a tax by raising the tariff-inclusive price to P_x^d, which is equal to $P_x^w + t$ if the tariff is a "specific" tariff or $P_x^w(1+t)$ if the tariff is an ad valorem tariff. At this price, domestic production expands to q_1^S, while consumption shrinks to q_1^D. Imports fall to $q_1^S q_1^D$.

The concepts of consumer and producer surplus are used in this context to assess the welfare effects of the tariff. Consumer surplus shrinks by area $a + b + c + d$; producer surplus expands by area a and government collects tariff revenue equal to area c. It is clear that the bulk of the tariff's effect is to redistribute income or economic wellbeing from consumers (who are the losers in this case) to producers and the beneficiaries of government expenditures funded by tariff revenue.

In order to assess the overall welfare effect, the benchmark model makes an assumption that may not always be true in the real world: it assumes that winners and losers attach equal value or utility to the transferred amounts. Hence, the loss of area a is worth as much to consumers as its gain is to producers. The same calculation is applied to area c, which transfers income from consumers to government. Under this assumption, the winners' gains "cancel" the losers' losses, implying that this income redistribution has no net effect on "national" welfare.

That leaves the effects captured by triangles b and d, known as the efficiency or "deadweight" losses. The first is the result of "trade diversion" from lower-cost world producers to higher-cost domestic firms and the second represents the loss of consumption brought about by the price increase. The net effect of the tariff is thus a welfare loss to the nation equal to area $b + d$. In the absence of the assumption of equal marginal utilities, the net result will be more or less negative, depending on whether consumers attach greater or lesser value to the transfer than the recipients.

The tariff creates welfare losses for the economy because it reduces the efficiency of resource utilization. It is an inefficient means of supporting home production, because it burdens consumers with higher prices. Any alternative policy that can achieve the same increase in domestic output without raising the price paid by consumers will be superior. As we shall see later, a per-unit production subsidy, equal to $P_x^w P_x^d$, the gap between the world price and the tariff-inclusive domestic price, achieves the same increase in production at lower welfare cost. The subsidy is a more efficient method of achieving the domestic policy objective, but it is also more transparent than the tariff and hence is politically less appealing.

Just because winners and losers value the transfer equally does not imply that the potential losers should not oppose the policy. Consider the following bargaining scenario. Could the losers compensate the winners in order to make them indifferent between the two trade regimes and still come away "better off" with free trade than with the tariff? Could the winners, on their part, compensate or "bribe" the losers to accept the tariff and still be better off with the tariff than with free trade?

In order to make producers and government outlay recipients indifferent between the two trade regimes, consumers would have to offer them compensation in the amount of areas a and c, respectively. Maintaining free trade would thus cost consumers area $a + c$, while the tariff regime costs consumers $a + b + c + d$. On the other side, producers and the government would have to pay consumers $a + b + c + d$ in order to make them indifferent between the two trade regimes. Clearly, this would be an inferior solution by the amount $b + d$. This "double-bribe criterion" is another way of showing the superiority of free trade.

The large country in partial equilibrium

The large country is able to influence world prices by changes in its behavior. It is a price "maker" rather than a price "taker" in world markets. When such a country raises or lowers its demand for imports, it forces foreign suppliers to adjust their prices. When the large country imposes a tariff, thus reducing its demand for imports, the world price of those imports falls. This "terms-of-trade" effect has positive implications for the country's welfare. It is, however, harmful to the rest of the world and is known for that reason as a "beggar-thy-neighbor" policy.

In Figure 2, two countries, A and B, both large enough in relation to each other to affect each other, trade good X. The left panel depicts the domestic situation in the importing country, A, while the right panel reflects conditions in the exporting country, B. The two curves in the middle panel represent A's net import demand and B's net export supply functions, respectively. Every point on each of these two curves is the difference between the respective domestic supply and demand at each respective price. Trade equilibrium occurs at the price at which the export supply forthcoming from country B just matches the import demand of country A. That price is P_x^w. At that price, distances $q_{0A}^S q_{0A}^D$ in the left panel, $q_{0B}^D q_{0B}^S$ in the right panel and $0q_0$ in the middle panel are equal.

As in the small-country case, imposition of an import tariff by country A may be depicted as a vertical addition to country B's export supply curve in the middle panel. If the tariff is a specific tariff, the tariff-inclusive supply curve will be parallel to the free-trade export supply curve. If the tariff is an ad valorem tariff, then the tariff-inclusive curve will have a steeper angle than the free-trade curve.

It is clear in the middle panel that consumers in country A will not want to maintain the free-trade level of imports, once the tariff is added to P_x^w. The quantity demanded falls to $0q_1$, forcing producers in country B to drop their price. In the

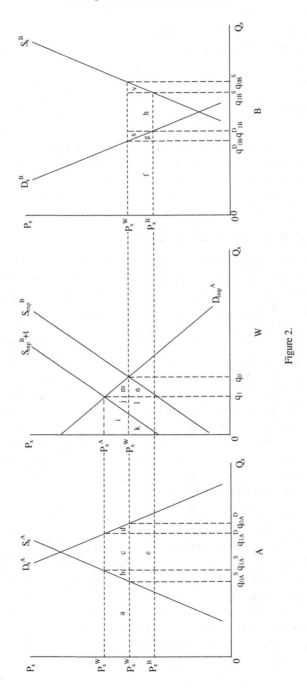

Figure 2.

new equilibrium, the price received by B's producers is P_x^B, the price paid by A's consumers is P_x^A, and the quantity traded, $0q_1$, in the middle panel is equal to $q_{1A}^S q_{1A}^D$ in the left and $q_{1B}^D q_{1B}^S$ in the right panel, respectively. While the difference between the two prices is once again equal to the tariff, in the large country case the tariff is added to a lower export supply price, implying that the domestic price in country A rises by less than the full amount of the tariff.

The welfare analysis proceeds along the lines discussed in the small-country case. Consumer surplus falls in country A by the area $a + b + c + d$. Producer surplus rises by area a and government revenue increases by area $c + e$. Under the assumption of equal marginal utilities among the parties involved, the area that remains after taking account of the internal income redistribution is equal to $e - b - d$. Area e is positive in the sense that it represents government revenue not paid by consumers. Rather, it is extracted from foreign producers through the decrease in B's supply price and thus represents a welfare transfer from B to A. Triangles b and d are the negative deadweight losses. The net effect on national welfare in country A depends on the relative magnitudes of the positive and negative elements. Hence, welfare may decrease as it did in the small country, but it may also increase if the gains from the terms-of-trade improvement are larger than the deadweight losses.

Thus, while the "optimal" tariff, that is, the welfare-maximizing tariff, is clearly zero for the small country, it may be positive for a large country. The optimal tariff is the tariff that maximizes $e - b - d$. A stronger terms-of-trade effect makes for a larger decline in P_x^B relative to P_x^W and thus for a smaller rise of P_x^A relative to P_x^W. This, in turn, reduces the deadweight losses and increases the transfer from abroad.[1]

Unlike the small country's tariff, trade protection by the large country imposes welfare losses on its trading partner(s). In country B, consumer surplus rises by area $f + g$, while producer surplus falls by area $f + g + h + s + v$. The net effect on national welfare in country B is given by area $h + s + v$, which represents a loss to the nation at large. Area $f + g$ is an internal transfer from producers to consumers, while area h is a transfer from B's producers to A's government and areas s and v are deadweight losses. The effect of A's tariff on world welfare requires an additional assumption about the equivalence of marginal utilities between the two countries. Then areas e and h are offsetting from the point of view of world welfare, so that the effect on world welfare is given by area $m + n$ in the middle panel, where m is the sum of areas b and d in the left panel and area n is the sum of areas s and v in the right panel. This is the deadweight loss to the world.

---

[1]For detailed discussions of the optimum-tariff argument for protection, see Heffernan and Sinclair (1990) and Vousden (1990).

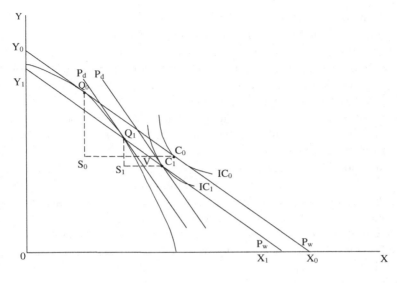

Figure 3.

Import protection in general equilibrium

The general-equilibrium version of the benchmark model considers the effect on the rest of the economy of protecting the import-competing industry. In the two-commodity framework, the rest of the economy is the export sector, Y. There are no non-tradable goods or services in the benchmark model. If the economy's productive resources are fully employed in the two sectors in Figure 3, then free-trade production occurs at point Q_0 and consumption at point C_0, with the world price ratio given by P_w. This is a relative price measuring the amount of Y that must be given up in order to obtain a certain amount of X. If the money prices of the two goods are P_x and P_y, then P_w and P_d express the ratios P_x/P_y for free trade and the tariff situation, respectively. When a small country imposes a tariff on imports of X, the world price ratio is unaffected, while the domestic price ratio rises to P_d. The angle between the two price lines represents the size of the tariff.

In the new equilibrium, domestic producers and consumers adjust their behavior in light of the new tariff-inclusive home price ratio, but the country continues to trade at the world price ratio, P_w. Production moves to point Q_1, where output of the good X has risen in response to the rise in its price; at full employment, this increase comes at the expense of a decline in output of good Y. Consumption retreats to C_1 on a lower indifference curve (IC_1), with less of both goods being consumed. Community welfare clearly has been reduced by the policy.

In the case depicted in Figure 3, the new "trade triangle" ($Q_1 S_1 C_1$) has shrunk along both dimensions, with exports and imports both smaller than before. This is a feature of import protection that is often overlooked in the policy debate: the tariff reduces not only imports, but exports as well. It causes the country to "de-specialize" along both dimensions.

In general equilibrium, community welfare is represented in terms of indifference curves.[2] Even without indifference curves, however, Figure 3 provides useful information about the welfare changes that have taken place. In the movement from C_0 to C_1, the fact that less of both goods is consumed would suggest a loss of welfare even without recourse to the community indifference curve.

It is possible under different sets of preferences, however, for the tariff to lower consumption of the import good, while raising consumption of the exportable product. The increase in the price of X gives rise to a substitution effect, which shifts consumption from X to Y. It also introduces an income effect, which tends to reduce consumption of both goods. Together, the two effects reduce consumption of X, but they work in opposite directions on consumption of Y. If the substitution effect dominates the income effect, consumption of good Y will rise.

Aggregate output (and income) in this economy can be measured in terms of either of the two goods. In terms of good X, aggregate output in the initial situation is given at the intersection of the free trade price line, P_w, with the horizontal axis at point X_0. Measured in terms of good Y, it is given at the intersection of the same price line with the vertical axis at point Y_0. After the tariff has been imposed, the level of aggregate output has declined to X_1, when measured in terms of X, and to Y_1 when measured in terms of good Y. While consumers will attempt to mitigate the negative welfare effects by substituting away from the product that becomes more expensive, their overall spending is nevertheless bound by an inferior budget constraint.

The welfare losses sustained by the country's consumers, as opposed to the country overall, are implicit in the relative sizes of the trade triangles. Under free trade, the country exported $Q_0 S_0$ units of good Y in exchange for imports of $S_0 C_0$ units of good X. After the imposition of the tariff, exports have fallen to $Q_1 S_1$ units and imports have declined to $S_1 C_1$ units. However, in the new equilibrium, consumers receive only $S_1 V$ units of those X-imports, while the rest goes to the government in the form of tariff revenue. The government may decide to distribute this quantity to consumers, but it may also elect to spend the tariff

---

[2]The assumptions underpinning the construction of community indifference curves are not uncontroversial. For additional discussion, see Markusen and Melvin (1984).

proceeds in ways that do not benefit consumers directly, but may still be expected to affect them indirectly as citizens of the country.

It is worth noting for future reference, that the benchmark model assumes trade to be fully balanced at all times. Exports pay for imports, so that the problem of lasting and unsustainable imbalances does not arise. Any incipient trade imbalance is immediately corrected by a change in the terms of trade.

A second important feature of the benchmark framework is that it is a single-period model, meaning that current output is completely absorbed or consumed in the current period. There is no saving and no recognition of depreciation and economic growth is taken as exogenous.

Effects of tariffs on factor prices

The Heckscher-Ohlin factor-proportions model provides additional insights into the adjustment process that follows imposition of a tariff. As the import-competing industry X expands production, it must offer higher wages and capital rentals in order to attract factors of production from the export sector. It can, of course, afford to pay higher wages and rentals, because the price of its product has risen from P_w to P_d. The Y-sector shrinks and releases labor and capital.

If the import-competing industry is relatively labor-intensive at the economy-wide factor-price ratio, then the proportion in which the export industry, Y, releases labor relative to capital at the initial factor-price ratio will be lower than the proportion required by the X industry at that same factor-price ratio. Consequently, wages will tend to rise relative to rentals in the move from point Q_0 to Q_1 in Figure 3. It is important to note that when factors of production are perfectly mobile between the two sectors, then this realignment of factor returns will take place throughout the entire economy. If factors are immobile, as in the specific-factors version of this model, then the tariff raises returns in the X-industry relative to the Y-industry.

Under complete factor mobility, the factor of production used intensively in the import-competing industry is the beneficiary of the protectionist policy, while the other factor is worse off. In other words, the tariff has implications for the distribution of income in the economy: it tends to redistribute income among the country's own factors of production. In the case at hand, workers throughout the economy benefit at the expense of capital owners and investors.[3] The distributional aspects

---

[3] Some of the implications of factor mobility are explored in the "specific-factors" version of the benchmark model, which typically assumes that capital is immobile in the short run. Consequently, the rise in labor demand by the expanding industry boosts wages throughout the economy, while capital rentals rise in the expanding industry, but fall in the contracting industry. In the long run, when capital becomes fully mobile, the economy adjusts toward the results discussed in the previous paragraph.

of the tariff, therefore, amount to redistribution first from consumers to producers and second in favor of factors of production used intensively in the protected industry.

In the small country, internal income redistribution and an increase in inefficiency are the main results of protection. In the large economy, an import tariff exerts downward pressure on the world price of the country's imports as the reduction in demand for those goods forces exporting countries to offer price concessions. This improvement in the tariff-imposing country's terms of trade brings about a cross-country redistribution of income from the trading partner to domestic residents.

For the large country, price line P_w in Figure 3 would thus rotate in a counterclockwise direction (not shown); it would become flatter, implying that the tariff reduces the world price of the import good. As a result, price line P_d in the figure would also become flatter than in the small-country case. Consequently the post-tariff consumption point would lie on an indifference curve located somewhere between the two curves given in the figure. Indeed, if the terms-of-trade gain exceeds the inefficiency losses discussed above, then the new consumption point will lie on an indifference curve higher than curve IC_0. The tariff will have improved welfare.[4]

As noted earlier, the optimum-tariff scenario is clearly an important argument in favor of protection. However, since country A's gains come at the expense of its trading partners, this policy is widely viewed as "beggar-thy-neighbor" in nature and is thus likely to invite retaliation from other countries.

Non-tariff trade policies

The foregoing has focused on tariffs as the instrument of protectionist trade policy. In this section we briefly examine non-tariff barriers such as import quotas and voluntary export restraints (VERs). While the basic welfare results continue largely unchanged, some of the many quantitative restrictions available to policy makers may actually generate results that are more costly to national and/or world welfare than their tariff equivalents.

Import quotas are quantitative restrictions imposed by importing countries, while voluntary export restraints (VERs) are quantitative restrictions imposed on their own exports by exporting countries (very typically under pressure from importing countries). A binding quantitative restriction is one that limits imports to an amount less than that brought into the country under free trade (quantity $q_0^S q_0^D$ in Figure 1 above). If the quota amount is set at $q_1^S q_1^D$, then there will be an excess

---

[4] See Markusen and Melvin (1984) for more on the general equilibrium framework.

demand at the free-trade price, forcing the domestic price to rise until the quantity imported just fills the gap between the demand and supply curves.

This quota is said to be "equivalent" to the tariff of Figure 1 and vice versa. As before, consumer surplus declines by area $a + b + c + d$, while producer surplus rises by area a. Under the usual assumptions about comparable marginal utilities, area a is an internal transfer and areas b and d are deadweight losses. What happens to area c, which denoted revenue collected by the government in the case of a tariff, now depends on how the quota "rents" are distributed.

Quota licenses may be auctioned off, in which case the government will collect quota rents equal to area c. Licenses may also be given away, in which case the rents accrue to the holders of the licenses, who obtain the product at the world price and sell it at the domestic price, P_x^d. If the holders are domestic residents, such as importing companies, and the assumptions pertaining to marginal utility comparisons hold, then area c will be a domestic transfer from consumers to importers. If the holders are foreign entities, then area c is a transfer abroad and the loss of national welfare expands to area $b + c + d$. From the national welfare point of view, therefore, this type of quota is clearly inferior to the tariff and to the auctioned quota. Voluntary export restraints have effects on welfare similar to those of quotas whose licenses are allocated to foreigners, except that under VERs the rents accrue automatically to foreigners, who produce the product at the world price and sell it at the importing country's domestic price.

Non-trade policies

It is clear that, with the exception of the optimum tariff, the protectionist policies examined above are all inferior to free trade. Their main effects are income redistribution among domestic interest groups and inefficiencies in resource utilization. There exist domestic policy alternatives that are capable of achieving the objective of raising domestic production at lower welfare cost. One such policy is the domestic production subsidy.

A subsidy per unit of production equal to the difference between the domestic and world prices in Figure 1 increases output to q_1^S. Producers sell that output at the world price — P_x^w — and receive a subsidy payment equal to the difference on every unit they produce, while consumers continue to pay the world price. Hence, there is no change in consumer surplus, while producer surplus again rises by area a. The cost of the subsidy to the government is area $a + b$. Under the stated assumptions about utility comparisons, area a is a transfer from tax payers to producers, while area b represents the efficiency loss to society.

Although free trade with domestic production subsidies is still inferior to free trade, the welfare costs are smaller than under any of the trade-based policies discussed above. The main problem with subsidies is that they are more transparent for the income redistribution that is involved and thus tend to be less popular with industry and more difficult to implement politically. In recent years, moreover, a consensus has emerged among the member countries of GATT/WTO that subsidies of this type are beggar-thy-neighbor policies, because they create employment at home at the expense of unemployment among trading partners. A series of "subsidy codes" has been negotiated among WTO members, which sharply restricts the use of production subsidies as a viable policy option.[5]

Export promotion

The preceding has dealt with trade policy intervention designed to protect import-competing industries from foreign competitors. In recent years, however, trade intervention designed to increase exports and to help domestic firms penetrate foreign markets has become an important preoccupation of governments. Export promotion policies include export subsidies, production subsidies to exportables industries, subsidized interest rates to finance exports and undervaluation of the domestic currency.

Export subsidies

An export subsidy offers domestic producers a payment for each unit of a commodity that is exported. It thus differs from a production subsidy, which is paid on each unit produced. Figure 4 provides a partial-equilibrium perspective on the effects of export subsidies. In the initial equilibrium at world price P_y^w, the country produces q_0^S units of commodity Y, consumes q_0^D units, and exports the difference. When the subsidy program is implemented, firms in a small country can sell all of their output in the world market at the world price and then collect the subsidy for every unit exported.

Together, these payments add up to a price-equivalent of P_y^d. Under these circumstances, there is no incentive to sell any part of their production domestically unless they can receive a price equal to the world price plus the subsidy. Hence, domestic consumers will be forced to pay P_y^d. It is important to note, however, that this outcome is possible only if consumers are prevented from importing the product at the world price.[6] This issue is examined in a later section.

---

[5] Although the stated objective of the subsidy (as of the other policies) is to raise output and employment in the import-competing sector, the underlying imperative is to preserve incomes in the sector.

[6] The European Union's variable levy on food imports is a noteworthy example of a policy that limits consumers' access to low-cost imports from world markets.

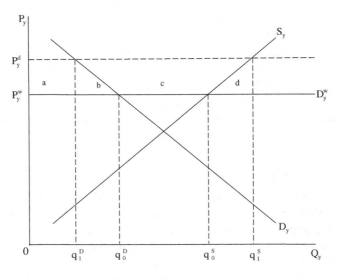

Figure 4.

In Figure 4, consumer surplus falls by area $a + b$, producer surplus rises by area $a + b + c$, and the cost of the subsidy to government is $b + c + d$. Assuming equal marginal income utilities across interest groups, area $a + b$ amounts to domestic income redistribution from consumers to producers with no effect on national welfare. Area c represents income redistribution from taxpayers to producers, while area $b + d$ takes income from taxpayers that does not go to any other group in society. This is the increase in inefficiency, the "deadweight" loss, brought about by the subsidy policy.

If, on the other hand, consumers are able to access the world market for good Y, they will continue to purchase $0q_0^D$ units, implying that the entire domestic output of the product will be exported and that the government will pay the export subsidy on the entire output. After accounting for internal transfers from taxpayers to producers, area d remains as the deadweight loss to society. Note that this is equivalent to a production subsidy in its effects and costs.[7]

---

[7]Note that an income subsidy equal to area $a + b + c$ paid directly to producers would raise producer surplus by the same amount, while leaving consumer surplus unchanged. The cost to taxpayers would be $a + b + c$. There would be no effect on national welfare. Output and exports of good Y would remain unchanged.

Exchange-rate protection

Exchange-rate manipulation offers countries a way of simultaneously promoting exports and protecting imports. Undervalued currencies make exports cheaper abroad, but more expensive at home, while imports become more expensive at home. This result is equivalent to the combined effect of export subsidies and import tariffs. For a small country, whose export prices are determined in world markets, a rise in the exchange rate (defined as the price of foreign currency in terms of the home currency) raises receipts per unit exported in terms of domestic money. In a diagram like Figure 4, currency undervaluation raises firms' export receipts to P_y^d, thereby encouraging greater production and a rise in exports. As under the export subsidy, home consumers end up paying the higher price.

On the import side, in a diagram similar to Figure 1, undervaluation raises the home price of imports at given world prices, thereby allowing domestic firms to expand production and sales. Consumers pay a higher price for imports and import-competing goods and services. The welfare effects of undervaluation follow the line developed for import tariffs.

Of course, at full employment it is not possible in our two-good economy for production in both industries to rise, unless the economy is growing. Hence, domestic export and import prices rise proportionately, with no change in relative prices, no change in the output mix, and no change in the trade balance. In real-world economies, however, exports and imports, the so-called "tradables" sectors, make up only part of total domestic output. Many other industries produce non-tradable goods and services, allowing production of both imports and exports to rise by drawing productive resources from these non-tradables sectors.[8]

While a small country is a "price taker" in the world markets for its imports and exports, a large country will depress world market prices of both imports and exports, as the undervaluation of its currency reduces its import demand and raises its export supply. On the import side, Figure 2 is a useful tool for assessing the effects. In the middle panel, effective foreign supply shifts left, not because the tariff imposes additional costs, but because the depreciation of the importing country's currency raises the price of imports in terms of the home currency. As we have seen, for the small country, that price will rise to fully reflect the extent of the depreciation.

In a recent study, Fletcher (2010) raises important concerns about the benchmark model's view of global competition, particularly with respect to its assumption that technological know-how is uniformly distributed across countries and that there are no economies of scale. We examine these issues in a subsequent section.

[8] The existence of large pools of under-employed labor in many developing countries generates wage behavior that is quite different from that envisaged in the benchmark model. See Lewis (1954).

For the large country, the drop in imports lowers their foreign-currency price, implying that the rise in their home-currency price is less than the depreciation.

When the country is large, a rise in exports exerts downward pressure on the world price, implying that the resulting rise in the home-currency price of those exports will be less than the undervaluation. From the point of view of the exporting country, the policy leads to a loss of national welfare. From the point of view of the importing country, the positive terms-of-trade effect hurts local producers, but brings larger gains to consumers and thus raises national welfare. Producer surplus will decline by area $f + g + s + h + v$, while consumer surplus will rise by area $f + g$, leaving a net welfare loss of area of $s + h + v$. Area h represents the welfare transfer from trading partners to the currency manipulator, while area $s + v$ reflects deadweight efficiency losses.

If there are countries in the world who are net importers of commodity Y, they will benefit from the repercussions of currency manipulation by a large country. Assume for simplicity that they import the commodity under free-trade conditions. Then a decline in the world price of good Y will raise consumer surplus by more than it reduces producer surplus and hence will raise national welfare.

3. Intra-Industry Trade

The benchmark model was designed to explain *inter-industry* trade, where countries' imports and exports belong to different industries and where domestic and foreign goods from the same industry are perfect substitutes. In the era following WWII, however, there has been an explosion of *intra-industry* trade, where countries' imports and exports contain goods belonging to the same industry, but where domestic and foreign goods from the same industry are no longer perfect substitutes. German car exports to France and German car imports from France may belong to the same industry, but they are subject to varietal differences that matter to consumers.

Intra-industry trade based on *product differentiation* may be horizontal or vertical. Horizontal intra-industry trade is the dominant pattern among advanced countries and is broadly characterized by two-way flows of end products of similar quality. Vertical intra-industry trade, on the other hand, takes place between advanced and emerging economies involving trade in end products that differ in quality (Linder, 1961; Lancaster, 1979). In this instance, varieties exported by advanced countries tend to be of higher quality than the varieties exported by emerging economies.

In recent years, however, vertical intra-industry trade associated with cross-border production networks has grown particularly rapidly. Here, the constituent activities of production are dispersed across two or more countries, each country taking responsibility for the stage or activity in which it has a comparative advantage. In this instance, finished end products may be exported by a country that imports some of the components contained in those end products. As the product goes through its various production phases, it may repeatedly cross borders. This modern version of vertical intra-industry trade is exemplified by the flow of automobile parts and components from the United States to Mexico and the movement of assembled automobiles from Mexico to the United States, or by the flow to China of electronic parts and components from a number of East Asian countries for assembly into finished products destined for shipment to the United States and other advanced-country markets.

The benchmark model's focus on factor endowments and factor intensities works very well in understanding inter-industry trade and both types of *vertical* intra-industry trade, but it is limited in its ability to explain horizontal intra-industry trade. The model's focus on factor endowments and factor intensities, makes it a very useful tool for analyzing inter-industry trade, where differences in factor proportions play a key role. As Lancaster (1979) has shown,[9] factor-proportions are also important in end-product trade between advanced and emerging economies. Here, a labor-abundant emerging economy has comparative advantage in the production of more labor-intensive varieties in a given industry, while its advanced trading partner can use its abundant supplies of skilled labor and capital to advantage by producing more technologically refined, high-quality varieties.[10]

The inability of the factor-proportions approach to explain *horizontal* intra-industry trade among advanced countries is due to the overwhelming similarities among those countries of factor endowments and factor intensities. The "new" trade theories, developed in the second half of the last century by Brander and Spencer (1981, 1984), Helpman (1984), Krugman (1979, 1981), and others were intended to overcome these difficulties in order to provide a better understanding of these trade patterns. In these trade models, economies of scale and imperfect competition, as well as product differentiation, play key roles.[11]

---

[9]See also Vousden (1990), p. 152.

[10]To Linder (1961), this type of specialization may emerge from variations in local usage based on factor endowments. To Vernon (1966), such differences tend to disappear in the course of the "product cycle." Fletcher (2010) sees this catching up by emerging economies as a major threat to the long-run competitiveness of high-income countries. It is a key element in his critique of free trade.

[11]For excellent selections from this literature, see Grossman (1992), Helpman and Krugman (1985), Kierzkowski (1984) and Krugman (1990).

Scale economies and product differentiation

On the demand side, the new theories explore the possibility that consumers may derive benefits from product variety, in which case *product differentiation* comes to play a key role. "Love of variety" is an important element in the contribution by Dixit and Stiglitz (1977), in which trade increases consumer welfare by increasing the varieties available within each product category. On the supply side, increasing returns to scale are introduced and with them the possible erosion of competition. In this world, each country's producers specialize in a subset of all varieties, thereby generating longer production runs in order to take advantage of cost-saving scale economies.[12]

When each country produces and exports a subset of varieties, while importing the rest, overall demand for each country's domestic brands tends to rise as its market expands into other countries. Some domestic demand for domestic varieties falls as home consumers shift to foreign brands; indeed, some domestic varieties may disappear as they are replaced by foreign substitutes. Production runs for the surviving varieties tend to expand, thereby enabling producers to exploit the cost savings inherent in scale economies.[13]

With horizontal intra-industry specialization, equilibrium outcomes depend on such factors as the number of countries involved, the length of production runs needed to reach optimum scale in each industry, and the degree of product differentiation. A large number of participating countries makes for a larger integrated market. Each firm needs to decide on the number of varieties to bring to market and in which country to market them. Since each firm is large and thus a price maker and since it typically faces demand conditions that vary across countries, profit maximization typically involves price discrimination across national markets.

Firms compete for market share across borders. Each has an interest in protecting its own market against imports of foreign varieties, while seeking to promote exports of its brand. The short-run effects of import tariffs work very much like those discussed in connection with Figures 2 and 3. Each firm faces an upward-sloping short-run supply curve, with capital fixed and labor mobile. A

---

[12] Scale economies that are internal to the firm tend to create incentives for large firm size and thereby undermine the perfect competition assumption of the benchmark model. Scale economies that are external to the firm encourage firm clustering and agglomeration of productive activities, which is also incompatible with the benchmark model. On this, see Barba Navaretti and Venables (2004).

[13] When the European Union embarked on its "Single Market" project in the 1980s, achieving scale economies in passenger vehicles and other industries in order to compete more effectively with the U.S. and Japan was an important objective. The prevailing view in Brussels was that countries had protected their national markets for "national champion" firms, thereby limiting the size of the market and hence the ability of firms to fully exploit scale economies. See Jacquemin and Sapir (1989) and Emerson *et al.* (1988) for further discussion. See also Mertens and Ginsburgh (1985).

tariff on imports of the foreign variety raises its price, reducing consumer surplus, while raising government revenue. The net effect is a welfare loss. The rise in the home price of the foreign variety shifts domestic demand toward the domestic brand, raising price and increasing output. There are additional repercussions and spillover effects, but our main interest is in the long run when capacity changes and scale economies are won or lost.

In the long run, domestic firms respond to the rise in price of the domestic brand by expanding productive capacity. If the economies of scale are internal to the firm, this increase in size reduces each firm's cost, implying that the new short-run supply curve has shifted out and down, enabling firms to cut prices on domestic brands and thereby improve their overall competitiveness.

The experience of foreign firms is likely to run in the opposite direction. The tariff imposed by the home country, reduces demand for the foreign variety and thus puts downward pressure on prices and production abroad (along the lines discussed in relation to Figure 2). If foreign firms respond by eliminating capacity, then their long-run costs rise along the slope of the long-run cost curve. There is a leftward displacement of the new short-run supply curve, a rise in costs and a rise in price. Each country's firms have an interest in fighting off encroachment on the size of their operations. The home country's tariff — sometimes referred to as a scale-snatching tariff — makes them less competitive and reduces their market share and is thus likely to meet with retaliatory countermoves.

As the foregoing suggests, the welfare effects of trade intervention are not easily generalized, given the importance of initial conditions on both the demand and supply sides.[14] We do, however, have some empirical evidence in the experience of the European Union, where many countries have historically employed industrial and trade policies to support and protect "national champion" firms in key industries, including motor vehicles. Both tariffs and non-tariff barriers have been employed to reserve national markets for home producers. Formation of the customs union was aimed at elimination of inefficiencies caused by trade barriers, while the Single Market project standardized competition policy across borders and removed many other distortions and impediments. Creating a large and uniform market was expected to reduce the overall number of firms, thereby allowing the survivors to expand production and reduce costs.[15]

---

[14] Vousden (1990) provides detailed analyses of a number of possible scenarios. See Mertens and Ginsburgh (1985) for a study of structural models with various combinations of market power and product differentiation.

[15] In preparing the Single Market project, European leaders established regulations preventing member countries from seeking "first-mover" advantages for their industries by means of subsidies and other forms of support.

When intra-industry specialization is vertical in the manner of Linder (1961) and Lancaster (1979), advanced countries produce and export varieties at the high-quality end of the spectrum and import varieties at the low-price, low-quality end from less advanced countries. For the majority of developing countries local markets are too small to allow exploitation of scale economies. Hence, access to the markets of large countries and to the world market more generally is critical. Export-led growth has been a very important policy model, particularly in East Asia.

We saw earlier that vertical intra-industry specialization may be the result of endowment differences. In addition, differences in technological know-how also play a role. The Heckscher-Ohlin (1966) model, on the other hand, assumes away such differences in knowledge. As Vernon's (1966) view of the product cycle predicts and as post-war economic history shows, advanced countries find it very difficult to protect their knowledge-based edge. Over time, the advantage conferred by their endowment of "knowledge capital" is eroded as emerging economies catch up. Often, technology is appropriated by foreign rivals before the costs of research and development have been paid off. Protection of intellectual property rights is thus a very important part of trade relations. Important strides have been made in recent years at the level of the GATT/WTO to create a global framework for the protection of intellectual property.

Some critics see in the gradual erosion of advanced-country competitiveness in vertical intra-industry trade a key argument against free trade; it explains to them why free trade "doesn't work" (Fletcher, 2010). They advocate tariffs just large enough to protect the advantages conferred by scale effects. Imposition of such tariffs, however, would not easily pass WTO muster. Concerns about WTO sanctions sometimes lead to voluntary export restraints (VERs). The United States, for example, employed political pressure to move the Japanese government to impose limits on motor vehicle exports to the United States. This transferred large quota rents to Japanese producers, who promptly used them to upgrade the quality of their exports. Moreover, unlike the Heckscher-Ohlin model, in which there is no allowance made for foreign direct investment (FDI), Japanese firms responded to "Japan-bashing" by establishing production facilities in the U.S.

Protection through VERs may provoke tariff-jumping FDI, which replaces imports from abroad with local production of foreign brands for the home market. In an earlier age, American firms responded to discriminatory trade liberalization in Europe in the fifties by moving production of their brands into Europe. From the point of view of firms in the importing country, this undermines the extent to which they are protected from foreign competition. From the point of view of jobs protection, the case is more complicated. The jobs "saved" by the tariff, will be lost once foreign firms begin production, but new jobs will be created in the production of foreign varieties. The welfare effects again depend on the specifics, especially with respect to similarities and symmetries of cost structures.

The foreign affiliates' cost structures are likely to be affected by offsetting forces. Their cost conditions will be higher if they produce only for the local market, meaning a smaller scale of operations. Costs will be lower if they can acquire labor at better terms than domestic firms, along the experience of Japanese auto producers in Tennessee relative to Detroit or American firms in Ireland relative to German and French firms in their respective high-wage markets. If affiliate costs are higher than in the pre-tariff situation, then domestic firms receive a measure of protection. If they are lower, imposition of the tariff worsens their competitive situation.

Production networks and vertical intra-industry trade and investment

Vertical intra-industry production sharing works particularly well among dissimilar economies, including economies with different factor endowments. But since the Heckscher-Ohlin model assumes that technologies are not only similar, but identical across countries, its usefulness in explaining this type of trade may remain limited. However, the modern version of vertical intra-industry trade occurs largely within cross-country production networks anchored by multinational companies. Those companies typically transfer essential technologies and capital to labor-abundant emerging economies, thus ensuring that technologies are "identical" where needed and that relative labor abundance is the key determinant of intra-product specialization.[16]

It clearly makes no sense for a member of a production network to impose trade restrictions of any kind on imports of parts and components that are brought in for further processing or assembly. Such restrictions would raise costs along the rest of the value chain. The argument against such imposts is provided by the theory of effective protection (Corden, 1966). On the other hand, countries may compete for a place in a production network by offering concessions and incentives in order to attract multinationals.

Ireland's support of its electronics industry is an important example. Such support can play a key role even when scale economies are external to the firm. Government may aim its support at improving the competitiveness of the network

---

[16]For a discussion of recent developments in "arms-length off-shoring," see Ando, Arndt and Kimura (2005).

and its constituents. This includes policies that lower transactions costs, costs related to infra-structural and administrative inefficiencies, and the like.

In key respects, vertical specialization has effects similar to technological change. Fragmentation and cross-border sourcing may be sector-specific or economy-wide. Like technical change, production possibility blocks like that pictured in Figure 3 shift out along the axis or axes representing the sectors in which change occurs. Vertical specialization may also be factor-specific, with advanced countries tending to outsource low-skill-labor-intensive elements of production, while emerging economies outsource capital- and technology-intensive elements of production. The results for employment, factor prices, and changes in the output mix are sensitive to the specific features of a given episode.[17]

4. Imperfect Competition

In the benchmark model, all markets are perfectly competitive. While some international trade, especially in some standardized components and commodities, may be reasonably treated as if it were perfectly competitive, much of modern trade in both goods and services involves markets with imperfectly competitive structures. A significant share of trade in both goods and services is in reality dominated by large multinational companies. We have already noted that internal economies of scale tend to promote the formation of large firms and the concentration of market power. In this section, we explore the implications of trade intervention in the presence of imperfect competition.

In a world of imperfect competition, it is much more difficult to find easy generalizations regarding the welfare effects of alternative trade regimes. We have already encountered this problem in connection with scale economies and it carries through to other departures from the assumptions of the benchmark model. When everybody is a price taker, "markets" resolve imbalances in ways that achieve socially optimal outcomes. Imperfect competition is a form of market distortion that undermines the ability of markets to achieve socially optimal allocations of an economy's resources. Monopolistic elements encourage firms to restrict output and raise price relative to the outcome under perfect competition. Hence, any trade policy which strengthens this power by reducing competition from abroad is likely to be welfare-reducing.

However, in an economy with multiple distortions, introduction of an additional distortion may raise or lower welfare, depending on whether it augments or offsets the effects of existing distortions. Removal of one among multiple distortions

---

[17] For specifics, see Arndt (1997), Arndt and Kierzkowski (2001), Deardorff (2001) and Feenstra (1998).

gives rise to similar ambiguities, which means that elimination of a trade barrier in an economy with multiple distortions may reduce rather than raise welfare. These considerations are aspects of the economics of the "second best" (Corden, 1974); they create significant problems for policy makers.

Although broad generalizations are not easily forthcoming in the presence of market distortions, economists have studied trade intervention in specific cases of imperfect competition.[18] In the next sub-section, we focus on monopoly, not because it is the most typical of imperfectly-competitive market structures in international trade, but because the cases chosen illustrate several policy themes.[19] If monopoly power is the ability to influence prices, to be a "price maker," then we have already encountered one example of such price-making power, namely, the "optimum-tariff" argument for large countries. That argument continues to be relevant in the context of imperfect competition.

Domestic monopoly

In Figure 5, a country's domestic import-competing industry is assumed to be a monopolist, whose product is a perfect substitute for goods produced abroad. The country is assumed to be small in relation to the world market. In autarky, the firm faces downward-sloping domestic demand, D, with associated marginal

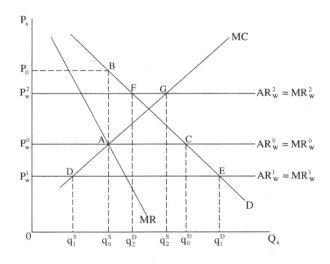

Figure 5.

---

[18]For a number of these studies, refer to the volumes listed in footnote 11.

[19]For applications to other forms of imperfect competition, see Kjeldsen-Kragh (2001).

revenue, MR. It produces an amount q_0^S, where marginal cost, MC, equals MR, and sells that amount at price P_0. Free trade and the resulting competition from abroad renders the firm's marginal and average revenue curves horizontal at the level of the world price, but the implications depend on the exact level of the world price.

If the world price is P_w^0, then the firm produces quantity q_0^S and sells it at that price, at which quantity demanded domestically is q_0^D. Hence, the country ends up importing an amount AC of the product. In this case, the move to free trade reduces price, but leaves domestic production unchanged, unlike the benchmark model in which domestic production falls. If the world price is as low as P_w^1, however, domestic production does decline and imports rise to DE. If the world price is as high as P_w^2, domestic production increases to q_2^S. At that price, the quantity demanded domestically is less than output and the firm exports FG units.

In all three cases, free trade eliminates the monopolist's ability to restrict output and raise price by forcing it to behave like a perfect competitor. This is the well-known function of free trade as an anti-trust instrument and may be the most powerful and compelling argument for free trade under imperfect competition. It is not surprising that domestic production may actually increase with free trade, given monopolists' tendency to restrict production in order to raise price.

Introduction of a tariff into this picture, raises domestic price in all three cases. As the intersection of the tariff-inclusive horizontal price line (not drawn) rises along the MC curve between point D and its intersection with the downward-sloping demand curve, domestic production rises, domestic consumption falls and imports decline. This outcome matches the results obtained with the benchmark model. It is important to note that the monopolist continues to be constrained to behave as a competitor for as long as domestic consumers are free to access the product at the world price and pay the tariff, that is, as long as arbitrage between the home and foreign markets is not restricted. As in the benchmark model, the effect of the tariff is to reduce net national welfare. It reduces consumer surplus, increases producer surplus and provides government with tariff revenue, but after accounting for domestic income transfers, there remain the typical deadweight losses.

If a tariff is introduced when the free-trade price is P_w^2, at which the firm is an exporter of the product, the firm can charge the tariff-inclusive price on units of the product sold domestically, but is constrained to sell all additional units in the world market at the world price. In that case, the firm effectively faces a kinked AR/MR curve. We return to this case after discussing Figure 6 below.

It was important in the preceding discussion that consumers' ability to arbitrage between the home and foreign markets be preserved in order to force the monopolist to behave like a competitor. In Figure 6, we suppose that the monopolist has the

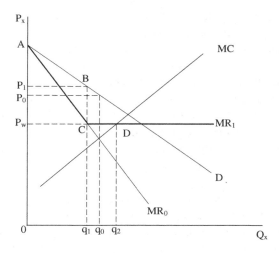

Figure 6.

ability to prevent such price arbitrage. Governments prevent arbitrage by means of import tariffs and other regulatory restrictions.[20]

Under the stated conditions, the monopolist produces quantity q_0 and charges price P_0 in autarky. When the economy is opened to trade on the export side, with world price at P_w, the monopolist's marginal revenue curve follows the bold kinked line $(ACDMR_1)$, descending initially from point A to C and then becoming horizontal at the world price. This curve intersects the marginal cost curve at point D, indicating a profit-maximizing output level of q_2. The firm sells Oq_1 units domestically at price P_1 and exports the rest at the world price. This profit-maximizing behavior may be viewed abroad as "dumping," selling a product at a lower price in the foreign market than at home. Such a policy might be pursued by countries seeking "export-led" growth. Domestically, this restrictive version of open trade reduces availability of the product and raises its price, to the obvious detriment of consumers.

Returning briefly to Figure 5, if a tariff is imposed when the world price is at P_w^2, the firm would again face a kinked marginal revenue curve, descending initially along the downward-sloping MR curve, becoming horizontal at the tariff-inclusive price $(P_w^2 + t)$, becoming vertical when it hits the demand curve, dropping down toward the world price line and becoming horizontal at that price line. Production would occur at point G, where the kinked MR curve intersects MC. Domestic

---

[20] See Mertens and Ginsburgh (1985), p. 157 for a discussion of such policies in Europe.

sales would occur at a price that would place home demand somewhere along the segment BF and the rest of the firm's production would be exported.

It is important to note the new context within which the analysis of the previous paragraphs takes place. In the benchmark model, there are no distortions under free trade in either the domestic or the world economy. Markets function efficiently and well. They can be relied upon to bring about the most productive utilization of national and world resources. In that model, the gains from trade arise simply from a more efficient allocation of productive resources. Trade intervention is thus welfare-reducing precisely because it interferes with market efficiency. In the benchmark model, trade intervention is the sole distortion in an otherwise undistorted world.

Monopoly, on the other hand, represents a distortion that interferes with the market's allocative functions and generates inefficiencies in resource utilization. In that distorted world, free trade introduces competition and thereby curbs or eliminates the distortion. As noted earlier, however, the theory of second-best (Corden, 1974) shows that in a world of multiple distortions it is not possible to say whether removal of one of those distortions improves or worsens welfare, just as it is not possible to say whether introduction of an additional distortion improves or worsens welfare.[21]

Foreign monopoly

Consider the case of a foreign, rather than domestic, monopoly supplier of a country's imports of goods or services. The essence of the argument, illustrated in Figure 7, is similar to the discussion of domestic monopoly. Under free trade conditions, the foreign monopolist, assumed to be the sole supplier of good X to the home market, produces output level q_0, where marginal cost and marginal revenue are equal, and sells it for price P_0. The foreign firm's monopoly profits are equal to area P_0ABC.

Ideally, the country's policy makers have an interest in breaking or at least curbing the monopolist's market power by imposing constraints on its price-making power. Recall, that in the example of the domestic monopolist, the price limit was provided by competition in the world market. In the present case, the country may decide to impose a specific tariff, the effect of which is to shift the marginal cost curve to MC + t. This new curve intersects the marginal revenue curve at

---

[21] Moreover, in the complex modern economy, many transactions do not take place in markets as defined in the benchmark model. This is especially true in financial markets, where many derivative products are traded over the counter. It is often difficult to say what the effect of such transactions is on economic efficiency and welfare.

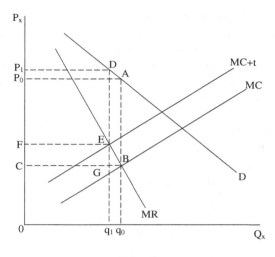

Figure 7.

output q_1, for which the monopolist charges price P_1 in the domestic market. The tariff allows the monopolist to raise the price paid by consumers and thus reduces consumer surplus by area P_1DAP_0. The firm's monopoly profits decline to area P_1DEF and the home country's government collects area FEGC in revenue, which it may recycle to consumers or use for other socially desirable purposes.

This type of tariff has come to be known as a "rent-snatching" tariff. Its effect is to raise national welfare, given that the government's rent receipts are larger than the loss in consumer surplus. Rents collected by the government will be larger than consumer surplus loss, provided that the MR curve is steeper than the D curve. Then, the reduction in quantity from q_0 to q_1 generates a larger vertical change along the steeper MR curve than along the flatter D curve.

However, while the tariff has redistributed some of the monopolist's profits to the home country's government, the two distortions — monopoly and tariff — together have further reduced the efficiency of resource utilization.

5. Other Market Distortions

Externalities

The benchmark model assumes that private and social costs and benefits are equal throughout the economy. In reality, positive and negative externalities abound, implying that the "private" demand and supply curves in Figures 1 and 2, on the basis of which producers and consumers make their respective decisions, do not correctly reflect costs and benefits to society. A well-known example is environmental pollution in agriculture and manufacturing, which raises social relative to private costs to the extent that private producers are not required to absorb the costs of environmental degradation. On the demand side, positive or negative externalities or spillovers may analogously separate private from and social benefits.

Economists agree that trade policy is generally not the best means of dealing with such externalities and that it is inferior to production and consumption taxes and subsidies, for reasons similar to those discussed in relation to production subsidies in Section 2. A tariff may achieve a socially desirable increase in output, if social costs are below private costs, but it does so by introducing a distortion on the demand side embodied in the higher prices consumers must pay.

Environmental and labor standards

In recent years, two issues seemingly unrelated to trade, have been introduced into the policy debate, in which opponents have argued that free trade can be "unfair" trade, especially between countries with very different environmental and worker protection standards. If countries like the United States have tough laws forcing firms to absorb the costs of environmental degradation and to protect workers from harsh and abusive conditions in the work place, then the resultant increase in private costs will place domestic producers at a competitive disadvantage relative to countries with more relaxed standards. This has led some to propose tariffs just large enough to offset such "unfair" advantages, much like an anti-dumping duty seeks to eliminate foreign price discrimination.

It is clear, however, that imposition of such a levy in the context of Figure 1 would create the welfare losses analyzed before, without having any direct effect on the externalities in the exporting countries. While a production subsidy to the domestic industry would also "level the playing field" without introducing a distortion on the side of domestic consumption, it too would have no direct impact on foreign "unfair" practices.

When such a duty is imposed by a large country, its effect is to reduce price and production abroad (as in Figure 2). If the objective is to penalize foreign firms for environmental degradation, then proponents may assert that the reduction in foreign producer surplus achieves that objective and, further, that the decline in output abroad serves to protect the global environment by shifting production from a high-polluting to a low-polluting country. It is even possible for the tariff to improve net welfare at home if the tariff is an optimum tariff.

If, on the other hand, the tariff is imposed in order to penalize the foreign country for abusive labor practices and inadequate worker protection, then the reduction in foreign production and rise in unemployment could worsen the plight of workers there. This has led some observers to propose that advanced countries like the United States might consider providing income transfers to poorer countries in order to help them pay for environmental and worker protection.

Preferential Free Trade Agreements (PTAs)

One of the most powerful conclusions of the benchmark model is that trade liberalization brings net welfare gains to a country regardless of whether its trading partners also adopt free trade. It makes the case for unilateral rather than negotiated free trade. In practice, however, the multilateral trade negotiations that have taken place since the end of WWII have from the beginning been based on reciprocity. Policy makers have found it easier to overcome domestic opposition to trade liberalization if they could show that opening their own markets was matched by more open foreign markets. Thus, in the public mind the perceived "cost" of lost import protection must be offset by the perceived gains from export promotion. Unfortunately, as the number of countries participating in multilateral trade negotiations has grown over the years, reaching a negotiated multilateral agreement has become more difficult and the negotiating process more protracted.

An important, but narrower and more limited form of negotiated trade liberalization occurs in the context of preferential trade agreements (PTA), the two most popular examples of which are the free trade area (FTA) and the customs union (CU). In both instances, trade among members is liberated, but in the FTA each country retains its own tariffs on trade with non-members. In the customs union, on the other hand, members adopt a common external tariff (CET) *vis-à-vis* non-members.

The main regional PTAs are the European Union (EU) and Mercosur, both customs unions, and the North American Free Trade Agreement (NAFTA) and the ASEAN Free Trade Agreement (AFTA). There are, in addition, numerous non-regional PTAs, such as those between the U.S. and Israel and between Singapore and the EU.

This form of selective and discriminatory trade liberalization may or may not increase national welfare, because it typically generates both positive and negative welfare effects. The positive effects are due to the shift from high-cost domestic production to lower-cost imports from member countries. This effect is known as "trade creation."

However, the lowest-cost member of the PTA may not be the lowest-cost producer in the world, in which case preferential elimination of the tariff in favor of PTA members diverts imports from lowest-cost non-members to higher-cost members. This cost-raising shift is known as "trade diversion." It follows that the net effect on the country's welfare depends on the relative magnitudes of trade creation and trade diversion.

In general, the larger the number of the world's low-cost producers included in the PTA, the greater the likelihood that the PTA will raise welfare. This insight provides an important explanation for the failure of the Latin American Free Trade Area (LAFTA), a discriminatory free trade area that excluded too many of the world's low-cost producers of too many products (including the U.S. and the EU). In that event, negative effects of trade diversion overpowered the gains from trade creation.

As noted in earlier sections, large countries are price makers and thus their welfare also depends on movements in their terms of trade. If a country entering a PTA is "large" in relation to other member countries, then the shift from domestic production to imports will tend to raise prices and this negative terms-of-trade effect introduces an additional welfare-reducing element.

On the other hand, to the extent that member countries are large relative to non-members, the diversion of imports will tend to reduce the price of imports from the rest of the world, providing members with potentially important terms-of-trade gains. Indeed, regional trade pacts may be beneficial from the point of view of small countries if, in addition to providing price-making power, they increase bargaining power in multilateral trade negotiations and multilateral institutions. The possibility that membership in a regional trading group may confer market power upon small countries, including influence over the group's terms of trade with non-member trading partners, is an important attribute of PTAs that has not been widely discussed in the literature (see Arndt 1968; 1969).

The lack of a common external tariff (CET) in a free trade area allows importers in a high-tariff member country to by-pass the domestic tariff by bringing in goods, parts and components from outside the area through a low-tariff member country. This is an evasive maneuver that is not possible in a customs union. In order to prevent such tactics, FTA members establish "rules of origin" (ROOs), also known as regional content requirements, which specify the percentage of an end product which must have been produced in member countries in order to take advantage of tariff-free passage across internal borders. Enforcement of these rules at road crossings, airports and seaports within NAFTA, for example, is so costly that roughly half of the intra-NAFTA trade that is eligible for the zero tariff does not take advantage of that privilege, because the costs of compliance exceed the tariff advantage.

This maneuver becomes increasingly cost-effective as the MFN tariff declines. At an average tariff of 4 percent, compliance costs can easily exceed that amount.

6. Concluding Comments

The case for free trade is at its strongest, but least relevant, when made in the context of a perfect economic environment. In such a world, protectionism introduces a distortion into an otherwise undistorted universe and thereby disturbs the "best" (most productive) utilization of productive resources. The inevitable and necessary consequence is a loss of welfare, as defined in that model. The benchmark model is useful not so much in providing a reasonable representation of reality, but in spelling out the many conditions that must be satisfied in order to nail down the case for free trade. It is useful, especially, in making clear that when resources are fully utilized, import protection or export promotion policies make some people better off, but only at the expense of making others worse off. We see such policies for what they are, namely, opaque approaches to income redistribution, among domestic interest groups in small countries and partly away from foreigners in large countries. Moreover, in bringing about income redistribution, trade intervention creates welfare-reducing inefficiencies.

In the presence of imperfect competition, a principal benefit of free trade may be simply that it introduces competition into the home market and forces the monopolist or oligopolist to behave like a competitor. It is a great anti-trust policy with which to tame and control domestic monopolistic elements. On the other hand, however, free trade may give foreign monopoly or oligopoly undesirably easy access to rents in the home market, in which case a tariff is useful in "snatching" back part of those rents. In the absence of workable anti-trust policies for dealing with globally concentrated industries, rent-snatching tariffs may some day become the last recourse for many an individual country.

Scale economies, especially when they are internal to the firm, nurture and promote imperfect competition. It is not always easy to say whether the cost savings inherent in larger firm size justify the adverse price changes introduced by attendant monopoly elements. Add various types of externalities into the brew and the welfare implications of any policy action, whether toward or away from freer trade, become even murkier. This is a challenge that has not only stymied economic analysis, but that handicaps policy-making as well.

Meanwhile, the world has made significant progress toward global free trade since the end of WWII, driven in part by policy and in part by cost-reducing innovations in transportation and communication technologies. Indeed, the degree of success is so extensive as to suggest that for many goods and services trade is now freer than the markets themselves. In many areas of economic endeavor, with the notable but not the only exception of agriculture, the trade barriers that remain are probably less detrimental to welfare than some of the other distortions, particularly those involving imperfect competition. One example is suggested by the banking and financial industries. It would be difficult to show that opening world markets even more completely to the global banking and financial oligopolies would bring greater welfare benefits to society, however defined, than would increasing the degree of competition and facilitating entry and, most importantly, exit.

References

Ando, M., S.W. Arndt and F. Kimura (2006), "Production Networks in East Asia: Strategic Behavior by U.S. and Japanese Firms." (Japanese version published, 2007.)

Arndt, S.W. (1997), "Globalization and the Open Economy," *North American Journal of Economics and Finance*, 8, 1, pp. 71–79.

_____(2004), "Global Production Networks and Regional Integration," in M.G. Plummer (ed.), *Empirical Methods in International Trade* (Northampton, MA: Edward Elgar).

_____and H. Kierzkowski, ed. (2001), *Fragmentation: New Production Patterns in the World Economy* (Oxford: Oxford University Press).

Barba Navaretti, G. and A.J. Venables (2004), *Multinational Firms in the World Economy* (Princeton: Princeton University Press).

Brander, J. and B. Spencer (1981), "Tariffs and the Extraction of Foreign Monopoly Rents Under Potential Entry," *Canadian Journal of Economics*, 14, pp. 371–389.

_____(1984), "Tariff Protection and Imperfect Competition" in H. Kierzkowski (ed.), *Monopolistic Competition and International Trade* (Oxford: Clarendon Press).

Caves, R.E. (1996), *Multinational Enterprise and Economic Analysis*, 2nd ed. (Cambridge: Cambridge University Press).

Corden, W.M. (1966), "The Structure of a Tariff System and the Effective Protection Rate," *Journal of Political Economy*, 74, 3, pp. 221–237.

_____(1974), *Trade Policy and Economic Welfare* (Oxford: Clarendon Press).

Deardorff, A.V. (2001), "Fragmentation in Simple Trade Models," *North American Journal of Economics and Finance*, 12, 2, pp. 121–137.

_____(2006), *Terms of Trade: Glossary of International Economics* (London: World Scientific).

Dixit, A.K. and J.E. Stiglitz (1977), "Monopolistic Competition and Optimum Product Diversity," *American Economic Review*, 67, 3, pp. 297–308.

Emerson, M. *et al.* (1988), "The Economics of Europe 1992: An Assessment of the Potential Economic Effects of Completing the Internal Market of the European Community," *European Economy*, No. 35/3.

Feenstra, R.C. (1998), "Integration of Trade and Disintegration of Production in the Global Economy," *Journal of Economic Perspectives*, 12, pp. 31–50.

Fletcher, I. (2010), *Free Trade Doesn't Work* (Washington, D.C.: U.S. Business and Industry Council).

Grossman, G.M., ed. (1992), *Imperfect Competition and International Trade* (Cambridge, MA: MIT Press, 1992).

Heffernan, S. and P. Sinclair (1990), *Modern International Economics* (Oxford: Blackwell).

Helpman, E. (1984), "Increasing Returns, Imperfect Markets, and Trade Theory" in R.W. Jones and P.B. Kenen (eds.), *Handbook of International Economics*, Vol. 1 (New York: North-Holland).

——and P.R. Krugman (1985), *Market Structure and Foreign Trade* (Cambridge, MA: MIT Press).

Jacquemin, A. and A. Sapir (eds.) (1989), *The European Internal Market: Trade and Competition* (Oxford: Oxford University Press).

Kierzkowski, H., ed. (1984), *Monopolistic Competition and International Trade* (Oxford: Oxford University Press).

Kjeldsen-Kragh, S. (2001), *International Trade Policy* (Copenhagen: Copenhagen Business School Press).

Kreinin, M.E. (1987), "Comparative Advantage and Possible Trade Restrictions in High-Technology Products," in D. Salvatore (ed.), *The New Protectionist Threat to World Welfare* (New York: North-Holland).

Krugman, P.R. (1979), "Increasing Returns, Monopolistic Competition, and International Trade," *Journal of International Economics* 9, pp. 469–479.

——(1981), "Intra-industry Specialization and the Gains from Trade," *Journal of Political Economy*, 89, 5, pp. 959–973.

——ed. (1986), *Strategic Trade Policy and the New International Economics* (Cambridge, MA: MIT Press).

Lancaster, K. (1979), *Variety, Equity and Efficiency* (New York: Columbia University Press).

Lewis, W.A. (1954), "Economic Development with Unlimited Supplies of Labour," *Manchester School of Economic and Social Studies*, 22, 2, pp. 139–191.

Linder, S.B. (1961), *An Essay on Trade and Transformation* (New York: John Wiley & Sons).

Markusen, J.R. and J.R. Melvin (1984), "The Gains-from-trade Theorem with Increasing Returns to Scale," in H. Kierzkowski (ed.), *Monopolistic Competition and International Trade* (Oxford: Oxford University Press).

Mertens, Y. and V. Ginsburgh (1985), "Product Differentiation and Price Discrimination in the European Community: The Case of Automobiles," *Journal of Industrial Economics*, 34, 2, pp. 151–166.

Pomfret, R. (1992), "International Trade Policy with Imperfect Competition," *Special Papers in International Economics*, No. 17 (Princeton University, August).

Vernon, R. (1966), "International Investment and International Trade in the Product Cycle," *Quarterly Journal of Economics*, 80, 2, pp. 190–207.

Vousden, N., *The Economics of Trade Protection* (New York: Cambridge University Press, 1990).

Chapter 2

On Discriminatory vs. Non-Preferential Tariff Policies

Sven W. Arndt

Abstract

In a recent paper published in this JOURNAL, Cooper and Massell [1] have argued that "customs union is necessarily inferior to an appropriate policy of non-preferential protection" (p. 745). This conclusion, the authors maintain, emerges naturally from the separation of the effect of customs union into two exhaustive components, the one a tariff reduction component and the other a pure trade diversion component. As the terms themselves suggest, the former incorporates the single potential gain from customs union.

These results depend crucially upon the assumption that the union is small and therefore incapable of influencing the terms of trade. Thus, the possibility that dominant terms-of-trade effects may endow the union with certain favourable outcomes which are not otherwise attainable need not be considered. It is the object of the present note to investigate the relevance of changes in the terms of trade to the conclusions reached by Cooper and Massell. It will turn out that even within the context of a model which resembles in most respects the one used by the authors, a positive terms-of-trade effect may indeed be dominant. However, and more important, it will be suggested that the relevant alternative to customs union is not unilateral, non-preferential tariff policy, but some form of international collusion. In the light of the latter, customs union may present the only effective solution to the problems of control and enforcement of "collective" policies.

JEL Classification: F11, F12, F15

Keywords: Customs Unions; MFN tariffs; General-equilibrium model

I

In order to develop the argument, it will be convenient to replace the single-commodity, Marshallian partial-equilibrium model employed by the authors with a more general analytical framework. There are three countries, A, B and the rest of the world, C. They produce two commodities, X and Y, such that A is the least efficient and C the most efficient producer of commodity X. In Fig. 1 *GH* represents the production possibilities of country A. The straight line passing through Q_o and C_o gives the free-trade international terms of trade, the price of X in terms

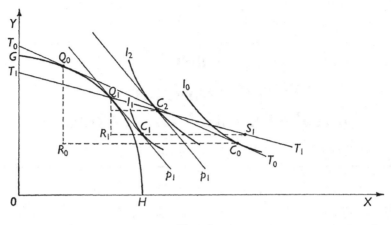

Figure 1.

of Y. Production equilibrium is established at Q_o, while consumption occurs at point C_o on indifference curve I_o.

Imposition of an *ad valorem* tariff of $C_1 S_1 / R_1 C_1$ has two effects. Assuming that A is sufficiently large and that the foreign demand for imports is not infinitely elastic, A's terms of trade improve, shifting from T_o to T_1. The internal price of X in terms of Y increases to p_1, such that $p_1 = (1 + t_a) T_1$, where t_a is the *ad valorem* rate of duty.

Following an implication of the Cooper–Massell model, it is assumed that when the authorities do not redistribute tariff revenues they consume the latter exclusively in the form of commodity X.[1] In the absence of revenue redistribution country A's citizens adjust to the tariff by moving production to Q_1 and consumption to C_1. They export $Q_1 R_1$ of Y for $R_1 S_1$ of X, giving up $C_1 S_1$ of X to the government in A.

As a result of the tariff policy country A's citizens are worse off than before, although their welfare would have decreased still further if the terms of trade had remained unchanged. However, the authorities in A could raise the welfare of the private sector above C_1 by redistributing the tariff proceeds as income subsidies. Such a policy would cause the private sector to move (approximately, due to the secondary effects on the terms of trade and the domestic price ratio) to point C_2.

---

[1] The demand and supply curves used by Cooper and Massell are private-sector curves. If the authorities attempted to exchange a portion of the revenues collected for commodity Y, and if they did so in the domestic market, where Y is cheaper, market equilibria would be disturbed. They could, of course, exchange commodities in international markets without any economic effects, given the authors' assumption of constant terms of trade. In our present case, however, this move as well as redistribution of revenues will alter the terms of trade.

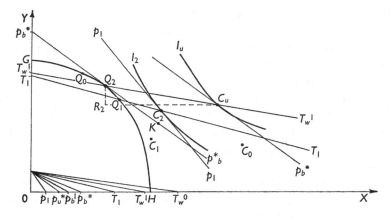

Figure 2.

Such redistribution of tariff revenues is a key aspect of traditional customs-union analysis as exemplified by Lipsey's classic paper [2].

Nevertheless, in the present case C_2 implies a welfare loss relative to the free-trade position. The gains associated with shifts in the terms of trade are insufficient to offset the losses due to the tariff itself. However, it is possible in principle for the terms of trade to improve by enough to produce a net welfare gain. It is well known that the tariff will leave the domestic price ratio unchanged, provided that the sum of the domestic marginal propensity to spend on imports and the foreign elasticity of demand for imports equals unity.

In order to compare the effects on welfare of the non-preferential tariff, on the one hand, and customs union, on the other, the essential features of Fig. 1 have been reproduced in Fig. 2. Following Cooper and Massell, we assume that the customs union comprises what are in Vanek's [3] terminology economies with similar structures: prior to union the two countries do not trade with each other.

If the common union tariff is prohibitive the intra-union price of X must rise to a level higher than p_b^*, the relative price of X at which country B ceases to trade and which, along with various other relevant price ratios, is indicated in the left corner of the diagram. At price ratios higher than this critical ratio trade reversal will have taken place in B, with the latter now exporting commodity X. The equilibrium intra-union price ratio will thus lie to the left of p_b^*, say, at p_u^*. The international terms of trade, which will rule in the absence of union trade with the outside world, are given by T_w^o. Country A will produce somewhere between Q_o and Q_1 on GH and through trade move to a point to the right of C_1, the exact location of which point will be determined by the tangency of the prevailing price ratio and an indifference curve. The latter will represent a higher level of satisfaction than the indifference curve which passes through C_1. Inspection of the diagram suggests that appropriate non-discriminatory tariff policies on the part of A would enable the country to reach identical levels of welfare. The claim that customs union is unnecessary thus seems to hold.

Now suppose that a tariff which is less than prohibitive had in fact been introduced. We may distinguish among three possible outcomes. Following the imposition of the tariff, the intra-union price of X may be greater than, equal to or less than p_b^*. In the first case the union countries will trade with each other, in the second country B is indifferent to trade and in the last case the two partners do not trade with each other.

We examine the last two possibilities first, not because they are most likely to occur, but because they are analytically simpler. Suppose, therefore, that the intra-union price is exactly equal to p_b^* and that the corresponding international terms of trade are given by T_w^1. Country B ceases to trade and country A's entire trade is conducted with the outside world. A will produce at point Q_2 and through trade move to some point such as K — assuming, as before, that the authorities retain all customs revenues. It appears once again that formation of the union was unnecessary and that simple manipulation of its non-preferential tariff would have accomplished the same ends for country A.

However, judgments regarding the efficacy of various policies which are based on comparisons of private-sector consumption points such as K and C_1 may be misleading. For, since at point K the authorities in A are not without tariff revenues, the size of the collections in the two cases must necessarily be compared. The authors themselves have made it one of their major arguments that the customs union destroys governmental tariff revenues and thus forces countries to either substitute alternative sources of revenue or cut erstwhile spending programmes. In either case this will tend to reduce private sector welfare.

Changes in total revenue collected are particularly significant in the present case, since A will either inherit country B's trade or conduct the entire amount of a vastly reduced world trade at highly favourable international terms of trade. In either case, revenue collections are likely to increase. Now, in the absence of detailed information about government programmes and expenditures, it is convenient to assume that these "programmes" constitute redistribution of revenue to the private sector. In the case of the pre-union non-preferential tariff imposed by A this would lead to consumption equilibrium at C_2. After customs union, on the other hand, country A is able to rise to a level of satisfaction given (approximately) by point C_u. The latter situation is obviously preferable to the former and, what is more important, cannot be reached by way of non-preferential tariff policy.

An analogous argument may be derived for the case in which both countries trade only with the outside world. We shall not develop it here. There remains, then, the possibility that the union partners will conduct trade between themselves. For this to occur, the union tariff must be of sufficient magnitude to produce an intra-union price of X greater than p_b^*. The corresponding terms of trade will be less favourable to country A than T_w^o, but more advantageous than T_w^1. The worsening of the internal price ratio and the improvement in the terms of trade will have opposite effects on A's welfare.

Production of X will increase in A, while that of Y will fall, and a portion of country A's total exports of Y will now go to the union partner. This portion will be exchanged at the internal union price ratio and will not provide the authorities with tariff revenue. The remainder of A's trade will go to the outside world in exchange for commodity X at the prevailing terms of trade. While it is not possible to identify the exact proportions of country A's trade without additional information about the other two countries, it is apparent from Fig. 2 that there exist a number of trading situations of this type which will produce equilibrium for country A on indifference curves which lie to the right of and thus represent higher levels of welfare than the curve passing through the highest point attainable with non- preferential tariffs. In the present instance that point is C_o.[2]

The foregoing discussion suggests that the terms-of-trade effect of the customs union may be of sufficient strength to produce a net improvement in welfare over any non-preferential tariff situation. What this implies necessarily is that the combined economic power of the two countries acting in unison may accomplish what one country acting in isolation cannot bring off.

II

We have seen that in some of the cases for which the above conclusions hold, trade between the union members will be small or altogether non-existent. The question obviously arises as to the necessity of forming a customs union. What country A really desires from country B is an appropriate protective policy against the outside world. If A can establish effective collusion with B formation of a customs union may, from the point of view of the present objectives, not be necessary.

---

[2] An alternative approach to this problem would be to retain the assumption that country A alone is too small to influence the terms of trade, and to suppose instead that the customs union which A joins is large. Then, among the many cases in which customs union would be preferable to unilateral tariff policy the following possibility is intuitively clear. If the union leaves the internal price ratio at its free-trade level, and if country A continues to trade with the outside world, it will be capable of reaching welfare levels which are unattainable with non-preferential tariff policies.

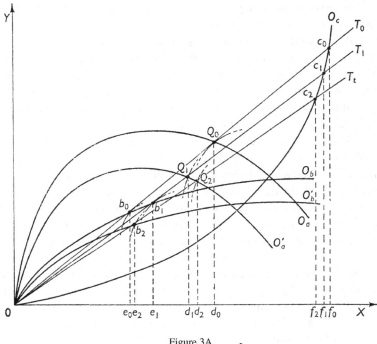

Figure 3A.

To investigate this possibility, the offer curves O_a, O_b and O_c for the three countries, respectively, have been drawn in Figs. 3A & 3B. In case 3A country A is initially the most efficient producer of Y, while in case 3B the two countries are assumed to possess equal efficiency. At free trade terms of trade, OT_o, country A exports $d_o a_o$ of Y to country C for Od_o of X, while country B exports $e_o b_o$ of Y for Oe_o of X the sum of the two countries' exports being exactly equal to Of_o.

After imposition of an *ad valorem* tariff country A's revenue-distributed offer curve is assumed to shift to O'_a, which causes the terms of trade to move to OT_1. Evidently A's trade with C is reduced as a result of the tariff while B's trade with C increases, although the growth of B–C trade is not enough in Fig. 3A to prevent total world trade in terms of both commodities from being contracted. From A's point of view, competition by B in A's export markets has reduced the effectiveness of unilateral, non-preferential tariff policy.

However, A's welfare may still increase even under these less advantageous circumstances, provided that the move from a_o to a_1 is accompanied by two conditions. It is clear that the greater is the size of B relative to A and the more elastic are the B and C offer curves over their relevant ranges, the greater the likelihood that A will lose as a result of the tariff. Further, given the various foreign offer

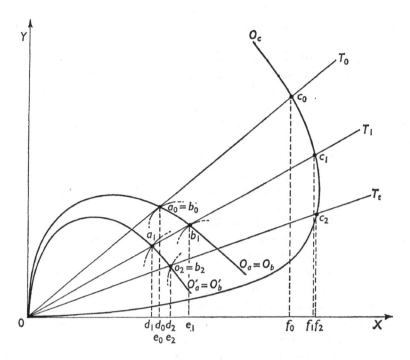

Figure 3B.

curves and the A-tariff, A is more likely to sustain a loss in welfare, the lower its own marginal propensity to spend on its export commodity. If Y is a Giffen good in A's consumption a_1 will be inferior to a_o.

In the present example case 3A leads to a decrease in welfare at a_1, while the analogous point in Fig. 3B involves an improvement in welfare. In both cases it is apparent that country A has fared less well than it might have with less competition from B. The latter country, on the other hand, experiences a clear welfare gain in both cases.

It is obviously to country A's advantage to induce country B to adopt restrictive trade practices. To illustrate these possibilities, let B impose an *ad valorem* tariff. Suppose, in order to reduce the number of curves in the diagram, that in Fig. 3B all aspects of B's situation are identically those of country A, so that the revenue-redistributed offer curves coincide. In both diagrams the terms of trade shift to OT_t. The new equilibrium locations are given by a_2, b_2 and c_2. B's tariff improves country A's welfare in both cases. Country B, on the other hand, gains only in case 3B. In the other situation B would be better off with unrestricted trade in the presence of the tariff in A.

Figure 3A thus illustrates the fundamental problem, namely, that the interests and therefore the policies of the two countries may not be compatible. Country A stands to gain from restrictive trade practices in B, but the latter is better off without such restrictions — provided that A maintains its tariff. The dilemma in which A finds itself in trying to improve its terms of trade is brought about by its inadequate control of the market for its export commodity. Its optimum trade policies and their effects are functions not only of the demand elasticity in C but also of supply conditions in B and of the latter's reaction to a given policy in A.

Country A will attempt to influence policy-making in country B. In view of the fact that the latter may have considerable inducement to pursue independent policies, country A may encounter formidable difficulties in this respect. It could attempt to handle this problem in a relatively loose arrangement along the lines of international commodity agreements, or in a tightly controlled and more restrictive set-up involving an international cartel. The difficulty is that neither alternative may provide effective control over the maverick who stands to gain from independent policies. In that case a customs union with common tariff and sufficient incentives may work where other arrangements do not.

In concluding their analysis, Cooper and Massell question the usefulness of the standard type of customs-union analysis with its emphasis on the trade- creation and trade-diversion effects of changes in "specialisation." This sort of analysis, they argue, "fails to show why a customs union may be acceptable when a tariff reduction is not, and it fails to analyse how a customs union may more efficiently serve the ends previously served by non-preferential protection" (p. 747). This criticism is well taken, but it may be misdirected, for we have shown that the relaxation of but one of the essential assumptions of the authors' analysis permits us to escape this criticism. Elimination of the assumption that neither the individual country nor the union possess significant bargaining powers with respect to the rest of the world brings out the possibility, which is doubtlessly empirically demonstrable, that the relevant alternatives to customs union must all involve the pooling of economic power and the extension of reciprocal advantages, and that union may provide the most workable of such arrangements. This is not to argue that other reasons for economic integration may not exist which are in the end equally, if not more, important. The foregoing discussion simply suggests a rationale for such integration without departing from the essential framework of customs-union analysis.

References

1. Cooper, C. A., and Massell, B. F., "A New Look at Customs Union Theory," *Economic Journal*, December 1965.
2. Lipsey, R. G., "The Theory of Customs Union: A General Survey," *Economic Journal*, September 1960.
3. Vanek, J., *General Equilibrium of International Discrimination* (Cambridge: Harvard University Press, 1965).

Chapter 3

Customs Union and The Theory of Tariffs

By Sven W. Arndt*

The standard analytical vehicle of customs union theory consists essentially of a two-commodity, three-country model of the trading world. Within this framework, two of the three countries form the union, while the third "country" comprises the "rest of the world." The latter is either assumed to contain a single country or, where several economies are involved, these are taken to be perfectly homogeneous, so that differentiation among them is immaterial to the analysis.[1]

Many significant results have been obtained with the aid of this apparatus, which has in spite, or perhaps because, of its basic simplicity taken the analysis of customs union a long way since the problem was first formalized by Viner [18]. Nevertheless, the model does suffer from the burden of several major constraints. Not the least of these involves the treatment of the non-union or outside world as a single unit. In the present paper, we shall develop a model that will permit us to break up the rest of the world into several heterogeneous components. The smallest version of this expanded model will contain four countries—two within the union and

two without—but the number of countries may be readily increased.

Among the principal results of this extension, the traditional conclusion of customs union theory that terms-of-trade movements will lead to deterioration in the welfare of the "outside world" will be shown to be of limited relevance to the multiple-country situation. It will be shown further that when exclusion from the union involves more than a single country, the incentives to elect nonmembership will be increased for some countries by the final form of the union. An attempt will also be made to demonstrate the superiority of customs union as a particular type of tariff policy.

· The model will be introduced in Section I; it will be used there to examine the case of the large union which imposes a prohibitive tariff. This will bring out the importance of movements in the terms of trade in determining the welfare effects of customs union. In Section II, the more general case of the nonprohibitive tariff will be taken up. Section III will deal with the existence of tariff policies as alternatives to customs union. A final summary concludes the paper.

I. Large Union: Prohibitive Tariff

The initial purpose of this section is to set out the framework of the analysis. Among the basic properties of the model is the assumption that full employment is maintained throughout and that factor supplies are fixed. Further, perfect competition is assumed to prevail. Commodities are homogeneous and mobile between countries without transportation

* The author is assistant professor of economics at the University of California at Los Angeles. He is indebted to William R. Allen for his valuable comments on an earlier draft. He is, of course, solely responsible for any remaining errors. Fellowship support from UCLA's Committee on International and Comparative Studies with funding from the Ford Foundation is gratefully acknowledged.

[1] See, for example, the papers by Lipsey [10] and Michaely [13]. Vanek [16] uses a similar framework, but he does attempt some generalizations beyond the three-country world. Cooper and Massell [4], on the other hand, conduct their analysis entirely in terms of a single-commodity, three-country model.

costs. Factors of production are perfectly immobile internationally. Tariffs are imposed for regulatory purposes only; all proceeds are returned to consumers as income subsidies. Individual tastes and preferences are such as to justify the use of community indifference curves.[2] Finally, all production transformation functions are assumed to be concave to the origin.

Suppose, then, that the world may be divided into two groups of countries producing commodities X and Y. Group W_A is the set of all actual or latent exporters of Y, while group W_B exports X. The groups are necessarily defined with reference to the prevailing terms of trade, for it is clearly possible that alterations in the international price ratio will introduce trade reversals which will cause countries to shift between groups.

An essential feature of the present model is its use of aggregate reciprocal demand functions. Such functions are constructed by taking the radial sum at various terms of trade of the offers of the members of a given group.[3] The shape of the aggregate curve is generally dependent upon the individual component curves; its smoothness increases with the number of countries and with the similarity among the underlying offer curves; its elasticity is determined by the elasticities of the individual curves. Where individual countries are small, changes in the

behavior of a single member of a group will leave unaffected the group reciprocal demand curve and thus the international terms of trade. A large country, on the other hand, will cause shifts in its offer curve to be reflected in the aggregate curve.[4]

Group W_A, the exporter of Y, may consist of one or more countries. We assume for simplicity, but without loss of generality, that it contains two countries, A_1 and A_2. Suppose further that A_1 is the lowest-cost producer of Y, so that it will be a supplier of Y and an importer of X at lower relative prices of Y than any other country. Specifically, if OA_1' and OA_2' are the countries' relevant offer curves, A_1 will be the sole exporter of Y at all terms of trade equal to or steeper than those given by the ray through point W (the line not being drawn to avoid cluttering up the diagram). Consequently, the group offer curve will be coincidental with A_1's offer curve up to point W, i.e., country A_2's curve is tangent to the line OW at the origin. When the price of X is high enough to cause country A_2 to become an exporter of that commodity, i.e., to produce a negative offer of Y, the country's demand

---

[2] This assumption is of special importance in view of the subsequent use of reciprocal demand curves. It is assumed that the distribution of income is held constant by the authorities. This is clearly a restrictive assumption which ignores, among other things, the possibility raised by Johnson [7] and Metzler [12] that tariff-induced changes in the terms of trade will alter the distribution of income. Its virtue lies in the fact that it eliminates the problem that tariff alterations and formation of customs union may cause the reciprocal demand curves of a given country to cross. For more detailed discussions of community indifference curves, see Michaely [13] and Vanek [17, Ch. 16].

[3] Aggregate reciprocal demand curves were implied by Graham [6] and have been derived by Becker [2] and Elliot [5].

[4] We may note the special case in which the members of a group possess identical offer curves. The resulting aggregate curve will be perfectly smooth and will possess the convenient property that the entry or withdrawal of one or more of these countries will leave the elasticity of the aggregate curve invariant with respect to a given price ratio. Kemp [9] has discussed this invariance in connection with various types of demand shifts. While he was concerned primarily with individual country offer curves, the present application is a natural extension of his analysis.

When offer curves differ among countries, the elasticity of the group offer curve will be determined by the relative propensities to consume importables in the component countries and by the individual shares in total group imports, on the one hand, and by a compensated price elasticity for the group, on the other. Both income and price effects will essentially be weighted averages of the individual component country terms. A disaggregated elasticity of demand has been derived for a single country composed of two individuals by Bhagwati and Johnson [3]. That analysis is readily adaptable to the present situation.

for the latter commodity must be added to the aggregate demand of group W_B.

At terms of trade flatter than OW, country A_2 begins to export commodity Y. The group reciprocal demand curve, OWW_A', reflects this increased supply of Y on world markets by moving away from OA_1' at this point. The intersection of OWW_A' and OW_B', which is group W_B's aggregate offer curve and which may be derived analogously, determines the world terms of trade. If the country curves had been free-trade curves, the resulting terms of trade would give the free-trade world price ratio as well as the internal relative prices in the various countries. If, on the other hand, OA_1', OA_2', OB_1' and OB_2' are all revenue-redistributed offer curves corresponding to various individual tariffs imposed by the four countries, then OWW_A' and OW_B' are the resulting group offer curves and OT_t measures the terms of trade of a tariff-ridden world. This latter case is in fact the one depicted in the first quadrant of Figure 1. Free-trade offer curves have, in general, not been drawn in order to keep the diagrams as simple as possible.

Let us assume, therefore, that quadrant 1 represents the situation as it exists prior to formation of the customs union. World-trade equilibrium is located at P, the point of intersection of the revenue-redistributed group offer curves. The terms of trade are given by OT_t. In this situation, different cost, demand, and tariff conditions will prevail within the various countries. To illustrate, the revenue-redistributed offer curve (OA_2') of country A_2 corresponds to an ad valorem rate of tariff of OM/MN. The internal price ratio in A_2 is indicated by RM. Point R represents equilibrium for that country. As Johnson [8, Ch. 2] has shown, the terms-of-trade line cuts the indifference curve which passes through R, whereas the internal price line is tan-

gent to that indifference curve. In the free-trade case, on the other hand, where internal and international price ratios are identical, the indifference curve passing through the equilibrium point will be touched by the common price line.

We may think of country A_1 as having imposed a higher ad valorem rate of duty, given by OK/KL and producing an internal price ratio of SK. At *constant* terms of trade, the internal price of X will be higher in A_1 than in A_2, given the higher rate of taxation in A_1. When countries are large enough to affect the terms of trade, however, differences in size will tend to offset (or augment) differential effects of varying tariff rates on prices.[5]

Suppose now that countries A_2 and B_2 form a customs union with prohibitive tariff. Countries A_1 and B_1 thus constitute the "outside world." In the latter, trade equilibrium will shift to P', the point of intersection of the revenue-redistributed offer curves of the truncated groups, provided that neither group reacts to the union by altering its tariff policies. The new outside terms of trade are OT_w; they represent a worsened trade situation for the country importing commodity Y.

In the third quadrant, OA_2' and OB_2' are drawn along with the countries' free-trade offer curves, OA_2 and OB_2. With a prohibitive external tariff the intra-union terms of trade will be OT_u. It would thus appear that the terms of trade facing A_2 and those facing its former group, and for

---

[5] The word "size" is used here in the broad sense, encompassing both demand and supply conditions. It is well known that a tariff will leave the internal price ratio unchanged if the sum of the marginal propensity to import in the taxing country and the foreign elasticity of demand for that country's exports equal unity. See, for example, Meade [11, p. 74]. This condition, however, holds strictly only for the case in which the given country is the sole supplier of the commodity; in the presence of competing suppliers the conditions must be amended to include the effects on third country offers of the given country's tariff policy.

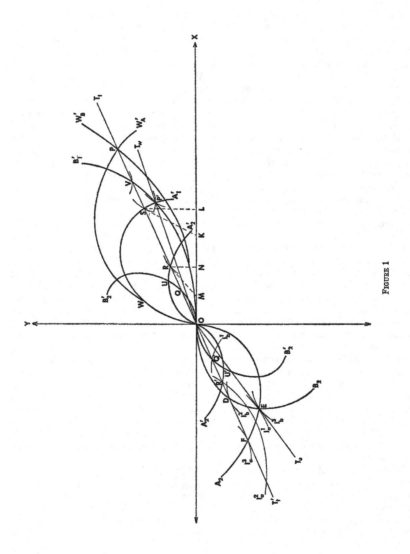

FIGURE 1

symmetrical reasons B_2 and its former group, have moved in opposite directions. This, however, need not always occur. It is possible that, for an appropriate choice of countries and, within these, an appropriate choice of ad valorem tariffs, the final intra-union terms of trade will move in the same direction as those in the outside world. As a special case, it is possible for the terms of trade in either the union or the outside to remain unaltered at OT_t while those in the opposite block take on a new value.

Finally, there is one case, namely, union of "similar" economies,[6] in which we can make unequivocal statements about the direction of the terms-of-trade shifts. For example, if two of a large number of countries in W_A form a union, the terms of trade outside the union will clearly move in favor of group W_A, and thus the intra-union price ratio *must* move in the opposite direction. In the absence of the latter increase in the relative price of X, the commodity will not be produced within the union.[7]

A significant aspect of customs union theory has been its attempt to predict the direction of terms-of-trade changes. Whether the terms of trade move in favor or against the "inside" or the "outside" is of considerable import not only to the respective union partners, but to those who remain nonmembers as well.[8] As the foregoing discussion makes clear, however, it is generally undesirable, if not meaningless, to deal with the "outside world" as a single entity when that world contains several distinct members. We can see in our present case of the prohibi-

tive tariff, that every movement of the terms of trade will be favorable to some countries and adverse to others. There is only one clear case and that involves union of similar economies in which *all* exporters of one commodity, say, Y, join the union. Then, indeed, will the relative price of X rise in the union and fall in the outside world, producing trade reversals in some countries and leaving both blocks with uniformly worsened terms of trade.

Country A_2, having moved from R ($=R'$) to E, is worse off after customs union. The total change in welfare may be separated into two components. The first, which tends to increase the country's welfare, is the result of tariff elimination with its increased specialization in production and its attendant readjustments of consumption. It is equivalent to a movement from R' and indifference curve I_a^2 to F and curve I_a^3 at *unchanged* terms of trade. Removal of the tariff produces a reallocation of resources in favor of Y and substitution in consumption toward X by changing the internal price ratio from MR to OT_t'. The second component, which tends to reduce A_2's welfare, arises from changes in the terms of trade from OT_t' ($=OT_t$) to OT_u. It may be shown in perfectly analogous fashion that both component movements are favorable for B_2, whose welfare is increased unequivocally. By joining the union, the country gains both because its volume of trade increases and because its terms of trade improve. In order to determine the net change in union welfare, intercountry comparisons will become necessary, except for the possibility that the gainer may be able to compensate the loser and still prefer the union.

The foregoing analysis may be applied to the changes which will occur in the outside world. The movement from S to P' constitutes a welfare improvement for A_1: its terms of trade improve and the

---

[6] In Vanek's terminology [16], union of countries from the same group constitutes union of similar economies. The opposite situation produces union of dissimilar economies.

[7] It remains to be seen in a later section to what extent relaxation of the prohibitive tariff alters this conclusion.

[8] Cf., for example, Mundell [15] and Vanek [16].

internal relative price of imports falls. The welfare of B_1, on the other hand, deteriorates as a result of the formation of the union. The positions of the two countries are affected only by terms-of-trade shifts, given the unaltered degrees of their trade restriction.[9] It can be seen that the attitudes of A_1 and B_1 toward formation of the union will be very different. B_1 will try to oppose the union, fearing a worsening in its terms of trade. Country A_1 will support the union, but

[9] The present case raises the following question: will the tariff levels in A_1 and B_1, which were established in accordance with the pre-union trading situation, be consistent with post-union conditions? Suppose that prior to the union country A_i is relatively small within group W_A and that group W_B's offer curve is highly elastic. A_i's ability to alter the terms of trade will be small and its optimum tariff low. Suppose, next, that several members of the two groups join a prohibitive customs union. This increases A_i's power within the newly constituted group W_A. Assuming that the reduction in the size of W_B has raised the curvature of its reciprocal demand curve, it follows that optimum strategy, especially in the absence of retaliation, may now lead A_i to increase its tariff; and if this is generally applicable to the countries on the outside, the average level of protection will increase.

But is this the general case; or is it possible for optimum tariff policy to require tariff cuts? Suppose that all members of W_A and W_B enter a prohibitive union except for countries A_2 and B_2. Quadrant 3 then shows the situation in the outside world after formation of the union. At unchanged pre-union tariffs, the terms of trade are given by the ray (not drawn) through U'. Through that point will pass indifference curves for each country which will be touched by their respective internal price lines. It has been shown by Johnson [8, Ch. 2] and others, that if at U' the offer curve of the passive country is tangent to the internal price line of the tariff-imposing country, the latter country cannot gain by altering its tariff. If, on the other hand, the offer curve *cuts* the price line of the taxing country from the side of the line which lies between that line and the taxing country's export axis, the tariff should be increased. In the reverse case, the tariff will have to be reduced since it will exceed its optimum level.

The point of intersection, U', will be determined by the rates of duty established in the two countries prior to formation of the union. These rates will be affected by the sizes of the two countries within their respective groups, by the elasticities of the various offer curves and by the past history of tariff competition. There is no presumption, therefore, that optimal tariff strategy for the countries on the outside will always lead to increases in the rate of protection.

should clearly refrain from joining it, for it has much to gain from its increased market power in the outside world.

II. *Large Union: Nonprohibitive Tariff*

When the union tariff is less than prohibitive, OT_u and OT_w in Figure 1 no longer represent the final terms of trade. As the tariff is lowered to nonprohibitive levels, substitution in production within the union toward the product whose price is rising, namely Y, and substitution in consumption toward the product whose price is falling, namely the import commodity X, will tend to push OT_u in a clockwise direction, while analogous adjustments in the outside world will rotate OT_w in a counterclockwise manner. These rotations, however, will stop short of bringing the internal price vectors in the two blocks into equality, unless both remove their respective external tariffs completely.

If we assume that all tariff changes which actually occur are those involving the union, then OA_1' and OB_1' will continue to represent the outside world's ruling offer curves. The union offer curves, on the other hand, will be altered as the external union tariff is reduced, producing nonzero excess demands within the union for the two goods at their new prices. For the extreme case of a zero tariff, OA_2 and OB_2 will be the relevant offer curves; in this case, the final terms of trade will be steeper than OT_t, given the relative magnitudes of the pre-union tariffs of the partners and the relationships between curves OA_2' and OA_2 and OB_2' and OB_2.

In the general case, the world terms of trade will fall somewhere between the latter ratio and OT_w, the exact location being determined by the final size of the union tariff. It is apparent that the two union partners will be induced to pursue conflicting objectives with respect to the optimum level of the common tariff. Country B_2's gain from union will be smaller, the lower is that tariff; that country will thus tend to resist reductions in the common tariff. A_2, on the other hand, would see its earlier losses reduced by lower external tariffs, and is thus likely to pursue trade liberalization. Resolution of the conflict will probably involve redistribution of union tariff revenues to the residents of country A_2 plus compensating transfer payments from B_2 to A_2. In the case at hand, we see that the potential for such transfer payments exists.[10]

III. *Customs Union and Alternative Tariff Policies*

The analysis of customs union has traditionally concerned itself with the conditions under which countries will find regional or group tariff discrimination preferable to unilateral tariff policy. Alternatively stated, the theory has attempted to define the range of situations in which regional free trade will be preferable from various points of view to generally restricted trade. In the development of the theory, however, it has been suggested that some members of a proposed union would be at least as well off, and quite possibly better off, if they unilaterally and nonpreferentially reduced their own tariffs. This point is implicit in Lipsey [10] and Michaely [13], and it constitutes the major argument of Cooper

and Massell [4].[11] In all three papers, terms-of-trade effects are assumed absent.[12] Hence, for each country acting on its own, the welfare-maximizing tariff is the zero tariff. For any given country, a small customs union may or may not be as beneficial as unilateral freeing of trade, depending upon whether the lowest-cost producer of its importable commodity becomes a member of the union or remains outside.[13] What remains to be established is whether these conclusions are applicable to the case of the union which is large enough to alter the terms of trade.

Consider Figure 2. Let $OW_A{}^o$ and $OW_B{}^o$ represent the group offer curves consistent with various tariff levels in various countries, but with no trade restriction in countries A and B.[14] For the latter two countries, the relevant offer curves are OA^o and OB^o, respectively. The world terms of trade are given by OT_o; A is in equilibrium at point $Q_a{}^o$ on indifference curve $I_a{}^o$, while B is at $Q_b{}^o$ on $I_b{}^o$. It is possible for either country to raise its welfare by imposing an *appropriate* tariff, particularly if neither the other country nor the countries making up the rest of the world retaliate. Thus, if country A alone imposes a tariff such that OA' becomes its revenue-redistributed offer curve, $OW_A{}'$ constitutes the new A-group reciprocal demand curve and OP_a gives the new world terms

---

[10] When its external tariff is less than prohibitive, the union will collect tariff revenues, which may be shared by the residents of the union in a variety of ways. Since the welfare of the member countries will be affected by the particular distribution scheme adopted, the willingness of a given country to participate in the union will be influenced, among other things, by its share in union tariff revenues.

As for the transfer payments from one member country to another, it has been shown by Meade [11], for example, that the introduction of such payments will produce shifts in offer curves due to the fact that national expenditure will no longer equal national income.

[11] For an argument supporting customs union as a form of coalition see Arndt [1].

[12] Vanek [16] is an exception as far as this assumption is concerned.

[13] We are presently concerned solely with the specialization and terms-of-trade arguments of customs union. It is recognized that whatever the benefits or losses associated with these factors, there may be numerous other reasons which may favor a particular customs union.

[14] The curvature of the group offer curve has been accentuated deliberately in order to clarify the exposition of the argument. Use of more elastic aggregate offer curves would produce crowding of the various points in the diagram, since the relative terms-of-trade shifts upon which much of the analysis is based would be correspondingly smaller.

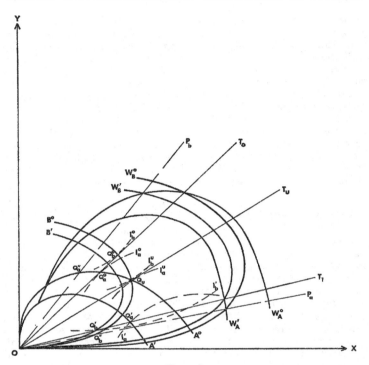

FIGURE 2

of trade. Country A's new equilibrium will be established at the point of intersection of OP_a and OA'; the welfare gain implicit in this policy is clear at once. Analogous remarks apply to country B and line OP_b. Retaliation by other countries, however, is likely to occur and hence to reduce or offset the favorable effects of unilateral tariff manipulation. This point can be ignored in the small union case, but it is of crucial importance in the present situation.

Assume next that both countries have in fact pursued past tariff policies and that OA' and OB' indicate their respective revenue-redistributed offer curves. OW_A' and OW_B' are the resulting group offer curves. The terms of trade are given by OT_1; A is now at Q_a' on indifference curve I_a' and B is at O_b' on I_b' A's welfare has improved relative to its no-tariff situation, while that of B has worsened. Starting with these conditions, and all other things unchanged, neither country's preferred strategy consists of unilateral, nonpreferential tariff *abolition*, since this would lead to inferior positions Q_a'' and Q_b'', respectively.

However, it may be equally impossible for either country to gain from further tariff manipulation. An increase in country A's tariff at point Q_a', for example, will shift the offer curves belonging to A and its group inward and move the terms of trade, OT_1, in a clockwise direction. The proportional displacement of the terms of trade will be smaller relative to the given proportional increase in the tariff, the smaller is the country within its own group and the larger is the number of trade reversals produced by the movements in the terms of trade. Trade reversals will inhibit the change in the terms of trade by placing pressure on $OW_B{}'$ to move inward and $OW_a{}'$ to move outward. In the limit, a tariff which causes OA' to shift while it leaves OT_1 unchanged will clearly reduce A_1's welfare.

As an alternative, suppose that the two countries form a union, initially with a prohibitive tariff. The union price ratio is then given by OT_u and trade equilibrium within the union is established at Q_u with A on indifference curve $I_a{}^u$ and B on $I_b{}^u$. Country B's welfare has improved relative to the initial tariff situation, while A's has worsened. It is possible, however, for appropriate transfers from B to A to enable the latter to reach indifference curve $I_a{}'$, thus making it indifferent between the union and the earlier tariff situation, while leaving union membership preferable to B. A marginally larger transfer payment will make customs union more desirable for both countries.[15]

The foregoing conclusion depends upon several assumptions. First, the pre-union tariffs were assumed optimum tariffs for the two countries. Second, it was noted in an earlier section that the particular elasticities of the various curves, as well as the relationships between individual countries and their groups will affect the final outcome; for example, our results will change if elasticities are such that the indifference curves associated with the pre-union tariffs intersect in the area below curve OA^o. Third, and most im-

portant for present purposes, the union tariff was prohibitive.

In order to examine the nonprohibitive case, we note the following. The price ratio in the outside world which results from a prohibitive union tariff may coincide with or it may lie on either side of OT_1, and this set of ratios clearly includes those which lie above OT_u. The actual relative position will be determined both by the sizes of the two countries and by their respective pre-union tariffs.[16] Assuming that union autarky produces terms of trade in the outside world which are flatter than OT_u, the intra-union price of Y will increase as the tariff is lowered; at unchanged outside tariffs, the price of Y will fall in the outside world. From the union's point of view, this has two important results. First, the lower tariff, and thus the more advantageous price of Y, will make the union increasingly more desirable to country A without eliminating its attractiveness to B, unless the final price ratio within B is equal to or worse than OT_1. Second, the tariff will produce revenue which the union can distribute as compensation to A. It would thus appear, that country A, having pursued an aggressive tariff policy prior to union, will display considerable interest in a moderate union tariff. The argument for the case in which the world terms of trade under union autarky lie above OT_u may be derived in analogous fashion. We see in this instance that A will push for high union tariffs.

We have assumed throughout that the rest of the world remains completely passive. Yet it is clear that the changes we have discussed will affect other countries. For instance, unilateral tariff re-

---

[15] As indicated in footnote 10, introduction of transfer payments will relocate offer curves and their origins.

[16] We recall that $OW_A{}'$ and $OW_B{}'$ correspond to the given pre-union, nonprohibitive tariffs in A and B, respectively. Complete withdrawal by the two countries from trade with the rest of the world will produce outside offer curves which lie inside $OW_A{}'$ and $OW_B{}'$.

duction by *A* will worsen the terms of trade of others in group W_A: these countries may thus initiate retaliatory tariff policies. Similarly, in the post-union world the countries in one of the groups will be worse off in the sense that the terms of trade will have moved against them; they too may retaliate. The union is thus likely to produce alterations in the tariffs of many countries, and, as shown earlier, not all of these changes will result in higher rates of protection.

IV. *Conclusion*

Whenever a customs union assumes proportions which provide it with sufficient economic power to influence the prevailing terms of trade, the resulting impact on welfare may either augment or offset the welfare changes due to preferential tariff reductions. Some of these possibilities have been investigated, particularly by Vanek [16], within the framework of a three-country model.[17] In the preceding sections we have attempted to widen the inquiry by moving away from the customary three-country analysis. Certain conclusions have emerged from this broadened investigation. First, it is no longer particularly meaningful—except for union among all of the exporters of a given commodity—to argue that the customs union will do one thing or another to the terms of trade faced by the outside world. Rather, shifts in the terms of trade will produce welfare gains for some countries and losses for others. Whether the net effect constitutes loss or gain is then a function of the welfare weights attached to the different countries (or, more correctly, to the different individuals who reside in these countries) and of the possibility of income transfers between countries.

[17] Mundell [15] has also examined the effects of tariff preferences on the terms of trade. See also his discussion of the effects of trade taxes [14].

Further, we conclude that it may be rational policy for some countries to push for the establishment of a given customs union, but nevertheless to refrain from joining that union. Increased market share and growth potential outside the union which accrue to a country as a result of the formation of the union will cause that country to elect nonmembership. Finally, we have seen that, viewed as one of several types of tariff policies, customs union may be superior to non-preferential tariff policy. Not only will there result welfare changes due to variations in the terms of trade, but the tariff revenues collected by a nonprohibitive union may be distributed in a variety of ways which again affect welfare of, and hence the desirability of, the union to a given country.

An interesting by-product of the foregoing analysis is the suggestion that optimum tariff strategy may dictate that some countries remaining outside the union reduce their prevailing tariffs. Much depends upon the extent of tariff warfare prior to formation of the union, and thus upon the dynamics of tariff competition about which very little is known. It is nevertheless intriguing to speculate about the extent to which the existence of the European Economic Community facilitated the Kennedy Round.

REFERENCES

1. S. W. ARNDT, "On Discriminatory vs. Non-preferential Tariff Policies," *Econ. Jour.*, Dec. 1968, 78.
2. G. S. BECKER, "A Note on Multi-Country Trade," *Am. Econ. Rev.*, Sept. 1952, *42*, 558–68.
3. J. BHAGWATI AND H. G. JOHNSON, "A Generalized Theory of the Effects of Tariffs on the Terms of Trade," *Oxford Econ. Papers*, Oct. 1961, *13*, 225–53.
4. C. A. COOPER AND B. F. MASSELL, "A New Look at Customs Union Theory," *Econ. Jour.*, Dec. 1965, *75*, 742–47.

5. G. A. ELLIOT, "The Theory of International Values," *Jour. Pol. Econ.*, Feb. 1950, *58*, 16–29.

6. F. D. GRAHAM, "The Theory of International Values Re-examined," *Quart. Jour. Econ.*, Nov. 1923, *38*, 54–86.

7. H. G. JOHNSON, "Income Distribution, the Offer Curve, and the Effects of Tariffs," *Manchester School*, Sept. 1960, *28*, 215–42.

8. ———, *International Trade and Economic Growth.* Cambridge 1958.

9. M. C. KEMP, "The Relation Between Changes in International Demand and the Terms of Trade," *Econometrica*, Jan. 1956, *24*, 41–46.

10. R. G. LIPSEY, "The Theory of Customs Union: A General Survey," *Econ. Jour.*, Sept. 1960, *70*, 496–513.

11. J. E. MEADE, *A Geometry of International Trade.* London 1952.

12. L. A. METZLER, "Tariffs, the Terms of Trade, and the Distribution of National Income," *Jour. Pol. Econ.*, Feb. 1949, *57*, 1–29.

13. M. MICHAELY, "On Customs Union and the Gains from Trade," *Econ. Jour.*, Sept. 1965, *75*, 577–83.

14. R. A. MUNDELL, "The Pure Theory of International Trade," *Am. Econ. Rev.*, March 1960, *50*, 67–110.

15. ———, "Tariff Preferences and the Terms of Trade," *Manchester School*, Jan. 1964, *32*, 1–13.

16. J. VANEK, *General Equilibrium of International Discrimination.* Cambridge 1965.

17. ———, *International Trade: Theory and Economic Policy.* Homewood 1962.

18. J. VINER, *The Customs Union Issue.* New York 1950.

Chapter 4

DOMESTIC DISTORTIONS AND TRADE POLICY

By SVEN W. ARNDT

WHEN a country possesses monopoly power in the international markets in which it trades, a competitive free trade situation will be characterized by a disparity between the domestic and foreign rates of transformation. Achievement of an optimal solution requires that this disparity be eliminated in a manner which does not simultaneously destroy the equality between the domestic rate of substitution and the domestic rate of transformation. To this end, the theory of optimum tariffs provides a criterion for appropriate intervention in foreign trade by means of duties and subsidies on trade. A tax-cum-subsidy policy of intervention in domestic production, on the other hand, is not appropriate, because in removing the existing distortion it creates a new inequality between the domestic rate of substitution in consumption and the domestic rate of transformation. Consequently, a tax-cum-subsidy policy of intervention is necessarily inferior to an optimum tariff.

Violations of Pareto optimality may be of domestic origin. A consumption externality destroys the equality between the foreign rate of transformation (which, however, remains equal to the domestic rate of transformation) and the domestic rate of substitution, while the presence of an externality or of monopolistic power in production creates a disparity between the domestic and foreign rates of transformation (although the equality between the foreign transformation rate and the domestic substitution rate is maintained). In all such cases intervention in trade is inappropriate, because it eliminates an existing inequality at the cost of creating a new distortion. In the case of the production externality, for example, a tariff produces a disparity between the domestic rate of substitution and the foreign rate of transformation, with the result that there may exist no tariff which is superior to free trade. In contrast, an appropriate tax-cum-subsidy on the domestic source of the distortion will eliminate the existing inequality without creating another. Consequently the tariff policy is necessarily inferior to an optimum tax-cum-subsidy policy of intervention.

The effects of domestic distortions on a country's welfare and the determination of optimal policies to eliminate such distortions were first investigated by Haberler [3] and later clarified and elaborated by Bhagwati [1, 2], Johnson [4], and Ramaswami [2]. These studies were confined

[1] I am indebted to Professor R. A. Mundell for helpful comments on an earlier draft. A research fellowship granted by the Ford Foundation and the UCLA Committee on International and Comparative Studies is gratefully acknowledged.

to trading situations consisting of two countries and two commodities and did not deal with multiple-commodity problems. The literature on multiple-commodity models, on the other hand, has not been concerned with the effects of distortions.[1] The question therefore emerges whether the results of the two-commodity studies of distortions carry over to the more general case. In the present paper we shall be concerned with the role of a non-traded commodity, the production or consumption of which may or may not be the source of the domestic distortion.[2] The argument is developed with reference to a small country for which it is shown that the presence of a non-traded good—which means that although the country faces given world prices, its production pattern is no longer determined by domestic and foreign rates of transformation independently of the shape of the preference function—modifies the usual results in several respects. In contrast to the two-commodity situation, production of the export commodity may rise or fall when trade is opened and, for the case of distortions in the export sector, trade will provide unequivocal welfare gains only if the production of the exportable commodity increases. It is shown that the presence of the non-traded good and the degree of its substitutability for the import good determine whether free trade will be superior or inferior to autarky.

1. Domestic distortions in a small country

Consider a country which produces two and consumes three commodities: commodity X_1 is traded for commodity X_2 in international markets in which the country possesses no monopoly powers, while commodity X_3 is produced and consumed entirely at home. One reason for the lack of trade in X_3 is that transportation costs may make its foreign price prohibitive; there exists in every country a large class of goods with this characteristic. Alternatively, the non-traded good may be a close substitute for the import commodity in which the country has a comparative disadvantage. In fact, to reduce the present case to the standard two-commodity situation it is merely necessary to assume that commodities X_2 and X_3 are perfect substitutes and that trade does not lead to complete specialization.

A. Distortions in the tradable goods sector

Whether a country gains or loses in moving from autarky to a competitive free trade situation will depend upon the location of the distortion. In the standard two-commodity case, in which Pareto optimality is

---

[1] Cf., for example, Kemp [5], Komiya [6], McDougall [7], Melvin [8], Mundell [9], and Samuelson [10].

[2] The paper deals explicitly only with distortions in production, but the analysis is readily adaptable to distortions in the consumption either of the traded or of the non-traded good.

violated in the production of the commodity in which the country has a true comparative advantage, free trade will unequivocally increase welfare if it leads to greater production of the distortion-ridden commodity.[1] We wish to determine whether this conclusion applies to the present more general case.

Fig. 1 lends itself to an examination of both the two-commodity and the three-commodity cases. Suppose initially that X_2 and X_3 are perfect

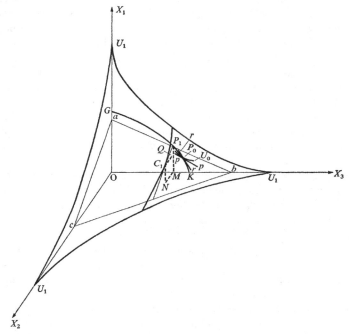

FIG. 1. Autarky equilibrium is located at P_0. Points P_1 and C_1 represent free trade production and consumption, respectively. At international terms of trade $(P_1 C_1)$, the country exports $P_1 Q$ of X_1 for $Q C_1$ of X_2.

substitutes, which means that we may ignore the third dimension and consider merely the $X_1 X_3$ plane, for we are essentially in a two-commodity world. GK gives the country's production possibility locus. The presence of an externality in the production of X_1 has raised the domestic market price (pp) of that commodity above its social rate of transformation (rr), causing the commodity to be underproduced. Autarky equilibrium is given by point P_0 on GK and on indifference curve U_0.

[1] See, for example, Johnson [4] and Bhagwati and Ramaswami [2].

Suppose that after trade has been established, the price ratio between the two commodities is given by ab, the international rate of exchange over which the country has by assumption no control. The changes in the nation's welfare which result from the move to free trade may now be separated into two components. First, with the original output mix unchanged, a welfare gain accrues to the country because it may, by trading some X_1 for X_3, move to an indifference curve which will lie (but which has not been drawn) above U_0; that is, there exists an indifference curve which is tangent to a line through P_0 and parallel to ab which represents a level of satisfaction higher than that indicated by U_0. Johnson [4] has called this gain the exchange or consumption gain. Second, the change in relative prices will affect the production mix itself. Assuming that factor prices are flexible and that resources are mobile, production equilibrium will move from P_0 to P_1.[1] At point P_1 the value of output in terms of the international exchange rate is necessarily higher than the value of output at P_0. Thus the exchange gain is in this instance reinforced by a production or specialization gain. The free trade consumption equilibrium (located on ab between P_1 and b) is therefore superior to the autarky situation.

In sum, when distortions are absent from a two-good world, a move from autarky to free trade yields a gain (which has a consumption and a production element); when distortions are present, a shift of output towards the industry with the distortion yields a gain, and a shift away, a loss, so that on balance there may be a gain or a loss. If, now, the industry subject to the distortion is the export industry, both forces make for a gain.

We wish to compare this result with the three-commodity case. Suppose, therefore, that X_2 and X_3 are not perfect substitutes, that X_2 is produced only abroad, and that X_3 is the home-produced commodity. The autarky equilibrium is again given by point P_0. However, pp is now one edge of a price plane relating the three commodity prices, and the U_i are indifference surfaces. In the absence of trade, the price plane of which pp is an edge will be so sloped in the $X_1 X_2$ and $X_3 X_2$ planes as to be tangent to the indifference surface U_0 at point P_0.

Now, suppose that trade is established and that ac is the international price ratio between X_1 and X_2. The ruling terms of trade must necessarily represent a welfare improvement: with production of X_1 and X_3 un-

---

[1] A potential source of domestic distortions is factor immobility coupled with factor price rigidities. Such cases have been analysed by Bhagwati and Ramaswami [2] and Johnson [4] in the context of a two-commodity world. The existence of a sector which produces goods entirely for internal consumption may, especially in underdeveloped countries, present obstacles to the free movement of factors of production and to the adjustment of relative factor rewards.

changed at P_0, the fall in the price of the import good produces an exchange gain; for by trading some X_1 for X_2 the country may move to an indifference surface located (but not drawn) above U_0, but below U_1. In addition, the country may gain from a relocation of the production equilibrium brought about by changes in the price relationship between exportables and the non-traded good, which will be the typical result of the initial change in the price of X_2. The fall in the price of that commodity will have two effects on domestic production and consumption. First, there will be substitution effects shifting demand from X_1 and X_3 to X_2, with the resulting excess supply greater for that commodity which is the better substitute for the importable good. Thus, if the competitiveness between X_2 and X_3 is greater than that between X_2 and X_1, substitution in consumption will lower the price of X_3 relative to X_1 so that on this count alone ab will be flatter than pp. In turn, changes in the price ratio pp will provoke substitution in production as producers adjust to demand shifts and thus tend to eliminate excess supply (in this case of X_3).

Second, the change in the price of X_2 will have a real income effect which will tend to increase the demand for the non-traded commodity, provided that it is not an inferior good. The strength of the real income effect depends upon the marginal propensity to spend on the non-traded commodity, and the greater the spending propensity relative to the substitution effect, the smaller the excess supply of X_3 and the greater the excess demand for X_3 which results from the opening of trade. The magnitude of the real income effect is also a function of a quantity weight determined by the proportion of national income devoted to the commodity for which the import good is a closer substitute. If, for example, X_2 and X_3 are strongly competitive in consumption and if at the time free trade is established the production of X_3 is higher relative to X_1, then the quantity weight will be correspondingly large. Finally, to these effects must be added the own-price elasticity of the home-produced good.

Whether the production of the exportable commodity rises or falls as a consequence of the opening of trade thus depends on spending propensities and substitution effects involving the non-traded commodity. This result differs substantially from the two-commodity situation in which the free-trade production pattern was determined independently of the shape of the preference function.[1] The greater the substitutability in

---

[1] In an analysis of the zero-distortions case in which a country produces all three goods, Komiya [6] has shown that price movements involving the non-traded commodity make the sign of the price elasticity of import demand ambiguous and raise the possibility of a positive elasticity even when the standard assumptions that imports are not inferior and that the elasticity of aggregate demand possesses the properties of individual elasticities are retained. For similar results, cf. McDougall [7]. Moreover, when three goods are produced

consumption between imports and the domestic good relative to the substitutability between exports and imports and the smaller the marginal propensity to spend on the domestic good, the greater the excess supply of the non-traded good and thus the greater the fall in its price; and for given propensities and consumption substitution effects, the required price change will be greater, the smaller the elasticity of substitution in production between exportables and the home good.

Suppose, then, that free trade increases the output of X_1 and reduces production of X_3 to the levels indicated by P_1. Free trade consumption equilibrium is given by the point of tangency (C_1) between the price plane abc and indifference surface U_1. The higher level of welfare associated with C_1 is due to both an exchange and a production gain. But while the introduction of trade has raised the country's welfare, the distortion has prevented the attainment of the optimum production mix and of the optimum volume of world trade.

Intervention in international trade is, however, not the appropriate policy to correct these unwanted effects of the distortion. If an export subsidy were to be imposed, it would increase the production of X_1, but only at the cost of creating a disparity between the domestic and foreign prices of exports. In the end, the ensuing situation will be inferior to free trade if the subsidy-induced production gain is more than offset by the resulting consumption loss. The optimal policy of intervention is clearly one which subsidizes directly the production of exports or taxes directly the production of the domestic good.[1]

We have until now dealt with the case in which the opening of trade leads to an increase in the production of the exportable commodity. If, however, the degree of substitution between imports and the non-traded good is sufficiently low relative to the substitutability in consumption between exports and imports and if the marginal propensity to spend on the domestic good is sufficiently high, the net effect of the improvement in the terms of trade will be an excess demand for the non-traded good and

with two factors of production, Kemp [5, ch. 6] has shown for the zero-distortions case that the price of the non-traded good will rise as a result of a rise in the import price of exports if both exports and the domestic product are either more capital intensive or less capital intensive than the import commodity. If the capital intensity of imports lies between those of the other two goods, the ratio of the changes in the prices of these two goods will be negative.

Melvin [8] has recently shown that the production surface in the case of a three-commodity, two-factor model in which complete specialization does not occur will be ruled, thus giving rise to a production indeterminacy, which in the case of a two-country situation makes it impossible to determine which country will produce what commodities without introducing specific demand assumptions. When all goods are produced, but one of them is not traded, the indeterminacy problem is in general solved.

[1] An analogous argument can be made for distortions in consumption. Suffice it to observe that a consumption tax on imports would have the same effects as a tariff as long as imports are not produced domestically.

38   DOMESTIC DISTORTIONS AND TRADE POLICY

thus a rise in its price relative to that of the exportable commodity. To the positive exchange effect on welfare must now be added a negative production effect and the net effect may go either way depending upon the relative strengths of the two components.[1]

From the preceding discussion the conclusion emerges that the results of the two-commodity case carry over to the broader situation with which we have been dealing. But the analysis does more than merely support the validity of the earlier results. It suggests three interesting generalizations. First, we have seen that a high degree of competitiveness between imports and home goods raises the probability that free trade will lead to production shifts in the direction of the exportable good in which the distortion is located and thus give rise to an unequivocal improvement in welfare. The greater, therefore, the competitiveness between the country's imports and its home-produced good, the less likely is the two-commodity result of 'specialization in the wrong direction' to occur. An adverse production effect becomes a threat only when the country's consumption is heavily biased in favour of a domestic good for which international markets offer very imperfect substitutes. As there exist in many countries large non-traded goods sectors, producing commodities which are likely to be competitive with imports, their presence effectively reduces the danger that a distortion-ridden export sector will lead to a situation in which free trade is inferior to self-sufficiency. This is, however, not to say that adverse production effects will not occur for countries with large domestic goods production.

Second, the size of the adverse production effect depends, *ceteris paribus*, on the rate of transformation in production between traded and non-traded goods.

Third, in a still more general case in which each country produces several exportable commodities together with a group of non-tradable goods, Haberler's concern with specialization and trade in a commodity in which the country has a true disadvantage is less urgent. When distortions are present in the production of exportables, the strong Haberler requirement that specialization take place in the commodity in which the country has a comparative advantage may be replaced by a much weaker and less stringent condition, namely, that free trade will unequivocally increase welfare if output expansion takes place at the expense of the non-traded commodity, even if such specialization does not occur

[1] Haberler [3] has called this specialization in the 'wrong' direction, but as Bhagwati and Ramaswami [2] have correctly pointed out, it is illegitimate, once domestic distortions are present, to argue that a country must in a two-commodity situation export the good in which it had a price advantage prior to trade. In the presence of a non-traded good the direction of change in production must in any case be separated from the direction of trade.

in the product in which the country has its greatest pre-trade price advantage.[1]

B. Distortion in non-tradable goods production

When the distortions under discussion are present in the production of the home good, it will be underproduced relative to the export commodity. The establishment of trade lowers the price of imports from its prohibitive autarky levels, and as price adjustments spread through the economy, the pre-trade production mix ceases to be appropriate unless the price ratio between exportable and domestic goods is unaffected by the new conditions. Apart from this special case, the results of the preceding section indicate that the price of exports will rise relative to the domestic good if the degree of competitiveness between commodities X_2 and X_3 is sufficiently high and the marginal propensity to spend on commodity X_3 is sufficiently low. An increase in the price and thus in the output of the exportable commodity creates in the present case a production loss which may or may not offset the exchange gain, depending, in addition to the factors previously mentioned, on the degree of distortion and on the ease of substitution in production between exports and the non-traded good. If, on the other hand, the price and hence the production of X_1 falls as a result of the opening of trade, the country will enjoy an unequivocal gain in welfare.

We are thus left with the interesting conclusion that (i) a country, whose export production is subject to distortions, may expect to gain from the establishment of free trade provided that the competitiveness between imports and the non-traded good is sufficiently high relative to the substitutability between imports and exports, while (ii) the existence of distortions in the non-traded goods sector requires, on the contrary, a low degree of substitutability between imports and home goods in order that an unequivocal gain be realized.

2. The choice of the export commodity

In the foregoing discussion, we specified at the outset that of the two domestically produced commodities X_1 was to be the tradable commodity. In the standard two-commodity model it is usually assumed that, while one of the two goods may represent the country's true comparative

---

[1] The existence of multiple commodities gives rise to the well-known problem of ranking commodities according to their 'comparative' advantages and disadvantages. The presence of swing commodities which a country may either export or import blunts the two-commodity distinction between production increases in the 'right' or 'wrong' direction.

Further, a detailed specification of this case must take into account the number of factors of production relative to the number of commodities produced and traded and thus the possibility of a production indeterminacy; it must also consider the relative degrees of distortion in the various tradable goods industries.

40   DOMESTIC DISTORTIONS AND TRADE POLICY

advantage, either good may become the country's export. It would thus seem that we have rather severely restricted the analysis.

However, this is not the case. Suppose, for example, that either one or the other but not both products may be exported, and suppose, further, that the establishment of free trade actually leads to exportation of X_3. Note that the fact that X_3 is being traded does not imply that specialization in its direction will take place. We cannot, in fact, determine the direction of specialization without first determining the degree of competitiveness between X_1 and the import good and X_3 and the import good. Given the degree of distortion in X_3, given the ratio of production of X_1 to X_3, and given the domestic expenditure propensities, the opening of trade will produce an unequivocal welfare gain if the competitiveness between X_3 and X_2 is sufficiently low. Our conclusions thus remain qualitatively unchanged.

3. Concluding remarks

The results of two-commodity studies thus carry over to the three-commodity case. But the introduction of a non-traded good provides greater precision, on the one hand, and leads to several generalizations, on the other. The precision accrues from our ability to specify under what circumstances the freeing of trade will lead to specialization gains and thus to unequivocal welfare gains. In the two-commodity case the output of the product in which the country has a true comparative advantage may increase or decrease depending upon the relationship between the domestic pre-trade distorted price ratio and the international terms of trade. In the present model we are able to predict the direction of specialization by examining the substitution and real income effects which relate the two traded commodities to the non-traded commodity.

The generalization derives similarly from the relationship between imported and home produced commodities. It has been shown that for given expenditure propensities, a sufficiently low degree of competitiveness between imports and domestic goods will bring about an unequivocal welfare gain consequent upon the opening of trade if the distortion is located in the non-traded commodity and that a high substitution effect is required when the distortion occurs in the production of exports.

REFERENCES

1. BHAGWATI, JAGDISH, 'The theory and practice of commercial policy: departures from unified exchange rates', Princeton University *Special Papers in International Economics*, No. 8 (Jan. 1968).
2. —— and RAMASWAMI, V. K., 'Domestic distortions, tariffs and the theory of optimum subsidy', *Journal of Political Economy*, lxxi (Feb. 1963).

3. HABERLER, G., 'Some problems in the pure theory of international trade', *Economic Journal*, lx (June 1950).
4. JOHNSON, H. G., 'Optimal trade intervention in the presence of domestic distortions', in Baldwin, R. E., *et al.*, *Trade, Growth, and the Balance of Payments* (Chicago: Rand McNally, 1965).
5. KEMP, M. C., *The Pure Theory of International Trade and Investment* (Englewood Cliffs: Prentice-Hall, 1969).
6. KOMIYA, R., 'Non-traded goods and the pure theory of international trade', *International Economic Review*, viii (June 1967).
7. MCDOUGALL, I. A., 'Tariffs and relative prices', *The Economic Record*, xlii (June 1966).
8. MELVIN, J. R., 'Production and trade with two factors and three goods', *American Economic Review*, lviii (Dec. 1968).
9. MUNDELL, R. A., 'The pure theory of international trade', *American Economic Review*, l (Mar. 1960).
10. SAMUELSON, P. A., 'The gains from international trade once again', *Economic Journal*, lxxii (Dec. 1962).

Part II

Fragmentation and Cross-Border
Production Networks

Chapter 5

Fragmentation

Fragmentation involves the decomposition of a production process into its constituent activities and the dispersion of those activities across national borders. It gives rise to cross-country production sharing and production networks. Under fragmentation, traded goods and services contain value added from more than one nation.

The ability to be "fragmented" into "production blocks," each capable of being carried out in a physically separate location, is in the first instance a matter of technology. Whether or not to take advantage of this facility, however, is an economic decision that depends on location-specific advantages, such as proximity to raw materials, factors of production, and markets. While the physical nature of production may remain largely unchanged, its organization undergoes significant transformation.

In addition to choosing locations for constituent activities, firms provide "service links" in order to facilitate communication and coordination and to allow for efficient and on-time transportation of parts and components within the network (Jones and Kierzkowski 1990). Hence, fragmentation will take place only where savings in production cost exceed the costs associated with service links.

When making their choices, firms must also determine whether to keep the dispersed activities under company management or to outsource them to independent contractors in so-called arm's-length relationships. The choice depends on economic as well as legal and institutional considerations; it involves trust, enforceability of contracts, and protection of intellectual property (Helpman 2006; Barba Navaretti and Venables 2004). A substantial proportion of cross-border production involves the foreign operations of the affiliates of multinational corporations, implying that a rising share of international trade is intrafirm trade.

Fragmentation, which has also been described as "breaking up the value-added chain," works particularly well between advanced and emerging economies and has grown rapidly in industries such as electronics, machinery, and textiles and apparel.

Key factors facilitating this development have been reductions in trade restrictions and other barriers and cost-cutting innovations in transportation and communications technologies. The rapid spread of international production sharing is changing trade patterns, trade balance accounting, and the interaction between trade, the exchange rate, and other macroeconomic variables.

The spread of production sharing implies that traded products increasingly contain parts and components from more than one country. Hence domestic value added to a country's exports is often significantly less than the value of those exports. Chinese exports of electronic machinery, for example, incorporate imported components. Similarly, the imports of many countries contain components made in those countries. United States imports of automobiles from Mexico, for example, carry large amounts of U.S.-made components.

Production sharing gives rise to a new form of intraindustry trade, in which parts and components and finished products belonging to the same industry or sector pass back and forth among countries. This vertical intraindustry trade differs from the more traditional horizontal intraindustry trade of different varieties of the same end product.

Analytical issues

The term *fragmentation* was first used in this context by Jones and Kierzkowski (1990). Alternative terminology includes intraproduct specialization and vertical specialization. The effects and implications of cross-border fragmentation may be examined from a variety of theoretical perspectives, including Ricardian, Heckscher-Ohlin (H-O), and imperfect competition (Arndt and Kierzkowski 2001). The first two are the workhorses of trade theory. In the Ricardian model, countries are differentiated by technology, so intraproduct specialization among countries participating in production sharing is determined by location-specific technological know-how. Countries with limited technological development will engage in low-tech production, while more advanced components and assembly will be produced in countries possessing the necessary technologies.

In the Heckscher-Ohlin framework, differences in factor endowments provide the basis for specialization, such that countries will specialize in activities that make intensive use of locally abundant factors of production. Labor-intensive component production and assembly will, therefore, be carried out in labor-abundant countries, other things being the same, while skill- and capital-intensive activities will be performed in more advanced countries. In that framework, fragmentation has effects on output, factor prices, trade, and welfare analogous to those associated with technological progress (Arndt 1997).

The factor-proportions view of vertical intra-industry specialization and trade is a key contribution of the H-O approach, which had been criticized in years past for its inability to explain horizontal specialization and trade. Indeed, it was this shortcoming that prompted the development of imperfect-competition models of international specialization and trade, in which consumers value variety and monopolistically competitive firms specialize in the production of variety. Intraindustry trade associated with production networks, on the other hand, consists of the movement across borders of parts, components, and end products belonging to the same a industry.

Factor endowments, however, are not the only type of location advantage. Others include distance, border, country size, infrastructure, legal and financial systems, and regulatory and other policies. The effects of these variables on trade in general have been studied with the aid of gravity models, which posit that trade between two countries will fall with distance and the thickness of the border; that country size measured in various ways affects bilateral trade positively; and that strong and transparent legal and institutional structures, ample infrastructure, and protrade regulatory policies increase trade.

The gravity equation is now beginning to be employed in the context of production networks, for the purpose of which it must be amended in a variety of ways. There is, for example, more than one distance to be accounted for. In addition to the distance between the importer and exporter of the final product, there is distance between countries supplying parts and components and the country in which the final good is assembled. Regional clustering of supplier nations (as in Southeast Asia) is a distinct location advantage.

Foreign direct investment

Production networks with developing economies typically require up-front capital formation, financed at least in part by inflows of foreign direct investment (FDI) and technology from advanced countries. Foreign investors erect production facilities and install infrastructure, bring in skilled workers, and transfer technology at levels of sophistication beyond those available in the country. While such activities violate several assumptions of the H-O model, that model is nevertheless useful in predicting the pattern of FDI flows.

The investment involved is vertical (VFDI), intended to support vertical or intraproduct specialization. In a world of cross-border production fragmentation, the H-O model predicts that VFDI will tend to flow from capital- and skill-abundant, labor- scarce countries to labor-abundant economies. The Ricardian model predicts that such flows will move from technologically advanced to technologically emerging economies.

As already noted, factor endowments are only one type of location advantage, and therefore cannot fully explain movements of FDI. Once again, the gravity model offers a way of accounting for additional location-specific considerations — including distance, country size, border effects, and various institutional and policy-related factors. The bulk of the existing empirical literature on FDI, however, covers periods dominated by horizontal foreign direct investment (HFDI), which prevails among advanced countries and which continues to be the dominant form of FDI.

According to this evidence, FDI responds positively to distance. The explanation lies in the fact that in horizontal specialization FDI is a substitute for exports. As distance and its costs increase, exports are replaced by on-site production for the local market and hence FDI flows rise. Vertical FDI, on the other hand, moves to support production sharing. Hence, when distance raises the costs associated with servicing a network, production sharing becomes unprofitable and FDI declines.

Multinational companies

While many multinationals go abroad to produce for the local market, an increasing number have become involved in production networks, a process in which affiliate operations play a key role. Often, the initial organizational structure follows a "hub-and-spoke" pattern, with affiliates in several countries trading directly with the parent company, but less with one another. As interactions become more sophisticated and infrastructure is developed, true networks evolve in which trade takes place among affiliates located in various countries, as well as between affiliates and local firms. This pattern is exemplified by Japanese multinationals operating in Southeast Asia (Kimura and Ando 2003).

Agglomeration of activities is important in this context, because it generates positive externalities. Clusters of multinationals operating in a given country or in several adjacent countries attract and train workers, improve access to finance and other services, and generate knowledge spillovers that raise productivity and reduce costs. The creation of such an environment benefits from supportive public policies and public investment in infrastructure. A classic example is Ireland and the electronics industry. Such an environment generates positive agglomeration effects, as workers with industry-specific skills migrate into the area and knowledge spillovers occur.

In this setting, local producers are encouraged to enter the industry as suppliers of goods and services to the multinationals. There is evidence that arm's-length trade is growing in Southeast Asia as foreign multinationals rely increasingly on local suppliers. For developing countries, this opens another path to industrialization.

Scale economies are important in production networks and are exploited by multinationals. Since neither the Ricardo nor Heckscher-Ohlin framework is capable of handling scale economies and externalities, the imperfect competition literature provides important insights. Scale economies come into play on both the production side and in the provision of service links among production blocks. If production of each part or component is concentrated in one location, for example, longer runs permit exploitation of internal scale economies at each location. Meanwhile, agglomeration and clustering of producers generate economies that are external to plant and firm.

In the provision of service links, the fixed costs associated with establishing a communications network can be spread over larger numbers of units and firms as the size of the network and the number of participating entities expand. Access to a service network encourages agglomeration of firms in a country or region. Where individual countries tend to be small, cooperative policies among countries are required to reap the benefits of agglomeration.

Productivity, employment, and wages

The spread of fragmentation has sounded political alarm bells in advanced countries about jobs and wages not only in manufacturing, but in services industries, as "offshoring" of call centers, help desks, programming, and ticketing operations has proliferated. There is no doubt that jobs of workers whose functions are shifted to foreign locations are lost. But if cross-border sourcing of components raises competitiveness and lowers prices of final products or services, thereby increasing sales and thus output, then jobs will be created elsewhere in the industry or more generally in the economy.

With respect to wages, there are two concerns. First, production sharing with low-wage countries may exert downward pressure not only on the wages of workers whose jobs are lost, but on wages generally in a "race to the bottom." Second, it may change the wage distribution against low-skilled workers and widen the wage gap between skilled and unskilled workers.

The available evidence is mixed, in part because it is not easy to separate the effects of fragmentation from those of technological change and of other factors affecting employment and wages (Feenstra 1998). The outcome further depends on the sector in which fragmentation occurs, on the skill ratios in the affected industries, and on the relationship of each skill category to capital. In a framework in which fragmentation occurs in many industries, moreover, there will be "onshoring" as well as "offshoring," so that jobs lost in one sector must be balanced against jobs gained in others. Under such circumstances, the problem is mainly one of matching unemployed workers with emerging jobs. This is the familiar trade-adjustment problem.

Regional integration

In recent years, regional production sharing and trade in parts and components has grown rapidly. This growth has been facilitated by preferential trade liberalization. While production sharing is generally welfare-improving under free trade and in preferential trade areas (PTAs), rules of origin that restrict the movement of components from outside the PTA can introduce significant elements of trade diversion.

Production sharing is changing the nature of regional integration, in that it requires deeper integration than the removal of tariffs and other restrictions on the flow of goods and services. It calls for liberalization of investment and for the cross-border movement of persons, as well as harmonization of technical standards, regulatory policies, and dispute settlement procedures. To the extent that cross-border integration of production at the level of industries reduces asymmetries and promotes convergence of business cycles, it helps pave the way for greater regional monetary cooperation, including monetary union.

When industries become linked across borders, production sharing tends to reduce the sensitivity of trade flows to exchange rate changes. Consider a depreciation of the Mexican peso against the dollar, which raises the price of imports of U.S.-made components for incorporation into passenger vehicles. When these vehicles are exported to the United States, the dollar's appreciation has an offsetting effect. Hence trade flows associated with production sharing are less sensitive to exchange rate movements than other types of trade. This has implications for intraregional exchange-rate arrangements (Arndt and Huemer 2007).

Fragmentation and interdependence

Production sharing allows countries to reap the benefits of increased specialization. In the context of standard trade theory, intraproduct specialization pushes out the production possibility curve and thereby allows countries to reach higher consumption frontiers. In this sense, its effects are analogous to those of technological progress and factor accumulation.

But it also links countries more closely to their trading partners and thereby reduces policy autonomy and increases interdependence. It goes well beyond trade in promoting economic integration by linking industries at the level of production. Countries are more open and thus more exposed to external shocks. A group of countries operating in a production network will experience similar shocks. As more industries become involved in networks, cross-country asymmetries decline. Business cycles tend to converge. The pressures — and incentives — for policy cooperation increase.

Fragmentation is an important feature of globalization. Products become internationalized, national markets are more closely linked to those abroad, economy-wide behavior patterns converge, and the domain of overlapping policy interests expands.

See also agglomeration and foreign direct investment; economies of scale; gravity models; Heckscher-Ohlin model; intrafirm trade; intraindustry trade; outsourcing/offshoring; Ricardian model; technology spillovers

Further Reading

Arndt, Sven W. 1997. "Globalization and the Open Economy." *North American Journal of Economics and Finance* 8(1): 71–79. Derivation of key results of fragmentation in terms of the Heckscher-Ohlin Model.

Arndt, Sven W., and Alexander Huemer. 2007. "Trade, Production Networks and the Exchange Rate." *Journal of Economic Asymmetries* 4(1): 11–39. Examines the effect of global production networks on the sensitivity of trade flows to exchange rates.

Arndt, Sven W., and Henryk Kierzkowski, eds. 2001. *Fragmentation: New Production Patterns in the World Economy.* Oxford: Oxford University Press. A collection of papers dealing with various aspects of fragmentation.

Barba Navaretti, Giorgio, and Anthony J. Venables. 2004. *Multinational Firms in the World Economy.* Princeton, NJ: Princeton University Press. A comprehensive study of the FDI, multinationals, and trade.

Deardorff, Alan V. 2001. "Fragmentation in Simple Trade Models." *North American Journal of Economics and Finance* 12(2): 121–37. Provides a more formal assessment of the effects of fragmentation.

Feenstra, Robert C. 1998. "Integration of Trade and Disintegration of Production in the Global Economy." *Journal of Economic Perspectives* 12(4): 31–50. Overview of theoretical and empirical issues related to fragmentation.

Helpman, Elhanan. 2006. "Trade, FDI, and the Organization of Firms." NBER Working Paper No. 12091. Cambridge, MA: National Bureau of Economic Research. A comprehensive overview of modeling multinationals.

Jones, Ronald W., and Henryk Kierzkowski. 1990. "The Role of Services in Production and International Trade." In *The Political Economy of International Trade,* edited by R. W. Jones and Anne O. Krueger. Oxford: Basil Blackwell, 31–48. Discussion of the role of service links in production networks.

Kimura, Fukunari, and Mitsuyo Ando. 2003. "Fragmentation and Agglomeration Matter: Japanese Multinationals in Latin America and East Asia." *North American Journal of Economics and Finance* 14(3): 287–317. An empirical study of Japanese MNCs operating in the two regions with a focus on behavioral differences.

Chapter 6

SUPER-SPECIALIZATION AND THE GAINS FROM TRADE

SVEN W. ARNDT*

An important facet of "globalization" is the spread of cross-border production, which is variously known as intra-product specialization, super-specialization, or production fragmentation. This advanced stage in the international division of labor works particularly well between high-wage developed and low-wage emerging economies. But it is precisely this context in which the practice has been criticized for destroying jobs and undermining wages.

This paper examines the welfare implications of this type of specialization on the part of labor-intensive, import-competing industries in advanced countries. The results will surprise the skeptics, for when import-competing industries abandon production of labor-intensive components, wages rise and industry employment and output expand. National welfare increases. For a large country, the terms of trade improve, raising national welfare still further. (JEL F11, F23)

I. INTRODUCTION

Around the globe, countries are being drawn ever more fully into the international trading system. In part, this merely reflects processes that have been underway for many years, but there are elements in the current phase of "globalization" that differentiate it from past episodes. One of those is the growing importance of what used to be called off-shore sourcing, but is also known as intra-product specialization, super-specialization, or production fragmentation.[1]

This paper examines the effect of super-specialization on wages, employment, output, and national welfare. The findings will be surprising to many, for intra-product specialization on the part of import-competing, labor-intensive sectors in high-wage countries increases industry employment and output, raises wages, and advances national welfare. If it generates terms

*This is a revised version of a paper presented at the Western Economic Association International 72nd Annual Conference, Seattle, Wash., July 1997. Helpful discussions with Henryk Kierzkowski and comments from participants at the Claremont workshop on "Globalization," at the University of Basel and from anonymous referees are gratefully acknowledged.

Arndt: C. M. Stone Professor of Money, Credit and Trade and Director, The Lowe Institute of Political Economy, Claremont McKenna College, Phone 1-909-621-8012, Fax 1-909-607-8008, E-mail lowe@mckenna.edu

1. Fragmentation is the term used by Jones and Kierzkowski (1997).

of trade changes, those are welfare-enhancing as well.

II. SPECIALIZATION BEYOND FINISHED PRODUCTS

The focus in this section is on offshore sourcing by the import-competing industry of an advanced country. The framework is the Heckscher-Ohlin (H-O) model. The initial conditions are featured in Figure 1, with X_o and Y_o representing the unit-value isoquants for final goods X and Y. The wage-rental ratio is (w/r). In an H-O setting, the high-wage country exports the capital-intensive commodity Y and imports labor-intensive X.

Production of commodity X is assumed to consist of two phases involving two distinct components, x_1 and x_2, whose expansion paths are represented in Figure 1 by rays $0x_1$ and $0x_2$, respectively. Activity x_1 is not only the more capital-intensive of the two but is more capital-intensive than the product as a whole. The factor proportion of overall production at point F is obtained by vector addition and represents a weighted average of the factor proportions of the component activities. Production of X_0 units of the finished product thus requires amounts of x_1 and x_2 given by isoquants (not drawn) at points G and H, respectively.

Starting with a situation involving trade in finished goods only, we ask what would hap-

Contemporary Economic Policy
(ISSN 1074-3529)
Vol. XVI, October 1998, 480–485

©Western Economic Association International

FIGURE 1

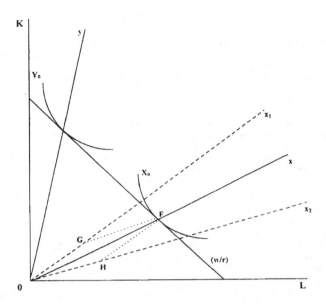

pen if reductions in coordination and other costs brought about by innovations in transportation and telecommunications, as well as liberalization of tariffs and other trade barriers, create incentives for the international dispersion of component activities without impairing quality control and other advantages associated with single-site production. Suppose, in particular, that there exists a labor-rich, low-wage country capable of supplying component x_2 at significant cost savings and that these cost advantages lead domestic firms to abandon x_2-production in favor of imports.[2]

This extension of the international division of labor into component activities reduces costs in the X-industry. Costs will be lower so long as the amounts of capital and labor embodied in exports of x_1 used to pay for imports of x_2 are smaller than the amounts of capital

and labor needed to produce x_2 at home.[3] In what follows, the cost of assembly is assumed to be incorporated in the cost of producing component x_1.

If the country is assumed initially to be small, then prices of goods X and Y are exogenous and the cost-savings do not lead to lower goods prices. Hence, adjustment takes place solely via changes in relative factor prices.[4] When x_2-production is abandoned, production conditions in the X-industry are fully embodied in the x_1-isoquants. If component x_2 were available free on world markets, then point G would give the full factor-cost of producing X_o units of X.

---

2. We assume that, for the usual reasons, factor-price equalization has not been achieved between the two countries. For present purposes, it is not important whether domestic firms set up their own production facilities abroad, in the manner of multinational companies, or whether offshore sourcing proceeds at arms length.

3. Imports of x_2 may, of course, be paid for by exports of Y rather than x_1.

4. Large countries will generate terms-of-trade effects as a result of component specialization. Those effects are discussed below. The present example suggests that in small countries facing declining world prices for finished products like X, industries may improve their survival chances by shifting production of their least efficient activities to the trading partner. From this perspective, offshore sourcing is an alternative to protection as a means of helping industries compete in the markets for final goods.

When x_2 is not free, but must be paid for with exports of x_1, the total quantity of capital and labor needed to produce X_o units of X will be larger than the amounts indicated at point G. In the presence of cost savings, however, the new unit-value isoquant will be closer to the origin than X_o. It will lie along the ox_1 ray at or beyond point G. Offshore procurement of x_2 will be cost-effective as long as the total quantity of labor and capital utilized in x_1-production is less than the amounts given at point F. Suppose that, at the initial factor-price ratio, this new unit-value isoquant is represented by X' in Figure 2a.

The original w/r ratio is no longer compatible with cost conditions in the X-industry. The factor-price ratio must be tangent to the Y_o-isoquant and the relevant x_1-isoquant. That ratio is given by $(w/r)'$. Offshore procurement of the labor-intensive component thus raises wages and increases capital-labor ratios in both industries, as reflected by the new expansion paths, ox_1' and oy'.[5]

This increase in relative wages is an important result, suggesting that fears about the adverse effects on wages of offshore procurement and cross-border production involving low-wage countries may be misplaced. The intuition flows readily from basic considerations of comparative advantage.[6]

Abandoning x_2-production releases both capital and labor from relatively inefficient, labor-intensive activities. The effect is similar to the well-known consequences of labor-saving technical progress in labor-intensive industries.[7] It allows the X-industry to concentrate on making those parts of X in which its comparative disadvantage is smaller or its comparative advantage greater. The gap between prices and costs, opened by reductions in the

latter, is eliminated by an increase in the relative price of labor, the factor used intensively in x_1 relative to Y.

A. Output and Employment Effects

Considering the changes that have occurred thus far, and assuming that labor and capital remain fully employed, Figure 2b traces the aggregate effects of super-specialization for a given economy-wide resource endowment of E. The primed expansion paths are carried over from Figure 2a. Output of X rises to X_1, while Y-output falls to Y_1. The gap between prices and costs in the X-industry creates profit opportunities and hence generates incentives for expansion.[8]

This, too, is an important result for suggesting that predictions of job losses in labor-intensive import industries as a result of offshore sourcing of components from low-wage countries may not be fulfilled.

Certain types of jobs will, of course, be lost in the X-industry. These are the jobs involved in making component x_2. But more jobs are created in the other line of production (and in assembly of the final product) than are lost; hence, overall employment rises in the industry.

Such changes may, of course, pose adjustment problems for workers in both industries, but those problems are likely to be less severe for X-industry workers, who are re-assigned to x_1-production and thus remain in the same industry, than for Y-industry workers, who must make the switch between industries.

B. The Terms of Trade

When the country is large, the increased output of good X coming on the market and the reduction in Y-output will put downward pressure on import prices and upward pressure on export prices and thus improve the terms of trade.[9] Thus, intra-product specialization in the

---

5. For more detail on the nature of these adjustments, see Arndt (1997, 1998) and Jones and Kierzkowski (1997).

6. In the context of the present model, featuring perfectly mobile, homogeneous labor, the wage-rental ratio necessarily rises throughout the economy. That is unlikely to happen in a multi-factor world with imperfectly integrated labor markets. The thrust of the argument is that workers can be made better off and jobs can be created in an import-competing industry that engages in this form of specialization. Some or all of these effects may spread beyond the industry.

7. On the effects of technical progress, see, for example, Johnson (1971).

8. In the case examined, final goods prices remain unchanged, and hence the decline in costs creates incentives for the industry to expand. In many import-competing industries, final-goods prices come under pressure from falling world prices. In such cases, cost-savings due to component specialization may alleviate, if not reverse, those contractionary pressures.

9. The full effect on world prices cannot be determined without consideration of concomitant changes in the second country. That issue is not pursued here.

FIGURE 2a

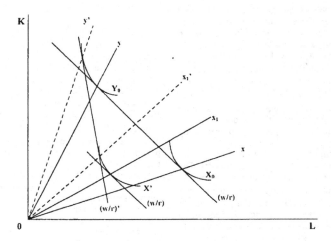

FIGURE 2b

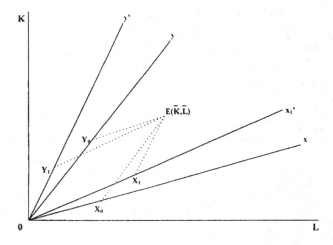

labor-intensive, import-competing industry improves the terms of trade of the advanced, capital-rich country.

The decline in the import price shifts the relevant x_1-isoquant out in Figure 2 (not drawn), while any increase in the export price would shift the Y-isoquant inward. Together, these price changes exert pressures on the wage-rental ratio opposite to those generated by component specialization. While cost reductions due to component specialization tend to raise X-output, terms-of-trade improvements reduce it. However, so long as the former effect dominates the latter, X-production will rise and Y-production fall.

C. National Welfare

We have seen that intra-product specialization in the country's import-competing sector raises industry employment and output and increases wages relative to capital rentals. It remains to determine the effect of specialization on national welfare. This is done in Figure 3, where the initial equilibrium for world price P_w is characterized by production at Q and consumption at C.

Super-specialization in X shifts the production possibility curve out along the X axis. To see the intuition, compare points T' and T''. The former represents the maximum amount of X that can be produced when intra-product specialization does not take place. If the introduction of offshore sourcing reduces the amount of capital and labor needed to produce X, then there will be labor and capital left over when the amount of X-output given at point T' has been reached. These resources may be used to produce additional amounts of X. Analogous considerations apply to other points on the production possibility curve. In general, the cheaper x_2-imports are relative to home production, the greater will be the displacement of the production possibility curve along the X-axis. The new production possibility curve is represented by TT''.

At initial terms of trade, P_w, the outward shift of the production possibility curve under intra-product specialization moves the production equilibrium to Q', confirming the earlier result that X-production rises while Y-production falls. Consumption moves to C', which lies on a higher indifference curve and thus

represents an improvement in national welfare.[10]

If the country is large, this combination of higher X-output and lower Y-output will cause the relative price of X to fall, rotating the terms of trade in a counter-clockwise manner to P_w'. This causes production to shift back toward good Y, to Q'', while consumption moves to C''. While production shifts partially back to the export good, the result is a further boost in national welfare.

III. CONCLUSION

Concerns that offshore production by labor-intensive, import-competing industries in high-wage countries is harmful to those industries do not appear to be warranted in the situations analyzed. Specialization at the level of components strengthens industries, allowing them to expand employment and output and causing wages to rise relative to capital rentals.

This type of specialization allows industries to slough off the activity in which they have the greatest disadvantage, thereby reducing production costs relative to prices. The emerging cost-price gap introduces profit opportunities and incentives to expand production. This type of innovation in the relatively labor-intensive sector raises wages. In the case examined, labor is homogeneous and perfectly mobile, so that the wage effect spreads throughout the economy. In situations with many types of labor and varying degrees of factor mobility, the effects of component specialization will spread less completely beyond the industry in question.

Changes in product prices matter. If the industry is competing with imports whose worldwide prices are falling, then component specialization can help it cope with those competitive pressures. If the country is large relative

10. One may ask why reallocation of productive resources away from the Y-industry in which the country has comparative advantage is not welfare-reducing. The answer is analogous to the case of technical progress in the import-competing industry. When that sector abandons the least advantaged activity, the effect is analogous to technological change. It reduces the extent of the industry's comparative disadvantage and thereby changes the optimal distribution of the economy's productive resources between sectors. The X-industry's reduced comparative disadvantage implies that the initial allocation of capital and labor in the Y-industry is excessive and must be reduced.

FIGURE 3

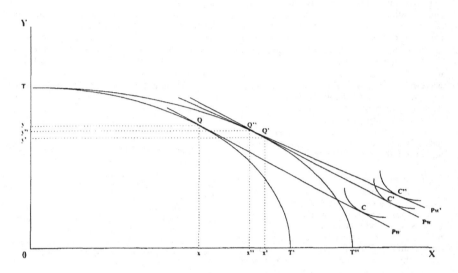

to the world market, then component specialization in the import-competing industry improves the terms of trade and thus adds further welfare gains.

Extending the international division of labor beyond final products to the realm of component activities thus opens up new welfare opportunities. It does so by reducing the comparative disadvantage of the labor-intensive industry.

Industries that retain the least advantaged of their productive activities undermine their overall competitiveness. Giving up the most disadvantaged activities and concentrating on doing what can be done better or best improves the utilization of resources and thus raises efficiency and welfare.

REFERENCES

Arndt, Sven W., "Globalization and the Open Economy," *North American Journal of Economics and Finance,* 8:1, 1997, 71–79.

———, "Globalization and the Gains from Trade," in Karl-Josef Koch and Klaus Jaeger, eds., *Trade, Growth, and Economic Policy in Open Economies,* Springer-Verlag, New York, 1998, 3–12.

Johnson, Harry G., *Two-Sector Model of General Equilibrium,* Aldine Atherton, Chicago, 1971.

Jones, Ron W., and Henryk Kierzkowski, "Globalization and the Consequences of International Fragmentation," mimeo, March 1997.

Chapter 7

Global production networks and regional integration

Sven W. Arndt

1. INTRODUCTION

Cross-border production sharing is probably one of the more important new elements in trade relations among countries. It occurs with or without the overlay of preferential trade liberalization. An example of the latter is the production networks of Japanese firms in Asia.[1] An example of the former is production sharing between Canada, the US, and Mexico in the North American Free Trade Area (NAFTA).

Production sharing based on intra-product specialization has been shown to be welfare-enhancing under conditions of free trade, while its effects are ambiguous in the context of a most-favored-nation (MFN) tariff regime.[2] This chapter examines the implications of production sharing in the context of preferential trade liberalization. Of particular interest is the case in which a free-trade area which is clearly trade-diverting under traditional circumstances becomes trade-creating with joint production.

Trade in components has important implications for the interaction between exchange rates and the trade balance. Trade tends to become less sensitive to exchange-rate changes and trade-balance accounting needs to distinguish between the value of total trade and trade in value-added.

When production sharing takes place between advanced and emerging economies, foreign investment flows occur and capacity accumulation typically precedes the onset of joint production. This introduces cycles into the behavior of the real-exchange rate and the current account. The real rate appreciates and the current balance deteriorates during the investment phase of the process, followed by real depreciation and current account improvement.

The rest of the chapter is organized as follows. Section 2 lays out the basic argument in a standard general equilibrium framework, while Section 3 examines key welfare effects of joint production in a partial equilibrium framework. Section 4 studies the effect of production sharing on the exchange-rate sensitivity of trade and discusses alternative measurements of the balance of trade. Section 5 deals with the real-exchange-rate effects of an investment cycle associated with the implementation of joint production. Section 6 considers exchange-rate regime choice. Section 7 concludes.

2.   TRADE LIBERALIZATION VERSUS ECONOMIC COOPERATION

While production sharing may take place across a broad range of trade regimes, it is not welfare-enhancing in every regime. It is unambiguously welfare-improving under conditions of free trade. It increases welfare by allowing specialization to be extended beyond finished products to the level of constituent production activities. In a standard Heckscher–Ohlin framework, variations in factor intensity across the components of a product imply potential gains from intra-product specialization, the magnitude of those gains depending on transport and coordination costs. Modern innovations in communication and transportation technologies have sharply reduced those costs and have thereby created new opportunities for profitable production sharing.[3]

In a tariff-ridden world, on the other hand, production sharing may reduce rather than improve welfare. A tariff on imports of the final product reduces the efficiency of resource allocation in the economy. While production sharing in that industry tends to mitigate the degree of comparative disadvantage of that industry and thus improves the efficiency of resource reallocation, it may not be able to fully offset the initial inefficiencies. Both the tariff and production sharing shift specialization toward the sector in which the country has comparative disadvantage, and the end result can be overall specialization in the wrong direction.

In Figure 8.1, points Q_0 and C_0 represent production and consumption in the presence of a tariff, t, on imports of finished product X. The size of the tariff is given by the wedge between the world price, P_w, and the tariff-inclusive domestic price, P_d. As shown in the literature cited above, production sharing in a sector has an effect similar to technical progress in that sector and shifts the production possibility curve out along the axis representing that sector. This shift is indicated by the move from point T to T' along the X axis.

When the country is small, these changes do not affect prices; the new production and consumption equilibria are located at points Q_1 and C_1, respectively, where the domestic price ratio is tangent to the new production possibility curve and an appropriate indifference curve. Output of the good subject to production sharing (X) thus increases at the expense of the second good (Y). Consumption falls to a lower indifference curve. The trade triangle shrinks.

It is apparent from the figure that welfare need not fall. Whether it rises or falls depends on the slope of the Rybczynski line (RR) relative to the slope of

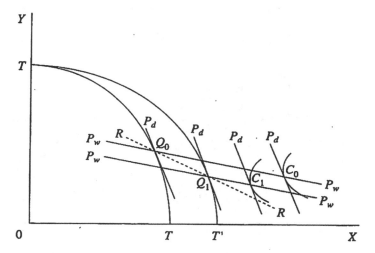

Figure 8.1   Production sharing and protectionism

the world price ratio.[4] When the line is steeper than the world price, welfare falls; it rises when the Rybczynski line is flatter than the world price.

When production sharing is introduced together with preferential tariff liberalization, welfare may rise or fall relative to the MFN level. While this is consistent with the well-known possibility that preferential trade arrangements may be net trade-creating or trade-diverting, production sharing mutes the trade-diverting tendencies of preferential trade liberalization.

In Figure 8.2, the analysis starts with an MFN tariff, domestic price P_d and production and consumption at points Q_0 and C_0, respectively. Introduction of a preferential trade agreement without production sharing generates intra-area price P_{pta} and moves production to Q_1 and consumption to C_1. Welfare declines, making this a trade-diverting free-trade area. Whether welfare declines or not depends on the intra-area price relative to the tariff-inclusive domestic price and the world price. As the intra-area price ratio becomes flatter and thus approaches the world price ratio, elements of trade creation expand, while the importance of trade-diverting elements declines. At a sufficiently flat price ratio, welfare improves relative to the MFN equilibrium.

This is a well-known feature of preferential trade liberalization. Suppose, however, that the partner countries engage in deeper economic integration, creating an economic area (EA) in which traditional preferential trade liberalization is combined with production sharing. The latter shifts the production possibility curve outward along the X axis from T to T', causing output to move to Q_2 and consumption to C_2. While this is still a trade-diverting

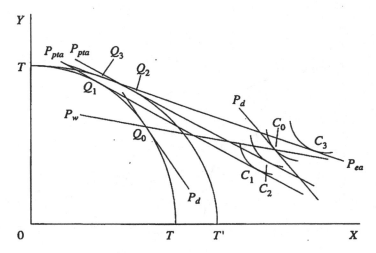

Figure 8.2 Production sharing and trade liberalization

arrangement, welfare falls by less than before. Thus deeper integration, which includes production sharing, mitigates the negative welfare effects of narrow preferential trade liberalization.[5]

Production sharing may, however, reduce the relative price of X and thus flatten the price ratio relative to its slope under the traditional PTA. By specializing in the components of product X in which each has comparative advantage, the two countries can improve productivity. We assume that this rise in efficiency is passed through to a lower intra-area price ratio, which is represented in Figure 8.2 by the flatter line P_{ea}. Production and consumption move to points Q_3 and C_3, respectively. This improvement in the country's terms of trade raises welfare.[6]

3. TRADE CREATION AND DIVERSION UNDER PRODUCTION SHARING

Implementation of NAFTA led to what were at times substantial shifts in trade patterns away from non-members to Canada and especially Mexico. In the automobile sector, for example, Mexico's share rose significantly, as Figure 8.3 suggests.[7] It would be tempting to interpret these shifts as evidence of trade diversion and hence of a welfare decline. Such a conclusion may appear warranted by the reasonable assumption that Mexico is the high-cost producer of automobiles.

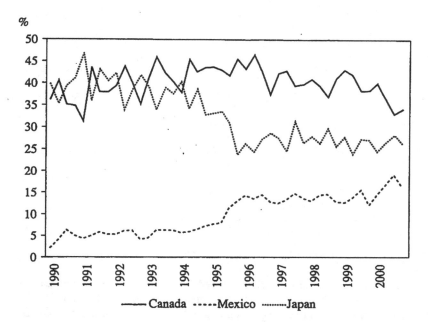

Figure 8.3   US motor vehicle import proportions

While trade diversion is certainly a possible outcome in the standard model of preferential trade liberalization, such an outcome is less likely in the context of the deeper integration associated with an economic area in which preferential trade liberalization is accompanied by production sharing. In that case, automobiles made entirely in Japan are replaced by imports from Mexico which contain parts and components made in the United States, with Mexico specializing in labor-intensive assembly. With both the US and Mexico specializing in activities in which they are respectively the low-cost producers, production sharing enables them to capture significant cost savings, so that trade diversion is now limited to activities in which Japan holds the edge.

Consider the situation depicted in Figure 8.4. In order to simplify the set-up, we assume linear supply curves for Japan, and for conventional production methods in Mexico and the United States. The term 'conventional' is used to denote that the good is produced in its entirety in each country, without resort to cross-border sourcing. We assume that Japan is the low-cost producer and Mexico the high-cost producer under these conventional conditions. Curves S_j and S_{mx} in Figure 8.4 represent supply conditions in Japan and Mexico, respectively.

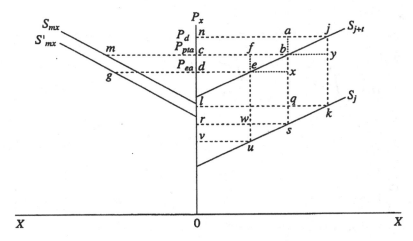

Figure 8.4 Trade creation and trade diversion

The starting situation is characterized by a specific non-discriminatory (MFN) tariff, t, imposed by the United States on all imports of product X. The full general equilibrium set-up was discussed above; here we focus on certain features of adjustment in a partial equilibrium context. The tariff-inclusive Japanese supply curve is given by curve S_{j+t}. The tariff-inclusive Mexican supply curve is not drawn, because the assumed magnitude of the tariff is such as to knock Mexico out of the US market. The rest of the picture, which would include US supply and demand curves, is not drawn in order to keep the figure simple and readable.

The initial price of X in the United States, P_d, is determined by the intersection between US demand (not drawn) and the sum of US and tariff-inclusive Japanese supply. At price P_d, Japanese exports to the US amount to nj in Figure 8.4. Tariff revenue collected by US authorities is given by rectangle $jkln$.

Implementation of a conventional free-trade area (that is, without production sharing) between the US and Mexico generates a lower price, such as P_{pta}, determined by the intersection between the aforementioned US demand curve and a new supply curve (not drawn) composed of $S_{us} + S_{mx} + S_{j+t}$. US imports rise to mb, with mc units coming from Mexico and cb units from Japan. Imports from Mexico partly replace imports from Japan, as well as US production. It is well known that the changes in price and output in conventional US production generate a transfer from producers to consumers and a net efficiency gain, which is a key element of trade creation.

The changes involving imports from Japan are the source of trade diversion. Trade diversion results from the inefficiencies associated with the switch of imports from Japan, which supplies the product along the low-cost supply curve, S_j, to Mexico's conventional producers, who supply the product along the relatively high-cost curve S_{mx}. As noted, before the PTA, US customs authorities collect tariff revenues equal to the area *njkl*. After implementation of the PTA, tariff revenues amount to *cbsr*. The lost revenue encompassed by rectangle *nabc* is compensated by the terms-of-trade gain given by *lqsr*. Area *nabc* is thus a pure gain in consumer surplus. The revenue loss contained in rectangle *bykq*, on the other hand, is a pure efficiency loss and thus represents the degree of trade diversion. The revenue loss represented by area *ajyb* is an internal transfer to consumer surplus. It is well known that the area of trade diversion may be larger or smaller than the sum of the areas representing trade creation, which makes the welfare effect of conventional preferential trade liberalization ambiguous.

Suppose that good X is made up of two components, x_1 and x_2, and that Japan possesses comparative advantage over the US not only in the final product, but in the production of each of the two components. Mexico is assumed to be at a competitive disadvantage *vis-à-vis* both countries in overall terms and in producing the first component, but to have comparative advantage with respect to the second component. In an endowment-based model, therefore, this information, together with Mexico's relative labor abundance, would imply that the second component is the labor-intensive component (of which automobile assembly is an example).

Introduction of production sharing represents a deepening of economic integration. We refer to this, more complex, type of integration as an economic area (EA). Under the stated assumptions, production sharing in such an area would have the US specializing in producing the first component and Mexico the second. Improvements in efficiency from production sharing may come in two forms. The ability to obtain certain components at reduced cost lowers production costs of the final product, which would be represented by downward shifts in both the US and Mexican supply curves. In this case, each country continues to produce the final product, but each unit of the final product contains imported components.

Cost reductions of the type discussed serve to lower the price of X relative to its level in the conventional PTA and hence generate improvements in welfare. In Figure 8.4, curve S'_{mx} represents such a cost-improving change in supply conditions in Mexico. This is a welfare gain, which helps offset elements of trade diversion.

The decline in price to P_{ea} reduces Japanese exports to the US to *de*, on which the US authorities collect *deuv* in tariff revenues. The revenue loss contained in area *cfed* is offset by the welfare gain associated with the terms-of-trade improvement of *rwuv*, so that *cfed* represents a net gain in consumer surplus, rather than an internal transfer from revenues to consumer surplus.

Area *fbxe*, on the other hand, is an internal transfer from revenues to consumer surplus and thus does not change overall welfare. Area *exsw* measures the extent of trade diversion in the move from the conventional preferential trade area to the economic area. The welfare gains appear to exceed the welfare losses, particularly since the lower price at which the US obtains imports from Mexico represents a pure consumer surplus gain.[8] The decline in the price of US-produced units breaks down into the usual internal transfer from producer to consumer surplus and a pure efficiency gain.

An alternative approach to exploiting the advantages of production sharing is to establish joint production facilities, which shifts some or all production of the product to new entities.[9] In that event, the supply curves representing conventional production remain unchanged, but there appears a new supply curve for joint production (not shown). This supply curve would be expected to lie below the two countries' respective conventional supply curves, but may lie above or below Japan's supply curve, depending on the degree of productivity improvement embodied in joint production. The extent of improvement depends on the initial gap between the US and Japan in x_1 production and on Mexico's edge in x_2 production.

The market now clears at the intersection (not shown) between the US demand curve and the sum of the joint supply curve, the conventional supply curves for the United States and Mexico, and the tariff-inclusive Japanese supply curve. It is clear that the market-clearing price, P_{ea}, will lie above relevant segments of the Japanese tariff-free supply curve, as shown, which implies that elements of trade diversion will persist even at this deeper degree of economic integration. As noted, imports from Japan decline to *de*, and this reduction causes the Japanese supply price to drop to the level indicated by *v*.

The welfare analysis then follows the discussion of production sharing which reduces costs relative to conventional production. There is an efficiency loss as low-cost Japanese imports are replaced by joint production, which supplies the product at the equilibrium price. That price lies above the tariff-free Japanese supply price, typically even if the joint production supply curve itself lies below that Japanese supply curve. The efficiency losses are given by the area *exsw*. It is important to note that, under conditions of increasing costs, conventional producers will lose market share, but they need not disappear altogether.[10]

4.   THE EXCHANGE RATE AND THE TRADE BALANCE

Whether it occurs with or without preferential trade liberalization, production sharing affects the sensitivity of the trade balance to exchange-rate movements and requires additional care in interpreting changes in the trade balance.

In the standard model, currency depreciation reduces imports and raises exports, as the domestic-currency price of imports rises and the foreign-currency price of exports falls. The net effect on the trade balance is subject to a variety of influences and conditions, including the degree of pass-through. Production sharing changes the role of pass-through, to the extent that a country's exports enter into its imports and its imports become part of its exports. That is because the exchange-rate effect on the price of imports denominated in one currency is offset by the exchange-rate effect on the price of exports expressed in the other currency.

There are several layers of pass-through at work here, but suppose that the depreciation of the peso is passed through completely to an increase in the peso price of component imports into Mexico, which in turn is fully passed through to the peso price of the assembled vehicle. When the vehicle is priced in dollars, again assuming full pass-through, the dollar price will fall only to the extent that the vehicle contains Mexican value-added.

This is the important difference between trade involving goods of joint production and traditional trade in products made entirely at home. The smaller the share of Mexican value-added in a commodity imported into the United States, the smaller the effect of the peso depreciation on Mexican exports of the finished product and US exports of the components that go into it.

These considerations have implications for the behavior of the trade balance. Conventionally, a country's demand for imports is modeled as a function of home GDP, relative prices and the exchange rate. An increase in GDP and in relative inflation at home, and a nominal appreciation all raise the demand for imports and thus worsen the trade balance. A rise in foreign GDP, foreign inflation and domestic currency depreciation tend to improve the trade balance. Suppose, however, that Mexican imports from the US consist mainly of components for use in exports to the United States. Then, changes in Mexican GDP should have little influence on imports. Instead, it would be changes in US demand for imports from Mexico which would be expected to determine the rise and fall of Mexican imports. Thus US end-product imports become an important determinant of US parts exports and the importance of Mexican GDP declines.

Production sharing also affects the interpretation of changes in the trade balance, particularly with respect to the distinction between the value of trade flows across borders and the movement of value-added. When an imported automobile from Japan, valued at $20 000, is replaced by a vehicle of equal value from Mexico, which contains US-made components worth $15 000, combined with $5000 consisting of Mexican components and assembly, the value of US car imports does not change. Imports of foreign value-added, however, fall from $20 000 (on the assumption that the Japanese automobile was made entirely in Japan) to $5000. This suggests an 'improvement' in the US value-added trade balance of $15 000.[11]

Over time, as motor vehicle imports from Mexico expand, exports rise by $15 000 for every $20 000 increase in imports, for a worsening of the conventional trade balance of $5000 per vehicle. If the $15 000 of US-made components is netted out of the imported motor vehicle, on the other hand, the value-added trade balance 'improves' by $10 000 for each vehicle included in joint production.

5.   PRODUCTION SHARING AND FOREIGN DIRECT INVESTMENT

Implementation of cross-border production sharing is often preceded by flows of foreign direct investment (FDI) from the advanced to the emerging economy, accompanied by shipments of capital goods and other goods and services needed for the creation of productive capacity in the emerging economy. These initial flows affect the balance of payments and the exchange rate. In the FDI-receiving country, the investment boom increases demand for both tradables such as capital goods, and non-tradables such as construction services. There is upward pressure on prices in both sectors.

But while non-tradables prices may adjust freely to such pressures, the movement of tradables prices in a small, open economy is limited by competition in the world market. With given world prices of tradables, changes in tradables prices expressed in the domestic currency are brought about by fluctuations in the nominal exchange rate.

A rise in the demand for tradables, such as capital goods, is readily satisfied through increased imports, but the rise in the demand for non-tradables, such as construction services, can only be satisfied by moving productive resources into the non-tradables sector. If there are unutilized resources in the economy, they represent an important source. When full employment prevails, the additional resources must come from the tradables sector and this shift is brought about by an increase in the relative price of non-tradables. This represents a real appreciation of the domestic currency.

In Figure 8.5, the real exchange rate, expressed as the ratio of tradables to non-tradables prices, is measured on the vertical axis, and quantities of tradables and non-tradables are measured horizontally in the right and left panels, respectively. Starting at an initial equilibrium in which both markets are assumed to clear, an investment boom shifts out demand for both tradables (D_t) and non-tradables (D_n). As noted, the rise in tradables demand can be met at the initial exchange rate by an increase in imports, which is financed by the inflow of FDI. The rise in non-tradables demand, however, creates an excess

Global production networks and regional integration   139

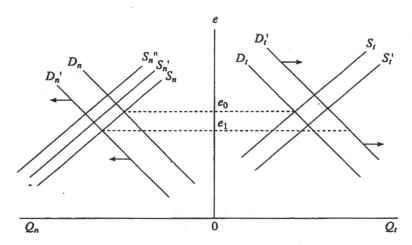

Figure 8.5   Real exchange rate patterns

demand at the initial exchange rate which can be resolved only by apprecia-tion of the currency in real terms from e_0 to e_1. This change allows domestic production of non-tradables to increase. The real appreciation contributes to the deterioration of the trade balance.

Thus an investment boom created by production sharing causes the capital-receiving country's currency to appreciate in real terms, while its current account deteriorates. As new productive capacity comes on stream, the real-exchange rate and the current account adjust once more. An increase in non-tradables capacity shifts that sector's supply curve out, thereby causing non-tradables prices to fall and the currency to depreciate in real terms. An increase in tradables capacity has no direct effect on the real-exchange rate, but the outward shift of the supply curve in the right-hand panel tends to reduce the current account deficit. The supply-side effect of the investment boom thus runs in the opposite direction to the earlier demand-side effect: it reduces the real exchange rate and improves the current account.

The extent of the exchange-rate adjustment depends on the magnitude of the capacity build-up in the non-tradables sector. If the bulk of investment goes into tradables, there will be a sustained real appreciation. The currency will remain 'strong,' perhaps even 'overvalued' in the view of some.

The expansion of capacity amounts to an increase in national income and wealth, which tends to raise the demand for both tradables and non-tradables. Demand in both sectors shifts out, as indicated by the arrows emanating from the outermost demand curves in the two panels. The rise in non-tradables demand tends to sustain the real appreciation and trade balance deterioration, while the rise in tradables demand leads to trade balance deterioration, but has no direct effect on the real exchange rate. How the real exchange rate and the current account evolve over time thus depends on the distribution of supply and demand changes between the two sectors. As noted, an investment boom that is heavily biased in favor of tradables will be accompanied by sustained currency appreciation and current-account improvement over the long run.

6. FIXED VERSUS FLOATING RATES

The aforementioned movements in the real exchange rate take place under both fixed and floating rates, but the burden of adjustment is distributed differently in the two regimes. In a floating exchange-rate regime, adjustments in the real rate may be brought about by changes in nominal rates, in non-tradables prices, or in both, assuming that world tradables prices are given. When the nominal rate is fixed, the entire burden of adjustment falls on non-tradables prices, which rise to bring about real appreciation and fall to induce real depreciation. These price movements may create political difficulties for incumbent governments. Rising non-tradables prices not only risk inflaming inflationary expectations, but may reduce real incomes, especially among tradables workers whose wages are held down by foreign competitive pressures.[12] The political difficulties are probably even more severe when the real rate needs to depreciate, because then prices and wages in non-tradables industries must fall.

When the country is large, changes in tradables demand and supply affect tradables prices in the world or in the free-trade area. Foreign tradables prices will tend to rise when the large country's demand for tradables rises during the early phase of the investment boom; they will tend to fall when productive capacity comes on stream in the large country and the world supply of tradables rises.

7. CONCLUDING REMARKS

Creation of an economic area, in which trade liberalization is combined with investment liberalization and cross-border production sharing, thus has both micro- and macroeconomic implications. Production sharing among members is capable of converting a trade-diverting free-trade area into a trade-creating one. Observed shifts of imports from low-cost non-members to higher-cost members do not necessarily imply trade diversion. By pushing specialization to the level of components, joint production among members may generate costs that undercut the low-cost outsider, if that country's cost advantage in the end product does not carry through to *all* of the component activities.

Production sharing tends to reduce the sensitivity of the trade balance to exchange-rate movements, because a country's exports are now linked to its imports, so that exchange-rate effects on one side of the trade balance are offset by changes on the other.

When production sharing takes place between advanced and emerging economies, foreign direct investment flows often precede joint production. These flows and the subsequent movement of components and products have important implications for the real exchange rate. In the FDI-receiving country, an investment boom tends to cause the real rate to appreciate initially and the current account to worsen, followed by real depreciation and current account improvement.

NOTES

1. See Kimura and Ando (2003) for new evidence on the extent of production sharing by Japanese firms in Asia and Latin America.
2. See note 3.
3. For a detailed analysis in the Heckscher–Ohlin framework, see Arndt (1997, 1998). For an assessment of cross-border 'fragmentation' in a Ricardian framework, see Jones and Kierzkowski (2001). See Deardorff (2001a, b) for an examination of fragmentation in a multi-cone context. See also Kohler (2001). For the role of service links in international production networks, see Jones and Kierzkowski (1990). Recent empirical studies include Egger and Egger (2001), Egger and Falkinger (2003) and Kimura and Ando (2003).
4. For details, see Arndt (2001).
5. It is clear that the first-best solution with and without production sharing is non-discriminatory trade liberalization.
6. While the overall welfare change depends on several factors, the main point is that deeper integration is welfare-improving relative to the base-line free-trade area.
7. This figure is taken from Arndt and Huemer (2001).
8. From Mexico's point of view, of course, it is a loss of producer surplus and thus a transfer of welfare to the trading partner.
9. When joint production is located in the emerging economy, direct investment inflows (FDI) may precede the onset of joint production. See Arndt (2002) for a discussion.
10. See Egger and Falkinger (2003) for a related treatment.
11. An important caveat, here, pertains to transfer-pricing practices by the multinationals involved in production sharing. These can affect the nature of pass-through and the value of trade. Where accounting practices distinguish between in-bond and regular exports, the distinction will be more readily apparent.
12. See Robertson (2003) for a study of Mexico.

REFERENCES

Arndt, S.W. (1997), 'Globalization and the Open Economy,' *North American Journal of Economics and Finance*, **8** (1), 71–9.
——— (1998), 'Super-Specialization and the Gains from Trade,' *Contemporary*

Economic Policy, **XVI** (October), 480–85.

Arndt, S.W. (2001), 'Production Networks in an Economically Integrated Region,' *ASEAN Economic Bulletin*, **18** (1), 24–34.

—————— (2002), 'Production Sharing and Regional Integration,' in T. Georgakopoulos, C.C. Paraskevopoulos and J. Smithin (eds), *Globalization and Economic Growth*, Toronto: APF Press, pp. 97–107.

Arndt, S.W. and A. Huemer (2001), 'North American Trade After NAFTA: Part I,' *Claremont Policy Briefs*, Claremont, CA, Lowe Institute of Political Economy, Claremont McKenna College.

Deardorff, A.V. (2001a), 'Fragmentation Across Cones,' in S.W. Arndt and H. Kierzkowski (eds), *Fragmentation: New Production Patterns in the World Economy*, New York: Oxford University Press, pp. 35–51.

—————— (2001b), 'Fragmentation in Simple Trade Models,' *North American Journal of Economics and Finance*, **12** (2), 121–37.

Egger, H. and P. Egger (2001), 'Cross-border Sourcing and Outward Processing in EU Manufacturing,' *North American Journal of Economics and Finance*, **12** (3), 243–56.

Egger, H. and J. Falkinger (2003), 'The distributional effects of international outsourcing in a 2 × 2 production model,' *North American Journal of Economics and Finance*, **14** (2), 189–206.

Feenstra, R.C. (1998), 'Integration of Trade and Disintegration of Production in the Global Economy,' *Journal of Economic Perspectives*, **12** (Fall), pp. 31–50.

Jones, R.W. and H. Kierzkowski (1990), 'The Role of Services in Production and International Trade: A Theoretical Framework,' in R.W. Jones and A.O. Krueger (eds), *The Political Economy of International Trade*, Oxford: Blackwell, pp. 31–48.

—————— (2001), 'A Framework for Fragmentation,' in S.W. Arndt and H. Hierzkowski (eds), *Fragmentation: New Production Patterns in the World Economy*, New York: Oxford University Press, pp. 17–34.

Kimura, F. and M. Ando (2003), 'Fragmentation and agglomeration matter: Japanese multinationals in Latin America and East Asia,' *North American Journal of Economics and Finance* **14** (3), pp. 287–317.

Kohler, W. (2001), 'A Specific-factors View on Outsourcing,' *North American Journal of Economics and Finance*, **12** (1), 31–53.

Robertson, R. (2003), 'Exchange rates and relative wages: evidence from Mexico,' *North American Journal of Economics and Finance*, **14** (1), 25–48.

Chapter 8

ASEAN Economic Bulletin Vol. 18, No. 1

Production Networks in an Economically Integrated Region

Sven W. Arndt

This article discusses an approach to "open regionalism" based on regional production networks and component specialization. Component specialization, or intra-product trade, has been shown to be welfare-enhancing. It creates jobs and raises output by improving competitiveness. It is one of the innovative features of the current phase of globalization. It offers groups of small countries opportunities to make regionalism work in ways which the traditional European model does not. It is less discriminatory and less inward-looking than the European model. It stresses regulatory reform and the creation of a single market early in the process of regional economic integration. The welfare gains flow from elimination of market distortions and minimization of trade diversion.

JEL Classification: F11, F13, F15

Keywords: Production networks; Fragmentation; ASEAN economic integration

I. Introduction

The process of regional integration has tended to follow a fairly set pattern. In the early stages, the focus is on liberalizing trade in goods. Subsequent initiatives address trade in services, the movement of labour and capital, co-ordination of regulatory and other policies, and monetary union. Each successive stage makes its inroads on national sovereignty and policy independence. Still, it is typically not until the very end of a long and drawn-out process that market segmentation may be said to have been effectively eradicated and the region can be truly called a single market. This article argues that the nations of Asia-Pacific might benefit from restructuring the process of regional integration so as to assign top priority to the spread of regional production systems.

There are significant reasons to doubt that a small grouping among any subset of countries in the Asia-Pacific region provides the basis for a viable preferential trade area of the traditional variety. Even when the static framework is broadened to allow for dynamic elements such as scale economies and endogenous growth, most arrangements would not pass the test on strictly economic grounds.

An important characteristic of the traditional approach to regional integration is that structural and market transformation are initially quite limited, so that the benefits of trade liberalization depend almost entirely on the extent to which existing resources can be used more efficiently. Significant changes in industrial structure typically do not take place until economic integration has reached the "deeper" stages. In the European Union (EU), for example, the Single Market project ("Europe 1992") occurred decades after the creation of the original customs union (European Economic Community or EEC) and free trade area (European Free Trade Area or EFTA) in the 1950s. It represented the community's response to the failure of the earlier phases of integration to eliminate market segmentation.

This article examines an approach to regional integration which allows industrial structure to change early in the process. The structural change envisaged here involves creation of regional production networks and dispersion of manufacturing processes across national frontiers. The result would be *regional* as opposed to *national* industries. Regional initiatives are more likely to be welfare-improving if they include economic integration based on cross-border production networks.

Section II develops the basic idea and establishes a benchmark example of traditional integration against which to evaluate the effects of the proposed alternative. Section III introduces regional production into the framework and assesses the welfare gains thereof. Section IV discusses varieties of cross-border procurement and the role of foreign direct investment (FDI) and multinationals in the context of regional production networks. Section V deals with trade liberalization in the presence of production networks to show how the latter tends to create pressures favouring non-discriminatory trade liberalization. It also considers the effect of offshore procurement on wages and employment. Section VI considers dynamic factors like scale economies. Section VII concludes.

II. Creating a Regional Economy

Regional economic integration has been an important part of the globalization of many national economies. While Europe provides the most complex example of the interplay of multilateral and regional forces, both the Western Hemisphere and the Pacific Rim have seen significant regional initiatives. Unlike Europe, however, most of these approaches have been more cautious, with members wary of becoming too involved with their trading partners and losing too much sovereignty and economic policy autonomy in the process. Although Mercado Commun del Sur (MERCOSUR) in the Southern Cone of Latin America has opted for customs union, most initiatives have been more circumspect. In the North American Free Trade Area (NAFTA), for example, members were content to settle for a free trade area and thus to retain greater trade policy independence. Although some observers have called for the deepening of NAFTA, including monetary integration, the political sentiment does not in general appear to be ready for that level of commitment to the regional option.[1]

This reluctance to commit more fully to the regional idea prevails in the Pacific area as well. In part, such sentiments are driven by concerns over the loss of national sovereignty, but in part they also reflect the fact that the standard regional arrangement may not be so obviously superior to less discriminatory, more plurilateral and multilateral approaches. There is general agreement among expert observers, for example, that the Association of Southeast Asian Nations (ASEAN) and its trade arrangement, the ASEAN Free Trade Area (AFTA), do not constitute an optimal economic area, because the elements of trade diversion are likely to dominate those of trade creation (Panagariya 1998).[2]

The countries of the Pacific Rim are quite aware of this constraint inherent in the traditional model of regional integration. They have reacted by exploring alternative approaches, which seek to contain the forces of trade diversion and to encourage trade creation. This is the avowed objective of "open regionalism", which strives for better balance between the benefits of preferential trade liberalization and the costs of damaging trade linkages with the rest of the world. The search continues for strategies that are less openly discriminatory than the traditional approach.

Any grouping of small countries in Asia-Pacific along traditional lines is bound to exclude the world's low-cost producers in many product categories and thus to ensure that trade diversion will dominate. That will certainly be true of products that tend to be highly skill-, research-, and capital-intensive. AFTA is no exception: a preferential trade arrangement which excludes Europe, the United States, Japan, Korea, Taiwan, and China is a virtual guarantee that trade diversion will dominate trade creation.

For many of Asia's economies, trade relations with countries unlikely to become members of a regional preference area are often more important than trade with neighbours. Countries may be neighbours, but their geographic proximity is often greater than their economic interaction. The United States and Japan may be farther away geographically, but they loom large as key trading partners. Recognition of this reality is one reason for the existence of the Asia-Pacific Economic Co-operation (APEC) forum, which covers a much larger area and includes all the major players of the region. But APEC has thus far not been able to solve the problem of how to make its vision of "open regionalism" work. There are at present more dreams than workable proposals for implementing the concept.[3]

The debate has followed traditional lines, which start with liberalization of trade in goods. There is hope, of course, that increased trade will spur industrial growth and development, but growth and industrialization are typically considered at the national level. Each country formulates trade expansion and growth policies according to national priorities. There is little or no co-ordination of policies among countries. It follows that national policies will at times be in cross-border harmony, but in conflict at others. To the extent that the growth goals pursued by the countries of the region are similar, their policies and actions will possess significant competitive elements.

Most emerging economies in the region have been pursuing export-led growth strategies in which selling into the United States and other advanced-country markets has played a major role. Their exports are very similar, because they all cater to demand developments in the same markets. When world demand rises for a

product — steel, textiles, apparel, consumer electronics, computer components, and so on — every nation moves to expand capacity in order to raise exports. Every country behaves quite properly as the small, price-taking member of the global economy, whose own capacity expansion will have no effect on world market conditions. But when the actions of all are cumulated, the impact on world markets and prices may not be trivial after all.

The products involved are "national" in the sense of being made more or less entirely inside a particular nation. If we take the case of ASEAN, for example, we find firms which engage in outsourcing, but outsourcing across borders is more typically carried out by extra-regional multinationals that operate in the region than by indigenous firms.[4] Cross-border sourcing faces obstacles from trade and other policy barriers, as well as communication and transportation costs, which tend to be higher between than within nations (Athukorala and Menon 1997). Cross-border production, in which indigenous firms from one member country invest in production facilities in another, is rarer still.

An important aspect of the current wave of globalization, however, is precisely the role that trade liberalization and innovations in communications and transportation technologies have played in facilitating it. Cross-border sourcing and offshore production of parts is now easier than ever. The main theme of this article is that emerging nations stand to reap welfare gains and improve competitiveness if they move away from the "national" model of industrialization policy toward more regional, collaborative perspectives.

The basic idea is to think of the region rather than the nation as the production base and to spread component production around the region in accordance with comparative advantage. The object is to raise efficiency, reduce production costs, and increase competitiveness, and thereby to gain market share for all the region's players. The key features of this argument are developed below in the context of a standard trade model.[5]

The Welfare Effects of Component Trade

It is well known that the move from most-favoured-nation (MFN) tariffs to preferential trading arrangements may raise or lower national welfare (Johnson 1967). The outcome generally depends on the relative magnitudes of the trade-creating and trade-diverting effects. The former arise in the shift from domestic production to more efficient sources in the Free Trade Area (FTA) partner country; the latter are associated with the shift from low-cost, non-member suppliers to higher cost, less efficient producers in the partner country. Net trade diversion becomes more likely as the cost differentials between partner country and non-members rise.

The following analysis starts with traditional static considerations of trade in end products. Dynamic elements are taken up in a subsequent section where it is shown that they, too, are more likely to be stronger in a properly constituted regional production network. The basic structure of the argument is illustrated in Figure 1, where curve TT represents the production possibility set of a small country. Prior to creation of the preference area, the country has a most-favoured-

nation tariff (MFN) on imports of good Y. The world price ratio is given by P_w, so that P_d is the tariff-inclusive domestic price ratio. The country produces at Q and consumes at C on indifference curve I, exporting final good X in return for imports of final good Y.

After implementation of the preference area, the relative commodity price will lie somewhere between the world price, P_w, and the initial MFN tariff-inclusive domestic price P_d. Let that price be P_{pta}. In general, the preference area is more likely to be trade-diverting as P_{pta} approaches P_d and thus moves away from P_w. Intuitively, net trade diversion takes place as the additional resource cost implicit in the difference between the world price and the preference area price exceeds the gain from the reduced cost implicit in the difference between the MFN price and the preference area price.

In the figure, the preference area is depicted to be trade-diverting, i.e. welfare-reducing. Production has moved to Q', while consumption is now located at C' on a lower indifference curve, I'. This is a well-known result which does not require extensive commentary. Its role is to serve as a benchmark for assessing the effects of cross-border component sourcing. Suffice to note here that for many groupings of emerging economies, the outcome is more likely to be welfare-reducing than welfare-creating because the world's low-cost producers of goods affected by the preference area will too often remain on the outside. The nations of ASEAN, for their part, are well aware of the problem.

It is often asserted that the repercussions enumerated above are too static and depend too much on existing conditions and structures. In particular, it is argued that a variety of dynamic effects, including scale economies, FDI, and endogenous growth, can more than compensate for the poor showing of the static analysis. While there is doubtless something to that argument, even the dynamic effects will often be limited by the small scale of national markets and the geographic area encompassed by the regional arrangement. Creation of a regional economy, with regionally structured production networks, is likely to be more beneficial than preferential trade liberalization

FIGURE 1
Regional Production Network

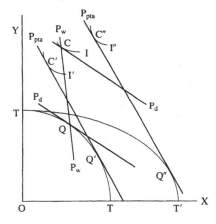

which leaves the member economies segmented. We turn to that issue in the next section.

III. Trade Liberalization versus Market Integration

While end products have traditionally played a dominant role in international trade, offshore sourcing of components and offshore assembly have grown rapidly in recent years (see, for example, Ng and Yeats 1999 and Yeats 2001). This growth has been made possible in part by reductions in trade barriers and in part by innovations in transportation and telecommunications technologies, which have sharply reduced the cost of co-ordinating cross-border sourcing and production.

The welfare implications of cross-border production have received considerable analytical attention recently.[6] It has been shown in a variety of modelling contexts that offshore sourcing or cross-border production of components can be strongly welfare-enhancing. It has been further shown that such foreign procurement creates jobs and expands output in the industries in which it occurs and that it frequently raises wages.

While the factors which determine these outcomes vary across models and empirical instances, the intuition is simple and compelling. If foreign sourcing of a component is cost-saving, then it improves the competitiveness of the end product of which it is a part. If the firm which makes the end product is a price-*taker*, then the reduction in production costs increases profitability and creates an incentive to expand output. If the firm is a price-*maker* in end product markets, the reduction in costs brought about by offshore sourcing enables it to lower price and thus gain market share. Once again, output rises.

In a Heckscher-Ohlin framework, competitiveness is equivalent to comparative advantage, and comparative advantage depends on resource endowments and factor intensities. When final products consist of multiple components whose production technologies differ, then factor intensities will vary across components. The factor intensity of the product itself is simply the weighted average of the factor intensities of its constituent parts. Varying factor intensities across components mean that countries' comparative advantage will vary across components, just as it varies across final products. A labour-rich, low-wage country will possess comparative advantage in labour-intensive components, and so on. These considerations apply with equal force to the factor-intensity of product assembly.

It follows that if countries involved in the regional trading initiative specialize in component production according to the dictates of comparative advantage, welfare will rise all around. The effect on productive efficiency of component specialization is similar to the effect of technical progress. In the industry or sector in which foreign sourcing of components takes place, a given input of resources is able to produce a larger output. In the context of the production possibility curve depicted in Figure 1, the effect of foreign sourcing is to shift out the curve along the axis representing the industry or sector in which it occurs. In the figure, that sector is taken to be the X-sector, which is this country's export sector. On the assumption that the country is a price-taker in goods markets, the effect of the outward shift of the production possibility curve is to move production from Q' to Q'' and consumption from C' to C'' on indifference curve I''. This represents an improvement in national welfare relative to regional integration without component specialization. It is clear that preference arrangements accompanied by component specialization are more likely to be welfare enhancing than those which are not.

Note that the move to foreign sourcing shifts the output mix away from the import good, Y, to the export good, X, as is evident in the relative positions of production points Q' and Q''. In other words, offshore sourcing enables the X industry to raise output.

Foreign sourcing may, of course, take place in either or in both sectors. If it occurs in the Y-sector only, then the production possibility curve shifts out along the vertical axis. It is easy to see that this restructuring is also welfare-improving relative to a preference arrangement without components trade. In this case, production of Y expands while production of X declines.

If foreign sourcing or production takes place in both sectors, then the outward shift of the production possibility curve will be less biased and welfare will improve once again relative to preference arrangements without component trade. In the context of a balanced expansion, output will tend to rise in both sectors, while employment of both factors will shift into the sector which uses the country's scarce factor relatively intensively.

An important feature of this regional rearrangement of production is that every country which moves to offshore procurement of components in which it has comparative disadvantage will experience an outward shift of its production possibility curve and a welfare improvement relative to the traditional case in which each country produces the entire product at home.

Thus, in the traditional European approach, the process of regional development is initiated by creating a system of discriminatory trade barriers designed to protect the region's producers from the outside's low-cost competitors. The focus is squarely on facilitating intra-regional trade rather than building a regional market and stimulating the creation of regional production networks and regional firms. Import-substitution matters more in the early goings than export promotion. If the programme gives rise to border-crossing investment, it is typically tariff-jumping investment on the part of the aforementioned outside competitors. Not surprisingly, markets remain substantially segmented and essentially national long after trade liberalization has been completed. As noted, Europe did not get to the "single market" project until more than three decades had elapsed.

The approach envisaged here starts with the creation of an integrated region whose purpose is not to protect regional producers from outside competition, but to enable the region's producers to become more efficient and competitive through location decisions that are not constrained by national frontiers. Trade liberalization is essential, but mainly to permit the unimpeded flow of components and end products within the region.

This type of trade liberalization is not discriminatory, because obstacles to the inflow of cheap components from non-members need to be removed as much as obstacles to the intra-regional flow of components. This is nicely consistent with the ideal of "open regionalism". The cost-saving consequences of the regional market serve not only to make indigenous producers compete more effectively in the region's market with outside competitors, but to enable the region's exports to compete in outside markets. If we return to the example of AFTA, its purpose then is not so much to create a protected regional market within which indigenous firms trade products, but an integrated arena in which production on a regional basis makes the region's products more competitive in world markets.

IV. Varieties of Cross-Border Sourcing

Offshore procurement of components can take place at arms length or through the activities of multinationals. The former approach will be most appropriate in the case of standardized parts sold in organized markets. This type of trade already exists, but more would take place if policy barriers and transactions costs were to fall further.

At the other end of the spectrum lies trade in components that are custom-made for particular products. Boeing and Airbus procure components abroad that are made specifically for particular airplanes and thus have no alternative uses. The maquiladora operations of American and other foreign firms in Northern Mexico represent an example of offshore final-product assembly. Assembly is procured offshore because it is relatively labour-intensive. In these instances, foreign procurement consists of foreign production carried out by partner companies or affiliates. This is where multinationals play an important role and where flows of FDI typically precede the flow of components.

The essential point here is that when costs of component production vary across countries, industrial strategies that rely on production sharing and production networking across national borders will generate welfare benefits that will exceed those available under strictly national approaches. For this approach to work, however, countries must not only remove border barriers to the flow of components, but create a regional regulatory framework that is neutral in its effects on location. Inasmuch as regional dispersion of production requires managers, technicians, and others from one nation to work in another, laws and regulations that facilitate the cross-border movement of such persons need to be implemented. The object here is not only to support the activities of third-party multinationals, but to encourage indigenous firms to become regional firms.

At the completion of this exercise, countries may be expected to be specialized in producing components for use not only at home, but throughout the region. This will make for longer production runs, as firms expand to supply their own and partner country needs. Longer runs open opportunities for scale economies that would not be available at lower output levels. The cost savings generated by scale effects improve competitiveness and thus permit output levels of final goods that will be larger than otherwise.

Component specialization clearly works well when end products are homogeneous, for it allows markets in components to develop. But it also applies to products which are differentiated by variety and thus have custom-made components. To the extent that consumers value variety, differentiated models of a given product type may be produced in different areas of the region, but component specialization can nevertheless play an important role in reducing costs and increasing efficiency and competitiveness. There may not be scale economies present in the assembly of the final, differentiated product, nor in the production of its customized components, but scale economies in the common components can contribute to cost savings.

V. Market Opening through Component Specialization

As noted earlier, Asia's policy-makers are seeking to avoid regional arrangements which upset their global trading partners. They are under pressure from the United States, the European Union and other advanced countries to open up their economies to imports. Their reluctance to comply is often based on the fear that without some protection from the competition of imports from advanced countries, they will not be able to move up the value chain towards more technologically complex, skill- and capital-intensive products.

While this argument has some merits, import protection may not be the best way to solve this problem. Tariffs imposed on imports of the end product protect all components, without distinguishing between components in which a country has comparative advantage and those in which it does not. It places the emphasis too heavily on making the entire product, rather than making the parts in which the country possesses comparative advantage. It is not necessary for a country to produce the entire product to become a world player in new, more advanced industries. The focus should be on parts and components, which use intensively the factors of production and the technologies with which the country is relatively well endowed.

These considerations apply to assembly as well. When assembly of an end product is skill-, capital-, and technology-intensive, it is most efficiently carried out by more advanced countries. The emerging economy should shy away from making the entire product, and concentrate instead on supplying components in which it has comparative advantage. Even when assembly lies within its comparative advantage domain, it may eschew production of the entire product, opting instead to import components in which it suffers comparative disadvantage.

The essentials of the argument are illustrated in Figure 2, in which good Y, measured vertically, is the country's import good. We suppose that this is the product in the manufacture of which the country wishes to become more proficient. Suppose that, in pursuit of that goal, the country has imposed an MFN tariff on imports of the full product, as a result of which the home price ratio, P_d, has risen relative to the world price, P_w.

In the figure, two tariffs of different magnitude

FIGURE 2
Component Specialization

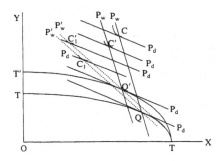

are considered. To minimize clutter in the figure, the two tariffs are assumed to produce the same domestic, tariff-inclusive price. That means that the larger of the tariffs is imposed on a lower world price of good Y, P_w. This tariff creates a large wedge between the world price, P_w and the home price. The smaller tariff creates the slimmer wedge between the domestic price and the world price P'_w. In the initial situation, production is at Q and consumption, respectively, at C and C_1.

Suppose that the Y-industry implements outsourcing of components in which it has comparative disadvantage, with the consequence that costs fall and the production possibility curve shifts out to TT'. For a small, price-taking country, relative world prices are unaffected by this move, and if tariff rates remain unchanged, then the domestic commodity price ratio is also unaffected. As a result, production moves to point Q' in both the high- and the low-tariff scenario. In the latter, consumption moves to point C'_1 on a higher indifference curve; in the former, consumption moves to point C' on a lower indifference curve. It is clear that the high tariff is inimical to the country's own welfare considerations.

Production Networks, Wages, and Employment

As noted above, employment and output will tend to expand in the sector which engages in cross-border sourcing of components. The effect of cross-border sourcing on relative factor prices depends on the sector in which it takes place. In the Heckscher-Ohlin context, it does not depend on the factor-bias of the sourcing innovation. If cross-border sourcing takes place in the labour-intensive sector, the wage-rental ratio rises; if it takes place in the capital-intensive sector, the ratio falls.[7]

Thus, if countries in Asia-Pacific switch to offshore sourcing in their import sector, which will tend to be the capital-intensive sector, then the wage-rental ratio will move against labour. That does not mean that wages will fall absolutely, but that they will rise less rapidly than capital rentals (or the wages of skilled workers, if skilled workers are the other factor).

If, however, cross-border sourcing is combined with reduction of tariffs on the imported good, then the consequent reduction in the price of Y will tend to raise the relative wage. Hence, trade liberalization in the Y-sector, combined with offshore sourcing of the capital-intensive component by that sector, will reduce the extent to which relative wages decline and may raise them if the tariff reduction is significant.

VI. Scale Economies and other Dynamic Elements

With some notable exceptions, the countries in Asia-Pacific tend to be small. The home market is too small to allow firms to fully exploit scale economies in many branches of manufacturing and services. While the region offers some opportunities for large-scale production, the various national economies are at present too segmented to make a single regional market. Even with a fully integrated market, however, access to the United States and to other large advanced economies is important. This ensures that the smaller countries of the region will continue to pay attention to their trade with the rest of the world.

If countries abandon the notion that every product must be fully produced at home, regional specialization at the level of parts and components offers not only the static welfare gains discussed in the preceding sections, but new opportunities to exploit scale economies. When every country produces its own components, production runs are likely to be small for the aforementioned reasons. But if production of a given component is allowed to take place in the country or countries where costs are lowest, then production runs will be longer and hence scale economies will become accessible.

For this structure to work, man-made and natural barriers must be removed and co-ordination and transportation costs must be brought down. Both policy-makers and the private sector have a role to play in this respect. Governments must eliminate policy obstacles which prevent firms from producing anywhere in the region. This task is clearly more complex than the traditional focus on the removal of trade barriers. The objective is not simply to free up the flow of goods, but to create an integrated regional production arena.

For its part, the private sector must invest in services networks that will permit firms to co-ordinate production across borders. If the conditions for a fully integrated regional economy are in place, then firms will be able to make plant location decisions from the regional rather than the national perspective. This will give them a competitive edge in the world market, where significant elements of market segmentation continue to exist.

Politicians and the public must abandon the habit of viewing the outflow of investment capital as inimical to national welfare. In an integrated regional production arena, investment by a firm in country A in a component-producing facility in country B may be more beneficial to the regional and international competitiveness of that firm than investment of the same magnitude in the home industry. Such investment outflows will make economic sense if the consequent reduction in the cost of an imported component cuts overall costs by more than the best domestic investment alternative. In that case, the effect of an outflow of capital is to shift out the domestic production possibility curve. Home output and employment rise when the industry invests abroad.

VII. Concluding Comments

The countries of Asia-Pacific continue to search for ways of making regionalism work for them. The traditional approach to regional economic integration, of which the European Union is the best example, does not appear to offer much in the way of benefits, especially for groupings of smaller countries which exclude the region's larger economies. The "European" approach is basically inward-looking, discriminatory, and import-substituting in its orientation. It tends to be preoccupied in its early stages with trade liberalization, leaving creation of a single regional market to later phases of the process. As the Europeans have learned, however, trade liberalization alone cannot eliminate market segmentation and thus cannot create the regional production arena that is essential for industrialization and development.

The approach suggested in this article places the focus on the development of regional production networks. The objective is to make the region's producers more efficient and competitive in regional and global markets. This is a more outwardly oriented approach, which is focused less on keeping third-party goods out than on facilitating exports to third-party markets.

Furthermore, whereas the traditional approach emphasizes comparative advantage at the product level, the proposed approach stresses comparative advantage at the level of parts, components, and assembly. A production network, spread throughout the region and based on component specialization, allows components to be produced and product assembly to be conducted according to the dictates of comparative advantage. Production costs are cut throughout the region, making the region's producers more competitive in world markets. The larger production runs permitted by component specialization make scale economies more accessible and thus add further to cost competitiveness. Implementation of a regional system of production networks requires harmonization of regulatory and other policies and the removal of barriers to the flow of services, persons, and finance. These changes need to be implemented early in the process of regional integration.

Note that nothing said thus far requires this regionalism to be discriminatory. It can be entirely "open". There is no need to limit production access to regional firms. Right of establishment can be available to all comers. Rules of origin make no sense in a framework in which the objective is to obtain parts and components, and to undertake assembly, where costs are lowest. If a preference area along traditional lines is pursued nevertheless, say, for political reasons, then component specialization is needed to reduce the likelihood of net trade diversion.

NOTES

1. See, for example, Courchene and Harris (2000) and Grubel (2000).
2. Traditional trade theory focuses on the gains from trade by assuming that countries' resource endowments are given. As economic integration deepens, FDI is also liberalized, and its consequences need to be taken into account (Athukorala and Menon 1997). In the traditional model of preferential trade liberalization, investment inflows into the region from non-member countries are motivated by the need to jump tariff barriers. Investment flows in and productive capacity is established in order to serve the local market. The focus in this article is on investment flows within the region, as well as inflows from outside the region, which facilitate the dispersion of production processes across national frontiers.
3. See Bergsten (1997) for an initial attempt to define the options under "open regionalism". Also see Srinivasan (1998).
4. See Ng and Yeats (1999) for a detailed accounting of the growth of components trade in Asia.
5. Although many of the insights can be established in the context of the familiar *partial equilibrium* framework, the model used here is one of *general equilibrium* in order to provide a simple view of economy-wide effects.
6. See Arndt (1997, 1998), Deardorff (2001), and Jones and Kierzkowski (2000, 2001) for detailed analyses. See also Krugman (1995).
7. For details, see Arndt (1997, 1998, 2001).

REFERENCES

Arndt, S. W. "Globalization and the Open Economy". *North American Journal of Economics and Finance* 8, no. 1 (1997): 71–79.
____. "Super-Specialization and the Gains from Trade". *Contemporary Economic Policy* XVI (1998): 480–85.
____. "Offshore Sourcing and Production Sharing in Preference Areas". In *Fragmentation: New Production Patterns in the World Economy*, edited by S.W. Arndt and H. Kierzkowski, pp. 76–87. New York: Oxford University Press, 2001.
Athukorala, P. and J. Menon. "AFTA and the Investment-Trade Nexus in ASEAN". *The World Economy* 20 (1997): 159–74.
Bergsten, C. F. "Open Regionalism". *The World Economy* 20 (1997): 545–65.
Courchene, T. J. and R. G. Harris. "North American Monetary Union: Analytical Principles and Organizational Guidelines". *North American Journal of Economics and Finance* 11 (2000): 3–18.
Deardorff, A. V. "Fragmentation Across Cones". In *Fragmentation: New Production Patterns in the World Economy*, edited by S. W. Arndt and H. Kierzkowski, pp. 35–51. New York: Oxford University Press, 2001.
Grubel, H. G. "The Merit of a Canada-US Monetary Union". *North American Journal of Economics and Finance* 11 (2000): 19–40.
Johnson, H. G. "The Possibility of Income Losses from Increased Efficiency of Factor Accumulation in the Presence of Tariffs". *Economic Journal* 77 (1967): 151–54.
Jones, R. W. and H. Kierzkowski. "Globalization and the Consequences of International Fragmentation". In *Money, Factor Mobility, and Trade*, edited by R. Dornbusch, G. Calvo, and M. Obstfeld. Cambridge, Massachusetts: MIT Press, 2000.
____. "A Framework for Fragmentation". In *Fragmentation: New Production Patterns in the World Economy*, edited by S.W. Arndt and H. Kierzkowski, pp. 17–34. New York: Oxford University Press, 2001.
Krugman, P. "Growing World Trade: Causes and Consequences". *Brookings Papers on Economic Activity* 1 (1995): 327–62.

Ng, F. and A. J. Yeats. "Production Sharing in East Asia: Who Does What for Whom, and Why?". Policy Research Working Paper No. 2197, World Bank, October 1999.

Panagariya, A. "Should East Asia Go Regional?". In *Economic Development and Co-operation in the Pacific Basin: Trade, Investment and Environmental Issues*, edited by H. Lee and D. Roland Holst. New York: Cambridge University Press, 1998. Shorter version published as "East Asia and the New Regionalism", *The World Economy* 17 (1998): 817–39.

Srinivasan, T. N. "Regionalism and the WTO: Is Non-Discrimination Passe?". In *The WTO as an International Organization*, edited by A. Krueger. Chicago: The University of Chicago Press, 1998.

Yeats, A. J. "Just How Big is Global Production Sharing?". In *Fragmentation: New Production Patterns in the World Economy*, edited by S.W. Arndt and H. Kierzkowski, pp. 108–43. New York: Oxford University Press, 2001.

Sven W. Arndt is the Director of the Lowe Institute of Political Economy and the C. M. Stone Professor of Money, Credit and Trade at Claremont McKenna College, California, U.S.A.

Chapter 9

Trade Diversion and Production Sharing

Sven W. Arndt[1]
The Lowe Institute of Political Economy
Claremont McKenna College

Abstract. This paper examines the repercussions of cross-border production sharing for the welfare effects of preferential trade liberalization. In a general-equilibrium context, a free trade agreement (FTA), which incorporates production sharing, raises the likelihood of welfare improvement. Thus, two members of a free trade area, who each have comparative disadvantage in the production of a final product relative to a non-member, may nevertheless enjoy net trade creation if they jointly possess comparative advantage in key components of that product. At a minimum, cross-border production sharing reduces the trade-diverting elements of an FTA. It follows, that rules of origin, viewed as constraints on cross-border fragmentation, augment the negative, trade-diverting elements of free trade areas.

JEL Classification: F11, F13, F15
Keywords: Trade diversion; Free Trade Areas; Fragmentation; Production networks

1. Introduction

As globalization spreads, markets are becoming more integrated across countries and economic activities more linked and intertwined. Continuing progress in trade and investment liberalization, as well as declining communication and transportation costs, play an important role in this process. As economies become more open and market access is improved, trade grows and production spreads across borders. As a result, end products entering into international trade contain parts and components from many countries.

The focus of this paper is on factors that inhibit and factors that encourage cross-border sourcing and their implications for the welfare effects of preferential trade liberalization. This is an important issue, because the welfare effects of cross-border production fragmentation are not independent of the trade policy regime. Under conditions of free trade in a standard trade model, for example, cross-border sourcing of components is welfare-enhancing. Its effects are analogous to those of technical progress. In the context of a most-favored-nation tariff regime (MFN), on the other hand, it may be welfare-reducing.[2]

The simplest models of preferential trade liberalization deal with trade in products that are produced entirely within national boundaries. Comparative advantage considerations then provide ready efficiency assessments and welfare calculations. In this framework, trade creation arises when imports of a finished or intermediate product from a partner country replace domestic production. Trade diversion, on the other hand, is associated with the shift of imports from low-cost outsiders to higher-cost FTA partners. In this context, the welfare effects of preferential trade liberalization are ambiguous.

Our interest, however, is in a deeper form of preferential trade liberalization, one that facilitates production sharing across borders. Here, the comparison of interest is not between the cost of producing an entire product in the countries involved, but comparison between fully home-based production in the non-member country and cross-border production sharing by the FTA members.

The intuition is that a country may be the world's low-cost producer of a product, without necessarily being the low-cost producer of every one of its components. When production of the product shifts from a nationally integrated set-up in the non-member country to a regionally fragmented production framework inside the preference area, the trade creating and trade diverting elements are rearranged in important ways.

The remainder of the paper proceeds as follows. Section 2 provides a brief review of the welfare effects of cross-border component sourcing under a variety of trade policy regimes. Section 3 employs a two-country general-equilibrium trade model to examine the effects of rules of origin, when these are interpreted as interventions designed to prevent optimal component sourcing. Section 4 examines the effects of cross-border component sourcing on domestic production and welfare in a simple partial-equilibrium framework. Section 5 employs a three-country, partial-equilibrium model to assess the extent of trade diversion in discriminatory trade liberalization with and without component specialization. Section 6 concludes.

2. Production Sharing, the Trade Regime, and Welfare

The welfare effects of cross-border fragmentation and production sharing have received considerable attention in the recent literature.[3] Under conditions of free trade, cross-border production sharing in either the import or the export sector of a small country unambiguously raises national welfare as it extends specialization from the level of products to that of parts, components and assembly. When it takes place in a large country, it generates terms-of-trade effects, which may augment or undermine the welfare effects of production sharing per se. Since it tends to increase domestic output in the sector in which it occurs, it turns the terms of trade in favor of the country when it takes place in the import sector and against it when it occurs in the export sector.[4] These tendencies are reinforced by complementary adjustments in the trading partner, when that country is also large. Then, output of the good subject to production sharing increases there as well, so that the price-depressing effects are enhanced.[5]

In a small country, cross-border fragmentation is also welfare-creating when it is part of a preferential trade agreement, and may thus turn an otherwise trade-diverting PTA into a trade-creating one. For large countries, the effects of production sharing on the terms of trade need to be taken into account along the lines discussed above.

The welfare effects of cross-border production fragmentation are ambiguous, however, when it is introduced in the context of most-favored-nation (MFN) trade policy. It is more likely to be welfare-reducing, the larger the wedge between the tariff-inclusive domestic price and the world price. Technically, the condition for welfare improvement is that the Rybzsynski line must be flatter than the relative world price in the standard general equilibrium trade model.[6]

Cross-border sourcing has potentially important implications for how we assess "exposure" to foreign competition of so-called non-tradables industries. When production is fragmentable, goods and services that are non-tradable as such, may contain parts and components that are. When a non-tradable good or service contains tradable parts and components, its insulation from foreign competition is reduced as the domestic factors of production employed in component production are exposed to competition from abroad.

Cross-border production sharing and component sourcing by non-tradables industries not only affect national welfare (by shifting out the production possibility frontier in a manner similar to technological progress), but also have implications for the real exchange rate, defined as the ratio of tradables prices to non-tradables prices. It is well-known that market-clearing conditions in the non-tradables sector play a key role in determining the real exchange rate (Arndt, 2004). Hence, when offshore sourcing of tradable components reduces costs and thus prices of non-tradables relative to tradables, the resultant increase in the ratio of tradables to non-tradables prices is equivalent to a depreciation of the country's real exchange rate. A shift to offshore sourcing in the non-tradables sector is thus accompanied by real depreciation of the country's currency.

The ability of non-tradables producers to use offshore sourcing of components to increase their competitiveness relative to tradables producers enables them to compete more effectively for domestic resources, and thereby raises output and employment in the non-tradables sector. Meanwhile, the depreciation of the country's real exchange rate, raises output in the tradables sector as well, implying that offshore sourcing by non-tradables industries raises output throughout the economy. The rise in tradables output and decline in tradables demand improve the trade balance.

3. Rules of Origin

Rules of origin, also known as domestic-content requirements, are designed to prevent producers in free trade areas from exploiting differences among members' tariff levels through cross-border sourcing of components from non-members. If country A has a lower tariff on component imports than its FTA partner, country B, the producers in A may use components from non-members to gain a competitive edge in B's markets. Rules of origin are policies specifically designed to control such offshore sourcing.

To the extent that rules of origin restrict country A's producers from third-country sourcing of parts and components, they cause the country's production possibility curve to contract relative to its optimal, unconstrained position.[7] We examine the welfare implications with the aid of Figure 1. Suppose that the production blocks represent the two countries, A and B, respectively, which have formed a free trade area and that P_{fta} is the intra-FTA relative price. Assume for simplicity that tastes are identical in the two countries, so that the initial equilibrium consumption bundle for each nation is given at point C_o. Production takes place at points Q_a and Q_b, respectively, with country A exporting good Y and importing good X. Suppose further that the conditions depicted by the two production blocks involve offshore sourcing by both countries of components from low-cost non-member sources.[8]

Suppose that country A enforces the rules-of-origin provisions of the treaty. Producers in country B have two options, depending on the relative sizes of applicable tariffs. They can continue to source components outside the FTA and pay the partner's tariff. They can, alternatively, shift the sourcing of components to FTA suppliers in order to avoid the partner's tariff on third-country value-added. The latter will be the preferred course of action, if the cost savings inherent in third-country sourcing are smaller than the tariff.

If the response is to shift component sourcing to intra-FTA suppliers, the effect is to shift B's production possibility curve inward along the X-axis to, say, $T_B{}'$. As a result, the intra-FTA price of X rises to $P_{fta'}$, which represents a worsening of country A's terms of trade. Production of good X rises in country A and falls in country B. Consumption in both countries moves to a lower indifference curve to reflect the welfare loss inflicted on both by country A's implementation of the rules-of-origin requirements.[9]

Free trade areas are known to generate both trade-creating and trade-diverting welfare changes. The latter may dominate the former and thus reduce welfare relative to an MFN tariff regime. The foregoing suggests that rules of origin introduce an additional element of trade diversion and thereby increase the likelihood that an FTA will be welfare-reducing.

The situation is made still worse, if country B elects to enforce rules-of-origin provisions against imports of good Y from country A that contain components from non-member sources. If country A responds by shifting to domestic, higher-cost components, then country A's production block will shift inward along the Y-axis and welfare will fall further in both countries.

Note, that while the common external tariff eliminates the need for rules of origin in customs unions, determination of a non-zero common tariff may require some countries to raise duties on component imports from non-members. To the extent that this change inhibits component sourcing from non-members, it has the effect of contracting members' production possibility curves along the axes of sectors engaged in such offshore sourcing and is thus welfare-reducing.

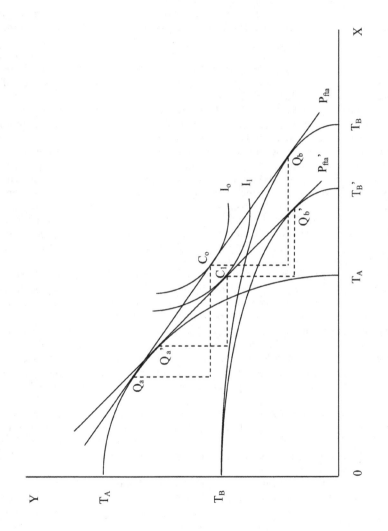

Figure 1

4. Production Sharing and Trade Diversion

As noted above, preferential trade liberalization can be welfare-reducing on balance. The question is whether cross-border fragmentation of production worsens or improves the welfare effect of traditional preferential trade liberalization. It will be recalled that in the traditional set-up, the shift of production from domestic producers to the partner country is an important source of trade creation, while the shift of production from the low-cost outsider to the partner country is the source of trade diversion. From this perspective, therefore, a NAFTA-induced shift of U.S. automobile imports from Japan to Mexico would clearly suggest trade diversion.

While such a conclusion is doubtlessly justified under the assumption that automobiles are produced in their entirety in every country, it is less automatic under conditions of cross-border fragmentation and production sharing between the partner countries. Automobiles imported by the U.S. from Mexico contain components made in the U.S. If Mexico is the low-cost producer of some component or of assembly, then the shift of those activities from Japan to Mexico is an element of trade creation. Any trade diversion can then arise only in the remainder of the production chain. If the U.S. is the low-cost producer of the components it supplies to Mexico, then the extent of trade creation is increased and the range of activities subject to trade diversion is further limited. The net welfare effect of the shift in production, which was once clearly negative, is now ambiguous.

The essential point of the foregoing is that unless Japan is the low-cost producer of every activity in the production chain, cross-border fragmentation and production sharing between the trade area partners reduces the trade-diverting elements of preferential trade liberalization. The intuition may be set out with the help of a simple numerical example. Suppose that the respective costs of the two components of a hypothetical product are $9 and $7 in country A, $10 and $4 in country J, and $17 and $1 in country M. When production takes place entirely within the boundaries of each country, a unit of product costs $16, $14, and $18, in the three countries, respectively, giving country J a comparative cost edge over the other two.

When countries A and M form a free trade area and engage in production sharing, with A producing the first and M the second component, joint cost of a unit of the good declines to $10. While, neither country is able to compete with country J without cross-border fragmentation, intra-product specialization enables them to become competitive.

In order to assess the supply-side implications of cross-border fragmentation and production sharing, we start with a partial-equilibrium representation of the import sector of a partner country. In Figure 2, curve DD represents domestic demand for the imported product, X, while domestic supply in the absence of cross-border fragmentation is given by curve S_{x1+x2}. The product is assumed to be made up of two components, x_1 and x_2, where production of the former is intensive in the country's abundant factor. Line S_{x1+x*2}, represents costs of production when the first

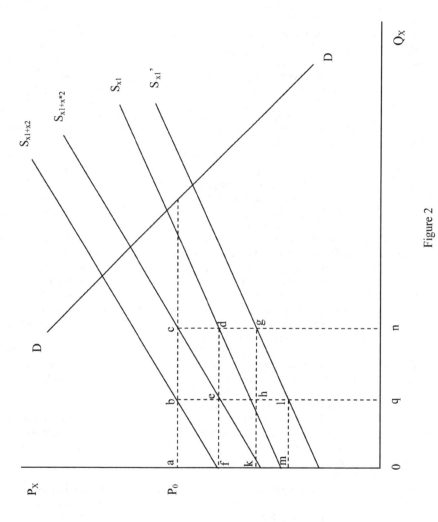

Figure 2

component, in which the country is assumed to have comparative advantage, is produced at home, and the second component is imported from a lower-cost foreign source.

The shift from local production to cross-border fragmentation, represented by the move from the first to the second supply curve, is welfare-increasing. If the country is small and the price of product X is given at P_o, then the gains from cross-border fragmentation accrue in the form of producer surplus (encompassed by area bckf) and increased employment (implicit in the rise in production from 0q to 0n). The value of X-production rises from 0abq to 0acn. Not all of this increase in value accrues to the country, however. The value of imported component x_2 is given by area acdf. The rise in domestic value added is therefore equal to the difference between areas ednq and abef.

Hence, both the quantity of X-production and the value of domestic production increase. While this is clearly positive from the point of view of the domestic industry, workers formerly engaged in producing component x_2 have lost their jobs. If those workers can find employment in production of component x_1, output of which clearly rises, they will remain employed in the industry and new workers may also be drawn into the industry.

The buffer provided by outsourcing can be seen if it is assumed that the world price of X is falling. In the absence of cross-border sourcing, domestic production of good X declines along supply curve S_{x1+x2}, with output and employment falling in the industry. Cross-border procurement of component x_2, on the other hand, shifts the supply curve out, moving production at the initial price to point c, so that when the negative world price shock occurs, domestic production declines along supply curve S_{x1+x2*}. It is evident, that cross-border fragmentation of production enhances the domestic industry's ability to fend off foreign competition.

The benefits conferred on domestic welfare by cross-border component procurement depend on several factors, including the share of imported components in total production. A rising share shifts down the S_{x1} curve to, say, S_{x1}, which raises the share of foreign value-added and lowers the share of domestic value-added and hence reduces the benefits from cross-border operations.[10]

The net effect also depends on the cost-savings inherent in offshore procurement. A rise in savings widens the gap between the top two supply curves, thereby increasing domestic production when the second component is imported and raising both employment opportunities and domestic value added.

5. A Three-Country Model of Economic Integration with Production Sharing

The focus in Figure 3 is on import demands and export supplies, that is, on the excesses between domestic demand and supply in importing and exporting countries, respectively. Demand curve $D_1D_2D_3$ represents the difference between domestic demand and domestic supply in country A. It is the country's net import demand curve. Curve D_3D_3 is the country's domestic demand curve; it becomes net import demand at point D_2, when domestic production goes to zero. Function S_{j+t} represents

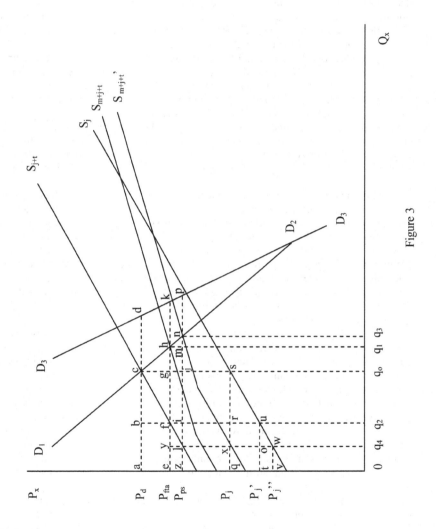

Figure 3

the tariff-inclusive net export supply of country J, while S_j is that country's pre-tariff net export supply. The initial MFN equilibrium, given at the intersection of net import demand and country J's tariff-inclusive net export supply, generates the domestic tariff-inclusive price, P_d, at which country A imports quantity $0q_o$ from country J. Output of X in country A is equal to the distance cd.

Introduction of a traditional free trade area between country A and country M reduces the price of X within the area to P_{fta}. This price is determined at the intersection between country A's import demand and supply curve S_{m+j+t}, which represents the sum of tariff-free export supply from country M and tariff-inclusive export supply from country J. Country A's total imports expand from $0q_o$ to $0q_1$, while imports from country J decline from $0q_o$ to $0q_2$. Imports from country M are equal to q_2q_1 (equal to fh). Domestic production in country A falls to hk. The reduction in country A's demand for imports from J forces that country to lower its supply price from P_j to P_j', providing country A with an improvement in the terms of trade.

Formation of the trade area generates the following welfare changes. Area acge represents domestic welfare transfers from government revenue to consumer surplus, while triangle cgh reflects welfare improvements due to trade creation and the consumption effect. Rectangle fgsr represents welfare losses due to trade diversion. It is clear that, terms-of-trade changes apart, the net welfare effect is ambiguous. It appears to be negative as drawn, with the magnitude of the area of trade diversion greater than that of the area of trade creation, but with steeper supply curves it will quickly turn positive. Inspection of the figure suggests further that the free trade area is more likely to be welfare-improving as the gap between supply curves S_{m+j+t} and S_j shrinks.

For large countries, formation of a free trade area will typically involve changes in the terms of trade, brought about by changes in the importing country's demand for goods from non-members. Area qrut (=abfe) gives the welfare gain due to the improvement in country A's terms-of-trade vis-a-vis country J. Terms-of-trade gains help offset welfare losses due to trade diversion.

Suppose that economic integration between countries A and M is deepened by introduction of cross-border component trade, such that country M is able to reduce production costs of good X by obtaining certain components at lower cost from country A. Reduced costs shift down country M's domestic supply curve (not shown), which in turn shifts out the country's export supply curve and thus curve S_{m+j+t} to, say, S_{m+j+t}'. This shift reduces the gap relative to country J's tariff-free supply curve.

Equilibrium moves from h to n, where the new joint export supply curve of countries J and M intersects country A's import demand. The intra-area price of X falls to P_{ps}. Relative to the initial MFN equilibrium, the area reflecting trade creation and consumption gains expands to triangle cjn, while trade diversion is now given by rectangle ljsx. The region of trade diversion thus shrinks vertically by rectangle fgji, but expands horizontally by rectangle lirx. It is clear that the net effect is ambiguous.

The first rectangle will expand and the second shrink as the supply curves become steeper.

In this process of adjustment, area fhmi is the welfare gain due to the lower price at which imports from country M are now available. Area lirx, on the other hand, is welfare-reducing because low-cost imports from Japan (equal to quantity li or q_4q_2) are replaced by higher-cost imports from country M.

The reduction in country A's demand for imports from J is now larger than in the case of a free trade area without production sharing, which forces country J to offer still deeper price concessions. J's supply price falls to P_j". The welfare gains due to this terms-of-trade improvement are given by area qxwv.[11]

Cross-border component sourcing thus allows country M to reduce costs and those cost savings redound to the advantage of consumers in country A.[12]   The magnitude of these benefits depends on the cost improvements brought about by cross-border production sharing between the area partners.   Greater cost savings generate a more pronounced downward shift of the S_{m+j+t} curve.

The analysis of cross-border production fragmentation has thus far focused on cost savings in the production of X in country M. As the discussion of Figure 2 suggests, however, country A may also enjoy cost savings if its producers are able to obtain low-cost components from country M. Then, A's domestic supply curve (not shown in Figure 3) shifts down, causing A's import demand curve to shift left in Figure 3. This shift reduces the price of good X still further, generating additional changes along all the margins discussed above.

Finally, cross-border fragmentation affects production of components. The shift of X-production from country A to country M reduces component production in country A. In the two-component example discussed above, the decision by country M to source component x_1 in country A raises production of that component in country A. Production of that component will rise still further if country A is able to achieve cost savings by procuring component x_2 from country M and thereby to raise its own X-output along the lines shown in Figure 2. These adjustments generate additional welfare effects.

Taken together, the various elements of the foregoing discussion serve as a reminder that in the presence of cross-border component sourcing, the shift of imports of a finished product from a low-cost non-member to a member complicates the welfare analysis.[13]

6. Concluding Comments

This paper has focused on the welfare effects of preferential trade liberalization which is accompanied by cross-border component sourcing. When trade involves finished products only, the extent of trade diversion depends on the differences among product prices in the countries involved. When production processes are fragmentable and trade integration gives rise to cross-border component sourcing, the prices of final goods are changed and the welfare calculus is altered. This possibility arises from the likelihood that a country may possess comparative advantage at the product level without commanding comparative advantage at every stage along the production chain.

This issue is explored in both partial- and general-equilibrium terms. It is shown that replacing imports of end products made in their entirety outside a free trade area (FTA) with products subject to production sharing inside the area may reduce the extent of trade diversion. Cross-border component sourcing among the partners of a free trade area is, thus, capable of converting a trade-diverting free trade area into a trade-creating one.

It is further shown that rules of origin, interpreted as policies to prevent efficient cross-border component sourcing, are welfare-reducing.

Notes

[1] Professor, Department of Economics, Claremont McKenna College; Address: 850 Columbia Ave., Claremont, CA 91711; Telephone: (909) 621-8012; Fax: (909) 607-8008; E-mail: lowe@claremontmckenna.edu. An earlier version of this paper was presented at a conference on "Structural Reform and the Transformation of Organizations and Businesses" at Homerton College, University of Cambridge, September 2003. Helpful comments from conference participants are gratefully acknowledged.

[2] See, for example, Arndt (2001, 2004).

[3] See, for example, Arndt (1997, 1998), Deardorff (2001a, 2001b), Jones (2000), Jones and Kierzkowski (2001) and Kohler (2001). See also Feenstra (1998) and Feenstra and Hanson (1996).

[4] Terms-of-trade effects of cross-border production sharing are examined in Arndt (2001). See also Deardorff (2001a).

[5] The implications of production sharing are examined in a two-country model in Arndt (2001).

[6] For a detailed workout, see Arndt (2004).

[7] Aspects of the analysis in this section will remind the reader of the "effective rate of protection." For an initial treatment, see Corden (1966). For a recent assessment, see Greenaway and Milner (2003) and for a comparative analysis of alternative measures of trade policy distortions, see Anderson (2003).

[8] In this framework, simplifying assumptions play an essential role. Implementation of a free trade area is thus often assumed to shift trade in its entirety away from the low-cost non-member country. Such an extensive reordering of production is due to the assumptions embodied in this model. In the next section, we use a three-country, partial-equilibrium framework to examine scenarios in which non-members continue to supply the FTA market, while sourcing of components and end products shifts to members.

[9] The focus here is on the effect of rules enforcement on the production possibility curve and through it on welfare. If B producers continue to source components among non-members and to pay A's tariff on those components, there will not be a single price of X in the region. There will be upward pressure on the price of good X

in A and downward pressure in B. The price differential between the two countries will reflect the size of the tariff and the share of third-country components in product X.

[10] This development is reminiscent of Hong Kong's experience in the electronics and textiles sectors, where the bulk of production has gradually shifted to the Pearl River Delta.

[11] It is apparent that the welfare gains due to terms of trade changes will vary over the range of possible FTA prices below the MFN price. The nature of the variations is governed by considerations similar to those involved in the theory of optimum tariffs. The elasticities of the relevant export supply and import demand curves are important here.

[12] These adjustments clearly have implications for trade, production and welfare in country M. There are strong, but not perfect, symmetries with the adjustments discussed for country A. For a closer examination of adjustment in a two-country framework, see Arndt (2001).

[13] Country J may also resort to cross-border component sourcing, in which case the analysis is further complicated.

References

Anderson, K., (2003), "Measuring Effects of Trade Policy Distortions: How Far Have We Come?" *The World Economy*, 26(4), (April), 413-440.

Arndt, S. W., (1997), "Globalization and the Open Economy," *North American Journal of Economics and Finance*, 8(10), 71-79.

_____, (1998), "Super-Specialization and the Gains from Trade," *Contemporary Economic Policy*, XVI(4) (October), 480-485.

_____, (2001), "Preference Areas and Intra-Product Specialization," in Paraskevopoulos, C., Kintis, A. and Kondonassis, A., *Globalization and the Political Economy of Trade Policy*, Toronto: APF Press.

_____, (2004), "Global Production Networks and Regional Integration," in M. Plummer (ed.) *Empirical Methods in International Trade*, Cheltenham, UK: Edward Elgar, forthcoming.

Arndt, S. W. and Kierzkowski, H. (eds.), (2001), *Fragmentation: New Production Patterns in the World Economy*, Oxford: Oxford University Press.

Corden, W.M., (1966), "The Structure of a Tariff System and the Effective Protection Rate," *Journal of Political Economy*, 74(3), 221-237.

Deardorff, A., (2001a), "Fragmentation in Simple Trade Models," *North American Journal of Economics and Finance*, 12(2) (July), 121- 138.

_____, (2001b), "Fragmentation Across Cones," in Arndt, S. W. and Kierzkowski, H., 35-51.

Feenstra, R. C., (1998), "Integration of Trade and Disintegration of Production in the Global Economy," *Journal of Economic Perspectives*, 12(4), (Fall), 31-50.

Feenstra, R.C. and Hanson, G. H., (1996), "Globalization, Outsourcing, and Wage Inequality," *American Economic Review*, 86(2), (May), 240-245.

Greenaway, D. and Milner, C., (2003), "Effective Protection, Policy Appraisal and Trade Policy Reform," *The World Economy*, 26(4), (April), 441-456.

Jones, R. W., (2000), *Globalization and the Theory of Input Trade*, Cambridge, MA: MIT Press.

Jones, R. W. and Kierzkowski, H., (2001), "A Framework for Fragmentation," in Arndt, S. W. and Kierzkowski, H., 17-34.

Kohler, W., (2001), "A Specific-Factors View on Outsourcing," *North American Journal of Economics and Finance*, 12(1), (March), 31-54.

Chapter 10

Production Networks, Exchange Rates and Macroeconomic Stability*

Sven W. Arndt

Abstract

As cross-border production sharing and multi-country production networks expand to cover more countries and more goods and services, questions arise about their implications for stability and adjustment in the open macro-economy. Participation in a production network ties a country more closely to other members of that network, thereby reducing cross-border asymmetries and promoting cyclical convergence. This strengthens the case for monetary cooperation and currency integration. On the other hand, if network activities are confined to a narrow, but non-trivial part, of the economy, then cross-border convergence may come at the expense of rising asymmetries within the economy. Rising asymmetries may compromise the effectiveness of monetary and fiscal policies. When the standard open-economy macro model is amended to take account of production sharing, the consequences for policy efficacy are similar to those arising from greater capital mobility. Further, production sharing may enhance or diminish the case for cross-border policy coordination, depending on whether it is broadly based or narrowly confined to specific sectors and industries.

JEL Classification: F15, F41, F42

Keywords: Production networks; Monetary cooperation; Exchange-rate regimes

1. Introduction

There has been a significant increase in production sharing since the early 1990s and with it a rapid rise of trade in parts and components. As a result, foreign value-added in countries' exports has risen sharply, as has the share of domestic value-added in imports.[1] In this process, exports and imports have become more directly linked and interdependent.

The trade patterns associated with production networks have a strong vertical intra-industry character, and vertical intra-industry trade is believed by many economists to promote convergence of business cycles. To the extent that cyclical convergence tends to reduce asymmetries among countries, it may strengthen the case for cross-border coordination of macro-economic policies and for fixed exchange rates.[2] If production sharing is centered in a specific region, say,

Southeast Asia, then there exists the potential for cyclical convergence within the region and hence enhanced opportunities for regional monetary and exchange-rate cooperation, including monetary union.[3] If, however, countries outside the region are part of the production network, then intra-regional monetary cooperation must include relations with the outsider. This is a particularly important issue for the nations of Southeast Asia, whose trade and network relations include major outsiders like the United States, Japan, and increasingly China.

Section 2 identifies several types of production sharing and their potential implications for exchange-rate and macro adjustment. Section 3 compares the efficacy of monetary and fiscal policies in the familiar Mundell-Fleming (M-F) model with an M-F model in which trade flows associated with production networks are accounted for. Section 4 considers the implications of these findings for monetary cooperation, and Section 5 offers conclusions.

2. Production Networks, Balance of Payments and Exchange Rates

A simple, bilateral form of vertical production integration occurs between two countries. Parts and components cross the border in one direction and assembled products flow in the other. More complex systems may involve hub-and-spoke arrangements between, say, a downstream assembly country and several upstream suppliers of parts and components, where trade flows from each of the latter to the former, without much trade among the latter. Fully articulated, multi-country production networks improve on the hub-and-spoke system by including trade among all members of the group. That is increasingly the case in Southeast Asia.

In NAFTA's automobile sector, American parts and components are exported to Mexico for assembly into vehicles that are then shipped to the United States. Here, only a minor portion of imported components is destined for use by Mexicans and only a few of the assembled automobiles are not shipped to the U.S. NAFTA's auto sector is also an example of hub-and-spoke production sharing, to the extent that Canada and Mexico each trade heavily with the United States, but where trade between them is minimal. In the aerospace sector, on the other hand, parts and components from several supplier nations flow into the United States for final assembly of the commercial jetliners.

Another hub-and-spoke example may be found in Japan's early production-sharing relations with several Southeast Asian nations in electronics and in other industries. More recently, Japan's interactions with many Southeast Asian countries, particularly in machinery trade, have taken on the character of a complex production network, as documented by Kimura and Ando (2003) and Ando, Arndt and Kimura (2006).

It is important to note that cross-border sourcing of parts and components allows the value of exports to differ from exported domestic value-added. The value of an automobile shipped from Mexico, of electronic machinery shipped from China or of airliners from the U.S., is significantly larger than Mexican, Chinese or U.S. value-added embodied in the respective products.

Network trade reacts differently to movements in prices, incomes and exchange rates than more traditional types of trade, because changes on one side of the trade balance are at least partly accommodated by changes on the other side. A shock leading to a decline in the demand for exported end products, for example, is partly absorbed by a decline in imported components, so that the effect on the trade balance and the domestic economy is attenuated.

The consequences of exchange-rate changes are also different, to the extent that variations in exchange rates affect both component imports and end-product exports or component exports and end-product imports. As a result, network trade turns out to be less sensitive to movements in exchange rates than other elements of a country's trade balance. That is because depreciation of its currency raises a country's cost of imported parts and components, but it also reduces the foreign-currency price of the exported end product.[4]

To capture these interactions, consider the following adaptation of a widely-used equation for the trade balance:

$$T = x[y*, e; m(y, e)] - m[y, e; x(y*, e)], \tag{1}$$

where x and m represent real exports and imports, respectively; y and y^* are domestic and foreign real GDP, respectively; and $e = E.P^*/P$ is the real exchange rate, composed of the nominal rate E and foreign and domestic prices, P^* and P, respectively. The additional elements in the expression are the direct links of exports and imports to each other.

In this set-up, a country's imports vary not only with home income, but also with foreign income through the direct link between imports and exports. Similarly, a country's exports vary not only with foreign income, but also with domestic income. In the typical demand-constrained view of exports and imports, we have come to associate domestic income as the dominant scale variable determining imports and foreign income as the dominant scale variable determining exports. With production sharing, the importance of domestic GDP relative to foreign GDP in driving a country's exports rises as does the importance of foreign GDP relative to domestic GDP in driving its imports.

Equation (1) shows further that changes in the exchange rate exert a more complex pattern of influences on the trade balance. Variations in the exchange rate now have two opposing effects on exports and on imports. The direct effect of currency depreciation, for example, raises exports and reduces imports as in the traditional model, while the linkage effect between exports and imports tends to counteract that tendency. Thus, while a depreciation of the home currency would, in the absence of production sharing, raise exports and thereby improve the current account, the fact that the rise in exports of finished products raises the demand for imported components increases imports and thereby worsens the trade balance, so that the net effect is smaller.

Analogously, in the absence of production sharing, a depreciation of the domestic currency is expected to reduce imports and increase exports and thereby to improve the current account (given suitable assumptions about the Marshall-Lerner condition). With production sharing, these effects are also present for non-network trade. For network trade, on the other hand, whether the depreciation reduces import demand depends on its effects on the demand for the country's exports. In arms-length transactions, the depreciation clearly raises the cost of imported components, which would be passed through to the price of the end product. But this rise in the home currency price of the end product will be counter-balanced by the depreciation's effect on the foreign-currency price of the end product. Meanwhile, the depreciation reduces the foreign-currency price of the domestic value-added contained in the country's exports. To the extent that the combination of these two effects raises the demand for the country's exports of the end product, there will be a rise in the demand for imported components.

The reduction of overall imports brought about by exchange-rate depreciation should consequently tend to be smaller when network imports are involved. Totally differentiating equation (1) yields the following:

$$dT = x_{y*}(1 - m_x)dy^* + [x_e(1 - m_x) - m_e(1 - x_m)]de - m_y(1 - x_m)dy, \quad (2)$$

where subscripted variables are partial derivatives, all of which are positive, except for m_e, the partial of imports with respect to the real exchange rate, which is negative. The effect of an exchange-rate change on imports is given by

$$dm/de = x_e m_x + m_e.$$

If it is negative, it will be smaller in the presence of network trade. But it may be positive, if the export-import linkage effect is larger than the direct effect of e on imports. Overall, equation (2) clearly shows that the effects of the three variables on the current account are smaller with than without network trade.

The transmission of shocks to the domestic economy is also attenuated. For example, to the extent that a rise in exports caused by a rise in foreign income is accompanied by rising imports, rather than rising domestic output, the transmission of foreign income shocks to the domestic economy is reduced. This strengthens the insulation of the domestic economy against foreign disturbances.

The previous discussion has been framed in terms of the real exchange rate, which suggests that the conclusions apply equally to movements in nominal exchange rates and in domestic and foreign prices. Foreign inflation, for example, raises the home-currency price of imports, including imported components (holding the nominal exchange rate constant). The latter rise increases the price of exported end products containing such components. While this represents an absolute price increase for the end product abroad, its relative price may actually rise by less than the foreign inflation rate to the extent that the price of domestic value-added has not risen.[5]

Similarly, domestic inflation, which in the absence of network trade would be expected to reduce exports and raise imports, will affect exports mainly to the extent of their domestic value-added contents and imports mainly to the extent that they are destined for domestic consumption.

The attenuated response of the foreign-currency price of the end product to exchange rate changes may look like incomplete pass-through, but it isn't. In the presence of bilateral production sharing, pass-through considerations apply mainly to the exporting country's value-added. This argument can be made more concrete in the following simple way. Let the price in country B of components made in country A be given by $p_b = E.p_a$, while the price in A of the end product is approximately $q_a = (1/E)[E.p_a + p_{vb}] = p_a + p_{vb}/E$, where p_{vb} is the cost of country-B value-added embodied in the end product. The exchange-rate effect on the foreign price is clearly limited to B's value-added in its own exports.

Of course, bilateral production sharing is a relatively simple form of cross-border intra-product specialization. In more complex cases, components may originate in third countries. Components made in Singapore, for example, are shipped to China for inclusion in electronic equipment destined for the U.S. market. In that case, $q_a = (1/E)[Z.p_c + p_{vb}] = (Z/E)p_c + p_{vb}/E$, where countries A, B, and C are the U.S., China and Singapore, respectively, and where E and Z are the yuan prices of the U.S. and Singapore dollars, respectively. Thus, if China's currency appreciates against the Singapore dollar to the same extent as its appreciation against the U.S. dollar, then the effect on the U.S. dollar price of Chinese exports is again attenuated and limited to Chinese value-added.

If China's currency remains unchanged against Singapore's, while appreciating against the U.S. dollar, then we obtain the traditional result of a more significant adjustment in the dollar prices of U.S. imports from China. Note, however, that as U.S. imports from China fall, China's imports of components from Singapore also fall. Hence, while China's appreciation against the dollar worsens its bilateral trade balance with the U.S., its overall trade balance deteriorates by less because of the decline in component imports from Singapore.

Hence, the extent to which appreciation of the Chinese currency translates into higher dollar prices of Chinese exports depends on whether the yuan appreciates against the currencies of its main supplier countries. If those currencies are tied to the dollar, so that the yuan appreciation against the dollar is an appreciation against the other currencies, then the effect on the dollar price of U.S. imports from China will be diminished by the extent to which the cost of China's imported components falls.[6]

These considerations have implications for exchange-rate strategy in countries which export to the U.S. or Japan indirectly via China. If their aim is to minimize the negative effects of a yuan appreciation against the dollar or the yen, they may wish to consider a float against the yuan, thereby allowing their currencies to depreciate against the yuan along with the dollar's depreciation. Alternatively, they may choose to price component exports in terms of the dollar. This is, in fact, the approach a number of countries in the region have adopted.

We conclude this section by noting that production sharing reduces the sensitivity of network trade to exchange-rate changes relative to non-network trade, with reactions heavily influenced by the share of local value-added embodied in network trade. Industries belonging to production networks appear to be more immune to exchange-rate volatility. At the same time, a country's balance of payments is buffered against shocks originating in the network, as exports and imports expand and contract together in response to changes in foreign incomes and prices.

3. Network Trade in a Familiar Open-Economy Macro Model

It is well-known that openness alters the effectiveness of monetary and fiscal policies in achieving employment and inflation targets. In the Mundell-Fleming (M-F) model, for example, the effectiveness of monetary policy is compromised in a small open economy with high capital mobility and a fixed exchange rate, but gains potency under floating rates with high capital mobility. In this section, we explore the effect of production sharing on these tendencies.

Money-market equilibrium is given by the familiar LM curve:

$$H/P = L(y, r), \tag{3}$$

where H is high-powered nominal money, P is the price level and y and r represent real output and the nominal interest rate, respectively.

The open-economy IS curve is amended by means of equation (1) above to represent the current account in place of the standard M-F specification, i.e., there is an additional term in the export and import functions:

$$i(r) + x[(y*, e; m(y, e)] - s(y) - m[y, e; x(y*, e)] = g, \tag{4}$$

where i is real capital formation, s is real saving, and x and m are real exports and imports, respectively, and g is the government surplus. The real exchange rate, e, is defined as before, namely, the nominal rate, E, adjusted by the ratio of prices, P^*/P.

We make similar adjustments in the balance-of-payments (BOP) equation:

$$x[(y*, e; m(y, e)] - m[y, e; x(y*, e)] + k(r - r*) = 0, \tag{5}$$

where k is the capital inflow and r^* is the foreign interest rate.

One consequence of the amendments embodied in equations (4) and (5) is to make the two curves flatter than they would be in the absence of network trade. The slopes are given by $dr/dy = [s_y + (1 - x_m)m_y]/i_r$ and $dr/dy = (1 - x_m)m_y/k_r$, for the IS and BOP curves, respectively. This result is of particular interest with respect to the balance-of-payments (BOP) curve, which becomes flatter in the M-F model as the international mobility of capital increases. As the importance of network trade increases and x_m rises, its effect on balance-of-payments adjustment is analogous to that of rising capital mobility. Thus, countries with insulated or repressed financial systems and thus faced with low capital mobility, may nevertheless have payments adjustment patterns typical of countries with open systems and high capital mobility, provided that the former are sufficiently linked to international production networks.

Thus, in a small country with a closed financial system domestic monetary policy is ineffective under fixed rates, regardless of the degree of involvement in global production networks. The potency of fiscal policy, on the other hand, rises under fixed rates as network trade becomes more important. Under floating rates, greater involvement in production networks enhances the efficacy of monetary policy, not only for the reasons known from the Mundell-Fleming model, but because the IS curve flattens out with network trade. The effectiveness of fiscal policy, however, is impaired by rising network trade, once that rise lowers the slope of the BOP curve relative to the LM curve.

It is important to note, however, that the network trade patterns that produce these results are those in which the country exports components and imports finished products, because then domestic income affects exports as well as imports. This means that the leakage of expenditure from the domestic economy is reduced.

4.   Challenges of Cross-Border Policy Cooperation

Production networking may segment parts of the economy from the rest, if it is sufficiently sector-specific and if it encourages location-specific agglomeration of productive resources. Vehicle and electronics industries centered in northern Mexico provide an example. The sectors involved in production networks tend to become more responsive to macro developments abroad and less responsive to those at home, implying rising cross-border, industry-specific cyclical convergence combined with intra-economy cyclical divergence. If cyclical convergence is sector-specific, asymmetries inside the economy are likely to rise, with part of the economy functioning like an enclave.

As noted, production sharing introduces a direct link between exports and imports, in addition to the traditional indirect link in which a rise of exports stimulates GDP and national income, which then feeds back to higher imports. The indirect link is weakened as the share of network trade rises in total trade, but the overall effect on imports is likely to become larger as the export elasticity of import demand rises relative to the product of the export effect on GDP and the income elasticity of import demand.

The impact of fluctuations in foreign economic activity on the balance of trade is attenuated, as changes in export demand brought about by fluctuations in foreign economic activity change imports in the same direction. By reflecting exports back into imports, network trade reduces the domestic repercussions of export shocks. Domestic monetary and fiscal policies, however, become relatively powerless in their ability to counteract cyclical fluctuations in network sectors. If monetary expansion cannot increase employment and output directly in the network sector, could it nevertheless be used to stimulate demand in the rest of the economy and thereby provide employment for resources idled in the network sector by a foreign disturbance?

Interestingly enough, the answer involves considerations that are very familiar from the literature on optimum currency areas, except that they are now applied to two segments of the same economy. If a collapse of export demand leads to a decline in economic activity in the network sector, while the rest of the economy enjoys high levels of employment, then a domestic expansionary policy will raise inflation pressures without doing much to improve employment in the network sector. The prescription of the theory of optimum currency areas is high factor mobility: factor movement from the network sector to the booming rest of the economy (Mundell, 1961).

This is the well-known asymmetry problem addressed by the theory of optimum currency areas. To the extent that introduction of production sharing increases asymmetries within the country, it undermines the suitability of the country as a whole for its common currency, while strengthening the case for a common currency between the network sector and the foreign economy.

The foregoing has assumed that networking is confined to a subset of industries or to a particular region in a country. If networking and production sharing are broadly diffused throughout the economy, on the other hand, then cyclical patterns of economic activity will converge among the country and its networking partner(s) and the consequent reduction in asymmetries strengthens the case for cross-border monetary cooperation. If production sharing takes place among neighbors in a larger region, then monetary cooperation among them could include a common currency arrangement. In Southeast Asia, on the other hand, production networking involves economies outside the region — including the United States, Japan and, increasingly, China. In that case, regional monetary cooperation will have to encompass a common strategy with respect to network partners outside the region.

Indeed, if the extra-regional trading partner dominates the production network, then the pros and cons of closer monetary integration of the regional group with that country would have to be addressed. The small nations of Southeast Asia have been struggling with this question for a number of years. An alternative to regionally coordinated approaches, however, is for each nation in the region to tie its currency to the outside network partner or to some basket of dominant network currencies, thereby effectively fixing all relevant bilateral rates. As the experience of Europe in the run-up to its common currency shows, however, countries are likely to fret over beggar-thy-neighbor currency manipulations, so that there probably is no alternative to a mechanism similar to the European Monetary System (EMS).[7]

5. Conclusion

The growth of production sharing may have implications for macroeconomic policy and adjustment in open economies. It is well-known that the effectiveness of monetary and fiscal policies in achieving output/employment objectives depends on the nature of the exchange rate regime and on the degree of capital mobility. Does it also depend on production sharing?

Production sharing may occur entirely among countries in a given region, such as the U.S., Canada and Mexico. For the nations of Southeast Asia, on the other hand, production sharing takes place with important extra-regional economies like Japan, the United States and, increasingly, China. It tends to reduce the sensitivity of the trade balance to variations in exchange rates, to the extent that imports of parts and components are re-exported in finished products or exported components return inside imported end products. Through the direct linkage between imports and exports, production sharing makes imports dependent on foreign GDP and exports on domestic GDP.

When production sharing is introduced into the standard Mundell-Fleming model, many of its conclusions regarding policy effectiveness continue to hold. However, production sharing tends to insulate the home economy from foreign shocks and disturbances. An important finding is that production networking tends to flatten the slopes of the IS and BOP curves and thereby exerts effects on the adjustment process that are similar to those of high capital mobility. Hence, countries with closed financial systems, but engaged in production networks, will display adjustment patterns similar to those of countries with open financial systems and faced with high capital mobility.

Finally, while production sharing may under the right conditions reduce macroeconomic asymmetries across countries and thus strengthen the case for monetary cooperation and monetary integration, it has the potential to increase internal asymmetries within the domestic economy which can undermine the suitability of the domestic economy as a common currency area.

Endnotes

*An earlier version of this paper was presented at the 2008 APEA conference in Beijing (December). Comments and suggestions from conference participants are gratefully acknowledged.

1. The effects of cross-border fragmentation have been widely studied. See, for example, Arndt (1997, 1998), Deardorff (2001) and Jones and Kierzkowski (1990) and Athukorala and Yamashita (2006). For production sharing in free trade areas, see Arndt (2001, 2004). The network activities of Japanese multinationals in Southeast Asia have been examined in Kimura and Ando (2003) and Ando, Arndt and Kimura (2006).
2. Chiquiar (2005) and Torres and Vega (2004) provide evidence of convergence between the United States and its North American trading partners.
3. For a discussion of monetary arrangements in North America, see Arndt (2006).
4. Arndt and Huemer (2006) find that network trade between the United States and Mexico is less sensitive to exchange-rate changes than trade in general.
5. Clearly, the end result will be affected by the way in which changes in component prices are passed through as they travel through the network. If transactions in the network are not fully arms-length, intra-firm transfer pricing becomes an issue. It will also matter whether traded goods are priced in local currencies or in some international currency, as is often the case in Southeast Asia for example. This is discussed later in this section.
6. Eichengreen , Rhee and Tong (2005) examine China's role in emerging trade patterns and the extent to which Chinese goods are crowding out the exports of other countries in the region.
7. In the aftermath of the Asian exchange-market crises of the late nineties, concerns have been expressed about financial attacks and contagion. It is

conceivable that participation in a production network may facilitate contagion-like transmission of shocks. This suggests that policies and institutions may be needed to provide first lines of defense, perhaps in the form of the service links discussed in Jones and Kierzkowski (1990). It also raises questions about sequencing of trade, financial and monetary integration. On this, see Pomfret (2005) and Rajan (2004) for useful discussion.

References

Ando, M., S.W. Arndt and F. Kimura (2006), "Production Networks in East Asia: Strategic Behavior by Japanese and U.S. Firms," Japan Center for Economic Research.

Arndt, S.W. (1997), "Globalization and the Open Economy," *North American Journal of Economics and Finance*, 8, 1, pp. 71–79.

———(1998), "Super-Specialization and the Gains from Trade," *Contemporary Economic Policy*, 16, 4, pp. 480–485.

———(2001), "Offshore Sourcing and Production Sharing in Preference Areas," in S.W. Arndt and H. Kierzkowski (eds.), *Fragmentation: New Production Patterns in the World Economy* (New York: Oxford University Press).

———(2004), "Trade Diversion and Production Sharing," *Journal of Economic Asymmetries*, 1, 1.

———(2006), "Regional Currency Arrangements in North America," *International Economics and Economic Policy*, 3 (3–4), December.

———and A. Huemer (2006), "Trade, Production Networks and the Exchange Rate," (Lowe Institute of Political Economy).

Athukorala, P.-C. and N. Yamashita (2006), "Production Fragmentation and Trade Integration: East Asia in a Global Context," *North American Journal of Economics and Finance*, 17, 3, pp. 233–256.

Chiquiar, D. And M. Ramos-Francia (2005), "Trade and Business-Cycle Synchronization: Evidence from Mexican and U.S. Manufacturing Industries," *North American journal of Economics and Finance*, 16, 2, pp. 187–216.

Deardorff, A. V. (2001), "Fragmentation in Simple Trade Models," *North American Journal of Economics and Finance*, 12, 2, pp. 121–137.

Eichengreen, B., Y. Rhee and H. Tong (2004), "The Impact of China on the exports of Other Asian Countries," NBER Working paper No. 10768, September.

Jones, R. W. and H. Kierzkowski (1990), "The Role of Services in Production and International Trade: A Theoretical Framework," in R.W. Jones and A.O. Krueger (eds.), *The Political Economy of International Trade*, (Oxford: Blackwell).

Kimura, F. and M. Ando (2003), "Fragmentation and Agglomeration Matter: Japanese Multinationals and Latin America and East Asia," *North American Journal of Economics and Finance*, 14, 3.

Mundell, R. A. (1961), "A Theory of Optimum Currency Areas," *American Economic Review*, 51, 4, pp. 657–665.

Pomfret, R. (2005), "Sequencing Trade and Monetary Integration: Issues and Application to Asia," mimeo.

Rajan, R. S. (2004), "Asian Economic Cooperation and Integration: Sequencing of Financial, Trade and Monetary Regionalism," mimeo.

Torres, A. and O. Vela (2003), "Trade Integration and Synchronization between the Business Cycles of Mexico and the United States," *North American Journal of Economics and Finance*, 14, 3, pp. 319–342.

Chapter 11

Trade, Production Networks and the Exchange Rate

Sven W. Arndt
Lowe Institute of Political Economy, Claremont McKenna College
Alex Huemer[1]
Lowe Institute of Political Economy, Claremont McKenna College

Abstract. This paper examines the effect of cross-border production sharing on trade and exchange-rate behavior. When a country's exports contain imported components, changes in exchange rates tend to have offsetting effects on imports and exports. Imports may fall, remain unchanged or even rise with depreciation, depending on the share of domestic value-added in exports. The effect of domestic and foreign GDP on imports and exports is also altered by production sharing. These behavior patterns are identified in trade in motor vehicles between the United States and Mexico with the aid of OLS and VEC techniques.

JEL Classification: F14, F15, F32
Keywords: Trade balance; Fragmentation; Intra-industry trade; Exchange rates: NAFTA

1. Introduction
Exchange rates, home and foreign prices, and home and foreign incomes are key explanatory variables in standard trade equations. The empirical evidence suggests overwhelmingly that exchange rates and incomes matter in determining the flow of trade. Domestic GDP helps explain imports, while foreign GDP influences exports. These findings apply to trade in end products and to intermediate products destined for use in the importing country. In recent years, however, the growth of cross-border fragmentation of production has generated trade patterns in which parts and components flow from one country to another, to be assembled into products that are then exported rather than used at home.

The object of this study is to assess the extent to which goods flowing within production networks alter the sensitivity of trade to the aforementioned determinants. The focus is on U.S.-Mexico trade, where we find that cross-border production

11

sharing reduces the responsiveness of trade to movements in the exchange rate and that a country's own GDP affects the demand for its exports.

The rest of the paper proceeds as follows. Section 2 sets out the basic analytical framework and discusses some stylized facts. The focus is on production sharing in the automobile sector between the U.S. and Mexico. Section 3 presents and assesses the empirical evidence; and section 4 concludes the study.

2. Trade Patterns under Cross-border Production Sharing

Production sharing between the U.S. and Mexico came into its own in the maquiladora program and continues under the North American Free Trade Agreement (NAFTA). It plays a key role in several industries, including textiles and apparel, motor vehicles, electronics, and processed foods. In its original manifestation in the motor vehicles sector, for example, Mexico's primary contribution was to assemble U.S.-made parts and components into finished automobiles destined mainly for the U.S. market. In more recent years, the nature of production sharing between the two countries has become more complex, as Mexican producers have begun to supply components, in addition to providing assembly. While U.S. firms play a dominant role in this relationship, multinationals from Europe and Japan are also active in Mexico.

Similar forms of interaction may be found in other sectors, including textiles and apparel, where cotton and various types of fibers are exported to Mexico, to be used in the manufacture of apparel destined for the United States. In the agricultural sector, raw produce is shipped to Mexico and returns to the U.S. in processed form. In this instance, the transformation is from imports of non-manufactures into exports of manufactures. We explore the implications of this phenomenon below.

2.1 Fragmentation and factor intensities

Cross-border production sharing pushes specialization from the level of products to that of components. Hence, if factor intensities vary across the components of products, then the factor-proportions theory should be useful in explaining component specialization across countries. Labor-abundant countries like Mexico would be expected to specialize in labor-intensive components and labor-intensive assembly, while capital- and skill-rich countries like the United States have comparative advantage in capital- and skill-intensive components and skill-intensive assembly. These considerations have been examined in the recent literature on fragmentation; our focus here is on the key determinants of trade flows when production sharing is present.[2]

2.2 The role of GDP

According to the standard trade model, Mexican GDP is an important determinant of imports from the U.S., while U.S. GDP helps determine Mexican exports to the U.S. In the context of cross-border production sharing, however, Mexico's imports from the U.S. include parts and components for use not by Mexicans, but in the manufacture of exports to the U.S. For this type of import, variations in Mexican GDP should be unimportant, while U.S. GDP should play a larger role, because it determines the demand for imported automobiles. In this context, Mexico's demand for component imports is a derived demand, which rises when U.S. demand for automobile imports rises. Variations in Mexico's GDP would, of course, continue to explain traditional imports (which may include imported components for direct use by Mexicans). Hence, the relative importance of the two GDPs in explaining Mexican imports depends on the share of network trade in total imports.

Our expectation, therefore, is that the explanatory power of Mexican GDP falls and that of U.S. GDP rises as the share of network trade in the dependent variable rises. These response patterns should be apparent in a comparison, for example, of imports of auto parts and components with merchandise imports generally. We test this expectation by examining trade at both aggregate and sector-specific levels.

2.3 The exchange rate

Traditionally, appreciation of a country's currency raises imports and lowers exports, ceteris paribus. In the presence of production sharing, on the other hand, the rise in the peso price of U.S.-made components tends to raise the peso price of the Mexican end product, but the dollar price of that product is affected in the opposite direction by the peso's depreciation.[3] These offsetting tendencies affect the degree of pass-through and thus the sensitivity of trade flows to changes in the exchange rate. The extent to which the dollar's appreciation reduces the dollar price of the end product declines as the share of Mexican value-added in the end product declines.

Note, moreover, that the decline in its dollar price is expected to raise the demand for the imported end product, which in turn will raise the demand for imports of U.S. components. Here, an appreciation of the dollar *raises* the demand for U.S. exports. The traditional negative response of exports following a dollar appreciation continues to hold, of course, for products and components that are not part of the production-sharing loop. Thus, the net effect of the appreciation on overall U.S. exports to Mexico may be negative, zero, or positive, depending on the share of production-sharing trade in total exports, the share of Mexican value added in exported end products, and the price elasticity of U.S. demand for the end product.[4]

2.4 Changes in the terms of trade

The trade-balance implications of terms-of-trade changes may also be affected by production sharing. Mexican inflation, for example, raises the demand for imports and reduces exports in the traditional model, causing the trade balance to deteriorate. Inflation raises the cost of Mexican value-added in motor vehicles shipped to the United States and thus reduces the U.S. demand for them. Such a decline in vehicle exports, however, reduces the demand for component imports from the U.S., which tends to mute the overall effect of the price change on the trade balance. Analogous considerations apply to the effects of price inflation in the United States. Together, the weakened or ambiguous influence of the nominal exchange rate and of relative prices suggests that the effect of the real exchange rate is also more tenuous.

3. Econometrics
The preceding discussion suggests, first, that the sensitivity of trade to the exchange rate declines with the rise of production sharing. Hence, in sectors with high shares of trade flowing within production networks, the exchange-rate effect should be weaker than in sectors in which network trade is low or absent. The sensitivity of trade in motor vehicles and motor vehicle components, for example, should be lower than that of overall manufacturing imports and exports. Second, the role of the component-importing country's GDP in explaining imports should decline and the role of the component-exporting country's GDP should grow as the importance of cross-border sourcing and of network trade rises.

Trade policy plays an important role in determining the feasibility of production sharing, particularly as it pertains to restrictions on investment flows, foreign ownership, and right-of-establishment issues. In the U.S.-Mexico case, NAFTA relaxed or removed a variety of restrictive policies pertaining to trade and foreign investment. Of course, other acts of trade liberalization, including completion of the Uruguay Round, helped reduce the costs associated with cross-border production sharing, and innovations in communications and transportation technologies made a major contribution to cost reduction.

As noted earlier, production sharing between the U.S. and Mexico predates NAFTA, and was already widespread under the maquiladora program. The focus of this paper is on the extent to which implementation of NAFTA has intensified cross-border linkages. However, shortly after the official inception of NAFTA in early 1994, Mexico experienced a major exchange-rate crisis, with significant disruptions of economic activity. The coincidence of these events raises potential problems for the empirical analysis, an issue which we explore more fully below.

3.1 Data analysis and regressions
The purpose of the empirical analysis is to explore the implications of production sharing for the key relationships of the standard trade model. The point is not to test alternative trade theories, but to compare the results when the model is applied to different categories of exports and imports, where a key feature distinguishing the trade categories is the relative importance of production sharing.

We take as our standard import-export equation a specification that includes GDP, the real exchange rate, and variables representing NAFTA on the right-hand side. We examine those relationships with quarterly data for bilateral trade between the U.S. and Mexico covering the period from the first quarter of 1989 to the fourth quarter of 2002.[5]

The basic model is then applied to U.S. trade with Mexico in three categories: exports and imports of manufactures, exports of non-manufactures and imports of non-manufactures excluding petroleum,[6] and imports of passenger vehicles and exports of motor vehicle parts and components. The degree to which the categories can be classified as traditional or non-traditional trade is summarized in Table 1. On the side of U.S. imports, non-manufacturing trade is the most traditional of the three categories, in that it contains virtually no network trade. It should thus display behavior most consistent with the predictions of the traditional model.

Imports of manufactures have a higher content of network trade, including motor vehicles, processed foods, textiles and electronics. They should thus display results that conform less well with, or deviate from, the predictions of the traditional model. Finally, motor vehicle imports are fully embedded in network trade and should thus display behavior that differs significantly from the traditional model.

On the side of U.S. exports, manufactures should display behavior that is most consistent with the traditional model, because the share of network trade is relatively small. The share is larger in non-manufacturing exports to Mexico, in view of the importance of exports of agricultural raw materials for use in the manufacture of processed food for the United States market and of cotton and textiles for use in the manufacture of apparel exports to the United States.

3.2 Statistical properties of the time series

Time series tests of the variables suggest that the logs of real imports, real U.S. GDP, and the real exchange rate, defined as the peso price of the dollar adjusted by the ratio of U.S. to Mexican wholesale prices, are all I(1) variables (Appendix Table A.1).[7] As reflected by the Engle-Granger[8] test statistics reported in the relevant tables, the I(1) variables appear to be cointegrated. This enables us to run the OLS regressions in level terms and thereby provides an easy means of assessing the nature of the long-run relationships involved.[9]

Still, the concern may be raised that the relationship is misspecified by the traditional OLS representation, particularly with respect to the designation of dependent and independent variables. Contemporaneous relationships may be statistically consistent, but erroneous representations of the true underlying relationships. For example, Torres and Vela (2003) present evidence suggesting that Mexican GDP may be a lagged or contemporaneous function of U.S. GDP, exports and the dollar exchange rate.

The traditional specification of the trade equation adopts the perspective that causality runs from GDP and the real exchange rate to exports and imports. The standard open-economy macro model, on the other hand, allows for the possibility that changes in exports may affect GDP. This raises another potential concern about causality: in the presence of production sharing, exports affect imports and imports of components may thus appear to Granger-cause[10] domestic output. Analogous concerns arise with respect to the direction of causality between bilateral imports and exports and the exchange rate. The correlation matrices presented in Appendix Table A.2 reflect both the strong contemporaneous co-movements and the common trends among our variables of interest. The real exchange rate is the exception.

We adopted two approaches to address these problems. First, we performed Granger tests to determine if consistent causality relations can be established among and across the variables of interest. However, Granger tests for inter-temporal causal relationships among the variables produced results which varied with the lag length. So much so, in fact, that no clear and consistent set of causal relations could be established using the Granger technique.

Second, remaining agnostic with respect to the question of causality, we estimated a vector-error-correction (VEC) specification of the relationship between the import and export series and their explanatory variables. The vector-error-correction estimations were constrained by the OLS-generated coefficients and then re-estimated in unconstrained form.[11] We calculated likelihood ratios (LR) for constrained (OLS) versus unconstrained representations. The likelihood of the import regression results was not significantly improved by the unconstrained VEC model, and so we accept the null hypothesis of the OLS representations for imports. However, the LR statistics indicated that the constraints on the export specifications were significant.

Moreover, the Durbin-Watson statistics from the OLS regressions gave consistent indication of error auto-correlation for the level regressions for exports. However, we show below that this apparent rejection of the OLS specification is likely to be spurious and due to an unconstrained error-correction component: the real peso-dollar exchange rate is weakly exogenous in the export model VEC specifications and, therefore, should not be included in the cointegrating vector. When corrected for the weak exogeneity of the peso, the trace and max-eigenvalue statistics indicate cointegrating relations for all our VEC specifications (with one notable exception), allowing us to reject non-cointegration of the VEC, and allowing us to further discount the probability of spurious regression for the level regressions.

Given the ambivalent causal relationships between the variables used in estimation, we thought it prudent to first identify contemporaneous relations with level OLS regressions. Lagged dependent and independent variables are present in the VEC model, and there the complex interrelations can be more carefully articulated.

3.3 Dealing with the effects of NAFTA

On the part of the United States, implementation of trade liberalization with Mexico during the period occurred in two significant steps in 1992 and 1994, as Figure 1 indicates. That figure presents the ratio of duty collections to the value of imports of manufactures, non-manufactures and passenger vehicles, respectively. There is a steep drop in duty collections in 1992, followed by another drop in 1994, and then a gradual decline over the remainder of the period. To underscore the preferential nature of these changes, we compare average duty collections on passenger vehicle imports from Mexico, Japan, and the rest of the world in Figure 2. Duty rates on imports from Japan are largely unchanged, while those for the rest of the world decline moderately and gradually over the period without any sharp reductions in 1992 and 1994.

A widely used approach to modeling the effect of NAFTA is by means of mean-shift dummies, which switch from zero to one in 1994, the year in which NAFTA went into effect.[12] As noted and as the figures suggest, however, there were two episodes of tariff liberalization vis-à-vis Mexico during the period. A simple 1994 dummy risks misspecification, particularly in view of the possibility that it may pick up effects associated with the beginning of the peso crisis.[13]

In order to test for the effect of trade liberalization prior to the official start date of NAFTA, we use a dummy for 1992 as an alternative specification. In order to further explore this issue, we use a two-stage dummy, which shifts to the value one in 1992 and takes on the value two beginning in 1994. We also tested regressions with an interaction term between the mean-shift variable and U.S. GDP on the right-hand side, but that specification did not significantly improve the fit or explanatory power of the model with dummies alone.

As an alternative to the dummy-variable approach, we employ the duty ratios of Figure 1 to construct a trade-liberalization variable defined as 1 plus the duty ratio.[14] We expect imports in each of the three categories to increase as the ratio of duty collections relative to the value of imports in each category declines. Hence, the coefficient is expected to be negative.

3.4 U.S. imports from Mexico

Table 2 presents regressions for U.S. imports from Mexico at the three levels of aggregation, with the four alternative specifications of trade liberalization during the period. The regressions are significant, reflecting the very high degrees of correlation among the variables noted earlier. Real U.S. GDP is significant in all regressions, with large coefficients across all levels of aggregation.

The real exchange rate carries the largest coefficient and greatest t-value for non-manufactures, the most "traditional" of the three categories (See Table 1). Its explanatory power is generally weaker as predicted for manufacturing imports and disappears altogether for imports of motor vehicles.[15] The results confirm our prediction that the influence of exchange-rate changes is eroded by the rise of network trade.

The effect of the NAFTA dummies varies across the import categories; it is significant for manufactures and motor vehicles, but insignificant for non-manufacturing imports. The latter result is consistent with the notion that the commodities contained in that category were least affected by NAFTA-based trade liberalization.[16] The sign on the fourth NAFTA variable, namely, the ratio of duties collected on each of the three categories of imports relative to the value of those imports is negative, as predicted: a decline in the ratio is a sign of trade liberalization and should thus stimulate imports (Table 2d). The coefficients are statistically significant in all three trade categories.[17]

3.5 U.S. exports to Mexico

U.S. exports are divided into manufactures, non-manufactures, and motor vehicle parts and components. This is not the only way to break up total exports into groups reflecting different production arrangements, but data constraints typically come into play. The main purpose here is to see whether the presence of network trade in the variable on the left-hand side affects the explanatory power of the widely-used export equation. The right-hand-side variables include the real exchange rate, Mexican GDP, and a NAFTA dummy. As noted above, manufacturing exports are the most "traditional" of the three export categories in that the share of goods destined for use by Mexicans is highest. Hence, this category should display behavior that is most consistent with the standard trade model. We expect the fit to be weaker for non-manufacturing exports, because the share of goods destined for use by Mexicans is smaller and the share of network trade is larger.[18] Finally, we expect the fit of the standard model to be relatively poor in the regression for exports of motor vehicle parts.

U.S. exports of goods destined for use by Mexicans should respond negatively to depreciation of the peso. For goods moving within production networks, on the other hand, the effect should be weaker. Hence, the exchange-rate coefficient may become insignificant for exports of non-manufactures and of motor vehicle parts. Indeed, the sign of the coefficient may turn positive, if depreciation of the peso raises U.S. imports of motor vehicles, which in turn raises the demand for U.S.-made parts and components. As discussed earlier, the power of Mexican GDP in explaining U.S. exports should fade as the importance of network trade rises.

Table 3 reports results testing these hypotheses. Our expectations with respect to the real exchange rate are largely confirmed. The response of manufactures exports, the most traditional of the three categories, conforms more closely with the predictions of the standard model than non-manufactures and motor vehicle parts. The latter, in particular, is closely tied to production sharing.

Our expectations regarding the role of Mexican GDP remain largely unconfirmed by the results, at least as far as significance levels are concerned. While the magnitude of the coefficient is smaller for non-manufactures than for manufactures, the coefficient in the regression for motor vehicle parts is larger in panels 2a and 2b. The results are more consistent with our expectations in panels 2c and 2d, in which U.S. GDP is added on the right-hand side. There, Mexican GDP is insignificant for U.S. exports of non-manufactures and carries weaker significance (but a larger coefficient) for exports of motor vehicle parts. U.S. GDP is significant in the regressions for all three categories. The magnitude of the coefficient rises as we move from manufactures to non-manufactures, but the level of significance declines and is weakest for motor vehicle parts imports.

As for the role of NAFTA, panel 2a reports results incorporating the 1994 NAFTA dummy in the standard export equation. As Figure 3 suggests, liberalization of trade in motor vehicle parts begins on the Mexican side in 1994. U.S. exports rise with the inception of NAFTA. We have no specific evidence of significant trade liberalization in 1992, apart from the duty reductions reported on U.S. imports.[19] However, to allow for the possibility of spill-over effects resulting from the U.S. reductions, panel 2b employs the two-stage specification of NAFTA, the coefficient of which is significant in all three regressions. The results are largely similar when U.S. GDP is added on the right-hand side of panels 2c and 2d.

3.6 Vector error correction results

As noted previously, VEC representations were also estimated for imports and for exports.[20] The import results are based on the specification presented in Table 2d. The duties/imports variable is our preferred representation of NAFTA, not least because it provides a continuous series for identifying the error-correction component of the model. There is, moreover, no empirical reason for preferring one of the other specifications (on a log likelihood basis). The VEC coefficient estimates are robust to sample size, lag length of the error-correction components, as well as the presence or absence of a constant term in the error-correction component.[21]

In the import equations, the cointegrating vectors display significant coefficients and have signs that are consistent with the OLS representations. The real peso is weakly exogenous to the system, and has very little significance, both contemporaneously and at various lags. However, in the VEC for imports of non-manufactures, the real peso is endogenous to the system, and so is included in the cointegrating equation. The common trend term is significant throughout for U.S. GDP, but less so for non-manufactured imports and not at all for aggregate manufactured and passenger vehicle imports.

The system of VEC equations generates impulse response functions. There is a positive import response to U.S. GDP changes, and a negative response to import duties. The size of both impulse responses increases as we proceed from manufactured imports to passenger vehicle imports, with the non-manufactured import response located somewhere in the middle. Apart from the exchange-rate effect on non-manufactured imports, there is only a slight impulse response running to or from the other variables, consistent with the results of our basic OLS regressions.

The export VEC specification is based on Table 3c[22], which is consistent with the time-line of Mexican trade liberalization. Here, both the real peso and U.S. GDP are weakly exogenous to the system and are thus relegated to the error-correction component of the specification. When OLS coefficients are used to calculate restricted versions of the VECs, the restrictions are non-binding, thus further mitigating our concerns about the adequacy of the OLS estimates.

For manufactured and non-manufactured exports, the impulse responses and coefficients are consistent with the OLS regressions. The significance of U.S. GDP in explaining U.S. exports to Mexico can now be seen in terms of its effect on the export error-correction response. Manufactured exports are weakly influenced by U.S. GDP, but only Mexican GDP is significantly influenced by deviations from the cointegrating vector. The reverse appears to be true for exports of non-manufactures, which are significantly positively influenced by Mexican GDP and trade liberalization, with U.S. GDP operating directly on non-manufactured exports and indirectly through its effect on Mexican GDP. Mexican GDP is not significantly influenced by U.S. exports of non-manufactures.

U.S. GDP was used in these VEC models in lieu of a direct measure of U.S. demand for commodities embodying exported components. However, in the case of motor vehicle parts, we do have just such a measure in passenger vehicle imports. When included in the cointegrating equation, passenger vehicle imports are significantly cointegrated with motor vehicle parts exports, while Mexican GDP is not. Table 10 presents the results, with Mexican GDP now relegated to a weakly exogenous influence on parts demand. Interestingly, the unconstrained estimate presents a cointegrating regression coefficient on passenger vehicles of 0.93, indicating a long-run relationship in which all but 7 percent of parts exports are fully embodied in passenger vehicle imports. The sign of the dummy term is now positive (though not significant), but that would appear to reflect the relatively greater significance of the NAFTA reforms to the importation of passenger vehicles, given the positive coefficient on error correction to that variable (and relatively insignificant response of parts exports to the same cointegrating relationship).

The VEC model has been applied in a number of open-economy macroeconomic studies. The suitability of the approach for identifying relationships between variables that are not macroeconomic aggregates (or between aggregates and specific commodity flows) is still unclear. However, the import relationships estimated are consistent with our OLS results and reinforce the conclusions reached. The export results reveal a relatively more complicated relationship, but indicate the importance of U.S. income changes in the determination of Mexican production, affecting Mexican component imports from the U.S., and ultimately impacting Mexican GDP. In the specific case of auto parts, Mexican GDP appears not to matter at all (or very little), with virtually all of the export demand being driven by the need for components for the production and importation of passenger vehicles for the U.S. market.

4. Concluding Remarks

The focus of this study has been to ascertain the extent to which the cross-border integration of production affects well-known relationships involving trade, the exchange rate, and key macroeconomic variables. An argument is developed which suggests that the sensitivity of exports and imports to the real exchange rate should decline when cross-border fragmentation expands and when the share of trade associated with production networks rises.

The evidence presented in this paper strongly supports that conjecture, showing that while the exchange-rate effect follows traditional lines for variables in which network trade is unimportant, the relationship fades as the share of network trade rises.

A country's imports may become less sensitive to movements in domestic GDP and more responsive to foreign GDP as the share of trade related to cross-border production sharing rises. The evidence indicates that the explanatory power of Mexican GDP is weaker and that of U.S. GDP stronger in the regression on motor vehicle parts exports to Mexico than in the other export regressions. From the VEC specification, we can identify the strong effect of U.S. GDP transmitted by U.S. imports of passenger vehicles.

The official start of NAFTA in 1994 was preceded by U.S. trade liberalization vis-à-vis Mexico in 1992. Regressions using dummies based on 1992 provide superior performance to those based on 1994, and a two-step dummy outperforms both in our import equations. In order to capture the continuity in trade liberalization over the length of the period, we construct a time series variable for the United States which relates duty collections to the flow of imports. The variable is significant and has the correct sign, suggesting an important evolving role for trade liberalization in the region. The export regressions confirm the role of NAFTA in U.S.-Mexico trade.

Table 1. U.S. Trade with Mexico

	Most Traditional	Semi-traditional	Least Traditional
Exports	Manufactures	Non-manufactures	Motor Vehicle Parts
Imports	Non-manufactures	Manufactures	Passenger Vehicles

Note: Traditional in this context refers to traded goods intended for final consumption or use by the importing country and not containing value-added of the importing country (parts and components). Least Traditional refers to traded goods with a high proportion of commodities used in production sharing networks, in this instance intended for final consumption in the United States.

Figure 1. Average U.S. ad valorem Duties on Mexican Merchandise Imports

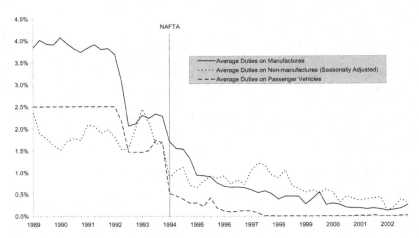

Source: USITC Trade and Duties; Authors' Calculations.

Figure 2. Average Ad Valorem US Duties on PV Imports

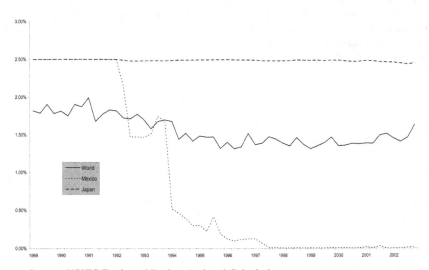

Source: USITC Trade and Duties; Authors' Calculations.

Figure 3. Average Mexican Ad Valorem Tariff on Imports of U.S. MV Parts (selected)

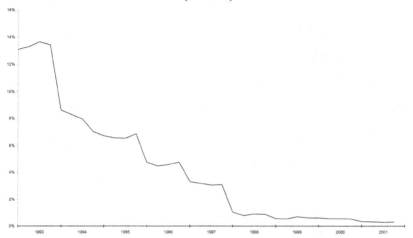

Source: USITC Trade Data, U.S. Commerce Department Tariff Data; Authors' Calculations.

Figure 4. U.S.-Mexico Manufactures Trade

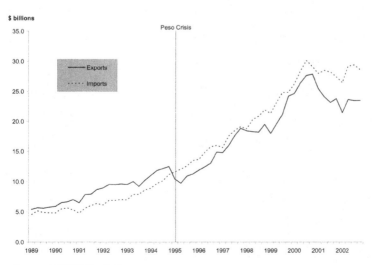

Source: USITC Trade Data.

Figure 5. U.S.-Mexico Non-Manufactures Trade

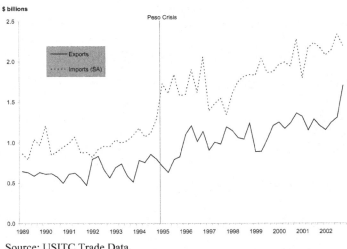

Source: USITC Trade Data.

Figure 6. U.S.-Mexico Passenger Vehicle Trade

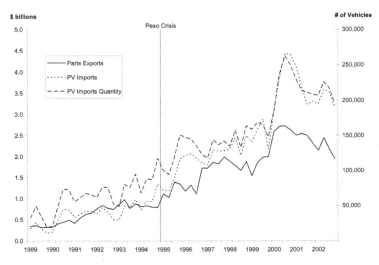

Source: USITC Trade Data; Authors' Calculations.

Table 2. Imports

(a)	Manufactures	Non-Manufactures	PV	(b)	Manufactures	Non-Manufactures	PV
C	4.98*** (5.74)	10.08*** (8.02)	0.07 (0.02)	C	2.25*** (4.92)	9.27*** (12.27)	-4.48** (-2.19)
GDP_U s	3.92*** (23.07)	2.13*** (8.52)	4.49*** (6.48)	GDP_U s	4.39*** (48.56)	2.32*** (15.53)	5.27*** (13.06)
Peso/$ Real	-0.01 (-0.12)	0.54*** (4.00)	-0.8 (-0.21)	Peso/$_{Real}$	0.33*** (4.76)	0.64*** (5.54)	0.5 (1.6)
D_{94}	0.23*** (5.7)	0.07 (1.21)	0.38** (2.34)	D_{92}	0.19*** (7.28)	0.04 (0.93)	0.33*** (2.78)
R^2	0.99	0.89	0.88	R^2	0.99	0.89	0.88
Adj. R^2	0.99	0.88	0.87	Adj. R^2	0.99	0.88	0.88
LL	72.72	50.95	-6.1	LL	78.8	50.64	-5.02
D-W	0.81	1.84	0.78	D-W	1.16	1.86	0.78
E-G	-3.00	-4.7	-4.02	E-G	-4.07	-4.69	-4.09

(c)	Manufactures	Non-Manufactures	PV	(d)	Manufactures	Non-Manufactures	PV
C	4.32*** (7.69)	9.85*** (9.79)	-0.97 (-0.36)	C	7.15*** (8.67)	11.99*** (7.99)	1.51 (0.41)
GDP_U s	3.99*** (35.33)	2.2*** (10.9)	4.61*** (8.47)	GDP_U s	3.49*** (21.57)	1.81*** (6.33)	4.23*** (6.00)
Peso/$ Real	0.15** (2.25)	0.59*** (5.11)	0.18 (0.59)	Peso/$_{Real}$	0.08 (1.15)	0.51*** (4.15)	0.04 (0.11)
$D_{92/94}$	0.13*** (8.51)	0.03 (1.2)	0.23*** (3.00)	$1 + \tau_i/M_i$	-11.57*** (-8.67)	-11.87** (-2.25)	-21.05*** (-2.69)
R^2	0.99	0.89	0.89	R^2	0.99	0.89	0.88
Adj. R^2	0.99	0.88	0.89	Adj. R^2	0.99	0.89	0.88
LL	83.55	50.94	-4.44	LL	84.16	52.77	-5.25
D-W	1.22	1.86	0.81	D-W	1.1	1.98	0.77
E-G	-4.21	-4.7	-4.16	E-G	-4.35	-5.02	-4.21

Number of Observations: 56 (t-stats in parentheses)

Table 3. Exports

(a)	Manu-factures	Non-Manu-factures	MV Parts	(b)	Manu-factures	Non-Manu-factures	MV Parts
C	12.59*** (11.13)	14.25*** (7.38)	4.87** (2.09)	C	11.69*** (12.04)	12.94*** (7.88)	7.7*** (3.48)
GDP_{Mx}	2.38*** (11.5)	1.28*** (3.61)	3.41*** (7.9)	GDP_{Mx}	2.52*** (13.98)	1.5*** (4.83)	2.87*** (6.98)
$Peso/\$_{Real}$	-0.37** (-2.38)	0.14 (0.58)	0.5 (1.15)	$Peso/\$_{Real}$	-0.17 (-1.28)	0.32 (1.6)	-0.22 (-0.66)
D_{94}	0.24*** (5.65)	0.19** (2.46)	0.38*** (3.72)	$D_{92/94}$	0.13*** (5.92)	0.09** (2.16)	0.3*** (5.39)
R^2	0.97	0.73	0.89	R^2	0.97	0.72	0.91
Adj. R^2	0.96	0.71	0.88	Adj. R^2	0.97	0.71	0.9
LL	61.95	30.36	8.34	LL	62.99	29.69	14.14
D-W	1.27	1.34	0.95	D-W	1.42	1.37	0.92
E-G	-2.55	-4.41	-2.76	E-G	-2.89	-4.34	-3.19

(c)	Manu-factures	Non-Manu-factures	MV Parts	(d)	Manu-factures	Non-Manu-factures	MV Parts
C	11.46*** (10.64)	13.12*** (7.00)	-1.5 (-0.54)	C	11.31*** (13.74)	12.78*** (8.36)	3.83 (1.66)
GDP_{Mx}	1.5*** (4.75)	-0.04 (-0.07)	1.41** (2.01)	GDP_{Mx}	1.36*** (4.7)	-0.07 (-0.13)	1.22* (2.00)
GDP_{US}	1.14*** (3.48)	1.63*** (2.67)	3.26*** (3.47)	GDP_{US}	1.29*** (4.69)	1.71*** (3.00)	2.42*** (3.39)
$Peso/\$_{Real}$	-0.4*** (-2.86)	0.04 (0.16)	0.56* (1.55)	$Peso/\$_{Real}$	-0.32** (-2.76)	0.1 (0.47)	0.08 (0.26)
D_{94}	0.16*** (3.7)	0.09 (1.13)	0.07 (0.58)	$D_{92/94}$	0.1*** (5.17)	0.05 (1.29)	0.2*** (3.41)
R^2	0.97	0.76	0.91	R^2	0.98	0.76	0.92
Adj. R^2	0.97	0.74	0.9	Adj. R^2	0.98	0.74	0.92
LL	67.92	34.04	14.27	LL	73.04	34.24	19.84
D-W	0.67	1.41	0.67	D-W	0.68	1.41	0.73
E-G	-1.92	-5.57	-2.43	E-G	-2.19	-5.59	-2.91

Number of Observations: 56 (t-stats in parentheses)

Table 4. Manufactures Imports $-8.06 - 3.32 \cdot GDP_{US} + 12.97 \cdot (1 + \tau_i / M_i)$

$$\quad\quad\quad\quad\quad\quad\quad\quad\quad\quad\quad\quad\quad (-14.02) \quad\quad\quad\quad (6.81)$$

Error Correction:	Δ(Manuf. Imports)	Δ(GDP_{US})	$\Delta(1 + \tau_i / M_i)$
Cointegrating Eq(-1)	-0.36**	0.02	-0.02***
	(-2.3)	(1.28)	(-3.16)
Δ(Manuf. Imports(-1))	0.03	-0.01	0.003
	(0.18)	(-0.52)	(0.62)
Δ(GDP_{US}(-1))	2.13	0.35**	-0.05
	(1.6)	(2.41)	(-1.21)
$\Delta[(1 + \tau_i / M_i)(-1)]$	3.97	-0.11	0.28**
	(1.03)	(-0.27)	(2.36)
Δ(Peso_{Real})	0.04	-0.002	-0.01*
	(0.74)	(0.23)	(-1.84)
Linear Data Trend	-0.04	0.005***	-0.0003
	(-0.53)	(3.7)	(-0.73)
R^2	0.17	0.13	0.28
Adj. R^2	0.08	0.04	0.2
Trace Statistic	36.5***		
Max-Eigenvalue Statistic	21.43**		
Log Likelihood	569.33		
Log Likelihood (d.f. adjusted)	564.37		
Number of Observations:	54		
(t-stats in parentheses)			

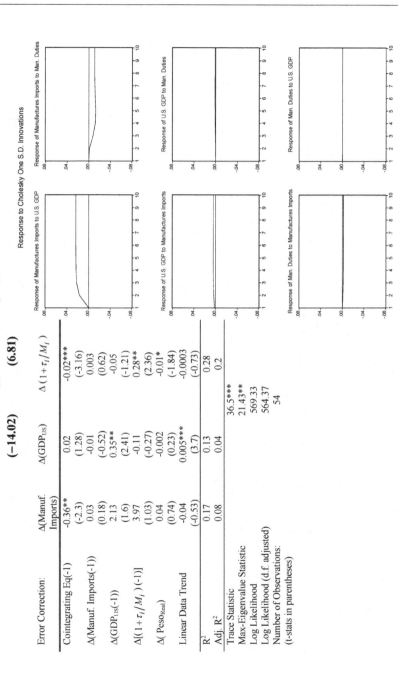

Response to Cholesky One S.D. Innovations

Table 5. Non - Manufactures Imports $- 14.85 - 1.25 \cdot \text{GDP}_{\text{US}} - 0.43 \cdot \text{Peso}_{\text{Real}} + 23.37 \cdot (1 + \tau_i/M_i)$

$$(-4.04) \qquad (-3.51) \qquad (3.99)$$

Error Correction:	Δ(N-M Imports)	Δ(GDP$_{\text{US}}$)	Δ(Peso$_{\text{Real}}$)	$\Delta(1+\tau_i/M_i)$
Cointegrating Eq(-1)	-0.8***	0.02*	-0.12	-0.01
	(-3.93)	(1.69)	(-0.93)	(-1.52)
Δ(N-M Imports(-1))	-0.1	-0.01*	0.13	0.003
	(-0.7)	(-1.83)	(1.38)	(0.93)
Δ(GDP$_{\text{US}}$(-1))	-3.28	0.31**	1.8	-0.003
	(1.25)	(2.35)	(1.1)	(-0.05)
Δ(Peso$_{\text{Real}}$(-1))	-0.21	-0.01	-0.19	0.001
	(-0.91)	(-0.48)	(-1.3)	(0.14)
$\Delta[(1+\tau_i/M_i)(-1)]$	3.82	-0.57	-4.67	0.07
	(0.54)	(-1.6)	(-1.06)	(0.45)
Linear Data Trend	0.04*	0.005***	-0.02	-0.0003
	(1.74)	(4.06)	(-1.6)	(-0.59)
R^2	0.46	0.21	0.12	0.05
Adj. R^2	0.4	0.12	0.03	-0.04
Trace Statistic	49.23**			
Max-Eigenvalue Statistic	28.41**			
Log Likelihood	595.76			
Log Likelihood (d.f. adjusted)	583.04			
Number of Observations:	54			
(t-stats in parentheses)				

Response to Cholesky One S.D. Innovations

Response of N-M Imports to Peso/$

Response of N-M Imports to U.S. GDP

Response of Peso/$ to N-M Imports

Response of N-M Imports to N-M Duties

Response of Peso/$ to N-M Duties

Response of Peso/$ to U.S. GDP

Table 6. PV Imports $-8.16 - 2.86 \cdot$ GDP$_{US}$ $+ 45.93 \cdot (1 + \tau_i/M_i)$
$$(-3.2)(4.15)$$

Error Correction:	Δ(PV Imports)	Δ(GDP$_{US}$)	Δ(1 + τ_i/M_i)
Cointegrating Eq(-1)	-0.43***	-0.002	-0.003***
	(-3.81)	(-0.86)	(-2.94)
Δ(PV Imports(-1))	0.27*	-0.004	0.001
	(1.88)	(-1.13)	(0.68)
Δ(GDP$_{US}$(-1))	-5.3	0.29**	-0.13***
	(-0.96)	(2.03)	(-2.75)
Δ[(1 + τ_i/M_i)(-1)]	9.42	-0.36	0.13
	(0.62)	(-0.92)	(0.96)
Δ(Peso$_{Real}$)	-0.41	-0.002	-0.001
	(-0.92)	(-0.14)	(-0.2)
Linear Data Trend	0.06	0.005***	0.0004
	(1.29)	(3.97)	(1.15)
R^2	0.24	0.2	0.22
Adj. R^2	0.16	0.12	0.13
Trace Statistic	30.7**		
Max-Eigenvalue Statistic	21.9**		
Log Likelihood	489.46		
Log Likelihood (d.f. adjusted)	479.92		
Number of Observations:	54		
(t-stats in parentheses)			

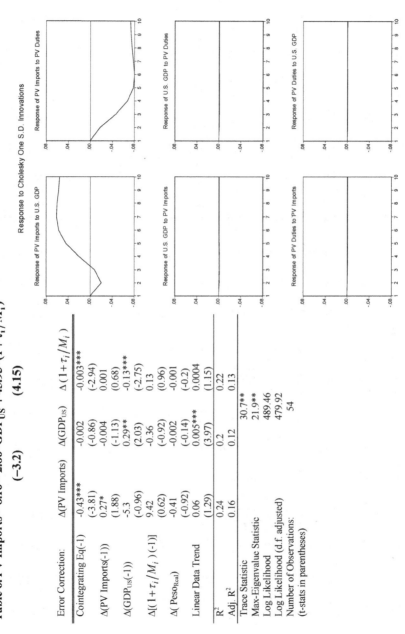

Response to Cholesky One S.D. Innovations

Table 7. Manufactures Exports − 9.73 − 2.9·GDP$_{Mx}$ − 0.11·D$_{92/94}$

$$(-19.75) \quad (-4.88)$$

Error Correction:	Δ(Manuf. Exports)	Δ(GDP$_{Mx}$)
Cointegrating Eq(-1)	0.01	0.29***
	(0.08)	(4.31)
Δ(Manuf. Exports(-1))	0.27	-0.01
	(1.39)	(-0.12)
Δ(GDP$_{Mx}$(-1))	-0.74**	-0.5***
	(-2.51)	(-3.58)
Δ(GDP$_{US}$)	3.41**	0.95
	(2.44)	(1.44)
Δ(Peso$_{Real}$)	-0.32***	-0.04
	(-2.77)	(0.83)
Linear Data Trend	-0.002	0.005
	(-0.2)	(0.8)
R²	0.42	0.75
Adj. R²	0.34	0.71
Trace	28.92*	
Max-Eigen Statistic	21.7**	
Log Likelihood	232.00	
Log Likelihood (d.f. adjusted)	224.68	
Number of Observations:	54	
(t-stats in parentheses)		

Response to Cholesky One S.D. Innovations

Response of Manufactures Exports to Mexican GDP

Response of Manufactures Exports to D92/94

Response of Mexican GDP to Manufactures Exports

Response of Mexican GDP to D92/94

Table 8. Non - Manufactures Exports $= 14.2 - 1.36 \cdot GDP_{Mx} - 0.07 \cdot D_{92/94}$
$$ (-4.6) \phantom{\cdot GDP_{Mx}} (-1.54)$$

	Δ(N-M Exports)	Δ(GDP$_{Mx}$)
Error Correction:		
Cointegrating Eq(-1)	-0.68***	0.03
	(-3.85)	(0.82)
Δ(N-M Exports(-1))	0.11	-0.002
	(0.55)	(-0.06)
Δ(GDP$_{Mx}$(-1))	0.08	-0.72***
	(0.19)	(-7.26)
Δ(GDP$_{US}$)	4.62	1.63*
	(1.27)	(1.99)
Δ(Peso$_{Real}$)	-0.27	0.04
	(-0.89)	(0.59)
Linear Data Trend	-0.02	0.002
	(-0.56)	(0.25)
R^2	0.31	0.59
Adj. R^2	0.22	0.54
Trace		31.95**
Max-Eigen Statistic		23.44**
Log Likelihood		175.02
Log Likelihood (d.f. adjusted)		168.09
Number of Observations:		54
(t-stats in parentheses)		

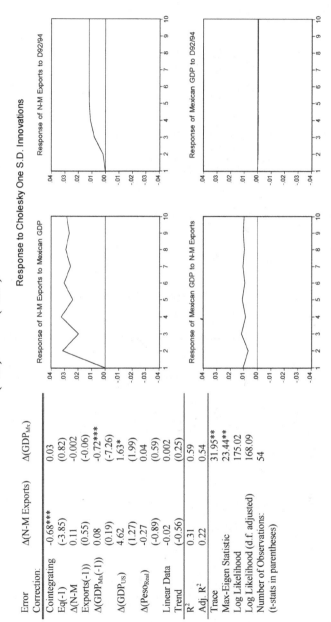

Response to Cholesky One S.D. Innovations

32 *THE JOURNAL OF ECONOMIC ASYMMETRIES* *JUNE 2007*

Table 9. MV Parts Exports $- 7.64 - 2.74 \cdot \text{GDP}_{\text{Mx}} - 0.45 \cdot \text{D}_{92/94}$
$$(-4.52) \qquad (-4.66)$$

Error Correction:	Δ(MV Parts Exports)	Δ(GDP$_{Mx}$)
Cointegrating Eq(-1)	-0.003	0.08***
	(-0.03)	(3.19)
Δ(MV Parts Exports(-1))	-0.27*	-0.08**
	(-1.75)	(-2.41)
Δ(GDP$_{Mx}$(-1))	-0.4	-0.62***
	(-0.96)	(-6.79)
Δ(GDP$_{US}$)	0.86	1.74**
	(0.26)	(2.39)
Δ(Peso$_{Real}$)	0.48	0.11
	(1.61)	(1.66)
Linear Data Trend	0.04	0.04
	(1.32)	(1.32)
R^2	0.17	0.67
Adj. R^2	0.07	0.63
Trace	19.19	
Max-Eigen Statistic	14.34	
Log Likelihood	172.6	
Log Likelihood (d.f. adjusted)	171.78	
Number of Observations:	54	
(t-stats in parentheses)		

Response to Cholesky One S.D. Innovations

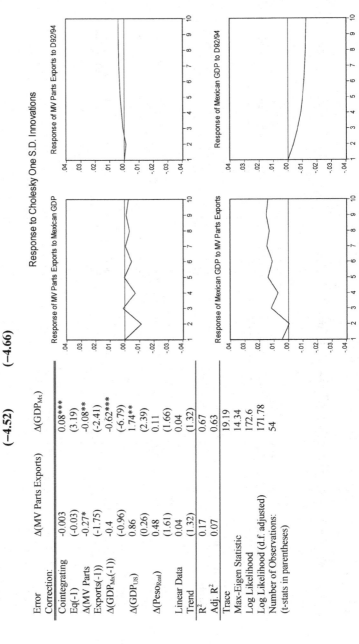

Table 10. MV Parts Exports + 0.1 − 0.93 · PV Imports + 0.15 · D$_{92/94}$

$$(-8.28) \qquad (1.42)$$

Error Correction:	Δ(MV Parts Exports)	Δ(PV Imports)
Cointegrating Eq(-1)	-0.06	0.46***
	(-0.73)	(3.35)
Δ(MV Parts Exports(-1))	-0.15	-0.04
	(-0.94)	(-0.15)
Δ(PV Imports(-1))	-0.13	0.3**
	(-1.37)	(1.95)
Δ(GDP$_{Mkt}$)	0.49	1.26**
	(1.23)	(1.99)
Δ(Peso$_{Real}$)	0.57**	-0.23
	(2.05)	(-0.52)
R²	0.22	0.27
Adj. R²	0.12	0.18
Trace		27.15*
Max-Eigen Statistic		20.41*
Log Likelihood		77.6
Log Likelihood (d.f. adjusted)		65.41
Number of Observations:		54
(t-stats in parentheses)		

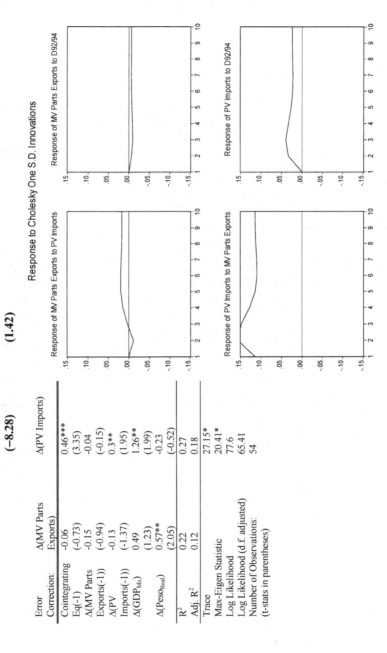

Response to Cholesky One S.D. Innovations

Response of MV Parts Exports to PV Imports

Response of MV Parts Exports to D92/94

Response of PV Imports to MV Parts Exports

Response of PV Imports to D92/94

Appendix

Table A.1. Unit Root Tests

Unit Root Tests		Augmented Dickey-Fuller		Phillips-Perron	
		Level	1st Difference	Level	1st Difference
GDP$_{US}$ (1995 = 100)	intercept	0.75	-5.09***	0.42	-5.13***
	Intercept+trend	-2.03	-5.09***	-2.17	-5.15***
GDP$_{MX}$ (1995 = 100)	intercept	-0.74	-3.33**	-1.2	-22.55***
	Intercept+trend	-3.0	-3.29*	-5.76***	-22.26***
Manufactured Exports	intercept	-1.28	-7.4***	-1.28	-7.4***
	Intercept+trend	-1.88	-7.43***	-1.94	-7.43***
Manufactured Imports	intercept	-1.6	-2.24	-1.31	-7.86***
	Intercept+trend	-0.52	-2.5	-1.56	-7.81***
Non-Manufactured Exports	intercept	-1.81	-5.69***	-1.65	-15.67***
	Intercept+trend	-5.16***	-5.63***	-4.87***	-16.62***
Non-Manufactured Imports (SA)	intercept	-1.2	-12.53***	-1.4	-14.52***
	Intercept+trend	-2.71	-12.41***	-4.62***	-14.32***
MV Parts Exports	intercept	-1.49	-9.51***	-1.6	-9.51***
	Intercept+trend	-2.47	-9.61***	-2.32	-9.68***
PV Imports	intercept	-1.6	-7.01***	-1.52	-9.91***
	Intercept+trend	-3.56**	-6.95***	-2.91	-9.98***
Real Peso/$	intercept	-1.76	-6.05***	-1.84	-7.88***
	Intercept+trend	-1.99	-5.99***	-2.18	-7.8***

All variables in log terms. All trade figures deflated with U.S. WPI.
Sample: 1989:Q1 – 2002:Q4

Table A.2. Correlation Matrices

	GDP$_{US}$	GDP$_{MX}$	Peso$_{Real}$	Man Ex	NoMan Ex	MVP Ex	Trend
GDP$_{US}$	1						
GDP$_{MX}$	0.95	1					
Peso$_{Real}$	-0.48	-0.63	1				
Man Ex	0.97	0.97	-0.58	1			
NoMan Ex	0.87	0.81	-0.36	0.85	1		
MVP Ex	0.94	0.92	-0.47	0.97	0.82	1	
Trend	0.99	0.95	-0.51	0.97	0.85	0.96	1

	GDP$_{US}$	GDP$_{MX}$	Peso$_{Real}$	Man Im	NoMan Im	PV Im	Trend
GDP$_{US}$	1						
GDP$_{MX}$	0.95	1					
Peso$_{Real}$	-0.48	-0.63	1				
Man Im	0.99	0.94	-0.43	1			
NoMan Im	0.92	0.89	-0.37	0.89	1		
PV Im	0.93	0.9	-0.4	0.96	0.84	1	
Trend	0.99	0.95	-0.51	0.99	0.9	0.95	1

	Man Ex	Man Im	NoMan Ex	NoMan Im	PV Im	MVP Ex
Man Ex	1					
Man Im	0.97	1				
NoMan Ex	0.85	0.86	1			
NoMan Im	0.83	0.91	0.79	1		
PV Im	0.93	0.96	0.8	0.84	1	
MVP Ex	0.97	0.96	0.82	0.84	0.95	1

Period: 1989:Q1 – 2002:Q4

Notes

[1]   Sven W. Arndt is a Professor at the Department of Economics at Claremont McKenna College and Director of the Lowe Institute of Political Economy. Alex Huemer is a Research Fellow at the Lowe Institute of Political Economy at Claremont McKenna College. Corresponding Author: Sven W. Arndt, Lowe Institute of Political Economy, Claremont McKenna College, 850 Columbia Avenue, Claremont, CA 91711-6420. Telephone: (909) 621-8012, Fax: (909) 607-8008, E-mail: lowe@claremontmckenna.edu. Earlier versions of these results were reported at workshops and conferences in Claremont, Beijing, Cambridge, U.K. and Tokyo. Helpful comments from conference participants are gratefully acknowledged. Thanks to Alan Winters for especially valuable comments and suggestions.

[2]   For detailed discussions, see Arndt (1997, 1998), Deardorff (2001), and Jones and Kierzkowski (2001). See also Feenstra (1998).

[3] Where multinational companies are involved, transfer-pricing policies may result in cost allocations that may differ from arms-length operations. We ignore the problem in what follows.

[4]   For a related study, see Landon and Smith (2007). These features have potentially important implications for the choice of the exchange-rate regime. The declining sensitivity of the trade balance to the exchange rate can be used as an argument to support floating exchange rates, because it reduces the effect of exchange-rate volatility on the volume of trade. It may, however, also be used against floating rates, because it reduces the importance of the exchange rate as buffer.

[5]   The trade data are taken from the International Financial Statistics of the International Monetary Fund (IMF) and publications of the U.S. Census Bureau, while import-duty information comes from the U.S. International Trade Commission (USITC). The latter two series are available in sufficient detail only after 1989 and undergo considerable redefinition in the Harmonized System classification after 2002.

[6]   Manufactures and non-manufactures are identified by their SIC/NAICS classifications. Non-manufactured imports from Mexico are net of oil and gas (which are subject to dollar pricing in the world petroleum market), and are seasonally adjusted with the Tramo/Seats methodology (to correct for seasonality in agriculture). Inclusion of petroleum (the largest U.S. non-manufactured import from Mexico) generates some non-manufactured import regression results that are similar to those for production-sharing trade, but for very different reasons. The dollar value of petroleum imports remains unaffected by real peso changes, since Mexican petroleum is priced in dollars.

[7]   Wholesale prices are used because measures of bilateral import and export prices were not available for Mexico.

[8]   See Engle and Granger (1991), pp. 81-111.

[9]   While the Durbin-Watson statistics are likely to indicate serial correlation in view of the relatively small size of our sample, the super-consistency properties of the OLS estimators assure rapid convergence as the sample size increases. When AR(1) terms are included in the regressions, the Durbin-Watsons and Q-statistics typically move into the desired range.

[10]   See Engle and Granger (1991), pp. 65-80, and Granger (1969).

[11]   The constraints are applied to the cointegrating vector coefficients. The method of Johansen and Juselius (1990) was adopted in estimating the VEC representation. Following Johansen (1992), a variant of the method of Pantula (1989) was used to identify the model rank of cointegration (consistently one) and to assess the role of the constant and trend terms in the cointegrating and error-correction components of the model.

[12]   Market anticipations of a policy shift may make the official start date an improper indicator of the impact of that policy.

[13]   It might be argued that NAFTA generated both a mean shift and a trend shift. We experimented with various specifications, including separate trend variables and interactions between the mean shift variable and U.S. GDP, interpreting the latter as the dominant trend variable. The results were uniformly inferior to those reported here. As noted earlier, the main variables in these bilateral trade relations are highly correlated and exhibit strong common trends. The fact that they are identified as of common order of integration and of being cointegrated argues against the need for an additional independent trend in the dependent variable. A theoretical motivation for inclusion of a trend found in the literature is based on the assumption of declining transport costs and/or border effects. In our specification, however, some of those effects are already controlled for in the duty rate variable and others in the trade liberalization dummies.

[14]   The measure is constructed for U.S. imports only, because comparable data were not available for Mexico.

[15]   There is the possibility of strong J-curve effects arising from the large real peso depreciation of 1994. However, the data are quarterly, which allows sufficient time to overcome most short-term demand inelasticities. Further, as figures 4-5 show, the balance-of-payments movements after the peso crisis do not suggest a J-curve effect; and Figure 6 shows that the subsequent slight decrease in passenger vehicle imports was consistent with a decline in import quantities, not a valuation effect arising from the depreciation.

[16]   Recall that the two-step representation of NAFTA switches to the value one in 1992 and to the value two in 1994.

[17]   We might be concerned about erroneously attributing to NAFTA effects stemming from the peso crisis of 1994, especially in the NAFTA measure used in Table 2d. The depreciation of the peso reduces the dollar value of U.S. imports and thus the dollar value of duty collections, especially when duties are of the *ad valorem*

type. However, examination of average U.S. dollar prices for passenger vehicle imports from Mexico indicates no significant deviation from trend over the period 1989-2002, thus limiting the likely significance of such concerns.

[18] The top six SIC/NAICS non-manufactured goods exported to Mexico by the United States over the period were various feed grains and cotton. While end-use of these commodities cannot be clearly identified, they comprise categories of commodities used in other types of production (baked goods, livestock, leather goods and apparel, etc.) likely to be exported back to the United States in some quantity.

[19] It is apparent, in the context of production sharing, that U.S. exports to Mexico will be affected by trade liberalization in two ways. First, liberalization on Mexico's part will encourage imports. Second, U.S. liberalization will encourage imports from Mexico and imports incorporating U.S.-made components will raise the demand for U.S. exports.

[20] Import results are reported in Tables 4 through 6; export results in Tables 7 through 10.

[21] Note that all the import and export categories have only one significant cointegrating vector.

[22] Separate estimates were made using the 1994 dummy, with little or no change in the overall result, and no qualitative change in the conclusions drawn from the use of the two-step dummy variables. Following Johansen (1995), the dummies were centered to prevent bias to the intercept variables.

References

Arndt, S. W., (1997), "Globalization and the Open Economy", *North American Journal of Economics and Finance*, 8(1), 71-79.

Arndt, S. W., (1998), "Super-Specialization and the Gains from Trade." *Contemporary Economic Policy*, October, XVI, 480-485

Davidson, R. and Mackinnon, J.G., (1993), *Estimation and Inference in Econometrics*, New York: Oxford University Press.

Deardorff, A. V., (2001), "Fragmentation in Simple Trade Models", *North American Journal of Economics and Finance*, 12 (2), 121-137.

Dickey, D.A. and Fuller, W.A., (1979), "Distribution of the Estimators for Autoregressive Time Series with a Unit Root", *Journal of the American Statistical Association*, 74, 427-31.

Engle, R.F. and Granger, C.W.J., (1991), *Long-Run Economic Relationships*, New York: Oxford University Press.

Feenstra, R. C., (1998), "Integration of Trade and Disintegration of Production in the Global Economy", *Journal of Economic Perspectives*, 12 (4), 31-50.

Granger, C.W.J., (1969), "Investigating causal relations by econometric models and cross-spectral methods", *Econometrica*, 37 (3), 424-38.

Hamilton, J. D., (1994), *Time Series Analysis*, Princeton: Princeton University Press.

Johansen, S., (1992), "Determination of Cointegration Rank in the Presence of a Linear Trend", *Oxford Bulletin of Econometrics and Statistics,* 54 (3), 383-397.

Johansen, S., (1995), *Likelihood-Based Inference in Cointegrated Vector Autoregressive Models*, New York: Oxford University Press.

Johansen, S. and Juselius, K., (1990), "Maximum Likelihood Estimation and Inferences on Cointegration—with Applications to the Demand for Money", *Oxford Bulletin of Economics and Statistics,* 52, 169-210.

Jones, R. W., and Kierzkowski, H., (2001), "A Framework for Fragmentation", in S.W. Arndt and Kierzkowski, H. (eds.), *Fragmentation: New Production Patterns in the World Economy*, New York: Oxford University Press.

Landon, S. and Smith, C.E., (2007), "The Exchange Rate and Machinery and Equipment Imports: Identifying the Impact of Import Source and Export Destination Country Currency Valuation Changes." *The North American Journal of Economics and Finance*, forthcoming.

Perron, P., and Phillips, P.C., (1988), "Testing for a Unit Root in Time Series Regression", *Biometrika,* 75 (2), 335-46.

Pantula, S. G., (1989). "Testing for Unit Roots in Time Series Data", *Econometric Theory,* 5 (2), 256-271.

Phillips, P.C., (1987), "Time Series Regression with a Unit Root", *Econometrica,* 55 (2), 277-301.

Pollard, P. S., and Coughlin, C. C., (2003), "Size Matters: Asymmetric Exchange Rate Pass-Through at the Industry Level", Working Paper 2003-029B, Federal Reserve Bank of St. Louis.

Torres, A. and Vela, O., (2003), "Trade integration and synchronization between the business cycles of Mexico and the United States", *The North American Journal of Economics and Finance,* 14(3), 319-342.

Chapter 12

Intra-industry Trade and the Open Economy[*]

Sven W. Arndt[**]

This paper explores the implications of cross-border production networks and vertical intra-industry trade for macroeconomic adjustment and for the effectiveness of monetary and fiscal stabilization policies. Vertical intra-industry trade introduces direct links between countries' imports and exports and thereby affects the manner in which trade balances respond to variations in exchange rates and to global shocks more generally.

The precise effects depend on whether the direct link runs from exports to imports or vice versa. In the U.S., for example, exports of auto parts and components rise with an increase of imports of passenger vehicles from Mexico. This produces a change in balance-of-payments adjustment similar to high capital mobility and raises the likelihood that a fiscal expansion will lead to appreciation rather than depreciation of the currency. In China and Mexico, on the other hand, a rise in exports of assembled end products raises imports of parts and components.

The differences in outcome are more pronounced under floating rates, because of the role of the exchange rate in the adjustment process. Direct export-import links undermine the impact of the exchange rate on the trade balance, hence necessitating larger changes in rates in order to achieve a given degree of adjustment and raising exchange-rate volatility as a result. In the case of both types of exchange-rate regime, vertical intra-industry trade weakens the response of the trade balance to price and income shocks.

JEL Classification: E63, F11, F41
Keywords: Fragmentation; Vertical intra-industry trade;
           Macroeconomic stability

---

[*] Received June 10, 2010. Accepted August 15, 2010. I am indebted for valuable comments to Hyejoon Im and to participants at the conference on Korea and the World Economy, IX.

[**] Claremont McKenna College, Robert Day School of Economics and Finance, 500 E. 9th Street, Claremont, CA 91711, U.S.A., E-mail: sven.arndt@claremontmckenna.edu

1. INTRODUCTION

Macroeconomic adjustment in the open economy depends critically on the impact of exchange-rate changes under floating and on price and income changes under both floating and fixed rates. Vertical intra-industry trade introduces direct links between countries' imports and exports and thereby alters the response of the trade balance to changes in prices, incomes and exchange rates.

In a simple example of vertical intra-industry trade, passenger vehicle components are shipped from the United States to Mexico, where they are assembled into finished products, which are exported back to the United States. In more complex patterns, exemplified by global electronics production, parts and components move among countries in Southeast Asia, as production moves through its various stages along the value-added chain. From Mexico's perspective, a rise in the demand for auto exports raises the need to import additional parts and components, so that the direct link runs from exports to imports. Exactly the opposite link pertains to the U.S., where the rise in auto imports generates a rise in component exports. In the multi-country case, a rise in the demand for exports of electronic end products from China gives rise to increased Chinese demand for component imports from Singapore, Taiwan, and other countries.

In the presence of vertical intra-industry trade, some of the imports that enter a country are not destined for final use in that country and the value of some exports exceeds the domestic value-added embodied in those exports. Part of a country's trade essentially "by-passes" the domestic economy and consequently alters trade-balance reactions to movements in prices, incomes, and exchange rates. It changes the manner in which shocks and disturbances are transmitted across borders, and has consequences for the effectiveness of traditional tools of macroeconomic stabilization policy.

The next section reviews some basic consequences for trade balance behavior that flow from vertical intra-industry trade. Section 3 explores the implications for macroeconomic stabilization policy of vertical intra-industry trade. Section 4 concludes.

2. NETWORK TRADE AND THE TRADE BALANCE

Depreciation of a country's currency tends to raise import prices expressed in the domestic currency and thereby to reduce imports, while lowering the foreign-currency prices of exports and hence raising exports. In the case of inter- and horizontal intra-industry trade, imports are destined for use by residents and the value of exports will have been largely generated in the home economy. When the Marshall-Lerner condition holds, the trade balance improves with depreciation.

However, when imports consist of components to be incorporated into exports, the effect of depreciation is to raise their price on the way in and to lower it on the way back out. In arms-length transactions, the higher price of imported components raises the cost of the final product, but that rise is offset when the depreciation reduces the foreign-currency price of the end product and of the components within it.[1] This suggests a reduced effect of the exchange-rate change on the trade balance compared to traditional "non-processing" trade. The effect of the depreciation on processing trade is limited to the domestic value-added embodied in processed exports.[2]

When depreciation reduces the foreign-currency price of domestic value-added in a country's exports and thereby raises foreign demand for exports, this rise in exports in turn raises demand for imported parts and components. Hence, processing imports actually rise rather than fall with currency depreciation, while ordinary imports fall. The processing balance of trade is

---

[1] In assessing the importance of this direct relationship, one needs to distinguish between "arms-length" trade and intra-firm trade that is subject to transfer pricing. Moreover, many emerging economies dependent on export markets in advanced countries tend to price their key exports in the currencies of large destination countries and thereby eliminate some of their exchange rates from the adjustment mechanism. For some discussion or arms-length vs. intra-firm vertical intra-industry trade, see Ando, Arndt and Kimura (2006).

[2] See Arndt and Huemer (2007) for an empirical study of U.S.-Mexico trade.

Sven W. Arndt

thus less sensitive to the exchange rate and this implies that the overall trade balance is less sensitive.

In the presence of production sharing, the equation for the trade balance may be written as follows.

$$b = x[y^*, e; m(y, e)] - m[y, e; x(y^*, e)], \tag{1}$$

where x and m represent real exports and imports of goods and services, respectively; y and y^* are domestic and foreign real GDP, respectively; and $e = EP^* / P$ is the real exchange rate composed of the nominal rate, E, and foreign and domestic price levels, respectively. What distinguishes this expression from the traditional trade equation, is that exports and imports are directly linked to each other. If the country is the United States, for example, then a rise in demand for passenger vehicle imports from Mexico leads to a rise of U.S. exports of vehicle parts and components. The effect of imports on exports is shown in the first bracketed term in equation (1). If the country is Mexico, a rise in exports of motor vehicles to the U.S. raises imports of components. That relationship is expressed in the second bracketed term of equation (1).

It is important to note that there is only one exchange rate in the present example of production sharing between two countries. In the more general case, a country's exports of the end product to another country may contain parts and components from third countries. That would be the example of electronic exports by China to the United States containing intermediates from Singapore, Taiwan and various Southeast Asian countries. In this case, it is necessary to consider movements in exchange rates between China and its supplier countries as well.[3]

2.1. Imports Linked to Exports

Total differentiation of equation (1) yields the following:

---

[3] See Arndt (2008) for a discussion.

$$db = x_{y'}(1 - m_x)dy^* + [x_e(1 - m_x) + m_e(1 - x_m)]de - m_y(1 - x_m)dy, \qquad (2)$$

where all partial derivatives except m_e are positive. In the case of trade between Mexico and the United States in motor vehicles, the amended feature from Mexico's perspective is the import term in equation (1), in which imports are a function of exports. When price levels are held constant, the real exchange rate changes one-for-one with the nominal rate. The effect of changes in the nominal rate on the trade balance is given by

$$\frac{db}{dE} = \frac{(dx - dm)}{dE} = x_e(1 - m_x) - m_e > 0, \qquad (3a)$$

where $0 < m_x < 1$ in order to allow for non-processing exports and for the presence of some domestic value-added in the country's processing exports. The magnitude of m_x rises as the share of processing exports in total exports rises, and that rise reduces the response of the trade balance to movements in the exchange rate.

It is clear from equation (1), that the effects on the balance of trade of the other components of the real exchange rate, namely, domestic and foreign inflation, may be explained in analogous ways. The influence on the trade balance of foreign inflation, for example, may be seen in expression (3a) if we substitute dP^* for dE : its effect is attenuated by the presence of network trade. Expression (3a) with $-dP$ replacing dE gives the result for domestic inflation. Its effect on the trade balance — deterioration — is weakened, because it affects the price of exports only to the extent of the share of domestic value-added in exports. Furthermore, to the extent that the higher cost of domestic value-added reduces exports of assembled products, it also reduces imports of parts and components.

The implications for the trade balance of changes in foreign GDP are also altered by production sharing. A recession abroad reduces foreign demand for the country's exports in the traditional manner $(x_y \cdot dy^*)$. If network trade is present, however, then the decline in exports is mitigated by a decline in

6   Sven W. Arndt

imports, reducing the overall effect on the trade balance. Moreover, the transmission of the shock to the rest of the economy is limited to the domestic value-added contained in the country's exports.

2.2. Exports Linked to Imports

Mexico and China are two important examples of countries with strong links from exports to imports. The trade of many countries in East Asia also has this characteristic. In other cases, however, a country's exports will be directly linked to its imports. In the simple bilateral example discussed above, the United States is in this position with respect to imports of finished automobiles from Mexico. The relevant condition for the trade balance response to the exchange rate is now given by:

$$\frac{db}{dE} = (dx - dm)/dE = x_e - (1 - x_m)m_e. \tag{3b}$$

When the U.S. demand for auto imports rises, it raises the demand for exports of auto parts and components. The terms containing x_m in expression (2) are relevant in this case. When the dollar appreciates, Americans demand more passenger vehicles from Mexico, because the peso's depreciation reduces the dollar price of Mexican value-added. This tends to worsen the U.S. trade balance, but by less than would be the case if the rise in U.S. imports had not directly raised U.S. exports. Countries involved in regional production networks may experience both types of linkage effects simultaneously.

These direct linkages between exports and imports complicate the analysis of exchange-rate pass-through. Consider, again, a depreciation of the peso against the U.S. dollar. As we saw earlier, for a given dollar price of U.S.-made components, the depreciation will raise their price in pesos and thus raise the manufacturing cost of motor vehicles. Meanwhile, however, the depreciation will reduce the dollar price of the vehicles, helping to mitigate the effect of the cost increase on their final price.

Moreover, the dollar price of the Mexican value-added embodied in the vehicle will fall, so that a depreciation of a given percentage will reduce the price of the imported vehicle by a smaller percentage than would otherwise be the case. It is not appropriate, however, to interpret this as weak or incomplete pass-through, because the pass-through applied to Mexican value-added is the relevant measure of the completeness of the pass-through.[4]

3. MACRO POLICY IN AN OPEN ECONOMY WITH PRODUCTION SHARING

The preceding discussion suggests that vertical intra-industry trade changes the behavior of the trade balance relative to traditional patterns involving inter- and horizontal intra-industry trade. In this section, we explore the implications of these tendencies for macroeconomic adjustment and stability and for macroeconomic policy. We do so by incorporating vertical intra-industry trade into the well-known open economy of the Mundell-Fleming model, which will serve as the benchmark model for comparison purposes. Given the established nature of this model, we see no need to review its major findings. For current purposes, the standard specification of money market equilibrium is retained as:

$$\frac{H}{P} = l(y, R), \tag{4}$$

---

[4] The presence of network trade can lead to overstatement of the volatility of trade volumes. If trade flows are measured in terms of the full value of exports and imports every time they cross a border, then there will be double-counting, the seriousness of which will rise with the frequency of the number of crossings during the manufacturing process. In the presence of production sharing, trade flows are better viewed in terms of value-added. See, for example, Wynne and Kersting (2009).

8

where H is high-powered money, P is the (constant) price level, y is real GDP, and R is the nominal rate of interest. With zero inflation, real and nominal interest rates are identical.

For goods-market equilibrium we incorporate direct linkages between imports and exports through network trade along the lines developed in equation (1):

$$i(r) + x[y^*, e; m(y, e)] - s(y) - m[y, e; x(y^*, e)] = g, \qquad (5)$$

where i is real investment, r is the real interest rate, s is real saving and g is the real budget surplus.

The balance-of-payments equilibrium condition of the benchmark model is also amended to include equation (1) as the specification of the current account:

$$x[y^*, e; m(y, e)] - m[y, e; x(y^*, e)] + K(R, R^*) = 0, \qquad (6)$$

where K represents net capital inflows, which are positive and negative functions, respectively, of domestic and foreign interest rates. As in the basic model, the assumption of stable prices allows us to ignore distinctions between nominal (R) and real (r) interest rates and nominal (K) and real (k) capital flows.

3.1. Direct Links: Exports to Imports

For countries in which the direct link runs from exports to imports only, the relevant expression for exports in equations (5) and (6) is $x(y^*, e)$. In that set-up, the main effect of vertical intra-industry trade is on the behavior of the exchange rate under floating rates.[5] When, for example, a monetary expansion lowers the interest rate and raises domestic income, causing both the current account and the financial account to deteriorate, the depreciation

---

[5] In other words, the slopes of the three curves are unaltered relative to the benchmark model.

needed to return the economy to equilibrium is larger in the presence of vertical intra-industry trade. This is evident in equations (5) and (6), where the depreciation increases both network and non-network exports, as expected. But while it reduces non-network imports, it raises network imports.

Another way to see this is to note that network trade tends to make the demand for foreign exchange less elastic with respect to the exchange rate than in the benchmark model. This results from the previously discussed fact that while a currency depreciation reduces the volume of imports, its positive effect on exports tends to raise processing imports, so that the net effect of a given exchange rate change on overall imports is smaller.

Hence, when a rise in domestic income raises the demand for foreign exchange, the lower exchange-rate elasticity of demand requires a larger adjustment in the exchange rate. The adjustments are $dE/dy = m_y/(x_e - m_e)$ in the benchmark model and $dE/dy = m_y/[(1-m_x)x_e - m_e]$ for production networking, when the direct linkage runs from exports to imports. The exchange-rate adjustment required to compensate for a change in domestic output on the trade balance is clearly larger. Hence, while the effect of disturbances like this on the trade balance is attenuated as the importance of network trade rises, the exchange rate must work harder in order to achieve a desired change in the trade balance.

This reduced sensitivity of the trade balance to the exchange rate suggests further that the critical values of the Marshall-Lerner condition will be harder to achieve as the importance of network imports in total imports rises.

A similar story applies to the response of the exchange rate to a fiscal expansion. The currency appreciates in both cases under high capital mobility, but the degree of appreciation is greater in the presence of network trade.

Foreign Shocks

A rise in foreign income affects the home trade balance less, because the rise in home exports is mitigated by the rise in imports through the direct link

10

between exports and imports in processing trade. Under floating rates, the currency must appreciate in both models in order to offset the expansionary effect of the rise in foreign income on the domestic economy.[6] However, the appreciation necessary to return the open economy to full equilibrium is smaller with vertical intra-industry trade than without. This is due to the fact that the foreign shock generates a smaller improvement in the home country's trade balance, which in spite of the reduced influence of exchange-rate changes on trade reduces the needed appreciation.

A foreign financial shock, such as a tightening of global credit conditions, reflected in higher foreign interest rates, $R^* = r^*$, tightens domestic credit conditions as capital flows out, causing domestic interest rates to rise and to dampen economic activity. The home country's financial account deteriorates to the same extent in the two scenarios. The home currency depreciates, which tends to stimulate economic activity. The net effect of these pressures is a permanently higher rate of interest and higher level of output. These results are identical to those in the basic model, except that the depreciation needed to bring the result about rises as the importance of vertical intra-industry trade in total trade rises.

Fixed Exchange Rates

Under fixed rates, there is no change from the benchmark model regarding the efficacy of monetary and fiscal policies. Monetary policy continues to be completely ineffective in the absence of sterilization, while the potency of fiscal policy as a tool of macroeconomic stabilization depends on the degree of capital mobility. High capital mobility enhances the power of fiscal expansion to close an existing output gap, because the strong reaction of capital inflows relative to the rise in goods and services imports puts pressure on the currency to appreciate. The central bank intervenes by purchasing foreign exchange and thereby raises domestic money supply. Low capital

---

[6] Much has been said about the relative immunity of the home economy to external output shocks in the Mundell-Fleming model. Our focus here, however, is to examine the consequences of production networks for the adjustment process. For a general assessment of Mundell-Fleming and alternative macro models, see de Grauwe (1997).

mobility has the opposite effect. The complete coincidence of outcomes derives from the fact that the elements of distinction between the two scenarios do not come into play.

The repercussions due to foreign income shocks, on the other hand, depend on the importance of the direct link between imports and exports. A positive foreign GDP shock causes a smaller improvement in the home country's trade balance than would be the case in the benchmark model, implying that the intervention-induced increase in the home country's money supply will be smaller and with it the expansionary effect associated with the foreign shock. A foreign liquidity shock, on the other hand, has identical reactions in the two models, once again because the elements of distinction between the two scenarios do not come into play.

3.2. Direct Links: Imports to Exports

Direct linkages may also run from imports to exports. As noted earlier, U.S. trade with Mexico in motor vehicles is an obvious example in which a rise in U.S. demand for imported automobiles directly increases exports of U.S.-made parts and components. When direct linkages run from imports to exports, the departures from the benchmark model's results are somewhat more complex.

It is well-known that balance-of-payments adjustment depends on the degree of capital mobility.[7] Capital mobility is crucial in determining whether a domestic fiscal expansion leads to appreciation or depreciation of a country's currency. Network trade with direct links from imports to exports has an analogous effect on balance of payments adjustment. In the presence of network trade, a rise in domestic GDP causes a smaller deterioration of the current account to the extent that the induced rise in imports provokes a rise in exports. Hence, a smaller increase in domestic interest rates is required in

---

[7] In other words, it depends on the slope of the BP schedule relative to the LM curve. High capital mobility flattens the BP curve, implying that a deterioration of the current account due to a rise in income requires a smaller increase of interest rates in order to provide the needed offset via financial account improvement.

12

order to offset the worsening of the current account. This means that countries with low capital mobility may nevertheless have relatively flat balance-of-payments curves if they are significantly involved in production networks.

Unlike capital mobility, however, network trade also changes adjustment in the goods-producing sector. The relevant ratio in the basic model is $dr/dy = (s_y + m_y)/i_r$, compared with $dr/dy = [s_y + m_y(1-x_m)]/i_r$ in the presence of network trade. In other words, network trade flattens the slope of the open-economy goods-market relationship.

Floating Rates

These differences, however, do not affect the efficiency of either monetary or fiscal policy in reducing an existing output gap under floating rates relative to the benchmark model. In other words, monetary and fiscal expansions of a given magnitude, respectively, have identical impacts on the home interest rate and on home income in the two scenarios. This may seem surprising, given the decreased responsiveness of the trade balance to variations in domestic income. However, under the assumption of identical money market structures in the two scenarios, the ensuing currency depreciations provoke relative adjustments in the balance of payments and the goods-producing sector that depend only on the marginal propensity to save. Given the same savings propensity across the two scenarios, the changes in interest rate and income will be identical.

The exchange rate, however, behaves differently in the presence of network trade. While the financial account responds identically to a change in the home interest rate, the trade balance reaction to the rise in income is weaker in the presence of network trade. On the other hand, a depreciation of a given magnitude also has a smaller effect on the trade balance. The net effect may be more or less depreciation with network trade, depending on the relative magnitudes of the marginal propensity to import and the sensitivity of imports to the exchange rate.

Fiscal Policy

For fiscal policy, the relevant condition is:

$$\frac{dE}{dG} = \frac{[(1-x_m)l_r m_y + l_y k_r]}{[x_e - (1-x_m)m_e][l_r s_y + l_y(i_r - k_r)]}. \tag{7}$$

The first term in the numerator is negative and shows the deterioration of the current account due to the rise in GDP brought about by the fiscal expansion, while the second term in the numerator is positive and shows the improvement in the financial account due to the rise in the home interest rate brought about by the expansion. The denominator is negative. When capital mobility is high (as measured by k_r) relative to the marginal propensity to import, then the expression is negative and the home currency appreciates.

The likelihood of appreciation is further enhanced by high values of the direct link from imports to exports (given by x_m). The difference between the benchmark model and network trade is thus incorporated in the term $(1-x_m)$, where $x_m = 0$ in the former. As the direct link from imports to exports rises, the negative term in the numerator of equation (7) becomes smaller, thus increasing the magnitude of the numerator. At the same time, the rise in x_m reduces the size of the denominator. Together, these changes increase the value of expression (7), suggesting that the home currency must appreciate by more in the presence of network trade than otherwise.

Monetary Expansion

In both models, a monetary expansion leads to the same lower rate of interest and the same higher level of income, for reasons similar to those given for the earlier case of links running from exports to imports. Thus, the current and the financial accounts both deteriorate, requiring depreciation of the domestic currency. Although the interest-rate change affects the financial account to an equal degree in the two models, the GDP increase creates a larger current account imbalance in the benchmark model. The deterioration

14

is smaller in the network-trade scenario, because the rise in imports due to the GDP increase induces a direct rise in exports.

Furthermore, a given change in the exchange rate has a smaller effect on the trade balance when there is vertical intra-industry trade, because the decline in imports following a depreciation induces a direct decline in exports. Thus, the depreciation needed to correct the imbalances will not be the same in the two models. It will be less under network trade if m_y is larger than m_e or if, for equal m_e and x_e, the marginal propensity to save, s_y, is small and the marginal propensity to import, m_y, is large.

Foreign Shocks

A recession abroad, represented as a shock to foreign income, y^*, has the same effects on domestic income and interest rates as in the benchmark model. It leaves them unchanged, meaning that the home economy is completely insulated from this type of external shock. In both cases, the home currency appreciates in order to neutralize the effect of the foreign shock. However, once again there are differences between the two cases in the workload carried by the floating exchange rate, which in this case needs to adjust more in the presence of network trade. This is consistent with our earlier finding in connection with direct links that run in the opposite direction.

A foreign credit squeeze, represented by a rise in interest rates abroad, brings about a capital outflow which causes domestic interest rates to rise. The home currency depreciates, which improves the trade balance so as to offset the deterioration in the financial account. While the interest-rate rise dampens domestic economic activity, the depreciation stimulates it. The net effect is a rise in aggregate output, as in the benchmark model. Whether the depreciation is larger or smaller than in that model is ambiguous and depends once again on the relative magnitudes of the marginal propensity to import and the exchange-rate sensitivity of imports.

Fixed Exchange Rates

When exchange rates are fixed, the effectiveness of monetary policy as a macroeconomic stabilization tool remains essentially unchanged from the benchmark scenario with respect to its effects on aggregate output and domestic interest rates. A monetary expansion temporarily raises income and reduces the rate of interest, but the deterioration of both current and financial accounts leads to pressures on the currency to depreciate. The resultant foreign-exchange market intervention by the central bank brings about a monetary contraction that continues until the original values of income and rate of interest have been re-established.

In the basic model, the efficacy of fiscal policy depends on the degree of capital mobility. Under high capital mobility, there are pressures on the home currency to appreciate. Intervention by the central bank leads to reserve accumulation and growth in the domestic money supply. This induced monetary expansion strengthens the effect on output of the fiscal policy. When capital mobility is low, on the other hand, intervention to prevent currency depreciation reduces the money supply, which tends to diminish the potency of the fiscal expansion.

In the presence of vertical network trade, the domestic interest rate tends to rise less than in the basic model, while aggregate domestic output grows by more. These results follow from the aforementioned change in slopes brought about by vertical intra-industry trade. Under high capital mobility, reserve accumulation will be larger with vertical intra-industry trade than without and reserve losses under low capital mobility will be larger as well than in the benchmark model.

The effects of foreign shocks may be summarized as follows. A rise in foreign income causes the home country's interest rate to fall and its GDP to rise and in each case the change is more pronounced than in the benchmark model. The explanation is fairly straightforward. The rise in foreign income stimulates exports to the same extent in both cases, giving rise to an improvement in the home country's current account. The resulting pressure

16

for the home currency to appreciate is met by central bank intervention in the foreign exchange market.

This intervention gives rise to an increase in money supply, which explains the decline in the interest rate and which stimulates the economy further. The consequent increase in home income raises imports in both cases, but the deterioration in the current account is less severe in the presence of network trade. Hence, income needs to rise more in order to complete the "automatic" adjustment under fixed rates. Overall, the foreign shock has a more pronounced impact on the home economy under conditions of vertical intra-industry trade.[8] There is, of course, reserve accumulation in both cases, but the accumulation is larger in the presence of vertical intra-industry trade when linkages run from imports to exports.

Finally, a tightening of liquidity abroad, represented by a rise in foreign interest rates, raises domestic interest rates and lowers domestic income in both scenarios. The decline in income is more pronounced with vertical intra-industry trade, meaning that a foreign liquidity crisis causes more damage in the domestic economy when that economy is tied to the outside world through participation in a production network.

The foreign liquidity crisis provokes an initial outflow of capital, which puts upward pressure on domestic interest rates and reduces interest-sensitive domestic expenditures. Pressures on the domestic currency to depreciate are met by central-bank intervention, which reduces the money supply. From the point of view of domestic macro stability, this is exactly the wrong outcome and will typically be sterilized by the monetary authorities. This result is interesting in light of recent global financial disturbances, in that a country's involvement in international production networks raises its exposure to foreign financial shocks. However, this exposure depends in part upon the nature of the linkages between its exports and its imports.

---

[8] The M-F model's ISXM and BP curves both shift out more than in Mundell-Fleming. Furthermore, since the BP curve always shifts more than the ISXM curve in response to this type of shock, the new intersection of the two curves occurs at a lower rate of interest than under Mundell-Fleming.

4. CONCLUDING COMMENTS

In traditional trade models, exports and imports are only indirectly linked to each other. A rise in exports, for example, stimulates domestic economic activity and raises domestic income, which in turn raises imports. Vertical intra-industry trade introduces direct links between exports and imports and thereby alters the behavior of the trade balance. It reduces the sensitivity of the trade balance to movements in exchange rates and to shocks and disturbances associated with various other variables. These repercussions have implications for macroeconomic adjustment and for the ability of monetary and fiscal policies to achieve employment and other objectives.

The reduced sensitivity of the trade balance to exchange-rate changes is important for adjustment under floating, where rate movements play such a critical role. We find that the exchange-rate changes needed to achieve a given degree of adjustment are consequently larger with than without network trade. In other words, network trade tends to raise the volatility of floating rates.

The trade balance also becomes less responsive to movements in income and in home and foreign prices. Increases in domestic income or domestic inflation both raise imports, but when direct linkages run from imports to exports, there ensues a rise in exports, which reduces the net change in the trade balance. This change in behavior is relevant to both floating and fixed regimes. One interesting result under fixed rates is that linkages from imports to exports tend to make a country more vulnerable to foreign financial crises.

Finally, we find that when direct links run from imports to exports, network trade has an effect on the adjustment process that is analogous to capital mobility. Hence, countries with increasing involvement in network production and trade tend to experience a rise in the potency of fiscal policy.

18

REFERENCES

Ando, M., S. W. Arndt, and F. Kimura, "Production Networks in East Asia: Strategic Behavior by Japanese and U.S. Firms," *JCER Discussion Paper*, No.103, 2006.

Arndt, S. W., "Production Networks, Trade Patterns and Exchange Rates," presented at APEA conference, Beijing, December 2008.

Arndt, S. W. and A. Huemer, "Trade, Production Networks, and the Exchange Rate," *Journal of Economic Asymmetries*, 4(1), June 2007. pp. 11-39.

De Grauwe, P., "Paradigms of Macroeconomic Policy for the Open Economy," in M. Fratianni, D. Salvatore, and J. von Hagen, eds., *Macroeconomic Policies in Open Economies*, Westport, CT: Greenwood Press, 2009.

Wynne, M., "The Financial Crisis, Trade Finance and the Collapse of World Trade," Annual Report, Globalization and Monetary Policy Institute, Federal Reserve Bank of Dallas, 1997.

Wynne, M. and E. K. Kersting, "Trade Globalization and the Financial Crisis," *Economic Letter*, 4(8), Federal Reserve Bank of Dallas, November 2009.

Chapter 13

Fragmentation, Imperfect Competition and Heterogeneous Firms

Sven W. Arndt

The earlier chapters utilize traditional trade theory models of perfect competition, constant costs, homogeneous goods, services and factors of production and an emphasis on trade at the sectoral or industry level. It is, of course, well-known that much of international trade takes place under conditions of imperfect competition, distorted markets and variable returns to scale, as well as heterogeneity of goods, services and factors of production. When these conditions prevail, the so-called new trade theory with its focus on imperfect competition, economies of scale, and product diversification provides a more appropriate analytical approach.[1]

Recent years have witnessed the rapid growth of a literature on trade with heterogeneous firms. Interest in the role of heterogeneous firms in international trade generally and in exports in particular has been stimulated by new empirical evidence suggesting that in many industries only some firms export and that among exporting firms only some engage in offshore production, i.e., behave as multinational producers.[2] While neither the new trade literature nor the literature on heterogeneous firms has been very concerned with fragmentation, both suggest expanded scenarios under which fragmentation may be implemented.[3]

Several chapters in this part conduct partial-equilibrium analyses of the effects of fragmentation on comparative advantage and on the pattern of trade at the sector or industry level using net import supply and demand curves. With some modifications, this approach is quite useful for the study of trade in the presence of heterogeneous firms. Figure 1 below presents a short-run, partial-equilibrium

---

[1]For more discussion, see chapter 1 in this volume. For major contributions to this literature, see Krugman (1979), Helpman (1984), Dixit and Stiglitz (1977) and others listed in Chapter 1.

[2]For recent reviews of this literature, see Helpman (2013) and Redding (2010) and for important contributions, see Melitz (2003) and Bernard *et al.* (1995).

[3]A recent paper by Gao and Whalley (2013) addresses the issue of fragmentation in a world of heterogeneous firms.

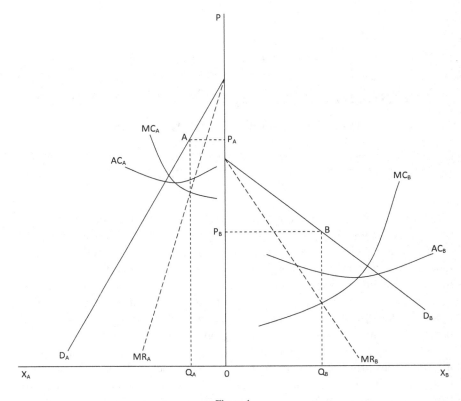

Figure 1.

view of two firms (A and B) producing differentiated products (or services) under conditions of monopolistic competition and increasing returns to scale. Each firm faces a downward-sloping demand curve for its variety, with the position and slope of the two curves depending on the degree of substitutability between varieties.

Following the example of the industry level analysis of the H-O model, there are two factors of production — capital and labor. The existing literature on trade and heterogeneous firms works with labor as the single factor of production. While this is in line with a venerable tradition of trade modeling, it seems rather restrictive for purposes of analyzing cross-border fragmentation and production networking by multinational enterprises.

In the absence of trade, equilibrium prices and output levels are at P_A, Q_A and P_B, Q_B, respectively, in Figure 1. The heterogeneity of the two firms is represented by different cost conditions, which play a key role in determining those price and output differences. There typically exists a multiplicity of causes

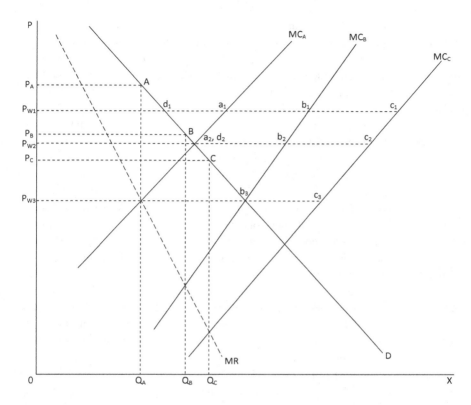

Figure 2.

of firm heterogeneity. In our case, firm B's lower cost and larger output could be the result of scale economies, but they could also be due to superior leadership, to better and/or more up-to-date technology, access to workers of higher quality, and so on. Product quality may also be a cause, with firm A producing a high-quality product for an upscale clientele, while firm B provides a cheaper product of lesser quality for a broader market.[4]

Figure 2 above is a reinterpretation of Figure 5 in Chapter 1 (p. 37 of this book). We consider three heterogeneous firms. Each firm should ideally be represented by a separate diagram along the lines of Figure 1 above, but in order to simplify and focus on cost conditions, we have consolidated the diagrammatic analysis. We assume that demand conditions are identically represented by the single demand and marginal revenue curves, with quantities of the three varieties measured along

---

[4]It is apparent that this set-up could be applied as well to analysis of a single multi-product firm.

the horizontal axis. Under autarky conditions and given marginal costs as drawn, firm outputs and prices are Q_A, Q_B, Q_C and P_A, P_B, and P_C, respectively.

While the three firms are monopolistically competitive in the closed economy, they may or may not possess monopoly powers in the world market. When free trade is introduced and international goods arbitrage works efficiently, all three firms are forced to behave as perfect competitors and to trade at the world price. When the world price is at P_{W1} (giving each firm a horizontal marginal revenue curve at that level), firm A is forced to lower its price. It raises output to point a_1 and the quantity supplied domestically to point d_1; it exports the quantity d_1a_1. The other two firms both raise domestic price, reduce sales to the home-market to point d_1 and become exporters. Exports constitute a major source of revenue for these firms. If the world price is at P_{W2} instead, firm A lowers price, raises output and domestic sales, but does not export. Firm B lowers price, raises output and domestic sales and exports (but less than in the previous case). Firm C raises price, raises production, reduces domestic sales and has smaller exports than at price P_{W1}.

If the world price falls below P_{W2}, firm A's output level falls below domestic demand for its variety, which leads to imports of foreign substitutes for that variety. At prices below P_{W2}, firms B and C continue to produce larger quantities than in autarky and to supply larger amounts to their respective domestic markets, but their exports are smaller than at higher world prices. At world price P_{W3}, firm A's output is identical to the pre-trade quantity, but that quantity is now too small to meet domestic demand and thus the firm or the country becomes an importer of that variety. Firm B provides larger quantities to the home market, but does not export. Firm C increases sales of its variety in the domestic market and continues to export, but the share of exports in total sales is smaller than before.

These results are broadly consistent with the new micro-data discussed in Bernard *et al.* (1995) and with the predictions of the heterogeneous-firm models (except that the literature on heterogeneous firms has focused on exports and says nothing about imports). It is important to recall the assumption that consumers are able to arbitrage between home and world markets, which forces suppliers to act as perfect competitors, as reflected in the horizontal marginal revenue curves at the various world price levels. If a firm can effectively prevent cross-border arbitrage of its variety, then it would have a kinked marginal revenue curve at various world prices, it would then service the protected home market at the monopoly price, and export any excess output at the world price.[5]

---

[5] See Figure 6 in Chapter 1 (p. 39 of this book) for a related discussion.

Modes of Fragmentation with Heterogeneous Firms

The simplest example of fragmentation is where a firm resorts to offshore procurement of a component or completion of a specific phase in the production of some end-product. In our discussion in earlier chapters of fragmentation at the sector level, this implied that in capital-rich, labor-scarce countries labor-intensive components or production activities are outsourced. In that context, offshore procurement takes place if it provides net cost-savings (i.e., greater savings in production costs than the additional outlays in service-link costs, at constant terms of trade).[6]

In Figure 3 below, we start where we left off in the previous figure: trade takes place at world price P_W. Firm A is an import-competing firm, producing OQ_{A1} and

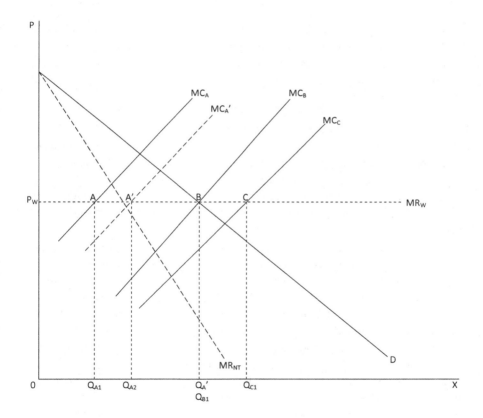

Figure 3.

---

[6]See Jones and Kierzkowski (1990) for a seminal contribution.

selling it in the domestic market. Imports of its variety are $Q_{A1}Q_{A'}$. Fragmentation reduces costs from MC_A to $MC_{A'}$, increasing output to Q_{A2} and reducing imports. Suppose that at world price P_W, firm B produces Q_{B1} units, which is just the right amount to satisfy domestic demand for its variety without leaving any excess to be exported or shortfall to be imported. There is no net trade, therefore in Firm B's variety. Note, however, that Firm B could employ fragmentation to reduce its production costs, shifting its MC curve to the right (not drawn) and thereby raising its output and starting to export. Finally, firm C may employ fragmentation to reduce its marginal costs (not shown). Since it is already an exporter of its variety, offshore procurement of one or more components raises both output and exports of its variety.

These results are consistent with those in earlier chapters when fragmentation was introduced by perfectly competitive export industries. So, the basic findings of the perfect competition model easily extend to the case of heterogeneous firms. It is important, once again, to keep in mind that when a firm resorts to fragmentation and offshore procurement, it becomes an importer of one or more components of the final product.

We consider next the case in which the fragmented activity is final assembly, as in the U.S.-Mexico case of cross-border fragmentation in the automobile industry. In Figure 3 above, in which firm A is depicted as an import-competing firm at the world price, the position and slope of the demand curve it faces depends, on the one hand, on competition from other varieties, like those produced by domestic firms B and C. It depends, on the other hand, on competition from foreign firms. An increase in foreign competition tends to push its demand curve inward and to flatten its slope.

Suppose that the "component" in which the firm has the greatest competitive disadvantage is labor-intensive assembly. The firm decides to outsource assembly of the final product to a labor-abundant, low-wage trading partner. The resulting decline in marginal cost (to a primed MC curve) increases output, as before. But in this case, the entire quantity of the final product sold in the home market by the firm is imported from the production-sharing partner, while a larger quantity than before of all other components is produced at home and then exported to the partner for assembly. This partner may be an affiliate or an arms-length firm.[7] This is another example of the extent to which the industry-level analytical approach of the papers in this section is amenable to application at the firm level.

---

[7]On the issue of affiliate versus arms-length outsourcing, see Kimura and Ando (2003) and Ando, Arndt and Kimura (2006).

References

(For additional references, see Chapter 1)

Ando, M., S.W. Arndt and F. Kimura (2006), "Production Networks in East Asia: Strategic Behavior by U.S. and Japanese Firms." (Japanese version published in 2007).

Bernard, A. B. and J. B. Jensen (1995), "Exporters, Jobs, and Wages in US Manufacturing: 1976–1987," *Brookings Papers on Economic Activity: Microeconomics*, pp. 67–112.

Dixit and Stiglitz (1977), "Monopolistic Competition and Optimal Product Diversity," *American Economic Review*, 67, 3, pp. 297–308.

Gao, Y. and J. Whalley (2013), "Heterogeneous Firms in a Product Fragmentation World," CES/IFO Working Paper No. 4229 (Munich), pp. 1–25.

Helpman, E. (1984), "Increasing Returns, Imperfect Markets, and Trade Theory," in R. W. Jones and P. B. Kenen (eds.), *Handbook of International Economics*, Vol. 1 (New York: North-Holland).

———(2013), "Foreign trade and Investment: Firm-Level Perspectives," NBER Working Paper 19057 (Cambridge, MA), pp. 1–29.

Jones, R. W. and H. Kierzkowski (1990), "The Role of Services in Production and International trade: A Theoretical Framework," in R.W. Jones and A.O. Krueger (eds.), *The Political Economy of International Trade* (Oxford: Blackwell), pp. 31–48.

Kimura, F. and M. Ando (2003), "Fragmentation and Agglomeration Matter: Japanese Multinationals in Latin America and East Asia," *North American Journal of Economics and Finance*, 14, 3, pp. 287–317.

Krugman, P. R. (1979), "Increasing Returns, Monopolistic Competition, and International Trade," *Journal of International Economics*, 9, 4, pp. 469–479.

Melitz, M. J., "The Impact of Trade on Intra-Industry Allocations and Aggregate Industry Productivity, " *Econometrica*, 71, 6, pp. 1695–725.

Redding, S. J. (2010), "Theories of Heterogeneous Firms and Trade," NBER Working Paper 16562 (Cambridge, MA), pp. 1–37.

Part III
Macro Policy Challenges in Open Economies

Chapter 14

Policy Choices in an Open Economy: Some Dynamic Considerations

Sven W. Arndt

University of California, Santa Cruz

Decision rules for stabilization policy in an open economy are examined under alternative specifications of the balance of payments. In particular, distinction between interest-sensitive debt capital and equity capital which responds to an activity variable alters the comparative static properties of instrument assignment. Various aspects of dynamic adjustment are further investigated in a context in which time is endogenous and in which the decision process minimizes a criterion function. It is shown that traditional one-to-one pairing of targets and controls may be inferior to assignment of clusters of instruments to some targets for specified time intervals.

JEL Classification: E61, E63, F41, F42
Keywords: Open-economy macro; Capital flows; Assignment problem

Like policy making in general, the formulation of macroeconomic policies in an open economy may be treated as a problem in decision analysis. In a widely used variant of a decision model first developed by Meade (1951) and Tinbergen (1952), the structure of the economy is laid out in terms of a number of important markets, and the conditions under which each market will be in equilibrium are specified. The decision problem then amounts to setting the economic controls in a manner which makes the actual values of key variables like employment and the balance of payments consistent with desired values. The link between state variables and controls is provided by the specified structure of the system, while the intervention of decision makers is governed by a set of rules designed to achieve a unique set of targets.

Submitted for publication March 16, 1970. Final version received August 25, 1971.

An earlier version of this paper was read to the Seminaire Jean Baptiste Say at the University of Paris-Dauphine. I am indebted to its members and particularly to Professor Pascal Salin for many valuable comments. I have gained much also from the suggestions of John Patrick and of Professors S. Black, E. R. Canterbery, R. Hawkins, L. Officer, A. Swoboda, and T. Willett. Any remaining errors are, of course, my sole responsibility.

Specification of targeted values or, more generally, of a criterion function, serves to introduce a normative element into the analysis by means of which actual values of controlled and noncontrolled variables may be distinguished from their desired values and which has the important consequence of justifying policy intervention even in cases which would, in the traditional definition of the term, be considered equilibrium situations, but in which the set of equilibrium values is inconsistent with perceived objectives.

Much of the important recent work in the analysis of internal-external balance derives its inspiration from the pioneering efforts of Meade (1951), Tinbergen (1952), and Mundell (1968). Within this framework, largely decentralized decisions are made in accordance with rules which assign to each target an instrument which possesses comparative advantage in manipulating that target. When all control variables are so assigned, it can be shown that the resulting policy mix will be stable.[1] The fixity of target values is an integral part of the analysis, for together with the assumption that decision makers hold no preferences—spatial or temporal —as among the chosen objectives, it obviates the necessity of constructing a social preference function.

A further virtue of the approach is that it permits the derivation of important results within an essentially comparative static framework in which decision makers may possess some knowledge about the detailed nature of aggregate functions, but in which they need know little more than the relevant excess demand functions.

The purpose of this paper is twofold. In Section I, in which the effects on assignment stability of alternative specifications of the capital account are examined, it is shown that disaggregation of capital movements into fixed-interest certificates and equities introduces an ambiguity into the decision mechanism, the resolution of which requires more detailed knowledge of the structural coefficients of the system. In Section II the fixed-target–fixed-time model is replaced by a framework in which decision makers minimize a criterion function subject to a set of constraints that explicitly incorporates adjustment speeds of the system and reaction speeds of the policy-making authorities. It is argued that when time horizons are endogenous, one-to-one pairing of control and state variables is not necessarily preferable; a case is sketched in which a decision rule assigns more than a single control variable to a given state variable for some interval of time, after the elapse of which some or all of the controls may be switched to another state variable. The one-to-one mapping of Section I, together with its constant and exogenous time horizon and its fixed set of targets, is seen to be a special case of a more general policy problem.

---

[1] Other contributions in this area have been made by Fleming (1962), Johnson (1965), Krueger (1965), Sohmen (1967), Jones (1968), Ott and Ott (1968), Patrick (1968), Cooper (1969), and Helliwell (1969).

I. Interest Rates and Income and the Determination of Capital Movements

In the literature on the assignment problem it has been customary in a manner following Mundell (1968) to assume that capital movements are uniquely determined by differentials among countries in interest rates.[2] This procedure is generally justified on the grounds that transactions on capital account which respond to variables other than interest rates are relatively constant in some short-run period, and may thus be ignored in short-run models. The major consequence of this approach is that capital movements are treated as portfolio transactions heavily dominated by claims lying near the short and liquid end of the spectrum, so that the short-term rate of interest becomes the relevant independent variable. By necessity this approach does not, and is not intended to, account for the flow of equity capital. This systematic exclusion from the analysis of certain phenomena is conceptually readily defensible, but the empirical relevance of a policy model that ignores equity flows rests upon verification of the implicit argument that transactions in equities respond to disturbances with greater adjustment lags than do those involving merchandise and services. The arbitrariness of the distinction between so-called short-term and long-term capital movements is underscored by recent empirical evidence that fluctuations in "activity variables" generated in short-term models give rise to statistically significant responses in international equity transactions.[3]

In the following discussion, transactions on capital account are dis-aggregated into those involving fixed interest-bearing securities that are assumed to respond to variations in rates of interest and into those properly classified as direct investment. The latter are assumed to vary with expected rates of return on investment, so that the direct investment inflow (D) is positively related to the excess of the domestic over the foreign expected real rate of return:[4]

$$D = D(r_d - r_f), \qquad D' > 0. \tag{1}$$

[2] See, among others, Krueger (1965), Sohmen (1967), Mundell (1968), Ott and Ott (1968), and Cooper (1969).

[3] Income or activity variables have been built into theoretical models of internal-external balance by Johnson (1965), Jones (1968), Patrick (1968), and Helliwell (1969); and in quarterly models of Canada and France, respectively, Rhomberg (1964) and Arndt (1970) have found some empirical evidence in support of the hypothesis that direct investment responds to variables other than the nominal rate of interest. In his recent study of the quarterly U.S. balance of payments, Prachowny (1969) shows that the industrial production index swamps the interest differential in a regression determining the outflow of direct investment capital. Moreover, his tests do not provide significant criteria for preferring the interest variable to the activity variable as principal determinant of equity capital movements.

[4] Relative rates of return must be corrected for relative risk factors; as a firm's investment in a foreign country rises in relation to its total investments, the growing concentration that is implied by further acquisition of claims in that country will be reflected in a rising risk coefficient.

With the introduction of equity transactions, the capital account is exposed to an additional source of variation, but it remains to be seen whether this alters the fundamental assignment rule according to which monetary policy serves best the external goal, and fiscal policy the internal. In figure 1, the A_0A_0-line is the familiar linearized internal-balance schedule, its negative slope indicating that the desired internal equilibrium can be maintained in the face of a cut in government expenditures (G) only by an expansion in the stock of money (H). Similarly, the foreign-balance schedule Z_0Z_0 has negative slope because a surplus in the trade balance occasioned by a reduction in the government's outlays must be compensated by a monetary expansion which, by lowering domestic interest rates, increases the outflow of interest-sensitive capital. The comparative advantage with which monetary policy affects the external balance is reflected in the steeper slope of the Z_0Z_0-schedule.

The two functions divide the quadrant into four zones, with the zones above A_0A_0 characterized by excess demand in domestic markets, while the zones above Z_0Z_0 represent an excess of payments over receipts in the external accounts. In each zone the short arrows indicate the direction in which the control variables must be moved in order to return the system from points in that zone to the equilibrium intersection between the two schedules. Consider, thus, the point Q at which the economy suffers from recession and from a payments deficit. In following the

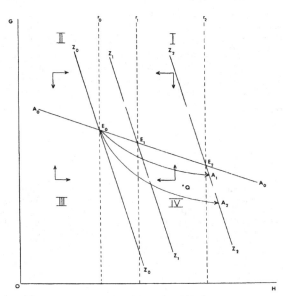

Fig. 1.—Internal (AA) and external (ZZ) balance for several relative expected rates of return (r) on equity investment.

prescribed program, the authorities increase government expenditures in order to increase domestic employment and income, while raising the degree of monetary stringency in order to attract the interest-sensitive foreign capital required to offset the worsening trade balance.[5]

As it is the objective of government during periods of recession to uplift the private sector's economic confidence, the fiscal expansion, if successful, improves the profit expectations of investors, and according to the preceding discussion, a relative increase in profit expectations tends to raise the inflow of investment capital. The effect of this inflow is to shift the foreign-balance schedule to the right and thus to change the extent of fiscal expansion and monetary laxity required for the attainment of joint balance. As the external-balance schedule is displaced in the direction of Z_1Z_1, the magnitude of the monetary contraction which will restore joint balance (now at E_1) is diminished, and the less stringent monetary requirements in turn have the effect of decreasing the magnitude of the necessary fiscal expansion.

While the movement, therefore, of the external-balance schedule to Z_1Z_1 alters the policy response, it does not affect its direction because the moving point Q is assumed to remain in zone IV. When Z_2Z_2 is the new foreign-balance schedule, however, the policy mix which achieves the new equilibrium combines fiscal expansion not with monetary contraction but with monetary expansion. If the authorities respond solely to observed excess demand conditions at Q without any knowledge of the shape of the functions or of the shift parameters in their arguments, they will initiate a monetary contraction, and the resulting inflow of interest-sensitive capital will, when added to the equity capital inflow, hasten the development of a balance-of-payments surplus. At the same time, the monetary stringency tends to slow the rate of growth of internal demand, though it is not possible without detailed dynamic specifications to judge the severity of this retardation. Further, although the crossover into a new quadrant and the consequent reversal in the required direction of one of the controls increases the presumption that equilibrium will not be achieved without oscillations, it is again not possible to ascertain from the information given whether and to what extent the stability of the system is endangered. It can be concluded, however, that the absence of some knowledge of the shape of functions and of shift parameters[6] diminishes the probability of a direct approach to equilibrium.[7]

---

[5] The means by which increased government expenditures are financed is of importance. If deficit finance is the chosen vehicle, the very act of increasing G will, in the absence of infinitely elastic international capital lead to an increase in the domestic interest rate, implying that a continuing deficit financed through open-market sales and thus a growing supply of bonds will put continuing pressure on the rate of interest.

[6] As we shall see below, not only the ZZ-schedule, but the AA-schedule as well, is likely to shift as a consequence of investment capital inflows.

[7] The shift parameter can represent a number of forces which would tend to shift the

The Expected Rate of Return and Policy Surrogates

A current reading on the distribution of private-sector profit expectations would represent an important input into the policy decision process. On the whole, this information is rarely available, and in its absence a number of surrogates have been proposed, among which the use of an "activity" variable has gained prominence.[8] In the present section a difficulty in the use of income or related variables is examined.[9]

Where an activity variable has been employed, the capital account has frequently been specified as follows:

$$K = K(i, Y), \qquad K_y > 0, \qquad K_i > 0, \tag{2}$$

where K is the total capital inflow and K_y and K_i the partial derivatives relating equity and interest-sensitive capital flows, respectively, to their principal determining variables. A noteworthy characteristic of equation (2) is the sign of K_y, which rests on the assumption that income is a highly substitutable proxy for the expected rate of return (r), so that variations in $(r_d - r_f)$ will be adequately reflected by variations in $(Y_d - Y_f)$. If, as in some variants of the accelerator model, profit expectations are determined by current economic activity or by expected future changes in activity which are directly related to current activity, the covariation between current income and expected profit differentials is probably substantial. But if, as is by no means impossible, expectations concerning future returns lead or lag variations in current activity, observed inflows of equity capital will have no uniformly positive relationship to current activity.

ZZ-function about. One of these is speculative expectations regarding the authorities' ability to maintain the given exchange rate. In a dynamic context, speculators' expectations can be related to the rate at which the nation's stock of foreign exchange reserves is being depleted as the policy measures taken at Q propel the system toward the ZZ-curve. Suppose that speculative capital outflows (K_s) are related to the time rate of decrease in reserves, $K_s = g(dR/dt)$. While the system is off the ZZ-schedule, reserves are declining, and the greater the delay in returning to external balance, the greater the total loss in reserves. The proportional reserve loss per unit of time is thus inversely related to the rate at which Q is pushed toward ZZ, and the slower that corrective movement, the greater the probability that speculative outflows of capital will shift the foreign-balance schedule to the left, thus compounding the requirement of monetary stringency. Introduction into the analysis of expectational changes therefore can severely undermine the all-important constancy of the market-balance functions. The last point applies equally to an economy facing an excess demand-cum-deficit situation, as in zone I. As it relates to the stability of the foreign-balance function, the relative rise in domestic prices brought about by the excess demand in goods markets tends to shift Z_0Z_0 to the left.

[8] The principal studies which have used activity variables are those of Johnson (1965), Jones (1968), Patrick (1968), Helliwell (1969), and Prachowny (1969).

[9] In a cogent analysis, Ablin (1968) has addressed himself to the proper specification of the income variable, considering among others the trend rate, the level, and the current rate of change of income.

The preceding is not a brief against income as a proxy for the expected return, but against the strong hypothesis $K_y > 0$. In the following, that hypothesis is replaced with the less restrictive hypothesis $K_y \gtreqless 0$.[10]

The consequences of the preceding analysis for correct assignment may be exposed with the aid of the following model, important features of which are the specification of the capital account and of the government's budget constraint. The supply of national output is assumed infinitely elastic, assuring a constant price level, and the exchange rate is assumed fixed:

$$E(Y, i) + F(Y, i) + G - Y = 0, \qquad 1 > E_y > 0, E_i < 0,$$
$$F_y < 0, F_i > 0; \tag{3}$$
$$F(Y, i) + K(Y, i) - B = 0, \qquad K_y \gtreqless 0, K_i > 0; \tag{4}$$
$$L(Y, i) - H = 0, \qquad L_y > 0, L_i < 0; \tag{5}$$
$$V(Y, i) - S = 0, \qquad V_y > 0, V_i > 0; \tag{6}$$
$$G = \Delta H + \Delta S, \tag{7}$$

where Y = national income, E = private expenditure, F = trade balance surplus, G = government expenditure, B = balance of payments, K = net capital inflow, L = demand for money, H = supply of money, V = demand for government securities, S = supply of government securities, and i = yield on government securities.

Equations (3), (5), and (6) describe the goods, money, and securities markets, respectively, and equation (7) gives the government's budget constraint under the assumption that all current expenditures are financed by supplying money or by supplying bonds. Under regimes of fixed

---

[10] Large movements of American funds into Canadian extractive industries during the fifties occurred in anticipation of future growth in the United States which was widely expected to create shortages in domestically produced raw materials. While such inflows tend to stimulate activity in the recipient economy, they may be inversely related to the relative rate of activity there, being determined instead by the relative expected profitability of investment in that country. In analyzing these flows into Canada, Wonnacott (1965) has differentiated between the "relative-cycle hypothesis," according to which equity capital inflows are positively correlated with relative current income expansion, and the "exporter's cycle hypothesis," according to which capital exports are positively correlated with a relative expansion in a country's income. The difficulties associated with the use of activity variables as proxies are compounded by the lack of synchronization of business cycles between countries. The strong hypothesis, $K_y > 0$, has the disadvantage of seeming to impart to the adjustment mechanism an inherent instability. Variations in income are the cause of variations in saving and investment. In case of specification (1), a flow of equity capital between two countries will have the effect of narrowing for any given level of world investment the gap between rates of return in the two countries, much as the flow of portfolio capital is assumed to eliminate gaps between national interest rates. Under the strong income hypothesis, on the other hand, a capital inflow occasioned by a country's relatively strong activity may widen still further the activity gap between the two countries, thus creating the incentive for more capital transfers in a process which appears to be self-perpetuating rather than self-limiting.

exchange rates, the stock of official reserves will increase and decrease with surpluses and deficits in the balance of payments, which raises the possibility that actual reserve changes $(dR/dt = B)$ may be inconsistent with desired reserves. In what follows, we shall assume that the authorities hold no specific reserve goals and that the domestic monetary effects of variations in reserve holdings are automatically neutralized.

The relevant equations of change are obtained by differentiation of equations (3), (4), and (5):

$$(1 - E_y - F_y)\, dY - (E_i + F_i)\, di = dG, \tag{8}$$

$$-(F_y + K_y)\, dY - (F_i + K_i)\, di + dB = 0, \tag{9}$$

$$L_y\, dY + L_i\, di = dH. \tag{10}$$

The determinant of the system is given by

$$\Delta = -(1 - E_y - F_y)L_i - (E_i + F_i)L_y, \tag{11}$$

and a sufficient condition for a positive determinant is that the propensity of the private sector to spend (E_y) be less than unity plus the propensity of the trade balance to worsen with an increase in income (F_y) and that the effect of variations in the rate of interest on expenditure be greater than its effect on the trade balance.

The object of the following manipulations is to discover the effects of monetary and fiscal operations on the variables Y, i, and B and to compare the results for $K_y > 0$ with those for $K_y < 0$.

$K_y > 0$:

$$\frac{dY}{dG} = -\frac{1}{\Delta}\left[L_i + (E_i + F_i)\frac{dH}{dG}\right] > 0, \tag{12}$$

$$\frac{dY}{dH} = -\frac{1}{\Delta}(E_i + F_i) > 0, \tag{13}$$

$$\frac{di}{dG} = \frac{1}{\Delta}\left[L_y - (1 - E_y - F_y)\frac{dH}{dG}\right] \gtrless 0, \tag{14}$$

$$\frac{di}{dH} = -\frac{1}{\Delta}(1 - E_y - F_y) < 0, \tag{15}$$

$$\frac{dB}{dG} = \frac{1}{\Delta}\left\{L_y(F_i + K_i) - L_i(F_y + K_y) - [(F_i + K_i)(1 - E_y - F_y)\right.$$
$$\left. + (F_y + K_y)(E_i + F_i)]\frac{dH}{dG}\right\} \gtrless 0, \tag{16}$$

$$\frac{dB}{dH} = -\frac{1}{\Delta}[(F_i + K_i)(1 - E_y - F_y)$$
$$+ (F_y + K_y)(E_i + F_i)] \gtrless 0. \tag{17}$$

An injection of government expenditure increases national income, a portion $(L_y\, dY)$ of the increased income being devoted by the public to augmentation of its holdings of domestic money. The increased demand for money pushes up the rate of interest if $dH = 0$, and it will raise the rate of interest even when $dH/dG = 1$, unless $(1 - E_y - F_y) \geq L_y$.[11] The balance of payments may improve or deteriorate as a consequence of official intervention. A monetary expansion will bring about an unequivocal deterioration in the balance of payments if $(F_y + K_y) < 0$. If $(F_y + K_y)$ is positive, and if, as before, we assume that $(E_i + F_i) < 0$, the condition for balance-of-payments deterioration becomes

$$\frac{(F_i + K_i)}{(E_i + F_i)} < -\frac{(F_y + K_y)}{(1 - E_y - F_y)}. \tag{18}$$

The effects on the balance of payments of fiscal expansion are governed by the manner of financing the government's expenditures. When $dH/dG = 0$, a sufficient condition for payments improvement is $(F_y + K_y) > 0$, whereas for $dH/dG = 1$, the balance of payments will improve if,

$$[(L_y + E_y + F_y - 1)(F_i + K_i) - (L_i + E_i + F_i)(F_y + K_y)] > 0. \tag{19}$$

$K_y < 0$:

Expression $(F_y + K_y)$ is now always negative so that income-sensitive capital flows can no longer be counted on to offset developments in the trade balance. A monetary expansion, which could in the previous case improve or worsen the balance of payments, now brings about an un-

[11] According to the budget constraint (7), government expenditure, dG, is to be financed either by money creation or by bond creation. When $dH = 0$, and assuming that initially $G = 0$, an increase in the rate of interest as given by equation (14) would be expected simply as the result of the greater supply of bonds. This has, among other things, important implications for the speed with which the rate of interest adjusts to its new level. Moreover, if the increase in government expenditure, and thus in bond supply, is required to maintain income at its desired higher level, a continuing budget deficit requires continuing additions to the outstanding stock of bonds, implying a sustained upward drift in the rate of interest. The majority of short-term models do not specify a government budget constraint (but see, for example, Ott and Ott [1968]). Under appropriate assumptions, the small-country model does not suffer from this weakness if additional supplies of bonds can be sold to the rest of the world at externally determined rates of interest. But for such a country a continuing budget deficit gives rise to a steadily rising international indebtedness, even while the capital imports, which improve the capital account, provide steady additions to the money stock. For a large country, the argument can be salvaged by the assumption that additional creation of bonds is so small relative to the outstanding stock that its effects are negligible. This assumption is analogous to assuming that the impact on the capital stock of new investment is negligible.

equivocal deterioration in payments. A budgetary expansion (with $dH/dG = 0$) worsens the balance of payments if

$$\frac{(F_i + K_i)}{L_i} > \frac{(F_y + K_y)}{L_y} . \tag{20}$$

Moreover, the payments balance deteriorates when, along with condition (20), government expenditure is accompanied by money creation.

Income-sensitive Capital and Domestic Economic Activity

The movement of international capital has important consequences for the balance of payments and thus becomes, as we have seen, a critical object of the policy makers' attention. Whether official interest extends to the domestic effects of foreign investment depends upon adjustment speeds. On the assumption that any period that is long enough to accommodate trade balance adjustments and the manipulation of such cumbersome instruments as fiscal policy is probably long enough to enable private decision makers to formulate and execute investment decisions, we consider in this section some domestic implications of direct investment flows.[12]

The inflow of investment capital, which has the effect in figure 1 of shifting the external-balance schedule to the right, supplements the pool of domestic savings and adds to the demand for resources. If idle resources and raw materials exist domestically, the increased demand for these will serve the useful purpose of pushing home income and employment to higher levels. In short, the *AA*-schedule will move down, implying that the fiscal stimulus needed for the achievement of internal balance has been reduced by the capital inflow, which plays a role similar to government expenditures in generating new demand.[13]

As the internal-balance schedule moves down, its points of intersection with the displaced foreign-balance schedule trace out the new equilibria

[12] For a country as large as the United States, the internal effects of these flows are probably quite small, as are also the repercussions on domestic monetary conditions of interest-sensitive capital flows. But for most other countries, characterized as they are by substantial openness both on current and on capital account, the domestic consequences of changes on capital account can be critical. Relatively large inflows that do not merely replace domestic investment may imply $E_y > 1$, a development that has important implications for the stability of the system.

[13] The stimuli will not be identical in all respects because the composition of GNP, which may be a social goal in itself, will be affected differently. That composition will be affected not only as between the private and public sectors or as between domestic and foreign ownership, but also as between the current and future current-account balance. When foreign direct investment takes place in the context of relatively high utilization of capacity—which is not the situation at Q—the trade balance is affected more immediately as the capital import gives rise to a merchandise import. If it is the direct investment inflow rather than an interest-induced inflow of capital that "finances" the emerging trade deficit, the schedule of future repayments is likely to vary accordingly.

toward which it is the objective of policy to push the system. The joint movement of the two functions will thus move the equilibrium in the direction indicated by the two heavy arrows A_1 and A_2, and in the aftermath of these shifts the actual location of the system (at some point similar to Q) may cross over into any of the other quadrants. The domestic repercussions of the capital inflow must be sufficiently great relative to total domestic activity to bring about significant displacements of the internal-balance schedule, but such displacement, even if small, begins to weigh more heavily as the equilibrium is approached.

The Stability of an Assignment

A policy assignment is said to be correct when instruments and targets are paired in a manner that exploits the comparative advantage of every instrument. To evaluate the relative effectiveness of monetary and fiscal tools and the stability of assignments in light of the foregoing discussion, figure 2 represents the essential features of the model, with balance in the goods and money markets indicated along XX and LL, respectively, and equilibrium in the balance of payments given along the BB-schedule. Schedule B_1B_1 reproduces the standard Mundellian case, while schedule B_2B_2 is one in which a strong positive relationship between income and equity inflows produces a negative slope.

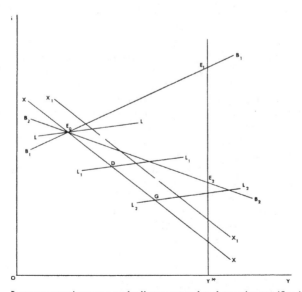

FIG. 2.—Instrument assignments and adjustment under alternative specifications of the capital account of the balance of payments.

It is assumed that income adjusts to excess demand in the goods market and that the rate of interest adjusts to excess demand in the money market, that is,[14]

$$\frac{dY}{dt} = k_1 X(Y, i), \qquad k_1' > 0, \tag{21}$$

$$\frac{di}{dt} = k_2 L(Y, i), \qquad k_2' > 0. \tag{22}$$

The system will exhibit stability if

$$\begin{vmatrix} k_1 X_y - \lambda & k_1 X_i \\ k_2 L_y & k_2 L_i - \lambda \end{vmatrix} = 0,$$

and stability is assured whenever $X_y < 0$; and for $X_y > 0$, the system will be stable provided that $-X_i/X_y > -L_i/L_y$ and $k_1 X_y < -k_2 L_i$.

According to the principle of effective market classification, the authorities adjust government expenditures in accordance with deviations of actual from target levels of income, and the money stock in accordance with deviations of actual from target values of the balance of payments, that is,

$$\frac{dG}{dt} = h_1(Y^* - Y), \qquad h_1' > 0, \tag{23}$$

$$\frac{dH}{dt} = -h_2(B^* - B), \qquad h_2' > 0. \tag{24}$$

Policy mixes that are consistent with these decision rules will achieve the stated objectives in both cases illustrated in the diagram, and other possibilities involving different relative slopes of the three functions may be similarly analyzed. Schedule $B_1 B_1$ obtains whenever $K_y \leq 0$, and in order to reach the new equilibrium indicated by E_1 on $B_1 B_1$, a budgetary expansion paired with a monetary contraction is required to shift XX and LL until they intersect in E_1. The assignment is stable.

But suppose that decision makers have no knowledge of the slopes of the functions. Their policy responses as defined by (23) and (24) are strictly to deviations between actual and desired values of income and of the balance of payments. At E_0 government expenditure shifts XX to the right. As $X_1 X_1$ shows, this leads to a higher rate of interest and to a payments deficit if $B_1 B_1$ rules, but to a surplus if $B_2 B_2$ rules. To these payments imbalances the authorities respond with increased monetary stringency in the first case and greater laxity in the second case. At point D, the same fiscal expansion produces a payments deficit in both cases,

---

[14] Under a fixed exchange rate, the level of official reserves adjusts to excess demand in the foreign exchange market. The domestic repercussions of that adjustment are assumed to be neutralized.

and in both the monetary controls are tightened. It is now apparent that the resulting increase in the rate of interest will be consistent with the final equilibrium rate if B_1B_1 rules, but not otherwise. In light of the ultimately lower rate of interest at E_2, the direction of monetary policy initiated at point D will at some other stage have to be reversed.[15]

The implications of these results may be briefly stated. First, if decision rules (23) and (24) are adhered to, the assignment will be stable in the comparative static sense. Second, the effect of reversals in the direction of monetary policy on dynamic stability cannot be ascertained without additional specification, and thus it cannot be determined whether such reversals increase the likelihood of oscillation around equilibrium. Third, since monetary stringency reduces the increase in income and employment associated with a given fiscal expansion, the total time interval required to achieve the desired goals is probably greater than it would have been had the authorities been aware of the downward slope of BB and thus expanded the money stock at the time of the fiscal expansion. Fourth, while reverse pairing is unstable for B_1B_1, it will be stable for B_2B_2. At points E_0 and D, a monetary expansion directed at internal balance generates a payments deficit that is removable by a fiscal expansion. The fiscal policy must be expansionary due to the dominance of favorable capital account effects. Thus, the reverse assignment is stable only if the authorities do not respond to the incipient trade deficit with the traditional budgetary contraction, and this assumes some knowledge of the shape of the functions.

The problem is more complex at G. Suppose the authorities react to the internal imbalance with a monetary expansion and to the external deficit with a fiscal injection. This raises the possibility of an intersection of XX and LL beyond the targeted level of income and, if Y^* indicates full employment, presents the authorities with an inflation/deficit situation. What happens at that point cannot be determined with the information given, for the changing domestic price level will shift all the functions.[16]

While the principle of effective market classification thus provides stable guidelines for policy action, the case of B_2B_2 demonstrates that such assignments are not unique in their stability. Indeed, the principle may generate a more roundabout and slower approach to equilibrium,

---

[15] Note that with G as the starting point, the ultimate requirement in both cases is a rise in the rate of interest from its initial level.

[16] A situation not shown in the figure, but one which is nevertheless of some interest, is that in which the slopes of the XX- and BB-schedules are reversed, making the latter steeper than the former. It can readily be shown that assignment according to rules (23) and (24) is unstable. If, on the other hand, the decision rules are less narrowly defined, stipulating simply that the fiscal instrument be paired with internal balance and the monetary instrument with external balance, then a fiscal contraction together with a monetary expansion can lead the system to the desired equilibrium. This, once again, would necessitate some knowledge of the structure of the system.

particularly when h_1 is very small. In that event, delays in the initiation of fiscal measures, combined with the pressing urgency which authorities may attach to achievement of the internal target, may induce them to assign monetary policy to the internal goal. As we have seen, such action contravenes (23) and (24), but it may nevertheless be stable. We turn to problems of this sort in the next section.

II. Some Aspects of a Dynamic Policy Model

Up to this point, policy makers have been assumed to hold uniform time preferences; no attempt was made to evaluate alternative time horizons in terms of their social desirability. The time horizon was exogenously determined. The present section examines some implications of replacing the earlier fixed-time model with a framework in which time itself becomes a target. When the time horizon is endogenous, the distinction between controlled and noncontrolled variables is blurred, and incompatibility among objectives may be as much a temporal as a spatial phenomenon. The effectiveness and comparative advantage of an instrument requires measurement in time-efficiency units as much as in terms of its total impact.

Suppose that in the following two-by-two model state variables are related linearly to controls:

$$x_{1t} = \sum_{t-\tau} \beta_{1it} a_{it} + u_{1t}, \qquad i = 1, 2; \tau = 0, 1, \ldots, \tag{25a}$$

$$x_{2t} = - \sum_{t-\tau} \beta_{2it} a_{it} + u_{2t}, \tag{25b}$$

where the x_{it} are the current values of state variables, the a_{it} current values of control variables, and the u_{it} represent the effect of "other" factors. Equations (25) may be expressed in convenient vector notation as

$$x_t = Ba_t + u_t, \tag{26}$$

where it should be noted that the first term on the right-hand side incorporates the lagged effects of policy actions. Positive values of the control variables are assumed to increase x_1 but to decrease x_2, the implication being that in cases in which higher values of both target variables are preferred, the effect of the constraints (25) is to generate a conflict situation.

In place of the assumption of Section I that the decision makers pursue fixed targets, we suppose that they seek to minimize the following loss function:

$$L(x, a) = \int_0^T \phi(t) F(x_1 - x_1^*, x_2 - x_2^*) \, dt, \tag{27}$$

where the functional is defined over the planning horizon T; $\phi(t)$ is a time-discounting function; and the x_1^* are the desired values of the state variables.[17] The integrand is assumed to be a quadratic function. In order to simplify the exposition and without loss of generality, we replace (27) with its discrete analogue, which is expressed in terms of its expectation to take account of uncertainty:[18]

$$E[L(x, a)] = E\left[\omega \sum_t \theta_{1t}(x_{1t} - x_1^*)^2 + (1 - \omega) \sum_t \theta_{2t}(x_{2t} - x_2^*)^2\right], \quad (28)$$

where ω indicates the relative importance to policy makers of achieving the first target. In the process of minimization of (28) subject to constraints (25), time enters once through the lagged impact of policy instruments on targets and again through the cumulative effect over some time horizon of the selected policies on the loss function.

The decision problem may now be contrasted with the earlier fixed-target approach to macroeconomic policy. Among the key differences between the two models, the following are particularly important.

First, the fixed-target approach assigns to both goals equal priority, while the loss function (28) permits discriminatory weighting of objectives through variations in ω. This is crucial inasmuch as it provides the most straightforward argument against one-to-one pairing of targets and instruments: as $\omega \to 1$, the optimal policy is one which assigns both control variables to x_1, for in the limit the effect of any policy which reduces $(x_2 - x_2^*)$ will not reduce the total loss, while any adverse effects of such a policy on the second target variable will enter the loss calculation with full weight. The values which ω assumes may be determined exogenously, or endogenously as when they are some function of the relative deviations of current from target values of the non-controlled variables,

$$\omega(t) = f\left[\frac{(x_{1t} - x_1^*)^2}{(x_{2t} - x_2^*)^2}\right].$$

A weighting scheme that varies over time implies that the nature of the assignment is variable as well, giving rise to time intervals during which both control variables may be used to reduce the numerator, a process

---

[17] While the loss function contains only noncontrolled variables, any instrument variable for which the authorities hold preferred or desired values may be included.

[18] For use of quadratic welfare functions in macroeconomic decision models, see Theil (1964) and Fox, Sengupta, and Thorbecke (1966). The former has provided an important means of dealing with uncertainty problems by developing the notion of "certainty equivalence." For an application of these techniques, see Brainard (1967).

which will serve in conflict situations simultaneously to increase the denominator.

Second, the time-discounting function $\theta(t)$ permits intertemporal discrimination among identical deviations between actual and desired values of target variables. To the decision maker a given deviation of actual from target values today may be more or less important than the same discrepancy tomorrow. Considerations of this sort are paramount when policy makers set target dates by which the criterion function is to be minimized. For if policies operate with variable lags, there will exist assignments that minimize the loss function over a given interval $t_0 t_k$ and that are thus preferred if decision makers select $\theta(t)$ such that coefficients associated with all $t > t_k$ are set at zero; but such assignments may lose their optimality for intervals defined by different $\theta(t)$.[19]

The time-discriminating function assumes special importance in the context of uncertainty. Inability to forecast accurately the behavior of the u_i or incomplete information on the B-matrix induces decision makers to place premiums on the near-future impacts of their policies. In such cases, as Theil (1964) has shown, the decision problem at time t is to set the control variables, a_i, for the first period, while hoping that the interval before the onset of the next period will produce new information on the basis of which the effectiveness of the chosen policy may be evaluated.

Third, the relationship between controlled and noncontrolled variables depends critically on the lag structure as given by the coefficient matrix B. In particular, the derivatives of Section I, dx_i/da_j, on which so many of the definitive policy prescriptions of that section depend, are there assumed to operate instantaneously. But in a model that incorporates lagged coefficients, a change in an instrument variable, with all other control variables held constant, will work its effect on a given target variable over noninstantaneous time, so that the effect as measured by the partial derivative will be the sum of the changes in the target variable over a number of elementary time units. This in turn implies that we can vary the magnitude—and in some cases the sign—of the partial derivatives by making arbitrary choices concerning the length of the relevant time interval. The short-run period of the preceding section is the result of such a choice. Choices of this sort will always be necessary, but it is the virtue of the present approach that it makes explicit this necessity and in so doing underscores the normative nature of such choices.

As we have noted, it is on the basis of the partial derivatives that evaluation of the relative effectiveness or comparative advantage of an

---

[19] The selection of $\theta(t)$ may be influenced by critical tests to which policy makers expect their policies to be subjected. Scheduled elections or international negotiations will bias decision makers in favor of policies that achieve maximum effectiveness prior to such events, even if the longer-term impact on target variables of such policies is weaker than that of slower-working alternatives.

instrument is based. It follows from the discussion of the previous paragraph that comparative advantage cannot normally be determined independently of the chosen time period, except in cases in which the lag structures associated with the instruments being compared are sufficiently similar. In cases not so characterized, reversals in comparative advantage are possible; that is, if control variable a_1 exerts most of its effect on target variable x_1 in $t + k$ time units, while a_2, which has a greater total effect per dose tends to generate its impact with greater lags, the ratio of the effectiveness of the two instruments will exceed unity over the interval defined by the $(t + k)$ time units and lie below unity beyond that interval.

Explicit treatment of the lag structure provides a simple means of resolving some of the problems inherent in stock-flow analysis.[20] If, in response to a change in relative world interest rates, adjustment occurs in existing asset portfolios, the time path of the balance of payments will reflect these movements of funds, even if, as in the case of a pure stock model, the capital account returns ultimately to its original position. It is this eventual disappearance of the stock effect which is stressed in a pure stock model, an emphasis which presupposes a decision concerning the time focus of the analysis. For in a stock model in which adjustment is not assumed to be instantaneous, it is not merely the fact that after the passage of some time $dB = 0$ that is of interest, but also the fact that during that time $dB/dt \neq 0$, the length of that interval depending upon adjustment speeds. It is of relevance that during the interval the loss function will reflect the ongoing capital transfers, the implication being that if the decision makers' time horizon, T, is contained within this interval, a policy that brings about stock adjustments will have served the goal of reducing the social loss associated with deviations of actual from target values.[21] That being the case, it is not strictly relevant that the stock adjustment cannot be permanent, any such argument really being a brief for the adoption of an alternative time horizon.

Finally, the nature of the lag structure can affect the stability of the system. In particular, the stability conditions of Section I do not take adequate account of lags in recognition, response, and adjustment, and rules like (23) and (24) equally ignore certain lags. If at time t the gap $(Y - Y^*)$ is what it is because the total effect of policies initiated in past periods has not as yet been registered, then decision makers acting in ignorance of this delayed reaction of the system may themselves overreact to the observed discrepancy and in consequence propel the system beyond

[20] For a cogent analysis of stock-flow phenomena, see Willett and Forte (1969).

[21] Such a policy need not, of course, be an optimal policy, that is, one that minimizes the criterion function. It may be added that the loss function will be affected by the attendant variations in official reserves if, in addition to other goals, the decision makers hold preferences with respect to reserve levels, and the loss function will further reflect the interest return flows occasioned by the reallocation of world portfolios. It is likely that the repatriation of earnings will again be determined by a lag structure.

its target. Some of the oscillations and reversals of policy actions which result from this may endanger the stability of the system.[22]

The fear of overreaction is compounded by uncertainty associated with the stochastic behavior of the u_i in equation (25), which suggests that the decision process may contain a built-in bias in favor of assigning priority to the variable with the greatest deviation of actual from desired values. This approach has the dual advantage that reduction or elimination of a relatively large gap has a greater impact on the welfare function (appropriate consideration being given to ω, θ, and B) and that moderate dosages of the two (or, in multiple instrument cases, of several) instruments applied to that target are less likely to cause overshooting. Such considerations clearly may create a presumption in favor of allocating more than one control variable to a single target,[23] and this presumption would, we suppose, be strengthened if it could be shown that, other things being the same, the lag structure contained nonlinearities such that the time path of a target variable when two control variables are assigned to it is more (or less) than the sum (or difference) of the lagged effects of the two instruments considered in isolation.[24]

In conclusion, several points may be briefly stated. First, introduction of an activity variable into the determination of capital movements creates an ambiguity in the shape of the foreign-balance function, which has the consequence of facilitating reversals of instrument assignments that are nevertheless stable. Whether such alternative assignments are more time efficient cannot be ascertained within the context of a comparative static model. But the analysis suggests that knowledge of the structure of the system enhances the power of the decision mechanism by permitting selection of the most time-efficient of alternative policy mixes.

Second, departures from one-to-one pairing may in selected cases be efficient. This presumption is supported and strengthened when the

[22] Overshooting of targets need not always be attended by disaster. Decision makers may not be entirely displeased if their attempts to eliminate a payments deficit produce a surplus, but they will surely be less content when expansionary policies designed to achieve full employment turn out to have been excessive and lead to inflationary developments. It is one of the major weaknesses of the quadratic preference function that it treats positive and negative deviations from target values symmetrically, but this failing may be moderated by setting $\omega = 1$ whenever $(x_2 - x_2^*) \geq 0$, where x_2 is the balance-of-payments surplus.

[23] This conclusion is in part a consequence of our having retained the Tinbergen-Mundell assumption that decision makers pursue unique values rather than ranges of values of the noncontrolled variables.

[24] For example, the private sector's expectations may exhibit nonlinear response patterns when fiscal expansion-cum-monetary contraction is replaced with expansion in both. This underscores the importance for effective use of the criterion function of prior estimates on the structure of the economy. The necessary information input is substantially more elaborate than the simple estimates of the signs of the partial derivatives in the Tinbergen-Mundell framework. As the discussion of the present section implies, without prior information on such things as the lag structure and the configuration of official preferences, the formal analysis would decline rapidly into taxonomy.

Tinbergen-Mundell fixed-target–fixed-time framework is replaced by a less restrictive criterion function. In the process of minimizing a quadratic loss function, which permits preferential ordering of goals and endogenous determination of the time horizon, decisions emerge which assign both control variables in a two-by-two model to one of the two state variables for an interval equal to or smaller than the time horizon.

Where the structure of the system is unknown, the correct approach in the Tinbergen-Mundell model is to manipulate each instrument in accordance with excess demand in the market to which it has been assigned, while minimization of the criterion function may require that both instruments be assigned to the greatest (weighted) deviation of actual from target values. The latter approach has the further advantages of generating a performance integral by which the effectiveness of policy may be evaluated, and of providing decision criteria even in cases in which the numbers of independent instruments and targets are not identical.

Third, the greater flexibility of the criterion function is achieved not without cost, for it virtually precludes the derivation of simple and unambiguous decision rules. One of the principal advantages of the Tinbergen-Mundell decision rules is their simplicity, particularly in the context of limited information on the structure of the economy. In gaining such simplicity, however, the analysis makes important concessions to rigidity. In the real world, policy makers may be observed to behave in contradiction of the decision rules stipulated in internal-external balance models, as, for example, when they assign both monetary and fiscal instruments to removal of internal imbalance, while ignoring external imbalance. This may be due to their not having discovered the Tinbergen-Mundell principle of efficient allocation of controls, or to the existence of temporal (θ) and atemporal (ω) official preferences and of lag structures (B) which are inconsistent with the essential neutrality implicit in the Tinbergen-Mundell framework. Under such circumstances, generation of decision rules by means of the more flexible criterion function would appear preferable, although the derivation of such rules requires a much greater input of empirical estimates on the structure of the economy.

References

Ablin, R. S. "Income, Capital Mobility and the Theory of Economic Policy." *Kyklos*, fasc. 1 (1968): 102–17.

Arndt, S. W. "Income and Price Adjustment and France's Basic Balance of Payments, 1961–1966." *Rivista Internaz. Sci. Econ. e Commerciali* 17 (May 1970): 429–48.

Brainard, W. "Uncertainty and the Effectiveness of Policy." *A.E.R.* 57 (May 1967): 411–25.

POLICY CHOICES IN AN OPEN ECONOMY   935

Cooper, R. N. "Macroeconomic Policy Adjustment in Interdependent Economies." *Q.J.E.* 83 (February 1969): 1–24.

Fleming, J. M. "Domestic Financial Policies under Fixed and under Floating Exchange Rates." *IMF Staff Papers* 9 (November 1962): 369–80.

Fox, Karl A.; Sengupta, J. K.; and Thorbecke, E. *The Theory of Quantitative Economic Policy.* Chicago: Rand McNally, 1966.

Helliwell, J. F. "Monetary and Fiscal Policies for an Open Economy." *Oxford Econ. Papers* 21 (March 1969): 35–55.

Johnson, H. G. "Some Aspects of the Theory of Economic Policy in a World of Capital Mobility." *Rivista Internaz. Sci. Econ. e Commerciali* 12, no. 6 (1965): 345–59.

Jones, R. W. "Monetary and Fiscal Policy for an Open Economy with Fixed Exchange Rates." *J.P.E.* 76, pt. 2 (July/August 1968): 921–44.

Krueger, A. O. "The Impact of Alternative Government Policies under Varying Exchange Systems." *Q.J.E.* 79 (May 1965): 195–208.

Meade, J. E. *The Theory of International Economic Policy.* Vol. 1. *The Balance of Payments.* London: Oxford Univ. Press, 1951.

Mundell, R. A. *International Economics.* New York: Macmillan, 1968.

Ott, D. J., and Ott, A. F. "Monetary and Fiscal Policy: Goals and the Choice of Instruments." *Q.J.E.* 83 (May 1968): 313–25.

Patrick, J. "The Optimum Policy Mix: Convergence and Consistency." In *The Open Economy,* edited by P. B. Kenen and R. Lawrence. New York: Columbia Univ. Press, 1968.

Prachowny, M. F. J. *A Structural Model of the U.S. Balance of Payments.* Amsterdam: North-Holland, 1969.

Rhomberg, R. R. "A Model of the Canadian Economy under Fixed and Fluctuating Exchange Rates." *J.P.E.* 72 (February 1964): 1–31.

Sohmen, E. "Fiscal and Monetary Policies under Alternative Exchange-Rate Systems." *Q.J.E.* 81 (August 1967): 515–23.

Theil, H. *Optimal Decision Rules for Government and Industry.* Amsterdam: North-Holland, 1964.

Tinbergen, J. *On the Theory of Economic Policy.* Amsterdam: North-Holland, 1952.

Willett, T. D., and Forte, F. "Interest-Rate Policy and External Balance." *Q.J.E.* 83 (May 1969): 242–62.

Wonnacott, P. *The Canadian Dollar, 1948–1958.* Toronto: Univ. Toronto Press, 1965.

Chapter 15

JOINT BALANCE: CAPITAL MOBILITY AND THE
MONETARY SYSTEM OF A CURRENCY AREA*

SVEN W. ARNDT

University of California, Santa Cruz

When two countries enter into a monetary union, the consequent
extension of their mutual dependence impinges upon the nature and
ordering of their economic goals and alters both qualitatively and
quantitatively the policy instruments in their individual and joint
possessions. The adoption of a uniform currency effectively removes
the monetary instrument from the individual country's arsenal, and
the freedom to employ fiscal controls is restricted because the transfer of monetary powers to the community constrains the available
means of financing government outlays. The latter constraints
operate even where each member country retains the right to issue
the common money, for monetary conditions within any country are
inseparably tied to conditions in the area at large.

The union's inception requires redefinition of individual and collective goals as well. While each member continues to strive for high
levels of domestic income and employment, the means by which each
seeks to achieve the internal objective have neighbourhood repercussions which exceed both in magnitude and profundity anything
that is likely to have existed when each acted in relative isolation. As
for the balance of payments, the currency union imposes a dicho-
tomy separating, as it does, the individual member's payments
balance with the rest of the union from that member's own and the
group's balance of payments with respect to the rest of the world.

In Section I below, the implications for internal and external
balance of various fiscal and monetary measures are examined in a
model in which two countries join in a currency union leaving a
third on the outside, and in which capital is perfectly mobile within

* Portions of this paper were completed while the author was Visiting Professor of Economics at the Johns Hopkins Centre for Advanced International
Studies in Bologna, Italy. I am greatly indebted to Professors Pascal Salin, Alexander Swoboda, Ray Canterbery and Jay Levin for their many helpful suggestions and comments, although any remaining errors are strictly my own.

the area but imperfectly mobile between the area and the rest of the world. The effect of the aforementioned policies on various targets is evaluated with and without the presence of wealth effects. The relevance of these considerations for the proper pairing of targets and instruments is briefly treated in Section II.

I A MODEL OF A CURRENCY AREA

The trading world is assumed to be composed of three countries, two of which – countries A and B – have formed a currency area, with the third country remaining outside but actively engaged in economic intercourse with the currency area. Within the area financial markets are completely integrated and a single currency acts as medium of exchange in both countries.

The system is described by the following four equations:

$$I(i) + T(Y,Y') + F(Y) + \alpha = S(Y) + \beta \tag{1}$$
$$I'(i) - T(Y,Y') + F'(Y') + \alpha' = S'(Y') + \beta' \tag{2}$$
$$L(Y,i) + L'(Y',i) + \theta = H \tag{3}$$
$$F(Y) + F'(Y') + K(i) + \lambda - B = 0 \tag{4}$$

where the price level is assumed constant and the external exchange rate fixed, and where Y and Y' represent current output in countries A and B, respectively; i is the area-wide rate of interest; and investment is represented by I, the intra-area trade balance by T, the external trade balance by F, saving by S, money demand by L, money supply by H, the external capital inflow by K, and the overall external balance of payments by B. Primed symbols denote analogously defined variables for country B. The α, β, θ and λ represent shift parameters. Thus, Equations (1) and (2) define equilibrium in domestic goods markets with the external sector of each country disaggregated into trade with the partner country, T, and trade with the outside world, F. This disaggregation is further reflected in the balance-of-payments equation in which F and F' sum to the total trade balance of the area with the outside. The capital inflow is not similarly disaggregated for the principal reason that the perfect mobility of capital within the area reduces the importance of that distinction.

There is no separate equation for the intra-union capital account, since with perfect capital mobility and in the absence of intra-area sterilization, the behaviour of the capital account may be ascertained

198   THE ECONOMICS OF COMMON CURRENCIES

directly from examination of the trade balance, T. However, while sterilization for purposes of offsetting the effects of intra-area trade imbalances does not take place, it is assumed that an area-wide exchange-equalization fund effectively sterilizes the repercussions of external payments disequilibria. It is assumed that the currency area is small relative to the rest of the world.

When differentiated totally, Equations (1) to (4) yield the equations of change.

$$
\begin{bmatrix}
-(S_y - T_y - F_y) & T_{y'} & I_i & 0 \\
-T_y & -(S'_{y'} + T_{y'} - F'_{y'}) & I'_i & 0 \\
L_y & L'_{y'} & (L_i + L'_i) & 0 \\
F_y & F'_{y'} & K_i & -1
\end{bmatrix}
\begin{bmatrix}
dY \\
dY' \\
di \\
dB
\end{bmatrix}
=
\begin{bmatrix}
d\beta - d\alpha \\
d\beta' - d\alpha' \\
dH - d\theta \\
-d\lambda
\end{bmatrix} \quad (5)
$$

where

$$S_y > 0, \quad S'_{y'} > 0; \qquad T_y < 0, \quad T_{y'} > 0;$$

$$F_y < 0, \quad F'_{y'} < 0; \qquad L_y > 0, \quad L'_{y'} > 0;$$

$$I_i < 0, \quad I'_i < 0; \qquad L_i < 0, \quad L'_i < 0; \qquad K_i > 0.$$

Any policy measure initiated in one country will affect not only that country's income and the external balance of payments, but in addition the area-wide interest rate and the level of income in the second country. Some implications of this interdependence are examined below.

The Impact of Fiscal Policy

The effect of an increase in government expenditures will vary with the manner of its financing. For simplicity we shall assume that tax collections support some basic level of government expenditures, but that all variations in fiscal policy made for purposes of achieving full employment or payments equilibrium are financed by supplying money or bonds or both. The government's budget constraint is thus

$$dG = dH + dS^* \quad (6)$$

where S^* is the stock of bonds.

The effect of an increase in government expenditures ($d\alpha$) on income (dY) in the first country is given in Equation (7) on the assumption that the money supply stays constant:

JOINT BALANCE 199

$$\frac{dY}{d\alpha} = -[(S'_{y'} + T_{y'} - F'_{y'})(L_i + L'_i) + I'_i L'_{y'}]/\Delta > 0 \qquad (7)$$

where the determinant of the system,

$$\Delta = -(L_i + L'_i)[(S_y - T_y - F_y)(S'_{y'} + T_{y'} - F'_{y'}) + T_y T_{y'}]$$
$$- I'_i[(S_y - T_y - F_y)L'_{y'} + L_y T_{y'}]$$
$$- I_i[(S'_{y'} + T_{y'} - F'_{y'})L_y - L'_{y'} T_y] > 0,$$

will be positive given the assumed signs of the partial derivatives. Further, the increase in country A's income is accompanied by an increase in the area-wide rate of interest:

$$\frac{di}{d\alpha} = [(S'_{y'} + T_{y'} - F'_{y'})L_y - T_y L'_{y'}]/\Delta > 0 \qquad (8)$$

The result that a fiscal expansion will raise the domestic income is well known from previous studies.[1] However, in a currency area, in which the relationships between the members exhibit strong characteristics of interdependence, a fiscal expansion in one country will generate significant repercussions in the rest of the area. As Equation (9) clearly indicates, an expansion in country A may bring about a recession in the partner country.[2]

$$\frac{dY'}{d\alpha} = [(L_i + L'_i)T_y + I'_i L_y]/\Delta \gtreqless 0 \qquad (9)$$

The likelihood that the initial effect of a boom in country A will be a downturn in country B is increased by a low area-wide interest-elasticity of demand for liquidity and a high interest-elasticity of investment demand in country B.[3] These interactions are presented diagrammatically in Figure 11.1, in which A_a and A_b represent equilibrium combinations of i and Y in the goods markets of the two

---

[1] For a review of the internal–external balance literature and for a detailed and exhaustive bibliography, see Whitman [5].

[2] This result was first shown by Mundell [3, Ch. 18 Appendix] for a two-country world. See also Kemp [2].

[3] The size of country A relative to country B is important, because a small L_i will produce a greater upward movement of the rate of interest in order to bring about the redistribution of liquidity required by the demand expansion in country A. The larger is country A and the more open its economy towards country B, the greater the chances that the positive trade effects will offset the negative effects on country B's level of income.

200   THE ECONOMICS OF COMMON CURRENCIES

countries, and in which L_T gives analogous combinations in the area-wide money market. External effects are ignored momentarily, but B_T represents external balance.

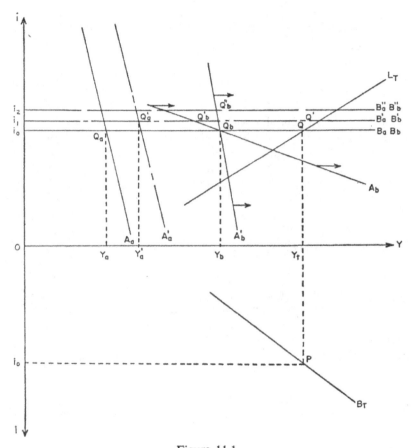

Figure 11.1

Curves A represent goods-market equilibrium. L_T gives the area-wide money market equilibrium. Curves BB show balance in intra-area trade. B_T gives external payments equilibrium.

The shift of A_a to A'_a disturbs the initial equilibrium established at points Q_a, Q_b and Q. At these points, the area-wide interest rate i_0 is consistent with absorption levels in the two countries of $O Y_a$ and $O Y_b$

and with the total demand for liquidity as indicated by Q on L_T. As a consequence of the expansion in country A the interest rate must rise, the extent to which it rises depending upon the slopes of the three functions. If goods market equilibrium in country B is given by the relatively interest-elastic curve A_b, the interest rate will rise to i_1, while a lower interest-elasticity of absorption (given by A_b) will cause the rate of interest to rise to i_2. Comparison of the two curves suggests that the initial depressing effect on country B's income of the expansion in country A will be greater, the more interest-responsive is absorption in country B.

This explains the effect of dα with the curve A_b held constant. However, the negative liquidity effect will tend to be partly or completely offset by the expansionary effect which is transmitted through the trade balance, T, and which serves to shift A_b and A'_b to the right; but it is clear from the figure that the magnitude of the export expansion required to offset the liquidity effect increases as the A_b-curve becomes flatter.

Thus, the use of fiscally expansive policies to alleviate problems of unemployment in one member of a currency area may create an aggravated employment situation in the partner country, a beggar-thy-neighbour outcome. Equation (9) provides the critical value at which country A's fiscal policy produces such undesirable effects.

In view of this conclusion, it is natural to ask whether fiscal expansion in one part of the union may not actually reduce total income and employment in the area taken as a whole. The condition under which that will be the case, i.e.

$$d(Y + Y')/d\alpha > 0,$$

is given by

$$-[(S'_{y'} + T_{y'} - F'_{y'})(L_i + L'_i) + I_i L'_{y'}] + T_y(L_i + L'_i) < -I'_i L_y.$$

One means of achieving this result is to make the interest-responsiveness of the community's demand for liquidity $(L_i + L'_i)$ sufficiently small while increasing country B's relative interest-elasticity of investment demand.

The conditions which determine the impact of country A's fiscal expansion on country B's income and employment also play an important role in establishing the effect of the policy on the overall balance of payments. That effect is given by

202   THE ECONOMICS OF COMMON CURRENCIES

$$\frac{dB}{d\alpha} = \{K_i[(S'_{y'} + T_{y'} - F'_{y'})L_y - T_y L'_{y'}] - F_y[(S'_{y'} + T_{y'} - F'_{y'})(L_i + L'_i) +$$
$$+ I'_i L'_{y'}] + F'_{y'}[(L_i + L'_i)T_y + I'_i L_y]\}/\Delta \gtreqless 0. \tag{10}$$

The first term of this expression is positive and represents the net capital inflow occasioned by the higher domestic interest rate which follows the fiscal expansion. The second term, which collects the effect of the growth in country A's income on its trade with the outside world, is negative. As is well known, the net effect of these conflicting forces may be to improve or worsen the balance of payments. However, as the third term, which may be positive or negative, is added, the overall balance of payments will improve if the fiscal expansion in country A brings about a sufficiently severe depression in country B. There is a second beggar-thy-neighbour element here, for in addition to drawing to itself a greater portion of the currency area's liquidity, country A obtains further benefits from country B's declining demand for, or increased generation of, foreign exchange reserves.

The Budget Constraint

We now examine the constraint which is imposed by the budget equation, Equation (6), and concentrate, first, on the case of deficit finance. The flow supply of bonds which accompanies the fiscal expansion, serves to increase the wealth of the community, where wealth is defined as the sum of physical capital K (assumed constant), money balances H, and bonds S^*, and where it is assumed that future tax liabilities arising out of financing the national debt are *not* discounted by the public

$$W = \bar{K} + \bar{K}' + H + H' + S^* + S'^*. \tag{11}$$

Variations in wealth tend to work their effects on several of the aggregate variables, including consumption, the demand for liquidity and the external accounts. Introduction of a wealth term generates both stock and flow adjustment; full equilibrium will not be achieved while the stock of wealth is changing.

Of primary interest here is the immediate and short-term effect of the steady growth of the public's holdings of government securities. For if we assume that the initial income level represents equilibrium for the system, so that the targeted level of income and employment can be *maintained* only if the budget deficit is itself maintained, there will be forthcoming a steady supply of bonds resulting in a steady change in the composition and the magnitude of the community's wealth.[1]

In the first place, the increase in wealth increases domestic consumption, the distribution of the effect depending upon the extent to which holders of bonds in the two countries alter their consumption and savings behaviour. The increase in consumption is introduced into the model by setting $d\beta < 0$, $d\beta' < 0$. Thus, the effect on income of a shift in the consumption function will operate in the same direction as that associated with $d\alpha$ and $d\alpha'$. Specifically,

$$dY/d\beta > 0, \qquad dY'/d\beta \gtreqless 0$$

and

$$dY'/d\beta' > 0, \qquad dY/d\beta' \gtreqless 0.$$

The wealth effect on consumption in country A thus supports the fiscal expansion in raising income, while the same fiscal expansion may have positive or negative repercussions for country B. But to the extent that a wealth effect which raises consumption expenditures emerges in country B ($d\beta' < 0$), it will serve to generate additional income there ($dY'/d\beta' > 0$) and thus tend to alleviate the possibly adverse initial effects of country A's fiscal expansion.

Second, the growth in the community's wealth, together with the mounting one-sidedness of portfolios which increasingly consist of bonds, tends to increase the demand for liquidity. This monetary effect is represented by the shift parameter in Equation (3), i.e. $d\theta > 0$. Algebraically, the effect is similar to that of a decrease in the money stock ($dH < 0$) and the reader is referred to Equations (12) to (15) below.

The monetary effect of the fiscal operation is thus to raise the rate of interest not only because a greater transactions demand is implied by the government's expansionary activity, but also because the steady change in portfolios generates a further demand for money balances.

Income in country A will continue to increase so long as the combined direct effect of the greater government demand and the wealth-induced shift in consumption expenditures exceeds the negative repercussions of the rise in the rate of interest on investment demand.

[1] For an analysis of wealth effects in a closed economy see Silber [4].

Variations in the rate of interest affect wealth through their effect on S^* (we would replace S^* and S'^* with S^*/i and S'^*/i). This so-called Metzler effect is assumed to be negligible.

As long as the interest rate continues to rise and thus exerts its contractionary impact on the system, the wealth effect adds a further dimension to the beggar-thy-neighbour attributes of the fiscal expansion in country A. Even if the initial impact of the expansion in country A is favourable to country B ($\mathrm{d}\,Y'/\mathrm{d}\alpha > 0$) – where we assume that country B is burdened with excess capacity and thus welcomes the expansionary pressures emanating from country A – the wealth-induced rise in interest rates eventually dampens the expansionary pressures.

The potentially disruptive implications of the wealth effect for both countries could be moderated by developments in the external accounts, if the rising rate of interest were permitted to attract foreign capital and thus to expand the currency area's money stock. But for as long as the authorities pursue sterilization policies, this will not occur.

The Impact of Monetary Policy

When wealth effects are not considered, monetary policy works according to well-established patterns: an increase in the money stock raises incomes in both countries and worsens the external balance. Specifically,

$$\frac{\mathrm{d}Y}{\mathrm{d}H} = -[(S'_{y'} + T_{y'} - F'_{y'})I_i + T_{y'}I'_i]/\Delta > 0 \tag{12}$$

$$\frac{\mathrm{d}Y'}{\mathrm{d}H} = [I_iT_y - (S_y - T_y - F_y)I'_i]/\Delta > 0 \tag{13}$$

$$\frac{\mathrm{d}i}{\mathrm{d}H} = -[(S_y - F_y)(S'_{y'} + T_{y'} - F'_{y'}) - T_y(S'_{y'} - F'_{y'})]/\Delta < 0 \tag{14}$$

$$\frac{\mathrm{d}B}{\mathrm{d}H} = \{-K_i[(S_y - T_y - F_y)(S'_{y'} + T_{y'} - F'_{y'}) + T_yT_{y'}] -$$
$$- F'_{y'}[S_y - T_y - F_y)I'_i - I_iT_y] - F_y[(S'_{y'} + T_{y'} -$$
$$- F'_{y'})I_i + I'_iT_{y'}]\}/\Delta < 0. \tag{15}$$

It is again noteworthy that while a monetary expansion will improve income and employment in both countries, such increases need be neither absolutely nor proportionally equal. Suppose, in Figure 11.1, that both countries are faced with identical absolute deviations of actual incomes from targeted incomes, i.e. $(Y^*_a - Y_a) = (Y^*_b - Y_b)$, which implies that country A has a larger relative gap to bridge. In view of the respective slopes of the two countries' internal schedules, country A's task of reaching Y_a^* is complicated by the relative steepness of its internal absorption schedule. It is clear that a monetary expansion which suffices to move country A to its target Y_a^* will bring about substantial inflationary pressures in country B. From the point of view of a member of the currency area the efficacy of monetary measures as a control policy is diminished as this type of 'dominance' of the rest of the area increases.

It follows that the magnitude of the overall payments deficit which follows the monetary expansion is also affected by the manner in which the two economies respond to the monetary stimulus. The overall trade balance with the outside world will deteriorate less severely if the country which responds more strongly to the monetary stimulus – in this case country B – has the smaller foreign trade coefficient – in this case $F_{y'}'$. [1]

Monetary Policy and Wealth Effects

As the expansionary monetary policy creates new money it also increases the community's wealth. The repercussions within the system may be analysed in a manner analogous to that employed in the case of deficit finance, the principal difference between the two situations being the impossibility for the interest rate to rise, although the downward pressures exerted on credit conditions are mitigated by the higher demand for liquidity occasioned by the growth in wealth. [2]

Comparison of the policy alternatives brings out several important differences. A fiscal expansion financed by bond sales gives rise to a wealth-induced increase in consumption expenditures which would tend *ceteris paribus* to reduce the level of government expenditure required to maintain the desired level of income and employment. However, as a result of the rising rate of interest the level of private

---

[1] It should be noted that country A can magnify the effect of the monetary expansion on its own income by redirecting country B's foreign trade to country A's own product, i.e. by increasing $T_{y'}$ at the expense of $F_{y'}'$.

[2] If the community diversifies its holdings among domestic (S_f^*) and foreign bonds (S_f^*) and domestic money balances (H), the monetary expansion gives rise to a continuing importation of foreign securities. This wealth effect on the capital account may be represented by specifying $d\lambda < 0$, which in turn implies that $dB/d\lambda = -1$. Thus, the impact of wealth changes on the balance of payments is to aggravate the deterioration brought about by the usual effects of the monetary expansion. Neither the external sector nor the internal economy can be in equilibrium while $dW \neq 0$.

206   THE ECONOMICS OF COMMON CURRENCIES

sector investment is diminished, raising the possibility that the net change in private absorption will be negative in which case larger doses of fiscal policy will be called for. This does not mean, however, that over some interval income cannot rise in the fiscally expanding country; it merely raises the possibility of an eventual decline in income.

If, on the other hand, the additional government outlays are financed by money creation ($dH/d\alpha = 1$), the aforementioned negative internal effects of the rising rate of interest will at least be mitigated. As a consequence, the positive wealth effect on consumption is supported by favourable interest rate-induced changes in investment expenditure. Any such net increase in private sector expenditure facilitates the maintenance of higher levels of income with smaller budget deficits, with the important consequence that, unlike the debt-financed fiscal stimulus, the present policy does not call for a 'permanent' budget deficit in order to maintain the desired level of income. In the case of a monetary expansion, wealth effects will occur while the money stock is increased from its initial to its final level, but these *changes* will end when the stock adjustment has been completed.

II ASSIGNING THE AREA'S INSTRUMENTS TO TARGETS

Many of the rules and conditions which determine the proper pairing of targets and instruments and which have been examined in the literature with reference to a single country or a two-country world, apply to the situation examined in Section I.[1] It is the purpose of this section to suggest a number of peculiarities which are a consequence of the addition of a 'third country'.

Among these the classification of targets and of instruments is of some interest. In a two-country world in which each member pursues an internal target of full employment and an external target of payments balance, and in which imperfectly mobile international capital provides each country with two policy instruments, one fiscal, the other monetary, one of the four control variables will be redundant. This outcome results from the symmetry of the balance of payments.[2]

[1] Cf. Whitman [5] for a survey of the literature on the single-country case, and Mundell [3, Ch. 18 Appendix] and Kemp [2] for the two-country case.
[2] The redundancy problem arises only if the payments goals are defined symmetrically so that one country's surplus is exactly the other's deficit, and if both are agreed on the speed with which the external target is to be achieved. With

JOINT BALANCE   207

The present situation is different in two respects. First, while it is still true that $T' = -T$, this condition does not insure that

$$(T' + F') = -(T + F),$$

if indeed the latter statement has any meaning at all. Consequently, each country may be concerned with both its intra-area trade balance and with its balance with the outside world, without there being any helpful symmetry. Thus, if each country worries about its 'internal' and its 'external' trade balance, the number of targets will exceed the number of available instruments. Second, perfect mobility of capital within the area effectively limits the monetary instrument to a single one, even if each member retains the right to issue the common money.

With the number of control variables limited to three, the number of independent targets is similarly limited to three, and the set consisting of $\{Y, Y', B\}$ suggests itself as a plausible selection. We shall assume therefore that the internal trade balance is not a policy target.

Monetary policy is normally considered the more efficient instrument for manipulation of the balance of payments. This is so because a monetary expansion worsens the trade balance by increasing income and the capital account by reducing the rate of interest, while a fiscal expansion worsens one while improving the other; and it may indeed produce a payments surplus if the capital inflow induced by the higher rate of interest is large enough to offset the deterioration in the trade balance. A fiscal expansion in a member country is more likely to produce an overall payments surplus if as a result of such an expansion income in the second country declines (see Equation (10)).

When wealth effects are considered, the monetary expansion which is required to achieve a desired reduction in the surplus will be smaller than otherwise because the wealth effect will tend to worsen both capital and current accounts. In the case of a fiscal expansion which is financed through bond sales, the capital account improves because the interest rate increases. The upward pressures on the rate of interest are perpetuated by the government's need to finance the

respect to the latter condition, redundancy will fail to emerge, for example, if one country assigns its monetary instrument to external balance, but, being the surplus country, does so at a speed which is inconsistent with the speed at which the second country's reserves are being depleted. In that event, the second country will have to employ the fourth instrument to change the *rate* of payments adjustment.

208   THE ECONOMICS OF COMMON CURRENCIES

deficit beyond the initial period, and the accumulation of bonds relative to money balances in private portfolios raises the public's price of accepting further additions to the stock of bonds.[1] This in turn suggests that the positive balance-of-payments effects of the fiscal expansion must come eventually to dominate the negative trade-balance effect, so that in the absence of a strong wealth effect on the consumption of foreign goods, a moderate policy of deficit finance can bring about a steady improvement in the external accounts.

Thus, a fiscal expansion aimed at internal balance will continue to exert its effects on the balance of payments even after it has achieved its domestic objectives, although it may, as we have seen, lead ultimately to a reduction in income. A fiscal expansion aimed at the balance of payments must similarly be continued because the positive payments effects are contingent upon a constant expansion of wealth and a continuing increase in the rate of interest. Once the fiscal policy is terminated and the portfolio adjustment completed (where the time required for such completion may be longer than the policy-planning horizon), the capital inflow will cease.[2]

An additional difficulty in assigning fiscal policy lies in deciding which country's fiscal instrument is to be used for what purpose. It is possible, as has already been noted, for fiscal expansion in one country to reduce not only income in the other country, but income in the area as a whole. Such a policy will not therefore be very useful in achieving the goal of higher community income and employment, although it can increase the income of the country using the policy. But this does not rule out completely the use of fiscal policy in the pursuit of internal objectives, because fiscal expansion undertaken in the second country need not have similarly unfavourable effects on the level of activity in the partner country. To see how this is possible, the following conditions may be compared:

$$\frac{dY'}{d\alpha} < 0 \qquad \text{if } T_y(L_i + L_i') < -I_i'L_y$$

---

[1] If the public is assumed to hold foreign bonds as well, the increase in domestic bond holdings induces some substitution of foreign for domestic bonds. Whatever the combinations of securities held, equilibrium in the markets described in Equations (1) to (4) implies equilibrium in the asset market.

[2] As all such models, the present one has the important weakness of ignoring changes in the capital stock, and the relationship between physical capital and other assets in the wealth equation.

JOINT BALANCE 209

$$\frac{\mathrm{d}Y}{\mathrm{d}\alpha'} < 0 \qquad \text{if } -T_{y'}(L_i + L_i') < -I_i L_{y'}'.$$

Both inequalities contain $(L_i + L'_i)$, but by suitable manipulation of the remaining partials one of the inequalities may be made to hold, the other to fail. For example, by making $|T_y|$ very large relative to $|I_i'|$, a fiscal expansion in country A can be made to raise income in country B, while a very small $T_{y'}$ relative to $|I_i|$ will cause income in country A to fall when country B undertakes domestic fiscal stimulation.

That being the case, there are considerable economies to be gained from the efficient assignment of instruments, and that can normally be accomplished by intra-area policy co-ordination. The community thus gains not only from the obvious need to co-ordinate policies in the joint monetary sector, but from co-ordination in the efficient allocation of the two fiscal instruments.

References

[1] Cooper, Richard N., 'Macroeconomic Policy Adjustment in Inter-dependent Economies', *Quarterly Journal of Economics*, Vol. 83, No. 1 (February 1969) pp. 1–24.
[2] Kemp, M. C., 'Monetary and Fiscal Policy under Alternative Assumptions about International Capital Mobility', *Economic Record*, Vol. 42, No. 4 (December 1966) pp. 598–605.
[3] Mundell, R. A., *International Economics* (Macmillan, New York, 1968).
[4] Silber, W. L., 'Fiscal Policy in IS–LM Analysis: A Correction', *Journal of Money, Credit, and Banking*, Vol. 2 (November 1970) pp. 461–72.
[5] Whitman, M.v.N., 'Policies for Internal and External Balance', *Special Papers in International Finance*, No. 9 (International Finance Section, Princeton, December 1970).

Chapter 16

INTERNATIONAL SHORT TERM CAPITAL MOVEMENTS: A DISTRIBUTED LAG MODEL OF SPECULATION IN FOREIGN EXCHANGE[1]

BY SVEN W. ARNDT

The role of speculative short term capital movements in balance of payments adjust-ment and in exchange market stability is examined. A theory of speculative behavior with a distributed lag model of expectation formation at its core is developed and empirically tested using the Canadian data for the period 1952–1960. Tests of an alternative but generically similar specification of the model are also presented and discussed.

1. INTRODUCTION

IN THE PRESENT paper we report the results of a study of the formulation of speculators' expectations about the future movement of the foreign exchange rate and the manner in which these expectations are translated into decisions to buy or sell foreign exchange. This problem has received some treatment in the literature. In several elegant and sophisticated theoretical models Baumol [1, 2], Canterbery [4], Einzig [6], Sohmen [17], Telser [19], and Tsiang [20] have dealt with the nature of speculative behavior. The emphasis of these studies was such, however, that the actual determination of the expected rate could be ignored.

In empirical models, on the other hand, the expected rate must be constructed in some way. This has generally been accomplished by the use of some proxy variable, such as the forward rate, to describe speculative expectations. But other variables may also be used. Some work along these lines has recently been done, notably by Kenen [10], Powrie [14], Rhomberg [15, 16], and Wonnacott [21].

In what follows we shall attempt to link expectations directly to observed variables. The theory in its simplest form is presented in Section 2. It is tested against the data of the Canadian flexible exchange period. In Section 4 the model is expanded to include other determining variables. Empirical estimates are also presented. The findings of this study are discussed in Section 6.

2. EXPECTATIONS AND SPECULATIVE DECISION MAKING

In the theoretical literature the analysis of speculative behavior has been concerned most prominently with the proposition, first enunciated by Friedman [7], that speculation can be destabilizing only if speculators on the average incur

[1] This study was supported by the UCLA Bureau of Business and Economic Research and by the UCLA Committee on International and Comparative Studies, the latter with funding from the Ford Foundation. The Western Data Processing Center provided computing facilities. Grateful acknowledge-ment is made to Professors Peter B. Kenen and John H. Williamson for comments on an earlier draft. They are, of course, absolved from responsibility for any·errors that remain.

losses. Let us assume, to begin the argument, that there exists a foreign exchange market which is characterized by perfect foresight and in which the price of foreign exchange, as determined by nonspeculative market forces, follows a perfect cycle; that is, the time path of the exchange rate is given by the sinusoidal function

(1) $r_1(t) = A \sin(\omega t + \varepsilon)$,

where r_1 is the rate of exchange, or the price in terms of the domestic currency of one unit of the foreign currency. If we assume further, that comparable short term interest rates in different international financial centers are maintained at identical levels as a matter of policy and that no forward market facilities exist, it follows that speculators will plan to sell foreign exchange at peaks of the cycle and purchase exchange at its troughs.

When the assumptions of certainty and of the perfectly cyclical time path are dropped, speculators will be uncertain about the turning points and thus about the precise moment at which transactions should be initiated. In his famous counter-example, Baumol [1] argued that since speculators will have knowledge of turning points only after they have occurred, it is possible that they will enter the market after the movement in the price has changed direction. Thus, speculative sales will take place during the downswing and purchases will be made during the upswing. Defining stabilization as the reduction of the frequency and the amplitude of price movements, Baumol concluded that his was a case in which speculation that was profitable, but not profit maximizing, was nevertheless destabilizing.

Baumol's model has been severely criticized, especially by Telser [19]. For us it forms a convenient starting point. To generalize the argument, it is useful at this point to change the focus of the analysis. Specifically, we examine the deviations of the actual current rate from some "expected normal" rate. We consider the following hypothesis:

(2) $S_t = \alpha(r_t - r_t^*) + u_{1t}$,

where S represents speculative capital flows (inflows are positive), r stands for the observed rate and r^* for the expected normal rate. The latter is not known directly and must thus be related to observables. For this purpose we propose the following hypothesis about the formation of exchange rate expectations:

(3) $r_t^* - r_{t-1}^* = (1 - \lambda)(r_t - r_{t-1}^*)$, $0 \leqslant \lambda \leqslant 1$.

Thus, current expectations are adjusted by a proportion of the deviation of the actual current rate from the previous expected normal rate. We may think of the change in the current rate—measured as the deviation from r_{t-1}^*—as consisting of a long term and a temporary or short term component. The ratio of these will be a function of the speculators' average time horizon. The longer the latter, the larger the short term component, which is measured by λ. Expectations will be adjusted according to the long term component of the change, i.e., in the proportion $(1-\lambda)$.[2]

Equation (3) may be solved for r_t^*:

(4a) $r_t^* = (1-\lambda) \sum_{i=0} \lambda^i r_{t-i}$,

(4b) $(1-\lambda) \sum_{i=0} \lambda^i = 1$.

Expressions (4) take the form of the familiar distributed lag function. The time shape of this lag is a descending geometric series and is given by (4b).[3] Substitution of (4a) into (2) and utilization of the Koyck [11] transform[4] yields the following estimating equation:

(6) $S_t = \alpha\lambda(r_t - r_{t-1}) + \lambda S_{t-1} + u_{1t} - \lambda u_{it-1}$.

Speculative capital movements are thus related to changes in the exchange rate and to the lagged value of the dependent variable. The coefficient associated with the latter is an estimate of the constant used in the weighting function.

3. SOME EMPIRICAL RESULTS

To test this model, we selected the years 1952–1960 of the Canadian flexible exchange rate period.[5] Ideally, one would like one's data to be available in neat categories separating speculative from nonspeculative movements. This is conceptually difficult and practically impossible. In Canadian balance of payments statistics for that period, total short term capital flows are divided into two sub-

---

[2] We may note, that in terms of the Hicksian concept of the elasticity of expectations, $E = (\Delta r^*/\Delta r) \cdot (r/r^*)$, $(1-\lambda)$ gives the coefficient of expectations.

[3] The discussion in the text has moved directly from the continuous function (1) to the discrete case of (4). For purposes of the subsequent empirical analysis this formulation is desirable. An expression for r_t^* where the lag is exponential may be derived analogously, however:

(5a) $r^*(t) = \beta \int_0^\infty e^{-\beta\tau} r(t-\tau) d\tau$,

(5b) $\beta \int_0^\infty e^{-\beta\tau} d\tau = 1$.

We take note of this relationship here; in the remainder of the paper we will be concerned with the discrete case only.

[4] For a related analysis, see Nerlove [13]. Distributed lag models are finding increasing application in econometric work. They have been used in studies of the consumption function, notably by Friedman [8] and Zellner [22].

[5] The data are balance of payments figures published by the Bureau of Statistics. They are on a quarterly basis and have been seasonally adjusted by the author using the Census Bureau Method II seasonal adjustment program.

categories, namely, "changes in Canadian dollar holdings of foreigners" ("changes") and "other capital movements" ("other"). The latter is a general catchall category which includes, among other things, a number of long term transactions plus the "errors and omissions" item which many other countries treat as a separate entry. Since details are not consistently available, it is impossible to construct a meaningful series giving speculative capital flows alone.

The difficulties associated with the construction of time series of speculative transactions are compounded by the fact that such a series would have to include not only "pure" speculation but speculative sales and purchases undertaken in conjunction with or as a byproduct of other balance of payments transactions, particularly leads and lags in payments by commercial importers and exporters. Thus, each one of the aforementioned subcategories of short term capital movements may be expected to contain a speculative component which cannot be isolated and presented separately.

Further, since speculative sales and purchases are generally assumed to be short term in nature, some importance attaches to the definition of what constitutes the short run. One may separate short term and long term capital movements by considering either the date to maturity of the traded asset or the motivation underlying the transaction. Thus, the purchase by a foreigner of a Canadian debt instrument with more than one year to maturity, the price of which the purchaser considers to be excessively subnormal and thus to rise in the near future, would be classified as a long term inflow on the first criterion, but as short term on the second. Motivations, of course, are difficult to quantify; individuals are often uncertain about their dominant motivation and may alter such motivation over time. For these reasons the date-to-maturity criterion is the one ordinarily employed.

Nevertheless, it is clear that this may introduce a substantial bias into the time series. In the Canadian case, the set of transactions most affected by this definitional problem consists of what the Bureau of Statistics calls "trade in outstanding securities" ("trade"). Most empirical workers have followed the Bureau's practice of excluding this item from short term capital flows.[6]

Since it was our purpose to explain speculative behavior, it seemed undesirable to exclude "trade" on a priori grounds. We decided to run some experiments using each one of the three subcategories, as well as various combinations of these, as the dependent variable. It turned out that "trade" and "other" flows gave approximately equal results; the performance of both surpassed that of "changes," and the total category composed of all these provided the most satisfactory outcome. On the basis of these results, it seemed clear that, if the theory was correct, "trade" contained a significant speculative element. As it appears in the equations below, S therefore includes "trade."

Finally, a choice needs to be made between bilateral Canada–United States capital flows and movements between Canada and the rest of the world. Again,

[6] Wonnacott [21], however, does consider these movements to be short term flows.

both alternatives were tried in preliminary runs and it was found that "global" flows gave better overall results. This is probably due to the fact that a significant proportion of Canada's third country transactions passed through New York markets.

The model was first tested using classical least squares (CLS). As will be seen, the calculated Durbin-Watson statistic leads to rejection of the hypothesis of serial correlation in the residuals. Similar conclusions were obtained when regression tests for correlation among the residuals were run. Griliches [9] and others, however, have pointed out that the d-statistic may be biased toward $2n/n - 1$ in distributed lag models. The presence of such bias will lead to inconsistent CLS estimates of the coefficient of the lagged dependent variable. To investigate the possibility of serial correlation in the composite error term, i.e., in $v_t = u_t - \lambda u_{t-1}$, we selected an alternative estimating procedure. Specifically, we made use of the "three pass least squares" method (3PLS) suggested by Taylor and Wilson [18]. The results obtained with Classical Least Squares are as follows:

$$S_t = 31.34 \, (r_t - r_{t-1}) + .72 \, S_{t-1} \qquad (R^2 = .59; \; d = 2.048) \, .$$
$$\quad (10.22) \qquad\qquad (.11)$$

Three Pass Least Squares yielded:

$$S_t = 32.30 \, (r_t - r_{t-1}) + .87 \, S_{t-1} - .08 \, u^*_{t-1} \qquad (d = 2.125) \, .$$
$$\quad (14.06) \qquad\qquad (.18) \qquad (.27)$$

The calculated residual term is u^* which falls out of the first and second passes of this method. Its coefficient is statistically insignificant. All other coefficients are significant and their signs follow theoretical expectations. One of the versions of the models tested included a constant term, but the latter failed in most cases to become significant. The value of the coefficient of determination, R^2, suggests that the model has significant explanatory power. In the light of our inability to test the model against a time series giving speculative flows only, this overall fit may be important. We see that a unit increase in $(r_t - r_{t-1})$ will lead to a short term capital inflow of \$31 million.

TABLE I

λ	r_t	r_{t-1}	r_{t-2}	r_{t-3}	r_{t-4}	r_{t-5}	Total
.72	.280	.201	.145	.104	.074	.053	.857
.87	.130	.113	.098	.085	.074	.064	.564

It is the coefficient of S_{t-1}, however, that is of particular interest. Going back to equations (4), we can now estimate the effect on expectations of a change in the current rate. Table I gives the weights assigned to the exchange rates in the six most recent quarters for $\lambda = .72$ and $\lambda = .87$, respectively. It is clear that speculators demonstrate considerable inertia and resistance to alterations in their current expectations about the normal rate. Thus, the expected normal rate may be assumed to change very slowly. In terms of equation (2), we see that the larger is λ, the smaller will be the effect on r_t^* of a given change in the current rate, the larger will be the resulting deviation of current from expected rate, and the larger, consequently, will be sales or purchases of foreign exchange by speculators. For example, as the current actual rate rises above the expected normal rate, the growing deviation of the two rates will produce increasing sales of foreign exchange. These sales will tend to inhibit further increases in the current rate. We conclude that speculators do not on the average wait for the turning points before entering the exchange market.

4. THE ROLE OF INTEREST DIFFERENTIALS AND OF THE FORWARD RATE

It has long been taken for granted by theoreticians and policy makers alike that, in addition to the expected and current exchange rates, speculators may be influenced by interest differentials among the relevant financial centers. More generally, and since our dependent variable includes all short term capital flows, it has been argued that the latter will contain an interest arbitrage component. In some recent studies, Bell [3] and Kenen [10] have examined various United States short term flows for interest sensitivity. Their contradictory findings are well known. However, as Cohen [5] has suggested, these contradictions are more apparent than real and arise in part from differences in theoretical emphasis and in research technique.

In this section we present several alternative attempts to test the interest sensitivity of short term capital flows.[7] We have chosen the difference between Canadian and United States three months treasure bill rates as the representative variable. We shall consider the covered (B) and uncovered (C) interest differentials as two alternative forms of the model. The model as given in equation (2) above is now respecified as follows:

$$(7) \qquad S_t = \alpha_1(r_t - r_t^*) + \alpha_2 C_t + u_{2t} .$$

Combining equations (4) and (7), and utilizing the Koyck transform, we obtain:

$$(8) \qquad S_t = \alpha_1 \lambda(r_t - r_{t-1}) + \alpha_2 C_t - \alpha_2 \lambda C_{t-1} + \lambda S_{t-1} + u_{2t} - \lambda u_{2t-1} .$$

Analogous results are obtained for B when the latter is substituted for C in equation (7).

As it stands, equation (8) is overidentified. In particular, the coefficient associ-

---

[7] Given the definition of S, we will be measuring not only the response of speculators, but that of covered interest arbitragers as well.

ated with the lagged interest variables may be estimated directly, or it may be obtained from estimates of the coefficients of the current interest variable and the lagged dependent variable. In general, the two estimates will be different. To avoid this difficulty, we make explicit use of the nonlinear constraints imposed on the coefficients: apart from the sign, the coefficient of the lagged interest variable is the product of the coefficients of the current interest variable and of the lagged dependent variable. The presence of nonlinearity in the parameters requires the use of a nonlinear estimating technique.[8]

TABLE II
FREE ESTIMATES

Variable	Uncovered Differential		Covered Differential	
	Equation (8)	Equation (9)	Equation (8)	Equation (9)
S_{t-1}	.55	.74	.73	.75
	(.13)	(.10)	(.12)	(.11)
$(r_t - r_{t-1})$	34.01	33.39	32.29	32.19
	(9.65)	(11.35)	(12.65)	(12.44)
B_t	—	—	5.13	—
			(15.38)	
B_{t-1}	—	—	−9.64	—
			(14.93)	
C_t	64.05	—	—	—
	(23.18)			
C_{t-1}	−33.84	—	—	—
	(22.38)			
$B_t - B_{t-1}$	—	—	—	7.97
				(15.38)
$C_t - C_{t-1}$	—	51.43	—	—
		(21.25)		
R^2	.71	.62	.56	.56
d	2.143	2.125	2.027	2.047

In Table II we present the free estimates for equation (8) using B and C alternatively.[9] Table III presents nonlinear estimates for that model. In both tests the coefficients of $(r_t - r_{t-1})$ and S_{t-1} are several times their respective standard errors. As for the interest variables, the signs are as predicted, a fact which is, for purposes of testing the explanatory power of the model, particularly important in the case of the lagged value of the variable. While the coefficient associated with the latter

[8] The computer program which was used for this purpose is based on Marquardt [12].

[9] Specifically, C is the Canadian three months treasury bill rate, i_c, minus the comparable United States rate, i_u; $B = (i_c - i_u) - (r' - r)/r$ where r' is the forward exchange rate, and where the forward premium is taken in per cent per annum to make it comparable to the interest differential.

is statistically insignificant where free estimates are used, the nonlinear estimate becomes significant for the uncovered interest differential. This does not make the latter unequivocally superior to the covered differential, however, since there was probably some multicollinearity present in this case: the spot exchange rate appears in the first three terms of the equation.

TABLE III

NONLINEAR ESTIMATES

| Parameter | Equation (8) | |
	Uncovered Differential	Covered Differential
λ	.55	.72
	(.17)	(.12)
α_1	70.50	45.74
	(28.17)	(19.56)
α_2	79.46	7.08
	(10.32)	(9.36)

Finally, introduction of the uncovered interest differential reduces the size of the coefficient of S_{t-1}. With $\lambda = .55$, the weights attached to the most recent six quarters are .45, .248, .136, .075, .041, .023, respectively. Even in this case, the impact of past periods is relatively important. It is possible, however, that the presence of multicollinearity caused this low estimate of λ. We will see below that substitution of first differences restores the value of λ to its earlier levels. Nevertheless, we note the possibility of this outcome.

It is also quite likely that the estimating equation is one of a system of simultaneous equations. While this is probably true of all of our models, the introduction of the two interest rates and of the forward rate vastly increases this possibility.

Close inspection of the foregoing results suggests still another possible formulation of the influence of interest differentials. It is especially apparent in the case of the uncovered differential that the coefficients of the current and lagged values are each other's negative. It may thus prove instructive to combine the terms and to test the following version of the model, which is here given for C. An analogous equation may be written for B.

$$(9) \qquad S_t = \beta_1(r_t - r_{t-1}) + \beta_2(C_t - C_{t-1}) + \lambda S_{t-1} + \varepsilon_t .$$

The estimates for equation (9) have been included in Table II above. We find again, that the uncovered differential produces better results. This would tend to reinforce our preference for C as the more relevant explanatory variable. As for the coefficients of the remaining variables, they are largely unchanged from previous models and are several times their standard errors. We note, moreover, that the value of λ is .74, which is consistent with most of our earlier estimates.

We may conclude, therefore, that interest rate considerations play a significant role in determination of these capital flows. This result tends to be consistent with the findings of Kenen [10], although the different approach of the latter study makes detailed comparison hazardous. Bell [3], on the other hand, was generally unsuccessful in attempts to establish a significant relationship between short term flows and interest rates.

Bell did find strong correlation, however, between various short term capital flows and United States exports. Kenen rejected the significance of such trade credit. For our data, the simple correlation coefficient between the trade balance and S_t was $-.50$. While simple regression of S_t on the trade balance produced significant results, however, the coefficient associated with the latter became insignificant when the variable was added to the full model. Multicollinearity may have been present in the model.

5. SHORT TERM CAPITAL FLOWS AND THE TREND EXCHANGE RATE

If our models are correctly specified and if the estimates of λ are consistent, we may conclude that the expected rate will change very slowly over time and that the actual rate will fluctuate about this expected rate, with short term capital flows tending to inhibit the magnitude of these fluctuations. This relationship suggests the following experiment, the outcome of which may support our earlier arguments that speculative flows will tend to reduce the variance of r.

We computed the trend exchange rate, which in this particular case has a moderately negative slope, and used this rate in place of the expected normal rate in earlier models. Clearly, this implies substitution of a new weighting function for that employed in (4b). Deviations of spot and forward rates from the trend rate were then tested in several alternative specifications of the model. The following case, using seasonally unadjusted data for the period 1951–1960, provided the best overall result:

$$Y_t = 76.14 \, X_{1t} + 48.95 \, X_{2t} + 26.28 \, X_{3t} - 22.62 \, X_{4t} - .57 \, X_{5t}$$
$$\quad (13.70) \qquad (20.08) \qquad (8.29) \qquad (6.74) \qquad (.11)$$
$$\quad - .41 \, X_{6t} + 45.25 \, X_7 + 68.11 \, X_8 - 7.82 \, X_9 \qquad (R^2 = .90) \, ,$$
$$\quad (.11) \qquad (20.25) \qquad (20.99) \qquad (22.67)$$

where Y is short term capital movements; X_1, the uncovered interest differential (Canada–U.S.); X_2, the covered interest differential (Canada–U.S.); X_3, the deviation of spot rate from trend rate; X_4, deviation of forward rate from trend rate; X_5, net long term capital movements; X_6, the net current account; and X_7–X_9, seasonal dummy variables.

All coefficients, except one associated with a seasonal dummy, are several times their standard errors and all signs correspond to theoretical expectations. While the equation is in all probability one of a system of simultaneous equations, the overall result is nevertheless interesting for several reasons. First, both covered and uncovered interest differentials enter the equation with significant coefficients.[10] Second, deviations from the trend rate of both the spot and forward rates produce "desirable" capital flows. For example, an increase in the spot rate relative to the trend rate induces sales of foreign exchange. This result would tend to confirm the conclusion that speculators operate with a strong sense of normality with respect to the level of the exchange rate.

As for the relationship between short term flows, on the one hand, and current account and long term capital account transactions, on the other, the inverse correlation may be partially mechanical and partially behavioristic. In the former instance, it may arise from the double entry accounting technique used in compilation of Y. Lags in the reporting process and the inclusion of errors and omissions loom foremost in this category. The foreign exchange market is not directly affected by these offsetting "short term capital movements." The extent of this interrelationship may nevertheless be of importance when policy attempts to cure balance of payments deficits are based on the manipulation of specific component flows.

One may expect, however, to find tendencies toward offsetting among the various subaccounts which have some behavioral content. For example, it is known that during the fifties Canadian municipal and provincial governments and Canadian corporations borrowed heavily in United States markets. Frequently, the proceeds of these operations would not be immediately or completely repatriated. Payments to foreigners of interest and dividends may be similarly retained in Canada. Considerations including tax incentives, interest differentials, exchange rate expectations, and others may have been the underlying reasons for this behavior. As a result, a short term outflow wholly or partially offsets the long term capital inflow entered on the opposite side of the ledger, and similarly, a short term capital inflow offsets the current account import. Further, Bell's findings that the extension of trade credit explains a large proportion of short term flows offers another possibility, although we found no significant relationship when the trade balance was substituted for X_6 in the present model. Since there is probably a substantial amount of intercorrelation among the independent variables, this result may not be conclusive. Finally, it is likely that many of these offsetting relationships have a fairly significant seasonal component.

In summary, we see that, apart from possible statistical complications, this equation and its results are illustrative of the balance of payments approach to "equilibrium" in the foreign sector as opposed to the so-called exchange market approach. The former is the approach employed by most countries today. Its weakness, from our present point of view, is that, while these short term capital "movements" are responsive to exchange and money market phenomena, they affect the

---

[10] The simple correlation coefficient between these two variables is .28.

exchange rate only in a very indirect sense. We might say that in the absence of incentives to relend long term loans on short term, the repatriation of these funds would have affected the exchange rate and that, offsetting these movements for the present, such flows have a "stabilizing" influence.

6. CONCLUDING REMARKS

In the preceding sections we have examined a theory of speculative behavior which seems to be supported by the Canadian data. Some difficulties nevertheless remain, indicating the need for further work. One of the major problems in the analysis was posed by the choice and availability of data. Since separate time series for speculators' sales and purchases could not be produced, total short term capital flows were tested for the speculative component.

The various estimates for the expectations coefficient suggest that speculators are on the average exceedingly reluctant to alter their views about the expected normal rate. A given change in the current exchange rate produces a relatively minor adjustment in expectations. Consequently, increasing deviations of the current rate from the expected normal rate set up capital flows which tend to limit the movement of the actual rate relative to the expected rate.[11]

It is probably the case that a stable general economic environment is an important prerequisite for stabilizing speculative capital movements. One would expect periods of political instability and uncertainty to exert downward pressure on the value of λ. An Exchange Equalization Authority, that had demonstrated its ability and willingness to undertake smoothing operations without attempting to maintain any one rate of exchange, would be expected to constitute a stabilizing element in the exchange market. It is noteworthy, for example, that speculators reacted with striking reluctance to the growing economic uncertainty and political instability in Canada during 1961 and early 1962.

In a stable environment, therefore, our theory predicts—and the data tentatively support this conclusion—that speculators' expectations will be a slowly changing variable which possesses considerable inertia, and that speculative sales and purchases will have a dampening effect on movements in the exchange rate. If these results should turn out to be applicable to other countries, they may be of relevance to the current debate on reform of the international monetary system.

[11] It is sometimes said [21] that public opinion was subject to strong "parity psychology," assuming an exchange rate of 1.00 as normal. We attempted to fit models using the parity rate or deviations from that rate. We were not particularly successful especially when the period as a whole is considered.

70 SVEN W. ARNDT

REFERENCES

[1] BAUMOL, W. J.: "Speculation, Profitability, and Stability," *Review of Economics and Statistics*, XXXIX, No. 3 (1957), 263–271.

[2] ———: "Reply," *Review of Economics and Statistics*, XLI, No. 3 (1959), 301–302.

[3] BELL, P. W.: "Private Capital Movements and the U.S. Balance of Payments," *Factors Affecting the United States Balance of Payments*, Joint Economic Committee, 87th Congress, 2d Session (1962), 395–482.

[4] CANTERBERY, E. R.: "Foreign Exchange, Capital Flows and Monetary Policy," Princeton University, *Studies in International Finance*, No. 15 (1965).

[5] COHEN, B. J.: "A Survey of Capital Movements and Findings Regarding their Interest Sensitivity," *The United States Balance of Payments*, Joint Economic Committee, 88th Congress, 1st Session (1963), Part I, 198–208.

[6] EINZIG, PAUL: *A Dynamic Theory of Forward Exchange* (London: Macmillan), 1961.

[7] FRIEDMAN, M.: *Essays in Positive Economics* (Chicago: University of Chicago Press), 1953.

[8] ———: *A Theory of the Consumption Function* (Princeton: Princeton University Press), 1957.

[9] GRILICHES, ZVI: "A Note on Serial Correlation Bias in Estimates of Distributed Lags," *Econometrica*, XXIX, No. 1 (1961), 65–73.

[10] KENEN, P. B.: "Short-term Capital Movements and the U.S. Balance of Payments," *The United States Balance of Payments*, Joint Economic Committee, 88th Congress, 1st Session (1963), Part I, 153–191.

[11] KOYCK, L. M.: *Distributed Lags and Investment Analysis* (Amsterdam: North-Holland Publishing Co.), 1954.

[12] MARQUARDT, D. W.: "An Algorithm for Least-Squares Estimation of Non-Linear Parameters," *Journal of the Society of Industrial and Applied Mathematics*, II, No. 2 (1963), 431–441.

[13] NERLOVE, MARC: *Distributed Lags and Demand Analysis for Agricultural and Other Commodities* (Washington: U.S. Department of Agriculture, Agricultural Marketing Service), 1958.

[14] POWRIE, T. L.: "Short-term Capital Movements and the Flexible Canadian Exchange Rate, 1953–1961," *Canadian Journal of Economics and Political Science*, XXX, No. 1 (1964) 76–94.

[15] RHOMBERG, R. R.: "Canada's Foreign Exchange Market: A Quarterly Model," *International Monetary Fund Staff Papers*, VII, No. 1 (1960), 439–456.

[16] ———: "A Model of the Canadian Economy under Fixed and Fluctuating Exchange Rates," *Journal of Political Economy*, LXXII, No. 1 (1964), 1–31.

[17] SOHMEN, E.: *Flexible Exchange Rates: Theory and Controversy* (Chicago: University of Chicago Press), 1961.

[18] TAYLOR, L. D., AND T. A. WILSON: "Three-Pass Least Squares: A Method for Estimating Models with a Lagged Dependent Variable," *Review of Economics and Statistics*, XLVI, No. 4 (1964), 329–346.

[19] TELSER, L. A.: "A Theory of Speculation Relating Profitability and Stability," *Review of Economics and Statistics*, XLI, No. 3 (1959), 295–301.

[20] TSIANG, S. C.: "A Theory of Foreign Exchange Speculation under a Floating Exchange System," *Journal of Political Economy*, LXVI, No. 5 (1958), 399–418.

[21] WONNACOTT, P.: *The Canadian Dollar, 1948–1958* (Toronto: University of Toronto Press), 1965.

[22] ZELLNER, A., D. S. HUANG, AND L. C. CHAU: "Further Analysis of the Short-Run Consumption Function with Emphasis on the Role of Liquid Assets," *Econometrica*, XXXIII, No. 3 (1965), 571–581.

Chapter 17

Regional Currency Arrangements in North America

Sven W. Arndt

1. Introduction

Currency arrangements in North America have varied over the decades, during which both Canada and Mexico have experimented with fixed and flexible exchange rates. Mexico has suffered full-blown exchange-rate crises, while Canada has not. Both have had to deal with a neighbor, who dominates economic relations and economic conditions in the region.

Steps have been taken in North America in recent years to enhance economic cooperation, but the focus has been on trade rather than monetary relations. A decade after the introduction of NAFTA, a new debate is underway over its achievements and shortcomings. Projects under discussion include rewriting the rules of origin, deepening real-sector integration in the direction of customs union, and greater monetary cooperation, including both unilateral or cooperative currency union. The debate is most animated in Canada and least in the United States.

During such debates, whether in North America or South-East Asia, questions inevitably arise about the lessons to be learned from the European experience. It is by now fairly clear, that while Europe offers useful lessons, both positive and negative, the North American situation differs from Europe in several important respects. One is the extreme imbalance in economic size among countries; a second involves the much greater diversity in the degree of economic development among the partners; and a third pertains to the relative importance in trade and regional economic activity of cross-border production sharing and production networks. These differences have implications not only for the available policy choices in North America, but for the relevance of some of the optimum currency area (OCA) criteria.

The rest of the paper is organized as follows. Section 2 reviews the main arguments pertaining to the choice of currency arrangements. Section 3 considers several key implications of the recent experience. Section 4 examines production networking in the region and its implications for the relevance of the OCA perspective. Section 5 concludes.

2. Key Issues in the Debate[1]

The theoretical issues relevant to currency arrangements have been debated since the early contributions by Mundell (1963), McKinnon (1963), and Kenen (1969). In the early days, the focus was more on goods and services markets, than on financial sectors, reflecting in part the fact that European capital markets were just becoming unfettered from capital controls. The background of relatively high MFN tariffs and limited integration of financial markets, affected the magnitude of the costs and benefits to be expected from regional integration, including regional monetary integration.

Since then, huge strides have been made in the multilateral reduction of barriers to trade, FDI and financial flows. Further, technical innovations have brought about substantial reductions in communication and transportation costs. Together, these developments have allowed goods, services, and asset markets to become more closely linked, for shocks to travel faster, and for adjustment processes to spill over national borders. The result has been that market integration has often raced ahead of inter-governmental coordination of regulatory and other policies. Financial institutions, for example, have been able increasingly to cross borders and hence jurisdictions, while agreement on who should monitor and regulate them is yet to be achieved.[2]

The cornerstone criteria for successful monetary union are well-known and will not be discussed in detail here. Suffice it to recall the basic argument, which is that in the presence of significant asymmetries among countries, loss of floating exchange rates will force adjustment onto variables like wages, prices, employment and output. To minimize politically unpopular adjustment patterns, considerations based on Mundell (1963) call for cross-border factor mobility. Considerations based on McKinnon (1963) suggest that very open economies make better candidates for currency union, especially if they are major trading partners. As the subsequent debate has pointed out, whether trade raises or reduces asymmetries among countries depends at least in part on whether it is mainly inter- or intra-industry in nature.[3]

Kenen (1969) adds diversity as a criterion, suggesting that economies with diversified production and trade structures are likely to be better candidates for monetary integration, because shocks are likely to be more diversified in nature and more diversifiable in terms of impact.

An important feature of the original OCA arguments was their focus on the real side of the economy. As the debate has evolved and inter-country financial linkages have grown, concerns about financial adjustment and financial stability have come to the fore, particularly in policy arrangements involving developing economies, whose financial sectors, though very open, tend to be relatively underdeveloped and fragile.[4] This is relevant to North America, where economic development among the three countries ranges from highly developed to emerging, thus requiring policies to bridge much larger gaps than existed in the original European arrangements. When it comes to monetary union, the differences in terms of financial sector development are also much larger than among the countries which formed the EMU. The United States and Canada are financially mature and integrated into the world economy, while Mexico's financial system, though linked to the United States, is relatively immature and burdened by "original sin" and "fear of floating."

The conclusion to be drawn from the contemporary discussion is that North America is less than fully, but nevertheless substantially ready for closer monetary cooperation. There is significant market integration among the three countries; wages and prices are quite flexible, and there is considerable cross-border factor mobility.

While factor mobility was important in Mundell's original assessment, there has always been a question of adjustment speeds to changes in exchange rates, on the one hand, and responses involving the relocation of labor and capital, on the other. In contemporary North America, prices and wages are less sticky than in Europe and labor and capital are more mobile. Prices and wages are more market-driven. Capital is freely mobile among the three countries. Skilled labor is mobile into the United States, especially from Canada, a fact which gives rise to concerns about "brain drain" in that country. Unskilled labor is also mobile, at least from Mexico to the United States.

The question, nevertheless, is how useful an adjustment mechanism such factor movements provide, particularly in the short run. Compared to the guest-worker programs adopted by many European countries in the sixties and seventies, which appeared to possess considerable short-run flexibility, cross-border labor movements in North America would be expected to be slower and thus offer somewhat more promise as a vehicle for long-run structural rather than shorter-run cyclical adjustment. It is not easy to make a case for factor mobility as an efficient alternative to exchange-rate based responses, which brings the discussion back to the seriousness of asymmetries. This question is taken up in Section 3.

The three economies of North America are each other's major trading partners and the small economies are also quite open. Chart 1 shows the evolution of Canada's and Mexico's trade with the United States. Both ratios grew rapidly during the last two decades of the 20th century, peaked at the end of the century, and have been declining since. Chart 2 gives a slightly different perspective,

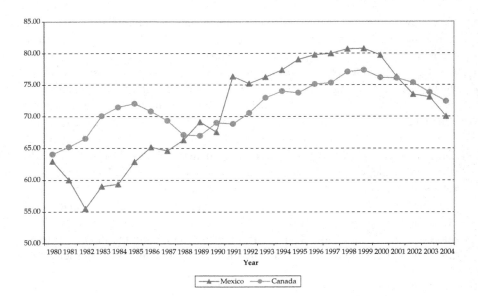

Chart 1. Regional Openness (Ratio of X + M with US to X + M with the world; scale by 100).
Source: UN Comtrade

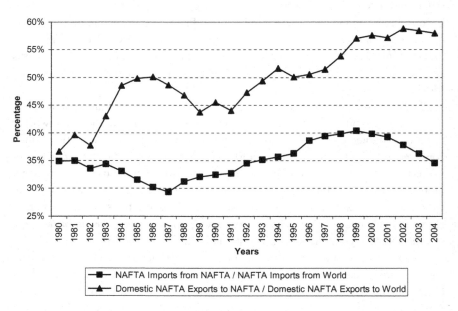

Chart 2. Aggregate NAFTA Import and Export Manufactures Ratios.
Source: UN Comtrade

focusing on the development of regional trade in manufacturing among the three NAFTA countries. It is important to note the decline since the late 1990s in intra-NAFTA imports, a decline that is particularly pronounced for the U.S. and Mexico. Overall, however, the behavior of intra-regional trade underscores the continuing integration of the region's economies.

Kenen's diversity criterion is the most problematic and ambiguous of the three. Diversity is deemed to be desirable because it makes the economy less vulnerable to shocks in particular sectors or industries. If diversified industries are subject to different types of disturbances, the negative shocks originating in any one sector may be counter-balanced by positive shocks in others. To the extent that factor mobility is needed to facilitate adjustment, it takes place within the country, where labor mobility among sectors and regions is often higher than across borders. That would be true of the U.S. and Canada, for example.

While it is certainly true that the U.S. and Canada, in particular, are diversified in terms of the variety of goods and services that are produced, consumed and traded in the overall economy, there is considerable regional concentration of many of these activities, which reduces the diversity within regions relative to diversity in the country overall. This is easily seen in the concentration of manufacturing in Eastern Canada, and especially Ontario, and the concentration of agriculture and mining in the Western provinces. These regional differences are replicated in the United States. In Mexico, too, much manufacturing is located in the Northern states, particularly in the maquiladora sector and in other activities catering to the U.S. market. These inter-regional asymmetries have long been of concern to analysts, some of whom have suggested that instead of a horizontal division, the continent should have been divided vertically into two currency unions.

As the debate has evolved over the years, increasing attention has been paid to the role of capital mobility. The arguments are familiar. The key feature relevant to the current discussion are the conclusions pertaining to monetary policy sovereignty. This is a hot issue in Canada, as well as Mexico. Both theory and the empirical evidence suggest, that in the presence of high capital mobility small countries lose their ability to run independent monetary policies under fixed exchange rates.

This has been a topic of considerable discussion in Canada, where the central bank's economists, in particular Murray (2000), have defended floating rates. While there have been periods during which Canadian monetary policy appeared to follow U.S. policy, there have been significant policy differences between the two countries in recent years. Along with many other central banks, the Bank of Canada has pursued an explicit inflation-targeting policy and has shown considerable tolerance for significant movements of the exchange rate against the U.S.

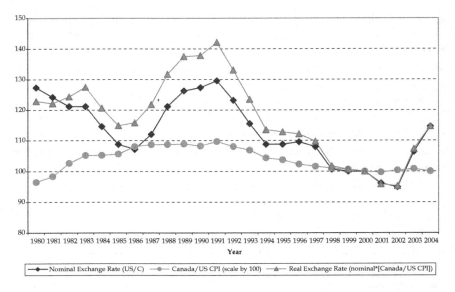

Chart 3. Canada — Nominal and Real Exchange Rates (2000 = 100).
Source: IMF/IFS

dollar. (See Chart 3 below.) A similar approach has been pursued by the Bank of Mexico. As we shall see below, the substantial depreciation of the Canadian dollar against its U.S. counterpart in the 1990s has been attacked for undermining growth in high-tech industries.

The recent OCA debate has viewed fixed exchange rates — including dollarization and currency union with a low-inflation country — as a way for inflation-prone countries to import price stability. As Chart 3 shows, this is not an issue in Canada, where monetary policy has succeeded admirably in maintaining low inflation rates. Indeed, the ratio of Canada's CPI (WPI) to that of the United States has been falling since the early nineties.

As Chart 4 shows, however, inflation in Mexico has been rising relative to both Canada and the United States. It has been rising as well in relation to some third-country competitors, which has helped erode Mexico's share in U.S. markets, and it is part of the explanation of the relative fall in intra-regional trade, noted in Charts 1 and 2.

In recent years, the discussion of alternative exchange-rate regimes has voiced concerns about the viability of soft pegs for emerging economies. This argument may be of relevance to Mexico, but not to Canada. Both Canada and Mexico have experimented with fixed rate systems, but only Mexico has experienced

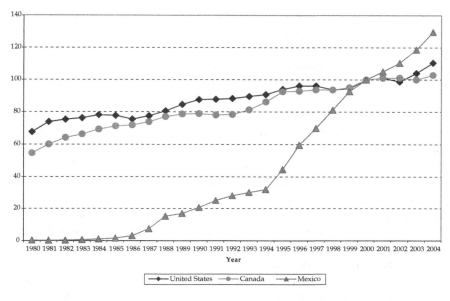

Chart 4.   Producer/Wholesale Prices — Index Number (2000 = 100).
Source: IMF/IFS

exchange-rate crises.   Canada carries considerable amounts of foreign-currency denominated debt and has run sizeable current account deficits, but these have not provoked crises.

Lessons from Europe

There are two sets of lessons to be learned from Europe.   One concerns the way Europe approached monetary unification, particularly with respect to sequencing of trade, financial and monetary integration and the gradual deepening of integration towards EMU. The second pertains to experience since inception of EMU, particularly with respect to the viability of the Maastricht criteria and the efficacy of the Stability and Growth Pact.

With respect to sequencing, the question is whether trade liberalization and creation of a common and single market must necessarily precede monetary integration or whether the latter might at some point be introduced in order to facilitate further real-sector integration.   In other words, have real- and financial-sector integration and reduction of asymmetries proceeded far enough in North America to make monetary integration a viable option, particularly if it can become a catalyst for further real integration?   There is widespread concern that NAFTA has been deficient in a number of ways, that the benefits it has delivered have fallen short of expectations, while costs have been larger than anticipated, all of which suggests to some that the agreement is in need of significant revision. There is evidence, for example, that the dispute settlement system is not working as expected and that compliance with rules of origin is so costly and burdensome that it is causing significant amounts of trade to by-pass NAFTA altogether.[5]

If the European approach to sequencing is the relevant model, then further initiatives in pursuit of deeper real-sector integration are in order. These would include movement toward a customs union and greater harmonization of regulatory, competition and dispute-settlement procedures. These would be followed by a gradual shift toward fixed rates, in the manner of the European Monetary System (EMS). If, however, the U.S. proves unwilling to proceed in a coordinated manner, then Canada and Mexico could elect to unilaterally or jointly fix to the U.S. dollar and bring their policies and practices into conformity with the new regime.

The second lesson to be learned, concerns Europe's experience with monetary union since the introduction of the Euro. Have the various OCA concerns raised in the preceding pages been an issue? Have asymmetries interfered with monetary policy at the ECB level? How important is the fiscal indiscipline issue? Are countries violating the SGP's limits because they are not getting the monetary policy they need? Are the Maastricht conditions appropriate for North America? To what extent would the United States be willing to share control over monetary policy? To what extent would the United States allow itself to be bound by a Stability and Growth Pact? What would be the consequences if the U.S. violated the conditions of such a pact? More generally, what are the implications for the common welfare of policy indiscipline in large member countries? Conversely, what are the implications for individual countries of policy constraints imposed by the group?

Can Europe Learn from North America?

In North America, cross-border production sharing has played an important role from the outset of regional integration. Europe, on the other hand, is just now entering a phase of deepening by means of production sharing. As Chart 5 shows, the Europe-15 group of countries has gone through "de-regionalization" since the early nineties as the share of intra-group trade has fallen relative to total trade. Chart 6 provides the explanation: much of the growth in the group's trade has been with the recently admitted members (and a good portion of that has involved production sharing).

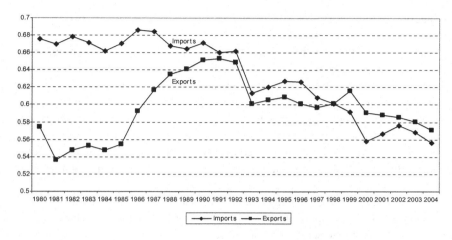

Chart 5. Intraregional Share of EU-15 Aggregate Imports and Exports.
Source: UN Comtrade

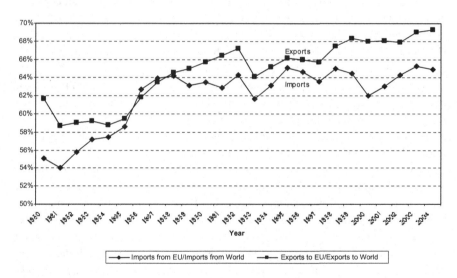

Chart 6. EU 25 Regional to World Import & Export Ratios.
Source: UN Comtrade

3. New Perspectives on an Old Problem

During the 1990s, the Canadian dollar depreciated against its U.S. counterpart. (See Chart 3 above.) It has recently recovered part of that lost value. Among Canadian observers, the sustained "undervaluation" of the currency has raised concerns about its effects on Canada's longer-run competitiveness. The argument may be stated as follows.

The sustained depreciation of the Canadian dollar has provided an important measure of protection to a variety of Canadian industries facing foreign competition. These include the resource-based industries, which suffered from depressed world prices of raw materials. The decline of the value of the home currency, gave these industries room to raise prices and wages, without suffering the competitive consequences that would have manifested themselves under fixed rates. Analogous competitive shelter was provided to non-resource based industries, many of them in the so-called "old manufacturing" sector, where they enjoyed a measure of protection from competition from emerging economies.

While this may have enabled these industries to sustain higher levels of activity than would otherwise have been possible, it also implies that the Canadian economy overall failed to move scarce productive resources into newer, more technologically advanced manufacturing. The weak Canadian dollar also raised the cost of imported technology, on which Canada relies heavily. In this sense, exchange-rate policy provided shelter to existing sectors at the expense of more modernization. This argument has been vigorously pushed by economists like Courchene and Harris (2000), and just as vigorously rejected by others, including economists at the Bank of Canada.

The evidence does not provide support for this argument; and even if it did, it may merely suggest, as McCallum (1999, 2000) has noted, that Canada needs a stronger dollar and not that it needs monetary union with the United States. What is, nevertheless, interesting about this argument is the importance it attaches to the role of the exchange rate in stimulating economic growth.[6]

In the course of this debate, economists at the Bank of Canada have steadfastly supported floating rates.[7] They have based the argument on the importance of the buffer function of flexible exchange rates. They have claimed on the basis of econometric modeling that the behavior of the exchange rate vis-a-vis the U.S. dollar can be adequately explained in rather traditional ways.[8] They have also disputed another argument sometimes used in support of official unilateral dollarization, namely, the assertion that a significant amount of de facto dollarization already exists. Murray and Powell (2003) argue that while the U.S. dollar circulates alongside the Canadian dollar, especially in border areas, and is used in certain types of activities, there is no evidence of creeping dollarization.

A key element in the Canadian debate, and in Mexico as well, is the political dimension. A broad segment of Canadian public opinion is concerned about the loss of national identity. In the presence of Canadian anxieties about U.S. cultural and economic dominance, the economist's efficiency and cost/benefit arguments are puny by comparison. In view of the indifference toward coordinated approaches in Washington, the prospects for monetary integration are dim.

The situation is somewhat similar, but also somewhat different in Mexico, where analogous anxieties about the Big Gorilla in the north exist, but where domestic institutions and policy discipline may be too frail for a go-it-alone strategy. While the quality of monetary policy has improved sharply in Mexico, the political environment is still too fragile to ensure *continuity* of policy discipline. There may thus be a case for a unilateral fixed-rate policy with the dollar in order to "lock in" certain policy reforms, provided that a political agreement to abide by the constraints on domestic policy independence can be reached. It is not clear that the current political environment in Mexico can generate such a consensus.[9]

4. Evolving Economic Structure

In this section we consider a feature of North American economic integration that distinguishes it from the original European experience, although much less from the situation since the most recent EU enlargement. This is the growing importance of cross-border production sharing across a range of industries. In the North American automobile sector, for example, parts and components made in the U.S. are assembled in Mexico into finished products and then exported to the U.S. In the same sector, production sharing is so intense between the United States and Canada, that special vehicles ferry automobiles at various stages of completion back and forth across a bridge between Detroit and Windsor. Similar multiple shuttling takes place in the furniture industry between Southern California and North-Western Mexico.

Production sharing began decades ago between the United States and Canada in the original auto pact. It was followed by the Canada-U.S. free trade agreement (CUSFTA) and then by NAFTA. Before NAFTA, the maquiladora program gave impetus to cross-border coordination of manufacturing activities between the United States and Mexico.

The trade flows generated by production sharing represent a new form of intra-industry trade. In Europe, trade among the countries of the EEC and EFTA was "intra-industry" in nature, but it was characterized by two-directional flows of "varieties" of finished products. Peugeots went from France to Germany, while Mercedes vehicles moved in the opposite direction. Production sharing adds a new dimension to intra-industry trade.

Production sharing has a number of implications. In the context of a preferential trade area, it improves the odds that a given PTA will be net trade-creating rather than trade-diverting (Arndt 2001). If a preferential trade arrangement is introduced where production sharing takes place with non-members, rules of origin tend to be welfare-reducing. Indeed, as noted, recent evidence suggests that compliance costs with NAFTA's rules of origin are so onerous, that a significant share of North America's cross-border trade avoids NAFTA and pays the MFN tariff.

Cross-border production sharing also has implications for the choice of monetary arrangements. It tends to support convergence and synchronization of business cycles and it affects the relationship between trade flows and exchange rates, as well as other variables in the traditional trade equation.

In a number of industries, specialization around the world has been pushed down from the level of end products to that of components and constituent activities. In the auto sector, for example, parts and components made in the U.S. are shipped to Mexico for assembly into finished passenger vehicles, most of which are then exported to the United States. Similar developments are taking place in electronics, machinery, textiles and apparel and furniture.

This type of intra-industry (intra-product) trade tends to reduce asymmetries between trading partners, certainly at the level of industries and sectors and possibly at economy-wide levels. Industry-specific shocks now affect production in all participating countries. If cross-border linkages occur across a broad range of industries, then the effect of production networks will foster cyclical convergence at the level of the aggregate economy.

It is, of course, possible that production sharing may be limited to particular sectors, in which case the reduction in asymmetries across borders in that sector, may be accompanied by greater asymmetries between that sector and the rest of the economy. In Canada, for example, this could contribute to a further widening of the gap between cycles in the Western and Eastern provinces. If industries concentrated in the province of Ontario engage in production sharing with their Eastern U.S. counterparts, or if industries located in the northern states of Mexico become more closely involved in production networks with U.S. firms, then this may widen asymmetries between such regions and other regions within their economies. The evidence to date suggests that production networks are contributing to convergence of business cycles.[10] (See Charts 7 and 8.)

As noted, production networks affect the relationship between trade flows and exchange rates, relative prices and incomes. They introduce a new direct relationship between exports and imports. Traditionally, an exogenous rise in the demand for a country's exports stimulates domestic output and raises income, which in turn boosts imports. This relationship also holds in the presence of production sharing, but to the extent that exports contain imported components, a rise in export demand has a direct effect on imports.

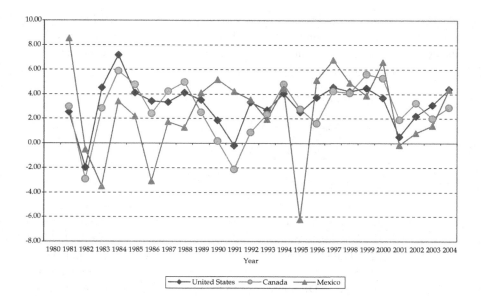

Chart 7.   Real GDP Growth Rate (Percentage).

Source: IMF/IFS

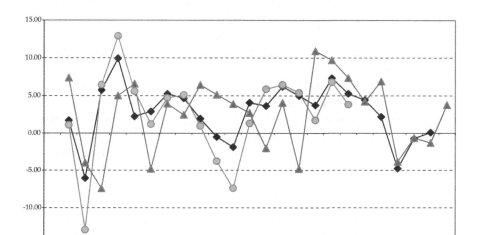

Chart 8.   Changes in Manufacturing Production Indices (Percentage).

Source: UN Comtrade

This implies that imports are affected not only by changes in domestic income (in the traditional direct manner), but by changes in foreign incomes as they raise the demand for a country's imported components needed to service the increased demand for exports.

$$M^*_{\text{parts}} = \overset{-}{\alpha_1} e + \overset{+}{\alpha_2} Y_{MX} + \overset{+}{\alpha_3} X_{pv} \tag{1}$$

$$X_{pv} = \overset{+}{\beta_1} e + \overset{+}{\beta_2} Y_{US} \tag{2}$$

$$\therefore M^*_{\text{parts}} = \overset{-}{\alpha_1} e + \overset{+}{\alpha_2} Y_{MX} + \overset{+}{\alpha_3}(\overset{+}{\beta_1} e + \overset{+}{\beta_2} Y_{US})$$

$$= (\overset{-}{\alpha_1} + \overset{+}{\alpha_3}\overset{+}{\beta_1}) e + \overset{+}{\alpha_2} Y_{MX} + \overset{+}{\alpha_3}\overset{+}{\beta_2} Y_{US} \tag{3}$$

This relationship is modeled very simply in equations (1)–(3), where Mexico's demand for parts imports (M^*_{parts}) is a negative function of the real exchange rate (e) and a positive function of domestic income (Y_{MX}) and exports of the finished product (X_{pv}). The latter, in turn, are a positive function of the real rate and of U.S. income (Y_{US}). Substituting equation (2) into equation (1), yields equation (3), a result which gives U.S. GDP a new role in determining Mexico's imports along with Mexico's GDP. In this setting, the coefficient on the real exchange rate may be negative, as in the traditional case, but it may also be insignificant or positive. It will be positive as Mexican value-added in passenger vehicle exports to the U.S. rises.

We would thus expect network-related imports to behave differently relative to more traditional imports, where the key characteristic of such imports is that they are not destined for re-export.

In auto trade between the United States and Mexico, U.S.-made parts and components are imported by Mexico for incorporation into finished vehicles, which are then shipped to the United States. Under normal circumstances, a depreciation of the peso against the dollar would be expected to raise the peso price of U.S.-made components and thus reduce demand. The higher price of imported components raises the peso cost of the vehicle into which they are incorporated. At the original exchange rate, this raises the dollar price of the vehicle. But the decline of the dollar price of the peso acts as an offset. The dollar price of the imported vehicle is pushed up by the increase in the peso price of components and pushed down by the depreciation of the peso.

The net effect on the dollar price of imported automobiles depends on the share of Mexican value-added in those vehicles. Mexican value added includes assembly and Mexican parts and components. When parts imports are destined for use by Mexicans and vehicle exports consist entirely of Mexican value-added, peso depreciation reduces imports, raises exports and improves the trade balance.

As the share of imported components intended for incorporation into exports rises, the response of trade to peso depreciation weakens as compensating changes on the two sides of the trade balance tend to mute the effect. To the extent that Mexico's vehicle exports contain Mexican value-added, the dollar price of exports falls as a result of the peso depreciation. This, in turn, raises the demand for vehicle imports from Mexico and thereby raises the demand for U.S.-made components. There are two forces operating on parts imports, therefore. On the one hand, the demand for parts for use by Mexicans falls, while the demand for parts to be incorporated into vehicle exports rises. The net effect depends on the share of imports for domestic use and on the share of Mexican value-added in vehicle exports. The response of imports to peso depreciation may thus be negative, positive or zero.

The foregoing helps explain the degree of pass-through of exchange-rate changes to domestic import prices. The peso depreciation will be reflected in lower dollar prices of vehicle imports only to the extent of embodied Mexican value-added. A simple view of this relationship may be sketched as follows.

$$P_c^* = EP_c \tag{4}$$

$$P_{pv}^* = P_c^* + VA^*$$

$$= EP_c + VA^* \tag{5}$$

$$P_{pv} = P_c + VA^*/E \tag{6}$$

$$dP_{pv} = dP_c + dVA^*/E - (VA^* \cdot dE)/E^2$$

$$= dP_c + (VA^*/E)(dVA^*/VA^*) - (VA^*/E)(dE/E)$$

$$dP_{pv}/P_{pv} = (P_c/P_{pv})dP_c/P_c + [(VA^*/EP_{pv}](dVA^*/VA^*) - [(VA^*/EP_{pv}](dE/E)$$

$$= \lambda dP_c/P_c + (1 - \lambda)dVA^*/VA^* - (1 - \lambda)dE/E \tag{7}$$

Let $dVA^* = dP_c = 0$; then

$$dP_{pv}/P_{pv} = -(1 - \lambda)(dE/E), \tag{8}$$

where P^* and P are prices expressed in pesos and dollars, respectively, E is the peso price of the dollar, VA^* is Mexican value-added, c stands for components, pv denotes passenger vehicles and λ is the share of imported components in vehicle exports.

Thus production sharing adds a new explanation for the observed weakness or absence of pass-through.[11]

The decline in sensitivity to exchange-rate changes of some trade flows has implications for the choice of exchange-rate regime. If trade becomes less sensitive, then the buffer function of flexible rates becomes less important, but so does the claim that floating rates destabilize trade.

5. Concluding Remarks

The pros and cons of greater monetary cooperation in North America have received extensive attention in recent years. The three countries in the region have taken steps toward closer economic integration through NAFTA. They meet many of the basic pre-conditions for monetary union — not perfectly, but reasonably well. They are each other's major trading partners in most dimensions and their economies are strongly linked across goods, services and asset markets and to a lesser extent at the level of factor markets.

Most empirical studies see gains from monetary integration, which tend to be easier to measure than the costs. That is due in part to the fact that the cost of lost policy independence is difficult to assess.

While the debate over policy continues, de facto integration moves forward. Among the more interesting developments in the past decade or so has been the rapid expansion of cross- border production networks, both within the region and beyond. The available evidence suggests that in the course of the process, cyclical and structural asymmetries among the countries are declining, thereby eroding a major argument against common currencies.

Furthermore, the evidence suggests that network-based trade tends to be less sensitive to variations in exchange rates, a result which reduces the importance of a floating rate's buffer function.

These are developments, the thrust of which should further diminish the economic obstacles to currency union. But while the economic pre-conditions are positive, the political environment is quite hostile. The attitude in Washington is one of indifference, while popular opposition in Canada and Mexico is based on cultural and political considerations. This is quite the reverse of the conditions that prevailed in Europe, where the economic case was often less than compelling, but where integration proceeded nevertheless because political forces pushed it along.

Acknowledgments

An earlier draft was presented at the workshop in Vienna on "Regional and International Currency Arrangements," sponsored by the Austrian National Bank and the Bank of Greece, February 24–25, 2006. I am indebted to Steven Kamin and

Pierre Siklos and to participants at the Vienna workshop for valuable comments, to B.J. Dechsakulthorn and Maria Tzintzarova for valuable research assistance, and to Alex Huemer for useful discussions.

Endnotes

1. For a detailed assessment of the options available to Canada, see Arndt (2003).
2. See, Mayes (2005), for example.
3. See, among others, European Commission (Emerson, 1990), Eichengreen (1997) and Krugman (1993).
4. See, for example, Berg and Borensztein (2000) and Hausmann *et al.* (1999).
5. In a recent study, Kunimoto and Sawchuk (2005) suggest that utilization of NAFTA hovers in the neighborhood of plus or minus fifty percent, meaning that for a significant share of intra-NAFTA trade the costs associated with MFN tariffs are lower than compliance with NAFTA's rules of origin.
6. Grubel (2000) has also been a forceful critic of Canada's recent exchange-rate regime, but for reasons that have more to do with hysteresis and the role of labor unions.
7. See Amano and van Norden (1993), Murray (2000), and Murray, Schembri and St-Amant (2003), for example.
8. The main causal variables in this model are the inflation differentials and relative prices of energy and non-energy products.
9. In this context, Austria's experience with a fixed-rate system involving the German mark is an extremely valuable case study (Arndt, 1982). It is doubtful that Mexico is capable of meeting those standards, in which case some version of a floating rate system is superior.
10. See, for example, Chiquiar and Ramos-Francia (2005) and Torres and Vela (2003).
11. See, for example, Knetter (1993), Goldberg and Knetter (1997), and Krugman (1987).

References

Alexander, V. and G.M. von Furstenberg. "Monetary Unions — A Superior Alternative to Full Dollarization in the Long Run." *North American Journal of Economics and Finance* 11, 2 (2000): 205–225.

Amano, R. and S. van Norden. "A Forecasting Equation for the Canada-U.S. Dollar Exchange Rate." In *The Exchange Rate and the Economy*. Ottawa: The Bank of Canada, 1993, pp. 266–71.

Arndt, S.W. *The Political Economy of Austria.* Washington, D.C.: AEI Press, 1982.

_____. "Super-specialization and the Gains from Trade." *Contemporary Economic Policy* 16 (1998): 480–85.

_____. "Offshore Sourcing and Production-Sharing in Preference Areas." In *Fragmentation: New Production Patterns in the World Economy.* Edited by S.W. Arndt and H. Kierzkowski. New York: Oxford University Press, 2001, pp. 76–87.

_____. "The Pros and Cons of North American Monetary Integration." In R.G. Harris (Ed.), North American Linkages: Opportunities and Challenges for Canada (Calgary: University of Calgary Press, 2003), pp. 391–418.

Arndt, S.W. and A. Huemer. "North American Trade After NAFTA: Part I & II." *Claremont Policy Briefs.* Claremont: Lowe Institute of Political Economy, April and July 2000, pp. 1–4.

Bayoumi, T. and B. Eichengreen. "One Money or Many? Analyzing the Prospects for Monetary Unification in Various Parts of the World." Princeton: *Studies in International Finance* 76 (1994).

Berg, A. and E. Borensztein. "The Choice of Exchange Rate Regime and Monetary Target in Highly Dollarized Economies." International Monetary Fund Working Study No. 29, February 2000a.

_____. "Full Dollarization: The Pros and Cons." IMF *Economic Issues* 24 (2000b).

Carr, J.L. and J.F. Floyd. "Real and Monetary Shocks to the Canadian Dollar: Do Canada and the United States form an Optimum Currency Area?" *North American Journal of Economics and Finance* 13 (2000): 1–19.

Chiquiar, D and M. Ramos-Francia, "Trade and business-cycle synchronization: evidence from Mexican and U.S. manufacturing industries," *North American Journal of Economics and Finance* 16 (2005), 187–216.

Courchene, T.J. and R.G. Harris. "North American Monetary Union: Analytical Principles and Operational Guidelines." *North American Journal of Economics and Finance* 11, 1 (2000): 3–18.

De Grauwe, P. *The Economics of Monetary Integration,* Sixth edition. Oxford: Oxford University Press, 2005.

Eichengreen, B. *European Monetary Unification: Theory, Practice, and Analysis.* Cambridge: MA: MIT Press, 1997.

Emerson, M. [*et al.*] "One Market, One Money: An Evaluation of Forming an Economic and Monetary Union." *European Economy* 44 (1990).

Frankel, J.A. and A.K. Rose. "The Endogeneity of the Optimum Currency Area Criteria." *Economic Journal* 108, 449 (1998): 1009–25.

Goldberg, P.K. and M. Knetter, "Goods Prices and Exchange Rates: What Have We Learned?" *Journal of Economic Literature,* 35 (1997), 1243–1272.

Grubel, H.G. "The Merit of a Canada-U.S. Monetary Union." *North American Journal of Economics and Finance* 11, 1 (2000): 19–40.

Gylfason, T. "Fix or Flex? Alternative Exchange Rate Regimes in an Era of Global Capital Mobility." *North American Journal of Economics and Finance* 11, 1 (2000): 173–189.

Harris, R.G. *Determinants of Canadian Productivity Growth: Issues and Prospects.* Discussion Paper No. 8. Ottawa: Industry Canada, December 1999.

_____. *The New Economy and the Exchange Rate Regime.* Discussion Paper No. 0111. Adelaide: Centre for International Economic Studies, Adelaide University, March 2001.

Hausmann, R., M. Gavin, C. Pages-Serra, and E. Stein, "Financial Turmoil and the Choice of Exchange Rate Regime," IADB, mimeo (1999).

Hochreiter, E. "Exchange Rate Regimes and Capital Mobility: Issues and Some Lessons from Central and Eastern European Applicant Countries." *North American Journal of Economics and Finance* 11, 2 (2000): 155–171.

Kenen, P.B. "The Theory of Optimum Currency Areas: An Eclectic View." In *Monetary Problems of the International Economy.* Edited by R.A. Mundell and A. K. Swoboda. Chicago: University of Chicago Press, 1969, pp. 41–60.

Knetter, M.M. "International Comparisons of Pricing-to-Market Behavior." *American Economic Review* 83 (1993): 473–486.

Krugman, P. "Pricing to Markets When the Exchange Rate Changes." In *Real Financial Linkages in Open Economies.* Edited by S.W. Arndt and J.D. Richardson. Cambridge, MA: MIT Press, 1987, pp. 49–70.

Kunimoto, R. and G. Sawchuk, "NAFTA Rules of Origin," (mimeo, 2005).

McCallum, John. "Seven Issues in the Choice of Exchange Rate Regime for Canada." *Current Analysis.* Toronto: Royal Bank of Canada, February 1999, pp. 1–10.

_____. "Engaging the Debate: Costs and Benefits of a North American Common Currency." *Current Analysis.* Toronto: Royal Bank of Canada, April 2000, pp. 1–9.

McKinnon, R.I. "Optimum Currency Areas." *American Economic Review* 53 (1963): 717–25.

_____. "On the Periphery of the International Dollar Standard: Canada, Latin America, and East Asia." *North American Journal of Economics and Finance* 11, 2 (2000): 717–25.

Mayes, D.G., "Financial Stability in a World of Cross-Border Banking," (mimeo, 2005).

Mundell, R.A. (1961), "A Theory of Optimum Currency Areas," *American Economic Review,* 51, pp. 657–65.

Murray, J. "Why Canada Needs a Flexible Exchange Rate." *North American Journal of Economics and Finance* 11, 1 (2000): 41–60.

Murray, J. and J. Powell, "Dollarization in Canada: where does the buck stop?" *North American Journal of Economics and Finance* 14, 2 (2003): 145–172.

Murray, J., L. Schembri and P. St-Amant. "Revisiting the case for flexible exchange rates in North America." *North American Journal of Economics and Finance* 14, 2 (2003): 207–240.

Torres, A. and O. Vela, "Trade Integration and synchronization between business cycles of Mexico and the United States," *North American Journal of Economics and Finance,* 14, (2003), 319–342.

Tower, E. and T.D. Willett. "The Theory of Optimum Currency Areas and Exchange rate Flexibility." Princeton Special Papers in International Economics, No. 11, May 1976.

Wagner, H. "Which Exchange Rate Regimes in an Era of High Capital Mobility?" *North American Journal of Economics and Finance* 11, 1 (2000): 191–203.

Appendix

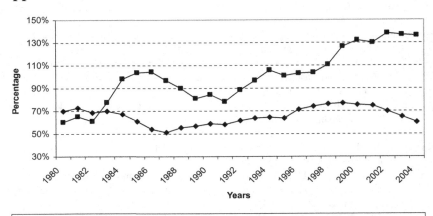

Chart 1A. Manufactures Machinery and Transport Equipment NAFTA Imports and Exports/RoW Ratios.
Source: UN Comtrade

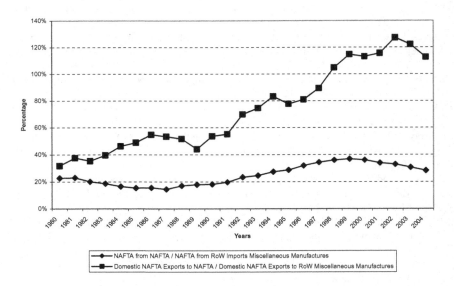

Chart 2A. Manufactures Miscellaneous Manufactures NAFTA Imports and Exports/RoW Ratios.
Source: UN Comtrade

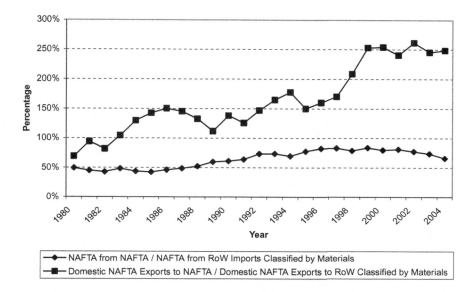

Chart 3A. Manufactures Classified by Materials NAFTA Exports and Imports/RoW Ratios.
Source: UN Comtrade

Chapter 18

Adjustment in an Open Economy with Two Exchange-Rate Regimes

Sven W. Arndt[1]
Claremont McKenna College

Abstract. This paper examines adjustment in a model with three economies, two exchange-rate regimes, and varying capital mobility. In the benchmark scenario, the U.S. dollar fluctuates against the euro and the Chinese yuan, but capital mobility is high in the former and low in the latter case. This generates offsetting exchange-rate adjustments, which affect the efficacy of U.S. fiscal policy. In the next two scenarios, the yuan is fixed against the dollar. Rate pegging by a large country like China "interferes" with U.S. macro adjustment and undermines U.S. policy autonomy.

JEL Classification: F31, F32, F41
Keywords: Open-economy macro; Exchange rate-regimes; U.S.-China payments adjustment; Production networks

1. Introduction

In recent years, the United States has operated under a mixed exchange-rate regime containing both fixed and floating elements. The country is officially classified as a "floater," which accurately describes the nation's official policy.[2] However, it has been unable to prevent a large country – China – from pegging its currency to the dollar.[3] If China were a small country, this policy would have no meaningful consequences for the United States. But China is not small and hence its exchange-rate management does have implications for the U.S.

This paper explores the consequences of China's exchange-market intervention for U.S. monetary and fiscal policy. It does so with an open-economy model of a country which has a floating rate with one trading partner and a fixed rate with a second trading partner. The two trading partners are the European Monetary Union (EMU) or "Euroland," whose currency is the euro, and the People's Republic of China, whose currency is the yuan or RMB. The dollar floats freely against the euro, while its relationship to the yuan is managed by the central bank of China. This gives the U.S. a *de facto* "mixed" exchange-rate regime.

Section 2 presents the model and works out a benchmark scenario in which both exchange rates are fully flexible. In Section 3, China fixes its currency to the dollar and recycles dollars accumulated in the process of intervention by purchasing U.S. Treasury securities directly from the Federal Reserve. This is the "non-sterilization" scenario. In Section 4, intervention dollars are recycled in the open market for U.S. Treasury securities. This is the "sterilization" scenario. Section 6 concludes.

What distinguishes China from the many other countries that have pegged their currencies to the U.S. dollar is that the People's Republic is large enough to affect macro adjustment in the American economy. Its exchange-rate management has the capacity to interfere with the effectiveness of U.S. macro stabilization policies and to compromise the flexibility of the dollar against other currencies.

2. An Open Economy with Floating Rates

The basic frame of reference for the analysis that follows is the textbook model of the open economy, modified to provide a three-country perspective.[4] Specification of the U.S. monetary sector follows conventional lines:

$$H/P = L(y, i), \tag{1}$$

where L is the demand for real cash balances, y is real income and i is the nominal interest rate. P is the price level, which is taken as given in the short run, reflecting the well-known "sticky-price" assumption of many macro models. In the standard model, base money is specified as $H = D + R$, where D is domestic credit and R represents foreign exchange reserves held by the *domestic* central bank. In the case of China, however, it is the foreign central bank that holds reserves of the U.S. currency. Hence, the relevant expression is $H = D - R^C + TB^C$, where R^C represents dollar accumulation by the Chinese central bank through intervention in the foreign exchange market and TB^C represents purchases by the Chinese central bank of U.S. Treasury securities from the public.

Equilibrium in the goods-producing sector is specified along standard lines, except that the U.S. trade balance with each country appears separately in the equation.

$$I(i) + T^*(y^*, y, E^*) + T(y^C, y, E) - S(y) = - G, \tag{2}$$

where investment, I, is a negative function of the rate of interest, where U.S. trade with Europe, T^*, and with China, T, is positively related to each country's real GDP (y^* and y^C, respectively), negatively to U.S. real GDP (y) and positively to the two nominal exchange rates (E^* and E), expressed as the dollar price of the respective foreign currencies. U.S. private real saving rises with real GDP, and G represents the real government budget deficit.

There are, finally, two basic balance-of-payments equations:

$$T^*(y^*, y, E^*) + K^*(i, i^*) = 0 \tag{3}$$

and

$$T(y^C, y, E) + K(i, i^C) = 0, \tag{4}$$

where K^* and K represent capital inflows into the U.S. from Europe and China, respectively. Inasmuch as the current account is a flow variable, we count on capital flows rather than the stock-adjustment components of the financial account to provide ongoing funding for current account imbalances. Cross-country interest differentials should cause agents to borrow where interest rates are low and to lend where they are high. We assume that such financial intermediation between Euroland and the U.S. exhibits "high capital mobility," while financial flows between the U.S. and China are subject to low mobility, in part because they are more vigorously controlled and regulated by the Chinese authorities.

As written, equation (4) assumes that all capital flows between the U.S. and China are autonomous. This assumption is appropriate when the yuan is fully flexible, which is the scenario of this section. Subsequently, equation (4) will be amended to accommodate the fixed-rate scenarios.

We begin by assuming that both exchange rates are fully flexible. This is the regime that Washington policy makers have been working to achieve by pressing China to allow the yuan's value to be determined by market forces. As noted above, capital mobility is high with Europe and low with China.

Monetary Policy
A monetary expansion in the United States produces well-known results. The expansion raises U.S. income and thereby causes both trade balances to deteriorate. It lowers the rate of interest, bringing about capital outflows, which impact negatively on U.S. financial accounts with both countries. As a result, the dollar depreciates against both currencies. If we assume for the present that the marginal import propensities in equations (3) and (4) are roughly similar, then the current account deteriorations are roughly similar as well.[5] In view of Europe's higher capital mobility, however, the decline in the U.S. interest rate affects the financial account with that region more severely than that with China. Hence, the dollar's depreciation against the euro is relatively larger. In the main, however, this result is consistent with well-known findings that depreciation enhances the effectiveness of monetary policy in achieving a reduction in the U.S. output gap.

The essential features of the adjustment are depicted in Figure 1. Note that the shift in goods-market equilibrium, represented by the ISXM curve, is the result of changes in both exchange rates and that there are separate curves for balance of payments equilibrium between the U.S. and its two trading partners. The steeper curve (BP) reflects the assumption of low capital mobility vis-à-vis China, while the flatter curve (BP*) accommodates the high degree of capital mobility between the

U.S. and Euroland. The monetary expansion shifts out the LM curve, while the depreciation of the dollar against the two currencies shifts the ISXM curve out and the two BP curves down. In the new equilibrium, U.S. output is higher and the interest rate lower than initially. The resulting improvement in output and employment is stronger than in the closed economy. This is the outcome that would pertain if the U.S. succeeded in persuading China to allow its exchange rate to become completely market-determined.[6]

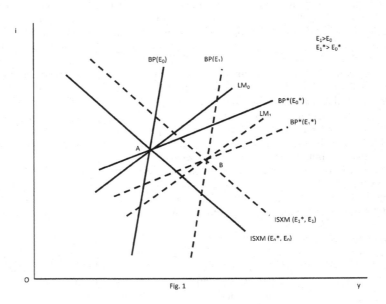

Fig. 1

Fiscal Policy

In the closed economy, a U.S. fiscal expansion shifts out the goods-market equilibrium curve along the stationary LM curve in Figure 2, raising output and the interest rate. In the open economy, however, the rise in output causes deterioration in both current accounts. The rise in the interest rate, on the other hand, improves the financial account with Europe by more than enough to offset the deterioration of the current account, therefore causing the dollar to appreciate against the euro. This, in turn, causes the goods-market equilibrium curve to shift inward, as indicated by the lower arrow, and the BP* curve to shift up to $BP^*(E_1^*)$. The result is to reduce the effectiveness of the fiscal expansion in achieving a desired reduction in the output gap.

With respect to China, on the other hand, the interest-rate increase is not large enough to improve the financial account by as much as the rise in U.S. output has caused the bilateral current account to deteriorate. The dollar is forced to depreciate

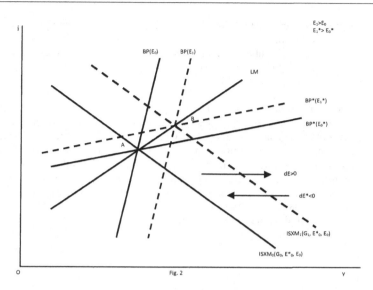

Fig. 2

against the yuan, pushing the goods-market curve out, as indicated by the upper arrow, and the BP curve to $BP(E_1)$. These adjustments, therefore, work in directions opposite to those associated with the dollar's appreciation against the euro. The net effect on the ISXM curve depends on the magnitudes of the relevant interest-rate and exchange-rate elasticities between the U.S. and Europe and China, respectively. If the forces indicated by the two arrows are equal, then the ISXM curve will not move from the position it reached with the initial fiscal expansion. That is the case depicted in Figure 2. The likelihood of little or no movement in ISXM rises as the values of the U.S. marginal propensities to spend on imports from the two trading partners and the exchange-rate elasticities of the two bilateral trade balances, respectively, converge toward each other.

When the adjustments are perfectly offsetting, the effectiveness of the fiscal expansion does not change relative to the closed-economy outcome. On the other hand, if the European results dominate, then the effectiveness of fiscal expansion will be weaker. It will be stronger, if the Chinese side of the adjustment process dominates.

3.   An Open Economy with Two Exchange-Rate Regimes

In this section we assume that China unilaterally pegs the yuan to the U.S. dollar. When the central bank intervenes in the foreign-exchange market and acquires dollars with yuan, it is assumed to convert those dollars into U.S. Treasury securities by purchasing them directly from the U.S. Federal Reserve.[7] It is important to keep in mind that intervention is carried out by the Chinese authorities rather than the

Americans. As they do so, the level of China's reserves will be changing, but in equilibrium there is no ongoing intervention in this scenario. In equilibrium, autonomous current account imbalances are exactly offset by autonomous financial flows. In this instance, R^C and hence H are clearly endogenous.

Monetary Policy
As before, a monetary expansion tends to put upward pressure on U.S. GDP and downward pressure on U.S. interest rates, causing deterioration in both current accounts and in both financial accounts. The Chinese authorities intervene in the foreign-exchange market by supplying yuan in exchange for dollars and use those dollars to purchase U.S. Treasury securities from the Fed. As a result, U.S. money supply shrinks until the initial rise in money supply due to the Fed's expansionary policy has been eliminated (as indicated by the westward arrow in Figure 3) and interest rates and GDP have returned to their original levels. The monetary policy is completely ineffective in the pursuit of higher levels of output and employment.

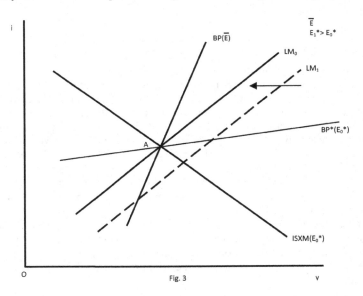

Fig. 3

It is worth noting in view of the flexibility of the dollar-euro rate, that the immediate effect of the policy is to push the rate up as it did in Figure 1. However, that higher rate and its effects on domestic income and employment is not sustainable, given the current account deficit with China, whose exchange-market intervention continues until the money supply has returned to its initial level.

While the end result is to an extent typical of fixed-rate regimes, the novelty here is that it occurs in the context of a free float between the dollar and the euro. The dollar depreciation against the euro, which would take place under floating rates, is prevented by the exigencies of a mixed-rate regime. The Chinese policy of pegging against the dollar has the effect of immobilizing the dollar against the euro. China's unilateral decision to attach its currency to the dollar prevents the U.S. from enjoying the benefits of monetary expansion under floating rates. In this situation, intervention by the Chinese central bank effectively makes the U.S. a non-floater.

Fiscal Policy
As before, a fiscal expansion shifts ISXM out and raises both GDP and the rate of interest. With high capital mobility between the U.S. and Europe, the resulting improvement of the financial account dominates the deterioration of the current account. The dollar appreciates against the euro, which shifts the ISXM and BP* curves in Figure 4 to the left, thereby reducing the potency of the fiscal expansion in the pursuit of high domestic output and employment. Meanwhile, the U.S. balance of payments with China deteriorates, because bilateral current account worsening exceeds bilateral financial account improvement. The Chinese authorities intervene to prevent the yuan from appreciating and then recycle the dollars acquired back to the U.S. by purchasing U.S. Treasury securities directly from the Fed. U.S. money supply shrinks, causing the LM curve to shift left in Figure 4. This reduction of liquidity has the effect of further limiting the expansion of output and employment.

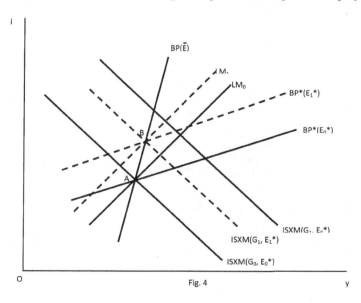

Fig. 4

4. The Foreign Central Bank Asserts Control Over the U.S. Money Supply

In this section, we assume that the Chinese authorities recycle intervention dollars directly into the U.S. financial system by purchasing Treasury securities from the public. In other words, the Chinese conduct "open-market operations" in the U.S. which have the effect of sterilizing the contractionary impact of their foreign-exchange market interventions on U.S. money supply.[8]

Monetary Policy
We now rewrite equation (4) as follows:

$$T(y^c, y) + K^C(i, i^c) + R^C = 0, \tag{4a}$$

where R^C represents the ongoing official capital inflow from China. It means that any excess demand or supply in the bilateral autonomous balance of payments is automatically accommodated by the Chinese authorities. In other words, the autonomous imbalance is made "permanent" by this recycling policy.

A U.S. monetary expansion shifts the LM curve out in Figure 5 and puts upward pressure on output and downward pressure on interest rates, worsening both current and capital accounts vis-à-vis Europe. The dollar depreciates against the euro, which enhances the effect of the monetary policy on output and employment. (The BP* curve shifts down to the right and the ISXM curve shifts out.)

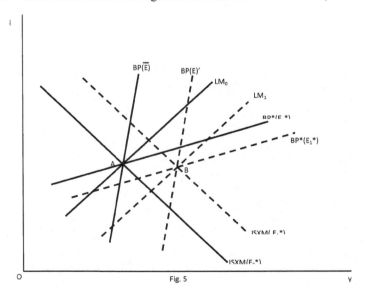

Fig. 5

The U.S. current account with China also moves into deficit and the bilateral autonomous financial account deteriorates as well. But this overall deterioration in the bilateral autonomous balance of payments is accommodated by dollar accumulation on the part of the Chinese central bank. The BP curve moves down to the right. The gap between the initial and new BP curves reflects the extent of the deficit in the autonomous balance of payments between the U.S. and China that must be financed by the ongoing inflow of official capital from China. At point B, a "permanent" payments deficit with China is financed by official Chinese accumulation of dollar-denominated securities.

Fiscal Policy

A fiscal expansion in the U.S. shifts the ISXM curve to $ISXM(G_1^*, E_0^*)$ in Figure 6, tending to raise output and interest rates. The dollar appreciates against the euro, given the assumed high capital mobility between the U.S. and Europe. The appreciation to E_1 shifts the BP* curve up and to the left and the ISXM curve moves back inward. These adjustments reflect a weakening of the effectiveness of the fiscal expansion.

With respect to China, the bilateral current account deteriorates and the financial account improves. The net effect is a deficit in the autonomous balance of payments with China. The central bank of China prevents the incipient appreciation of the yuan by intervening in the foreign exchange market. It then recycles the dollars acquired in the process back into circulation in the U.S. by purchasing U.S. Treasury securities from the public. The imbalance in bilateral payments is made permanent by this move and China continues to accumulate claims against the United States. Once again, the automatic adjustment mechanism has been shut down and the ongoing payments deficit is financed by Chinese reserve accumulation.

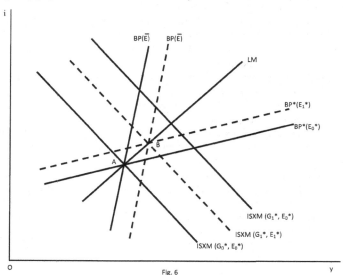

Fig. 6

5. Conclusion

In this mixed-regime model, the United States is neither a clear floater nor a full fixer, a condition which has ramifications for the effectiveness of monetary and fiscal policies in the context of cyclical stabilization. This paper has used a modified open-economy macro model to examine the implications. In an initial section, policy effectiveness is examined in the context of full flexibility of both exchange rates. The results are broadly consistent with the well-known benchmark model. However, high capital mobility between the U.S. and Europe, combined with low mobility between the U.S. and China, causes the two exchange rates to move in opposite directions in reaction to a fiscal expansion, with offsetting effects on policy effectiveness.

The paper next explores the case of a pegged yuan in the context of two scenarios. In the first, China recycles dollars absorbed in the process of exchange-market intervention by purchasing U.S. Treasury securities directly from the Fed, while in the second scenario the securities are purchased from the public. This allows China's pegging and recycling operations to "interfere" with the macro adjustment process within the United States. For example, even though the dollar is nominally free to fluctuate against the euro, the fact that China fixes the dollar-yuan rate "freezes" the dollar-euro rate. In another example, China's purchases of U.S. Treasury securities from the public essentially shut down the automatic adjustment mechanism associated with fixed rates.

Notes

1. Sven W. Arndt is Charles M. Stone Professor of Money, Credit and Trade at Claremont McKenna College. Comments from Tony Cavoli, and from participants at the meetings of the 2010 Asia Pacific Economics Association in Hong Kong and of the 2011 International Trade and Finance Association in Denver are gratefully acknowledged. Thanks to Saumya Lohia and Hao Tang for valuable research assistance and to the Financial Economics Institute at Claremont McKenna College for generous research support. Sven W. Arndt, Claremont McKenna College, Claremont, California 91711, sarndt@cmc.edu
2. According to the IMF (2008), the U.S. operates an "independently floating" exchange-rate regime. The evidence shows that this is so both *de jure* and *de facto*. China's regime is classified as a "fixed peg," meaning no bands. For more on the ongoing debate over exchange-rate arrangements, see Levy-Yeyati and Sturzenegger (2005), Reinhart and Rogoff (2004) and Shambaugh (2004).
3. In the Bretton-Woods system, rates were fixed in a coordinated, consensual manner, with each country committed to the defense of the agreed-upon rates. In the present case, China fixes to the dollar unilaterally. While China is not the first country to have done so, it is the first country large enough to generate serious repercussions for the U.S.

4. We use this model as the benchmark model because it is well-known. It is the model found in most undergraduate and graduate textbooks and it is the paradigm widely used by contemporary policy makers. That does not always make it the best analytical tool. Alternative model choices would include the New Open Economy Macro Models as expounded by Obstfeld (2001), Obstfeld and Rogoff (1995), Lane (2001) and Corsetti (2007) and the portfolio-balance model (Frankel, 1993; Devereux and Sutherland, 2007).

5. Production networking and processing trade between China and the U.S. may reduce the response of the trade balance to changes in certain variables, including the exchange rate and domestic GDP (Arndt (2010)).

6. It is important to note that many countries in Asia fix their currencies to the dollar; others price their exports in dollars. Many are participants in international production networks that either feed end products to the United States or engage the U.S. in reciprocal components trade. These linkages have implications for exchange-rate and macro adjustment. (See, for example, Arndt and Huemer, 2007.)

    Suppose, for example, that China allows the yuan to float against the dollar, but that Singapore fixes its currency against the dollar. Then a yuan appreciation against the U.S. dollar is also a yuan appreciation against the Singapore dollar. The U.S. dollar price of end products from China rises, but the yuan price of components from Singapore falls and with it the cost of end-product exports to the United States. If Chinese value-added contained in Chinese exports is small, then dollar depreciation against the yuan has repercussions only for a small part of the price of end-products from China. The effect of exchange-rate changes on the trade balance is reduced and with it the shift of BP due to a given exchange-rate shock.

7. We assume for simplicity that China pegs solely to the U.S. dollar and that it is a peg without bands. In reality, China is believed to operate a basket peg, with the dollar the dominant currency. China also has allowed the actual rate of the yuan to fluctuate. These departures from our simple peg will affect the magnitudes of various outcomes, but not the essential story. For further discussion of China's exchange-rate policy, see Frankel and Wei (2007).

8. In this section, we assume that sterilization is complete. A more realistic case would lie somewhere between this and the preceding scenario. See Obstfeld (1982) and Sarno and Taylor (2001), for example, for further discussion of the effectiveness of sterilization.

9. The fact that many of the components imported by China from third countries are incorporated into China's final-product exports implies that the "bilateral" current account deficit between the U.S. and the People's Republic is in reality a U.S. deficit with a multiplicity of countries. Indeed, only a relatively small part of the value of the trade imbalance between the U.S. and China is directly attributable to China as opposed to the countries that supply China with components and intermediate products. The importance of "processing" trade in China's overall trade is expertly examined in Xing (2011).

References

Arndt, S.W., (2010), "Intra-industry Trade and the Open Economy", *Korea and the World Economy*, December, 11(2), 1-18.

Arndt, S.W. and Huemer, A., (2007), "Trade, Production Networks and the Exchange Rate", *Journal of Economic Asymmetries*, June, 4(1), 11-39.

Corsetti, G., (2007), "New Open Economy Macroeconomics", *CEPR Discussion Papers*, November.

Devereux, M.B. and Sutherland, A., (2007), "Monetary Policy and Portfolio Choice in an Open Economy Macro Model", *Journal of the European Economic Association*, April-May, 5(2-3), 491-499.

Frankel, J.A., (1993), "Monetary and Portfolio-Balance Models of the Determination of Exchange Rates", in J.A. Frankel, *On Exchange Rates*, Cambridge, MA: MIT Press, 95-115.

Frankel, J.A. and Wei, S.-J., (2007), "Assessing China's Exchange Rate Regime", Cambridge, MA: National Bureau of Economic Research, Working Paper No. 13100.

International Monetary Fund, (2008), "De Facto Classification of Exchange Rate Regimes and Monetary Policy Framework", April.

Lane, P., (2001), "The New Open Economy Macroeconomics: A Survey", *Journal of International Economics*, August, 54(2), 235-266.

Levy-Yeyati, E. and Sturzenegger, F., (2005), "Classifying Exchange Rate Regimes: Deeds vs. Words", *European Economic Review*, August, 49(6), 1603-1635.

Obstfeld, M., (1982), "Can We Sterilize? Theory and Evidence", *American Economic Review*, May, 72 (2), 45-50.

Obstfeld, M., (2001), "International Macroeconomics: Beyond the Mundell-Fleming Model", *IMF Staff Papers*, Special Issue: IMF Annual Research Conference.

Obstfeld, M. and Rogoff, K., (1995), "Exchange Rate Dynamics Redux," *Journal of Political Economy*, June, 103(3), 624-660.

Reinhart, C.M. and Rogoff, K., (2004), "A Modern History of Exchange Rate Arrangements: A Reinterpretation", *Quarterly Journal of Economics*, February, 119(1), 1-48.

Sarno, L. and Taylor, M.P., (2001), "Official Intervention in the Foreign Exchange Market: Is It Effective and, If So, How Does It Work?" *Journal of Economic Literature*, September, 39(3), 839-868.

Shambaugh, J.C., (2004), "The Effect of Fixed Exchange Rates on Monetary Policy." *Quarterly Journal of Economics*, February, 119(1), 301-352.

Xing, Y., (2011), "Processing Trade, Exchange Rates and the People's Republic of China's Bilateral Trade Balances," Asian Development Bank Institute, Working Paper No. 270.

Chapter 19

Stabilization Policy in an Economy with Two Exchange Rate Regimes*

Sven W. Arndt

Abstract

This paper uses a flex-price open economy macro model to examine the effectiveness of U.S. monetary and fiscal policies when the dollar floats freely against the euro, but is fixed against the Chinese yuan. It is assumed that capital mobility is high between the U.S. and the Eurozone, but low between the U.S. and China. The model allows for short-run price flexibility and imperfect substitutability between domestic and foreign financial assets.

The focus is on the implications for the efficacy of U.S. macro stabilization policies of China's fixed-rate strategy. While many countries have pegged their currencies to the dollar, China is large enough to have an impact. It is shown that its large size enables China to impede the effectiveness of U.S. macroeconomic policies. Indeed, while the U.S. is officially tagged as an independent floater, Chinese intervention is capable of interfering with dollar-euro flexibility and thereby creates outcomes that are more consistent with policy under fixed rates.

JEL CLASSIFICATION: F31, F32, F41

KEYWORDS: Open economy macro; Exchange rate regimes; U.S.-China payments adjustment

---

*Comments from Tony Cavoli and Kar-yiu Wong and from participants at meetings of the International Trade and Finance Association, the Asia-Pacific Economic Association and the Association of Korean Economic Studies and at the 2011 conference of the Singapore Economic Review are gratefully acknowledged. For valuable research assistance and research support, respectively, I am indebted to Hao Tang and the Financial Economics Institute at CMC.

1. Introduction

A widely used approach in modeling the role of the exchange rate in open-economy macroeconomics is to assume that a country is either a pegger against the rest of the world or a floater. In that spirit, the International Monetary Fund (IMF) classifies the United States as an "independent floater." While this is an appropriate interpretation of (*de jure*) U.S. policy, it does not accurately reflect the country's *de facto* exchange-rate regime. That regime is a combination of floating rates against most countries and a fixed rate against the *renminbi* (RMB) or yuan, fixed by intervention of the Chinese monetary authority.

The object of this paper is to explore the implications of such a mixed exchange-rate regime for (i) the effectiveness of domestic macro stabilization policies and (ii) the transmission of foreign shocks and disturbances. The analysis is carried out with the aid of a medium-term open-economy macro model with prices and output both flexible (implying a positively sloped aggregate supply curve) and with capital mobility high between the U.S. and the Eurozone and low between the U.S. and China.[1] A final section examines the implications of production sharing between the U.S. and China for adjustment at the macro level. It is shown that China's exchange rate policy has material implications for U.S. macro policy autonomy and for the effect of foreign shocks on the U.S. economy. A particularly important consequence is that Chinese intervention, and the manner in which dollars are recycled into circulation in the U.S., interferes with the "automatic" adjustment mechanism in the American economy.

Section 2 provides an outline of the model and derives solutions for the benchmark scenario of a freely floating dollar against both currencies. Section 3 works out the mixed-regime scenario and provides an assessment of the U.S.-China policy debate over the causes of the bilateral current account imbalance. Section 4 focuses on the international transmission of economic shocks and disturbances in a mixed-rate regime and shows that fixing causes the U.S. economy to become more exposed to cyclical disturbances in China.. Section 5 examines the implications of production fragmentation between the U.S. and China and Section 6 concludes.

2. Freely Floating Rates Everywhere

In this section, the dollar is assumed to float freely against both the euro and the yuan. This is the preferred regime, according to Washington policy makers who continue to press China to allow the yuan to float against the dollar. The results of

---

[1] For an analysis of some of these issues in a sticky-price model, see Arndt (2011).

Global Economy Journal, Vol. 12 [2012], Iss. 2, Art. 7

this section will thus serve as a benchmark against which to evaluate the outcomes associated with the actual mixed-rate regime.

The model in this paper is one that is familiar to and used by most policy makers. It is based on the Mundell-Fleming (MF) model, but allows for price flexibility. Hence, rather than being flat, the aggregate supply curve is positively sloped. The broad effect of this change in structure is to reduce the response of income and employment to policy initiatives, because some portion of the energy of policy stimuli is absorbed into price changes. It also introduces an additional source of changes in real exchange rates.

The basic structure of the model is given by the well-known equilibrium conditions for the money market, the goods market and the balance of payments. The money market is specified as follows:

$$H/P = L(y, i), \tag{1}$$

where H represents the monetary base, P is a general price index, y is real gross domestic product, and i is a nominal interest rate or structure of nominal interest rates. The real demand for money, L, responds positively to income or output and negatively to the rate of interest.

Goods market equilibrium is specified as follows:

$$I(i) + T(y, y^*, y^\wedge; e^*, e^\wedge) - S(y) = -G, \tag{2}$$

where I is real capital formation, T is the trade balance or current account, S is private-sector saving, G represents the government budget deficit, y^* and $y^\wedge$ stand for Eurozone and Chinese GDP, respectively, and e^* and $e^\wedge$ represent the dollar's real exchange rate with respect to the euro and the yuan, respectively. The real exchange rate is defined as the nominal rate E (expressed as the dollar price of the respective foreign currency) multiplied by the ratio of the respective foreign price level to the U.S price variable, P. Investment responds negatively to the rate of interest; the current account worsens with a rise in U.S. income, but improves with foreign GDP and improves with a rise in either real exchange rate. Private sector saving is positively related to domestic GDP.

There are two balance-of-payments equilibrium conditions, one for the Eurozone, the other for China.

$$T^*(y, y^*, e^*) + K^*(i, i^*) = 0, \tag{3a}$$

and

$$T^\wedge(y, y^\wedge, e^\wedge) + K^\wedge(i, i^\wedge) = 0, \tag{3b}$$

Arndt: An Economy with Two Exchange Rate Regimes

where capital inflows respond positively to the domestic interest rate and negatively to the respective foreign rates. As noted above, capital mobility with Europe is assumed to be high, while that with China is low.

The aggregate supply curve is modeled as follows:

$$P = P(y), P_y > 0. \tag{4}$$

Monetary Expansion

The effects of a monetary expansion in the United States are summarized in Figure 1. The curves are familiar from the standard open-economy macro model, except that all slopes will generally be steeper as a result of the assumption of price flexibility. The steeper of the two balance-of-payments curves, B^B^ reflects the low degree of capital mobility vis-à-vis China. A monetary expansion shifts out the LL curve. The rise in domestic GDP and decline in the domestic rate of interest worsen both current accounts and both financial accounts. There is unambiguous pressure on the dollar to depreciate against both currencies. These depreciations shift the goods-market equilibrium and the two balance-of-payments functions to the right.

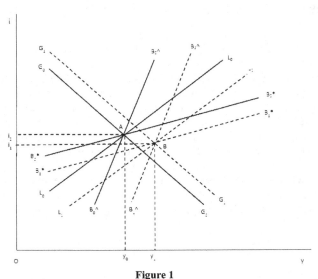

Figure 1

3

Global Economy Journal, Vol. 12 [2012], Iss. 2, Art. 7

At the new equilibrium, B, domestic income has risen, but by less than in the standard model, because the domestic price level has also increased. The magnitude of this price-adjustment effect depends on the slope (P_y) of the aggregate supply curve. The rise in U.S. prices implies that the dollar's real depreciation is smaller than the nominal depreciation with respect to both currencies. If purchasing power held before the shock, it no longer does in the new equilibrium. The relative magnitudes of the real depreciations depend on the values of both trade and financial account parameters.

Fiscal Expansion

The effects of an expansionary fiscal policy (dG>0) are summarized in Figure 2. The rise in government expenditures shifts out the goods market equilibrium function. The consequent rise in domestic GDP worsens both current accounts, while the rise in the domestic interest rate improves the financial account with the Eurozone by more than enough to offset the current account deterioration, but by less than is needed to offset the deterioration of the current account with China. There is thus pressure for the dollar to appreciate against the euro and to depreciate against the yuan. This has the effect of shifting the B*B* curve to the left and the B^B^ curve to the right. In the new equilibrium, they will have to intersect somewhere on the stationary LL curve. The exact location of that intersection depends on adjustment in the goods market.

The goods-market line is subject to two opposing pressures, with the euro depreciation tending to push it to the left and the yuan appreciation tending to push it to the right. The actual direction of movement depends on the relative strengths of these two effects. If they are equal, there will be no further movement of the GG curve and the final equilibrium will, as shown, lie at the point of intersection of the G_1G_1 and LL curves.

In that event, the policy's effectiveness will not differ from that of the closed-economy case. If dollar-euro adjustment is the dominant force, then the G_1G_1-line shifts left and policy effectiveness is weakened. If dollar-yuan adjustment dominates, then the line shifts to the right and policy effectiveness is strengthened.

Hence, ironically, low capital mobility between the U.S. and China, which is to a significant extent the result of capital and exchange controls in the latter, serves to strengthen the effectiveness of U.S. fiscal policy.

The dollar's real appreciation against the euro is reinforced by the rise in the domestic price level. The dollar's real depreciation against the yuan is made smaller than its nominal depreciation by the rise in the U.S. price level.

Arndt: An Economy with Two Exchange Rate Regimes

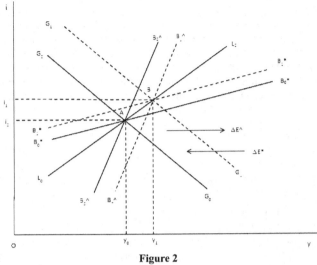

Figure 2

3. The Euro Floats While the Yuan is Fixed

In this section, it is assumed that China intervenes in the foreign exchange market in order to prevent the yuan's value from changing against the dollar. When the Chinese central bank intervenes to prevent the yuan from appreciating, it pulls dollars out of circulation, which has the same effect on U.S. money supply as would an intervention by the Federal Reserve. When the Chinese central bank uses these dollars to purchase U.S. Treasury securities in the open market, the effect is to offset the reduction in U.S. money supply brought about by the intervention itself. The result is well-known in the literature on sterilized exchange-market intervention: U.S. money supply is unchanged, the automatic adjustment mechanism for fixed-rate regimes is frozen, and the imbalance in the China-U.S. bilateral balance of payments is made "permanent".

The shift in the Chinese exchange-rate regime from floating to fixed requires a change in our specification of money market equilibrium. As in the previous case, base money is adjusted by the Fed through changes in domestic credit via standard open-market operations. When China intervenes to absorb an excess supply of dollars in the foreign exchange market, the result is to reduce base money in the U.S., very much like a Fed intervention (of selling yuan for

Global Economy Journal, Vol. 12 [2012], Iss. 2, Art. 7

dollars) would reduce base money. When the central bank of China follows up by purchasing U.S. Treasuries, the foregoing reduction in base money is offset.[2]

Monetary Expansion

The effects of a monetary expansion in the context of this mixed regime are summarized in Figure 3. The initial effect is to shift the LL curve to the right, which tends to reduce interest rates and raise domestic output and prices. With respect to the euro, both the current account and the financial account with the Eurozone deteriorate, thereby generating pressures for the dollar to depreciate against the euro. This tends to push both the GG curve and the B*B* curve to the right.

The rise in income and decline in domestic interest rates tend also to worsen both sides of the U.S. balance of payments with China. In order to prevent the yuan from appreciating against the dollar, the Chinese authorities intervene in the foreign exchange market in order to absorb the excess supply of dollars, after which they convert these dollars into U.S. Treasury securities. In combination, these two actions maintain the U.S. money supply at its new level.

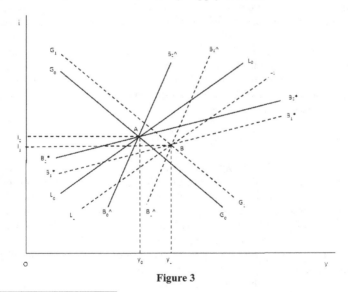

Figure 3

[2] For an intermediate scenario in which the Chinese authorities purchase Treasury securities directly from the Fed, see Arndt (2011). In that scenario, the automatic adjustment mechanism continues to function.

Arndt: An Economy with Two Exchange Rate Regimes

We rewrite the equilibrium condition for the U.S.-China balance of payments in order to reflect the fact that any imbalance in autonomous transactions will always be met by an offsetting transaction on official reserve account:

$$T^\wedge(y, y^\wedge, e^\wedge) + K^\wedge(i, i^\wedge) + R^\wedge = 0, \tag{3c}$$

where $R^\wedge$ represents the level of dollar reserves held by the Chinese authorities and where $dE^\wedge = 0$. While the nominal exchange rate is fixed, the flexibility of U.S. prices in this model makes room for changes in the real rate of exchange between the two countries.

Returning to Figure 3, we note that the new LL curve is now the anchor for the system in the sense that the new equilibrium must lie somewhere on that function. Suppose that the new goods-market and U.S.-Europe balance-of-payments curves meet at point B on the new LL curve. The combination of interest rate and income represented by that point leaves the autonomous U.S.-China balance of payments in deficit, i.e., the sum of the first two terms in equation (3c) is negative. This requires the Chinese central bank to accumulate dollars in perpetuity or until the U.S. central bank reverses its easy-money policy.[3] The $B^\wedge B^\wedge$ curve through point B thus reflects a balance of payments equilibrium in which a U.S. deficit in autonomous transactions is just covered by Chinese reserve accumulation.

At point B the dollar has depreciated against the euro in both nominal and real terms. It has remained unchanged against the yuan in nominal terms, but has *appreciated* against the Chinese currency in real terms. This appreciation is the result of the increase in the U.S. price level.

Fiscal Expansion

The effects of a U.S. fiscal expansion are summarized in Figure 4. The policy stimulus moves the GG curve to the right, tending to raise income and the rate of interest. As in the previous section, the rise in income causes both current account balances to deteriorate, while the higher interest rate attracts capital inflows from both countries. In the case of the Eurozone, where capital mobility is high, the improvement in the bilateral financial account exceeds the deterioration in the current account, thereby putting pressure on the dollar to appreciate against the euro. This appreciation causes the GG and B*B* curves to shift left. This is the familiar finding that high capital mobility reduces the effectiveness of fiscal policy.

---

[3] A later section considers some of the implications for the ongoing debate between the U.S. and China on who is responsible for and what should be done about the sustained current imbalances.

Global Economy Journal, Vol. 12 [2012], Iss. 2, Art. 7

On the Chinese side, low capital mobility limits the improvement of the financial account, so that the balance on autonomous payments deteriorates. Under floating rates, the dollar would depreciate against the yuan, thereby tending to strengthen the effectiveness of the fiscal expansion. The central bank of China prevents the yuan from appreciating by soaking up the excess supply of dollars and converting them into Treasury securities. The new B^B^ curve through point B represents a balance-of-payments equilibrium in which the deficit in autonomous transactions is just offset by reserve accumulation on the part of the Chinese authorities.

At point B, the dollar has appreciated against the euro in both nominal and real terms; it has remained fixed in nominal terms against the yuan, but has appreciated in real terms against the Chinese currency. This additional boost to the real value of the dollar worsens the imbalance between the U.S. and China, but it is important to keep in mind that this model does not take into account possible price increases in China.

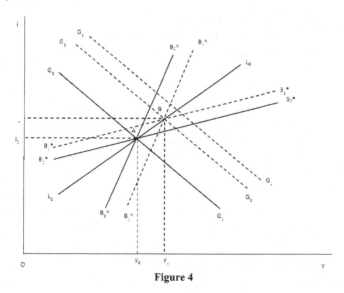

Figure 4

Lessons for the China-U.S. Policy Debate

The persistent China-U.S. current account imbalances continue to be a significant irritant in relations between the two countries. Many U.S. commentators and politicians tend to blame China's policy of fixing the yuan to the dollar at levels that may be too low. High and steadily rising levels of China's foreign-exchange reserves are cited as the primary piece of evidence that the yuan is undervalued. China's response has been to use the national income identity to argue that the problem is "made in the U.S.A." and arises from imbalances in the country's public finances and private sector saving and investment.

Although the model used in this paper is not fully suited to resolving the debate, it does offer some useful insights. First, the discussion in Section 2 shows that a flexible yuan would indeed restore balance in autonomous transactions. It does not say that there could not exist continuous current account imbalances, financed by financial account imbalances of equal magnitude and opposite sign. The cases captured by Figs. 1 and 3 taken together suggest that a shift by China from fixed to floating rates would cause the yuan to appreciate against the dollar, would reduce the bilateral current account imbalance, and would boost output and employment in the United States.

The discussion in earlier sections has underscored the role of low capital mobility between the U.S. and China in driving the results. Thus, another way in which China could alleviate the imbalance problem is to eliminate or reduce controls on capital movements, thereby allowing Chinese households, firms, and organizations to expand their portfolios toward foreign-currency-denominated assets. Paired with a fixed exchange rate, this policy would spread accumulation of foreign assets away from the central bank to the rest of the Chinese economy. Among the many benefits would be asset diversification and better returns. It would sharply reduce the gap between the current value of the yuan and its equilibrium or market-clearing value on the assumption that there is within China a pent-up private demand for dollar and other foreign assets. This reduction in the misalignment of the bilateral exchange rate would not only cool the rhetoric in Washington, but reduce the threat to small and medium-sized firms in China's leading export sectors of a move to greater exchange-rate flexibility.

As for the "made-in-America" argument, deficit reduction in the U.S. would have results opposite to those discussed in connection with Figure 4: it would reduce the bilateral imbalance. A rise in private sector saving, which has occurred in the aftermath of the financial crisis, would also have that effect. The downside of this strategy is that its short-run effect would be to reduce output and employment and thus to aggravate the economic situation in the U.S.

Finally, when the Chinese central bank recycles intervention dollars by purchasing U.S. government securities from the public or directly from the Treasury, it essentially neutralizes the forces that would work to restore balance in the foreign exchange market. The Fed might want to implement a strategy of selling Treasury securities directly to the Chinese authorities and thereby make room for the contraction of money supply that would follow.

Global Economy Journal, Vol. 12 [2012], Iss. 2, Art. 7

4. Cross-Border Transmission

Most economies have become significantly more open in recent years, with more extensive linkages among domestic and foreign markets for goods, services, and assets. One of the consequences may be that shocks and disturbances are more easily transmitted from one country to another, allowing for the usual caveats pertaining to transaction, transportation, and communication costs. In goods and services trade, an important contributor to this development has been the growth of cross-border production networks, which means that a downturn in demand in a country like the United States spreads to other countries not only via traditional "horizontal" channels, but by "vertical" channels along the value-added chain.

In the financial arena, greater market integration means that risky or contaminated assets held by financial institution in one country, create problems not only for the immediate parties involved, but for lenders and investors in third countries, who have provided funding to the process.[4] These often complex and opaque linkages are at least partly to blame for the growing role of contagion effects.

The nature and extent of cross-border transmission of shocks and disturbances depends on the exchange rate regime. In the model of this paper, flexible exchange rates provide significant insulation. In the first scenario, when the dollar floats against both currencies, a change in income growth in either China or the Eurozone has no effect on U.S. GDP or interest rates. Its only effect is to cause the expanding country's currency to appreciate against the dollar. This appreciation exactly offsets the stimulus emitted by the growth increase.

When the Chinese exchange rate is fixed along the lines of the second scenario, however, there is transmission. As shown in Figure 5, a rise in Chinese GDP initially shifts goods-market equilibrium and the U.S.-China autonomous payments curve to the right. Under high capital mobility, the dollar appreciates against the euro, which moves the new G and B* curves to the left. The B^ curve running through point B represents overall payments equilibrium between the U.S. and China (while the $B_1{}^{\wedge}$ curve represents equilibrium in autonomous transactions only). Hence, the distance between those curves represents the period-by-period decline in Chinese foreign-exchange reserves. Thus, a rise in Chinese growth raises U.S. GDP. In this model, at least, the rapid Chinese growth in recent years would not have had the beneficial effects on U.S. economic activity if there had been a floating rate between the two currencies.

---

[4] This recalls a feature of the European sovereign debt crisis, where suspect Greek government bonds undermine confidence not only in German and other European banks who made the initial loans, but in the U.S.-based money-market funds who provided some of the funding.

Arndt: An Economy with Two Exchange Rate Regimes

Finally, again in the second scenario of a mixed exchange-rate regime, faster growth in the Eurozone has no effect on the U.S. economy. Its only consequence is to cause the dollar to appreciate against the euro.

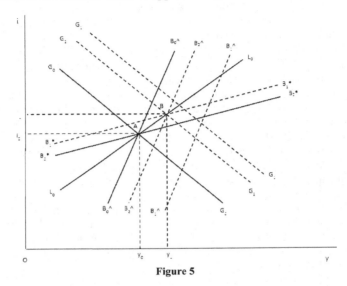

Figure 5

5. Production Sharing and Vertical Intra-Industry Trade

Cross-border production networks and vertical intra-industry investment and trade have grown rapidly in recent years, helped along by increasingly open and interlinked economies and important cost-saving innovations in transportation and communication technologies. As a result, trade in intermediates, parts and components has seen significant growth relative to other forms of trade. Indeed, the share of such transactions in total trade has become large enough to affect adjustment at the macro level. As Arndt & Huemer (2007) and others have shown, vertical intra-industry trade reduces the sensitivity of the trade balance and current account to movements in exchange rates. Arndt (2010) has argued that the growth of direct links between a country's exports and imports, which are typical of vertical intra-industry trade, alter response functions and adjustment patterns in a standard open-economy macro model of the Mundell-Fleming type.

An additional feature of vertical intra-industry trade is that it exposes *non-traded* goods and services directly to variations in exchange rates and to competition from abroad. This follows from the fact that production of non-traded goods may contain tradable components and non-traded services may contain

11

Global Economy Journal, Vol. 12 [2012], Iss. 2, Art. 7

tradable constituent activities. For example, X-ray procedures may not be tradable, but reading and analyzing X-ray images are tradable activities. Hence, the total cost of an X-ray procedure will rise with depreciation of a country's currency if image analysis is outsourced to a foreign operator.

It is possible to explore the implications of such developments in the context of the present model by rewriting equation (4) to include an exchange-rate effect. We assume that the share of components trade between the U.S. and China is large enough to imply that a dollar depreciation against the yuan shifts the aggregate supply curve up and we model that effect as follows:

$$P = P(y, E^\wedge). \tag{4a}$$

The main consequence is to introduce a direct effect of exchange-rate changes into the money demand function, so that variations in the dollar-yuan exchange rate move the LL curve under floating rates. As suggested earlier, another effect is to reduce the responsiveness of the GG and $B^\wedge B^\wedge$ curves to variations in exchange rates. This makes exchange-rate variability a less forceful instrument for payments adjustment.

6. Concluding Remarks

Over the decades, many countries have unilaterally fixed their currencies to the U.S. dollar. Countries in Latin America and in East Asia have been among them. Since they have tended to be small relative to the huge U.S. economy, their pegging policies have not aroused much concern in the United States. By and large, they have not seemed to interfere with U.S. policy-making autonomy.

The People's Republic of China also unilaterally pegs the yuan to the dollar, but its economy is large. As the ongoing debate over the implications of this policy suggests, it has become a major irritant to the U.S. From the point of view of many American businesses, the "undervalued" level at which the yuan is fixed gives China an unfair competitive edge in trade relations between the two countries. The policy also contributes to the large bilateral current account imbalance and to rising U.S. indebtedness to China.

A third issue, which has received less attention, concerns the extent to which unilateral pegging by China interferes with U.S. macroeconomic policy autonomy. This question is examined in the preceding pages with the aid of a medium-term open-economy macro model in which both prices and output are flexible. The focus is on the effectiveness of U.S. monetary and fiscal policies and the transmission of foreign disturbances to U.S. economic activity. A key assumption throughout is that capital mobility is high between the U.S. and the

Arndt: An Economy with Two Exchange Rate Regimes

Eurozone and other countries against which the dollar floats, but low between the U.S. and China.

The model is first solved for the system preferred by the U.S., namely, universal flexible exchange rates. This is the benchmark result against which the *de facto* alternative of a mixed-rate regime is compared. It is shown that China's pegging policy does affect the efficacy of U.S. macro policies, in part because China uses the dollar as its main reserve currency. By recycling intervention dollars into U.S. Treasury securities, China contributes to the "permanent" nature of the bilateral current account imbalance.

It is also shown that growth spurts from China to the U.S. have positive effects in the U.S. compared to growth spurts from the Eurozone. In the context of the recent recession in the U.S., that may actually have been a desirable result of China's policy.

An important element in U.S.-China trade relations is the importance of production networking and processing trade. These features are shown to affect the nature and efficiency of trade-balance adjustment in ways that do not exist in U.S. trade with the other countries in the model.

References

Arndt, S.W. (2011), "Adjustment in an Open Economy with Two Exchange-Rate Regimes," *Journal of Economic Asymmetries* (forthcoming).

_____ (2010), "Intra-Industry Trade and the Open Economy," *Korea and the World Economy*, 11 (3) (December).

_____ and A. Huemer (2007), "Trade, Production Networks and the Exchange Rate, *Journal of Economic Asymmetries*, 4, No. 1 (June).

Frankel, J.A. and S.-J. Wei (2007), "Assessing China's Exchange Rate Regime," NBER Working Paper No. 13100.

IMF (2008), "De Facto Classification of Exchange Rate Regimes and Monetary Policy Frameworks" (April).

Levy-Yeyati, E. and F. Sturzenegger (2005), "Classifying Exchange Rate Regimes: Deeds vs. Words," *European Economic Review*, 49 (6), (August).

Xing, Y. (2011), "Processing Trade, Exchange Rates and the People's Republic of China's Bilateral Trade Balances, Asian Development Bank Institute, Working Paper No. 270.

Chapter 20

Policy Challenges In A Dual Exchange Rate Regime[*]

Sven W. Arndt[**]

It is known that the effectiveness of macro policies depends on the exchange-rate regime. Pertinent models have typically considered either fixed or floating rates rather than mixed regimes. In recent years, however, the dollar has floated against most currencies, while being fixed against the yuan. This paper argues that a flex-price, dual-rate model consisting of the U.S., China and the Eurozone, combined with distinct adjustment patterns in tradables and non-tradables sectors and a tendency for policy makers to treat inflation in housing as pure asset inflation, provides a plausible explanation of the great moderation and its aftermath.

JEL Classification: E58, F32, F41
Keywords: Open-economy macro; Mixed exchange rate regime; Non-tradables; Asset inflation

---

[*] Received July 12, 2012. Revised August 1, 2012. Accepted August 8, 2012. The author is indebted to Chan-Guk Huh for valuable comments on an earlier draft and to participants at the AKES Conference on Korea and the World Economy, XI in Seoul, July 2012. Jing Wen provided able research assistance.
[**] Claremont McKenna College, 500 E. Ninth Street, Claremont, CA 91711, U.S.A., Tel: +909-607-7571, Fax: +909-621-8249, E-mail: sarndt@cmc.edu

Sven W. Arndt

1. INTRODUCTION

The effectiveness of macro stabilization policies is known to depend on the exchange rate regime. Monetary policy, for example, is ineffective in a small open economy with fixed exchange rates and high capital mobility, but very potent under floating rates. In the IMF's classification of exchange-rate regimes, countries are either floaters of various types or peggers of various types. In that scheme, the U.S. is officially classified as an "independent floater" (IMF, 2008; Fischer, 2001).

In the Bretton-Woods system, a country's currency was fixed against all member currencies, which at the time typically meant all major trading partners. The European Monetary System (EMS), on the other hand, was more of a mixed regime, with each member's currency fixed against every other member, but with the bloc of EMS currencies floating against the U.S. dollar and other major currencies.

Over the years, many small countries have tied their currencies to the dollar. Their small size vis-à-vis the U.S. meant that their currencies floated against other currencies in patterns beyond their control. China also fixes its currency against the dollar, but China is not small. The implications of this difference have recently been explored in the context of a short-run, sticky-price, Mundell-Fleming-type of model (Arndt, 2011) and of a medium-term model in which prices are flexible (Arndt, 2012). There it has been shown that China's unilateral exchange market intervention has significant effects on adjustment of the U.S. economy to domestic and foreign shocks and disturbances. It has also been shown that, unlike small countries, Chinese intervention interferes with U.S. policy autonomy.

This paper amends the aforementioned flex-price, dual-rate model by specifying the real side of the U.S. economy as consisting of tradables and non-tradables sectors. It argues that economic developments beginning in the early nineties and ending in the latter part of the first decade of this century were materially influenced by the mixed-rate regime, but that other considerations also came into play. The two-sector structure of the market for goods and services allows movements in relative prices to affect the allocation of labor and other scarce resources in the macro economy. In this model, price moderation due to foreign competition has larger effects on the tradables sector than on the non-tradables sector. The resulting relative price movements have important consequences.

A key component of the non-tradables sector is housing and in a high-employment economy, cost pressures arising in such an important sector are easily spread to the rest of the economy. At the time, however, the housing bubble was widely viewed as asset inflation and hence not as a sign of an overheating economy. In retrospect and with the benefit of hindsight, it would probably have been prudent to treat inflation in new housing, and in new structures more generally, as a sign of overheating.

The paper proceeds as follows. Section 2 outlines the basic model, focusing on the effects of a monetary expansion on economic activity when the output gap is large and when it is small. It assumes that capital mobility is high between the U.S. and Europe, but low with China. Section 3 takes a closer look at the interaction between tradables and non-tradables sectors as the economy moves toward and then surpasses the full employment level of output. It argues that high demand for non-tradables leads not only to price inflation in that sector, but to cost inflation throughout the economy. Section 4 summarizes the main elements and section 5 concludes.

2. THE THEORETICAL FRAMEWORK

The framework is an open-economy macro model in which prices are flexible and the economy is divided into tradables and non-tradables sectors. The focus economy is the U.S., whose currency fluctuates freely against the euro, but is fixed against the yuan.

The money market is modeled in the familiar manner, with real high-powered money, defined as nominal money supply (H) divided by the price level (P) equal to real money demand (L). The latter consists of transactions demand, as a positive function of real income (y) and asset demand, as a negative function of the interest rate on non-monetary assets (i).

$$H / P = L(y,\ i).\qquad(1)$$

Goods and services equilibrium is given by the following equation:

$$I(i) + T(y,\ y^{*},\ y^{c},\ e^{*},\ e^{c}) - S(y) = -G,\qquad(2)$$

where investment (I) is a negative function of the rate of interest (i); and the trade balance (or current account, (T) worsens with domestic output (y), improves with foreign incomes, and improves with a real depreciation of the dollar. Real exchange rates e^{*} and e^{c}, against the euro and yuan, respectively, are defined as the respective nominal exchange rates adjusted by ratios of foreign to U.S. price indexes. Domestic saving is a positive function of domestic income and G represents the government deficit.

As noted, an important difference between the Eurozone and China is the degree of capital mobility, which is assumed to be high with respect to the former and low with respect to the latter. The dollar-euro relationship is represented by the uncovered interest parity condition,

$$i - i^{*} = \frac{(E^{\text{exp}} - E^{*})}{E^{*}},\qquad(3)$$

where E^{exp} and E^{*} are the expected future spot and the current spot rate between the dollar and the euro, respectively. For present purposes, expectations are assumed to follow an AR process, so that a rise in the current spot rate unambiguously reduces the right-hand side of the equation.

Bilateral balance of payments equilibrium between the U.S. and China is represented by the following expression:

$$T^{c}(y,\ y^{c},\ e^{c}) + K^{c}(i - i^{c}) + R^{c} = 0,\qquad(4)$$

where K^c represents autonomous capital inflows from China in response to an increase in U.S. interest rates or a decline in Chinese interest rates and where R^c represents dollar accumulation by the central bank of China.

As noted above, prices are flexible and price movements involving tradable goods and services may differ from those occurring in non-tradables sectors.   The freedom of domestic firms to raise tradables prices is constrained by foreign competition.   Domestic import-competing firms cannot raise their prices without losing home market share, just as domestic exporting firms cannot raise prices without risking the loss of market share abroad.   Producers of non-tradable goods and services face much more limited pricing constraints.   Equilibrium prices in their markets are determined where domestic production satisfies domestic demand.

The overall price level is defined as follows:

$$P = \lambda p_t + (1-\lambda)p_n = \lambda(E^* \cdot p_t^* + E^c \cdot p_t^c) + (1-\lambda)p_n, \qquad (5)$$

where p_t and p_n are tradables and non-tradables prices, respectively; p_t^* and p_t^c are the euro and yuan prices of tradable imports from the Eurozone and China, respectively; and where λ is the share of tradables in U.S. GDP. With the nominal dollar-yuan rate fixed and assuming that tradables prices in foreign currency are given, the domestic price level will change for two reasons.   First, a change in the dollar-euro rate will change it and, secondly, variations in non-tradables prices will do so as well.

Production costs and thus price pressures are assumed to rise throughout the economy as the output gap shrinks. In the non-tradables sector, this leads to actual price increases. If we assume that the level of potential output is given, then domestic non-tradables prices rise with actual GDP, that is,

Figure 1   Adjustment in a Dual Exchange Rate Regime

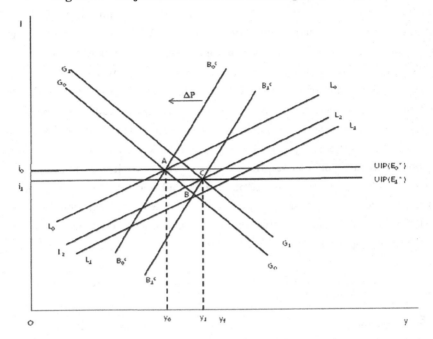

$$p_n = p_n(y). \tag{6}$$

In this model, a large output gap means that the main effect of monetary expansion is on output rather than prices. But as the output gap narrows, increasing portions of a liquidity injection will go into price increases rather than output expansion. In other words, the medium-run aggregate supply curve becomes steeper as the output gap falls. Thus, the coefficient p_{ny} rises as the output gap shrinks, meaning that non-tradables prices rise in a non-linear manner as the economy approaches full employment.

Figure 1 summarizes the effects of an expansionary monetary policy in a dual-rate regime. We focus on monetary policy, because our main interest is in understanding and assessing the Fed's role in the great moderation and its aftermath. The curves in figure 1 represent the money market (LL), goods and services equilibrium (GG), uncovered interest parity between the dollar and the euro (UIP), and the bilateral balance of payments between the U.S. and China (B^cB^c), respectively. The last curve is steeply sloped in order to reflect low capital mobility between the U.S. and China.

A monetary expansion in the U.S. shifts the LL curve to the right. The new LL curve's intersection with the initial GG curve achieves internal balance, but leaves an external disequilibrium with respect to both China and the Eurozone. The rise in U.S. economic activity worsens both current accounts, while the decline in the U.S. interest rate causes both financial accounts to deteriorate as well. The dollar depreciates nominally against the euro, moving the UIP curve down and the GG curve out. The nominal depreciation raises the dollar prices of imports from the Eurozone, tending to switch expenditure to domestic substitutes and strengthening the effectiveness of the monetary expansion in its ability to reduce the output gap and raise employment.

The rise in the dollar prices of imports has a direct effect on the U.S. price level, as shown in equation (5). Further, unless supply conditions in U.S. tradables sectors are infinitely elastic, the demand shift toward U.S. goods and services provokes cost pressures throughout the economy. The effect of any price increase in figure 1 is to shift the LL, GG and B^cB^c curves to the left, thereby tending to weaken the effectiveness of the monetary expansion (Arndt, 2012). This is because it is movements in the real exchange rate that determine the extent of expenditure switching. Against the euro, the dollar's real depreciation declines for any given nominal depreciation as U.S. inflation heats up. Against the yuan, where the nominal rate is fixed, the rise in U.S. prices is equivalent to dollar appreciation. These pressures on domestic prices typically become stronger as the output gap narrows, thereby gradually weakening the efficacy of the monetary expansion. The system approaches monetary neutrality.

In the yuan/dollar market, the central bank of China intervenes to prevent the yuan from appreciating, mopping up excess dollars in the process. This situation is reflected in the figure by the difference between the two B^cB^c curves. Under floating rates, the dollar would depreciate against the yuan and the bilateral payments curve would shift to the right to pass through a point like C. It is not point C, because the GG curve through C does not reflect the yuan appreciation that would occur under floating rates. With the rate fixed, the *autonomous* payments curve does not shift. The B^cB^c curve through point C represents the sum of autonomous and accommodating transactions. The gap between the two curves reflects the extent of Chinese dollar accumulation.[1]

In the "automatic" adjustment mechanism under fixed rates, the Chinese intervention that pulls U.S. money out of circulation weakens the stimulus generated by the initial money expansion. In the present case, however, this does not happen, because the Chinese authorities recycle their intervention dollars by purchasing U.S. Treasury securities from the public. Hence, the Chinese intervention not only annuls the price adjustment mechanism of floating rates by fixing the rate, but having fixed the rate, it short-circuits the adjustment mechanism of fixed-rate systems by sterilization and thus makes the bilateral payments imbalance "permanent."

It is in this sense that China would have to share the blame for the lack of adjustment in the U.S. economy, the persistence of current account imbalances, and the financial and economic upheavals that followed. It is also in this sense that China's exchange-rate policy is a beggar-thy-neighbor policy. For the rest of the world, meanwhile, the fundamental question is how to provide some degree of protection from and defense against risky and disruptive policies in large countries.

As noted earlier, stable foreign prices can be an important source of price moderation in the United States. Here, the size of the Chinese economy and the rapid emergence of China as a low-price supplier of a wide array of consumer goods played a key role. The ready availability of those goods was

---

[1] The rise in U.S. prices discussed above will actually shift the original B^cB^c curve to the left, as indicated by the horizontal arrow. The gap between this curve (not drawn) and the curve through point C represents the extent of intervention by the Chinese authorities. It also reflects the magnitude of the U.S. autonomous payments deficit with China.

due in part to the wide gap between Chinese production and domestic absorption, a gap which has sometimes been described as a savings glut. When Chinese export prices are stable and the yuan is fixed to the dollar, equation (5) tells us that the main sources of price inflation are reduced to dollar depreciation against the euro and price inflation in the Eurozone, on the one hand, and inflation in non-tradables in the U.S., on the other hand.

3. THE REAL EXCHANGE RATE IN A FULLY EMPLOYED ECONOMY

When the domestic output gap is large and the monetary expansion raises the demand for goods and services, the derived increase in demand for labor and other factors of production can be easily satisfied by drawing on unemployed resources. Any pressures on wages and other factor costs should thus be moderate. When the economy operates at high levels of employment, on the other hand, a rise in demand for non-tradables can only be satisfied by drawing productive resources away from tradables industries. A sustained rise in the demand for non-tradables, such as that seen in the years preceding the financial crisis, may be expected to raise wages and other factor prices, not only in non-tradables sectors but throughout the economy.

Since non-tradables producers face little or no foreign competition, they may pass on such cost increases to higher prices. Tradables producers, on the other hand, are limited by foreign competition in their ability to pass cost increases through to prices. Rising costs in the face of pricing constraints squeeze profits, forcing producers to limit production in both exportables and import-competing industries. Some firms deal with these pressures through offshore sourcing or even offshore production, while less competitive or agile firms leave the industry. Both types of actions tend to free up productive resources for transfer into non-tradables sectors.

Figure 2 provides a simple representation of the problem. The relative price of tradables is measured vertically as the ratio $p = p_t / p_n$, while the right

184   Sven W. Arndt

Figure 2   Policy Trade-Offs in a Two Sector Economy

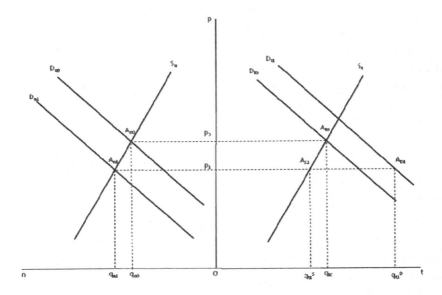

and left panels represent demand/supply equilibrium in tradables and non-tradables sectors, respectively. Note the important assumption embedded in the construction of tradables prices, namely, that the relative price between exports and imports — the terms of trade — remains constant.[2]

In the right panel, domestic demand falls with a rise in the relative price of tradables, while domestic supply rises. Since the price of non-tradables is in the denominator of the price ratio, the slopes of the two curves are reversed in the left panel in order to allow the demand for non-tradables to fall when the relative price of non-tradables rises and supply to rise. The horizontal axis measures quantity transactions in the two markets, respectively.

The figure represents a situation in which actual output is at or very near the full-employment level in this two-sector economy. Output combinations

---

[2] Under the circumstances prevailing in that period, we would expect U.S. export prices to rise relative to import prices, implying an improvement in the country's terms of trade.

depicted in the figure, therefore, represent combinations that lie on or near the economy's production possibility curve (not drawn). Hence, any increase of output in one sector must be accompanied by a decline in the other sector. Assume that points A_{n0} and A_{t0} at relative price p_0 represent an initial equilibrium. At the outset, therefore, domestic production of tradables is assumed to be equal to domestic absorption, so that the country's current account is in balance, with exports equal to imports.

Now suppose that a monetary expansion causes both demand curves in figure 2 to shift out. As discussed in the previous section, there will be upward pressure on both tradables and non-tradables prices, with the latter expected to be larger. This is shown in the figure as a decline in the relative price to p_1, at which the non-tradables market once again clears. The change in p — a real appreciation — must be large enough to return the non-tradables sector to equilibrium. Output has risen by drawing productive resources from tradables, where output has declined. In addition, there is now a current account deficit, equal to the gap between points A_{s1} and A_{D1}. This deficit is the result not only of the rise in demand for tradables, but also of the decline in their production in the U.S.

The figure reflects stylized facts that were widely noted and discussed, namely, that the U.S. current account deficit was large, was growing larger, and was seemingly permanent, while the dollar's international value remained surprisingly "strong." This combination of rising trade imbalance and strong or appreciating currency is critically important to the present argument. As noted, a rise in the price of non-tradables relative to tradables represents dollar appreciation in real terms. Conventional wisdom typically associates trade deficits with weak or weakening currency values. But in this context, the function of the real appreciation is to allow resources to be moved into non-tradables production, while bridging the resulting shortfall of domestic tradables output by reducing exports and raising imports.

At the time, however, the international strength of the U.S. currency was widely attributed to the dollar's role as reserve currency and to the importance of U.S. assets as "safe haven" investments. That argument undoubtedly has merit, but when dollar strength is accompanied by a deteriorating trade balance, that combination should raise alarm bells about resource pressures and overheating of the economy. It should not be automatically treated as benign.

4. PULLING THE PIECES TOGETHER

The highlights and essential elements of this paper's take on the economic ups and downs of the past two decades may be summarized as follows.

Adjustment in payments between the U.S. and the Eurozone went largely as expected under a floating rate system. Dollar depreciation made expansionary monetary policy more effective initially, along the lines taught in the standard textbook and as understood by policy makers around the globe. Unlike the textbook case, however, gradual closure of the output gap shifted more of the energy of monetary stimulation onto prices. Any rise in domestic tradables costs and prices due to expenditure switching diminishes the benefits of nominal dollar depreciation by reducing the extent of real depreciation. If the dollar-yuan rate had also been flexible, the tightening of resource constraints would have come faster and would have been more apparent. That would have put greater pressure on prices and might have been enough to alert the authorities to the dangers of overheating.

By fixing its currency to the dollar, China eliminated the payments adjustment mechanism that is typically associated with floating rates. The main consequence was that imports from China remained cheap in terms of dollars and those imports contained huge quantities of consumer goods in wide use among U.S. households. Having incapacitated the exchange rate channel as an avenue for external adjustment, the Chinese authorities then blocked the adjustment mechanism under fixed rate systems by sterilizing the contractionary effects of the money supply reduction brought about by the exchange market intervention.

The ready availability of imported consumer products spelled trouble for

U.S. tradables producers whose freedom to raise prices was limited. With the stimulus of an easy-money policy, U.S. demand continued to rise, the output gap shrank and U.S. GDP moved beyond what was then believed to be full employment (natural rate) output without significant pressures in popular price indexes. At these high levels of economic activity, the rising demand for non-tradables could not be met without drawing labor and other productive resources away from tradables. Pressures on wages and factor prices generally would be expected to rise throughout the economy in such circumstances. These cost increases represent additional threats to U.S. international competitiveness. Manufacturing and other U.S. tradables industries were shrinking and the current account was deteriorating.

The puzzle is why these developments failed to alarm U.S. policy makers? A possible answer may lie in the tendency among policy makers to interpret inflation in housing as pure asset inflation. A pure asset price bubble's principal direct effect is to raise wealth, some of which will eventually affect demand for goods and services. During the housing boom, however, the demand for new housing and new commercial property was in the first instance a demand for durable goods that needed to be produced and producing them requires inputs of labor, capital and other productive resources. In a high-employment economy such a sustained surge in demand is bound to be inflationary. This rise in non-tradables prices, together with a strong dollar, a shrinking U.S. tradables sector and a growing current account deficit should have provoked a better policy response than it did.

5. CONCLUDING REMARKS

The argument made in this paper is summarized in the preceding section. It seeks to understand macroeconomic developments in the U.S. economy since the early nineties. The mixed exchange rate regime makes a key contribution to the ultimate outcome, but other factors also play a role. China's exchange market intervention prevents the U.S. from enjoying a key benefit of floating rates, namely, timely adjustment of payments imbalances. Having fixed the rate, China again prevents normal adjustment patters from taking place by recycling intervention dollars back into the U.S. and thus effectively sterilizing the contractionary effects of the pegging operation. The large size of the Chinese economy and its ability to supply a wide range of products at stable prices is an important source of moderation in world tradables prices.

Distinction between tradables and non-tradables sectors helps in understanding these developments.   Variations in the relative price of tradables to non-tradables play a key role in shifting labor, capital and other productive resources between the two sectors.   As the U.S. expansion matures, relative inflation in non-tradables allows production in that sector to expand at the expense of tradables.   It is a key source of the dollar's continued strength and of the large U.S. current account deficit.

Housing is a major component of the non-tradables sector, not so much in the materials that go into dwellings and other structures, but in terms of labor and other factors of production needed to produce them.   Rapid inflation in housing prices and construction costs during the real estate bubble had major effects on the movement of relative prices in the U.S. economy and thus on the sectoral allocation of productive resources.   Hence, it is inappropriate to view this type of inflation as inconsequential for the real economy.

REFERENCES

Arndt, S. W., "Adjustment in an Open Economy with Two Exchange-Rate Regimes," *Journal of Economic Asymmetries*, 8(2), December 2011, pp. 11-22.

_____, "Stabilization Policy in an Economy with Two Exchange Rate Regimes," *Global Economy Journal*, 12(2), June 2012.

Fischer, S., "Exchange Rate Regimes: Is the Bipolar View Correct?," *Journal of Economic Perspectives*, 15(2), Spring 2001, pp. 3-24.

IMF, "De Facto Classification of Exchange Rate Regimes and Monetary Policy Frameworks," April 2008.

Chapter 21

The "Great Moderation" in a Dual Exchange Rate Regime[*]

Sven W. Arndt

Abstract

In the early nineties, the U.S. economy was emerging from a brief slump, monetary policy was easy, and economic activity recovered quickly during the decade, with GDP eventually reaching and then passing the consensus full employment level. Yet aggregate inflation remained surprisingly subdued. This moderation in prices at the aggregate level persuaded policy makers to allow the easy-money stance to continue in spite of the presence of inflation in non-tradables and in housing and construction in particular. This paper uses a flex-price, mixed-exchange rate model to examine some of the major contributing factors to economic developments in the two-decade period that ended in the financial meltdown and the great recession. It argues that Chinese exchange rate manipulation and China's preference for holding dollar reserves were important contributing factors. On the U.S. side, failure to understand the importance of differential inflation patterns in tradables and non-tradables sectors, and especially failure to see inflation in housing and construction as goods rather than asset inflation, allowed monetary expansion to last much longer than it should have.

JEL CLASSIFICATION: E58, F32, F41

KEYWORDS: Open-economy macro; Mixed exchange reates; Non-tradables; Asset inflation

[*]This is an edited version of the 2012 Presidential Address given at the annual meeeting of the International Trade and Finance Association in Pisa, Italy in May. I am grateful to the Association and the University of Pisa for giving me this opportunity and for the great discussion that followed my presentation. I am also indebted to Hao Tang and Jing Wen for competent research assistance.

1. Introduction

For two decades or more, the United States has operated within a dual exchange rate regime consisting of floating rates with the majority of its trading partners and a fixed rate with the Chinese yuan and a handful of other currencies. This *de facto* regime contrasts sharply with the *de jure* IMF classification of the U.S. as an independent floater.[1] This classification is an accurate description of U.S. policy and practice, because the People's Bank of China (PBoC) unilaterally manipulates movements in the bilateral exchange rate. This reality has important implications for macro adjustment and stability in the U.S. economy.

It is well-known that the effectiveness of monetary and fiscal policies depends on the nature of the exchange rate regime. But what is known about this issue has generally been explored in terms of models in which "the" exchange rate is either fixed or floating, rather than one in which both regimes exist side by side. The issue of policy efficacy in a dual-rate regime has been explored in two recent papers, the first examining the implications of China's fixing in a short-run, sticky-price Mundell-Fleming model (Arndt, 2010), and the second in a medium-run, flex-price model (Arndt, 2011).

The present discussion uses the flex-price model to explore the extent to which these exchange rate arrangements may have contributed to recent developments from the "great moderation" to the financial melt-down and the "great recession." A plausible case can be made that the dual exchange rate regime played an important role in shaping those developments, but a full explanation depends on the presence of other factors as well, including the sectoral structure of the U.S. economy, the nature of foreign competition, and policy makers' interpretations of and reactions to key economic indicators.

The paper proceeds as follows. Section 2 applies the model to the *de jure* case in which the dollar floats against both the euro and the yuan. The results provide a convenient benchmark against which to compare the dual rate regime in Section 3. Section 4 introduces and examines additional contributing factors. Section 5 concludes.

2. Fully Floating Rates Everywhere

In this flex-price version of the model there are three countries: the United States and trading partners China and the Eurozone. Capital mobility is assumed to be high between the U.S. and Europe, but low between the U.S. and China. The main features of the model are captured by equilibrium conditions for the goods

---

[1] See IMF (2008). See also Frankel and Wei (2007) and Levy-Yeyati and Sturzenegger (2005).

Global Economy Journal, Vol. 12 [2012], Iss. 4, Art. 1

and services sector, for the money market, and for the two bilateral payments balances.

The Basic Model

The real economy (henceforth the "goods market") is described by the GG equation:

$$I(r^{exp}) + T(y, y^*, y^c, e^*, e^c) - S(y) = - G, \tag{1}$$

where real investment expenditure (I) depends negatively on the expected real interest rate $r^{exp} = i - \pi^{exp}$, defined as the difference between the nominal rate (i) and the expected inflation rate. The overall trade balance or current account (T) is related negatively to real home GDP (y) and positively to real GDP in the Eurozone (y*) and China (y^c), and positively related to the dollar's real exchange rates with the euro (e*) and yuan (e^c). The real exchange rate is defined as $e^i = E^i.P^i/P$, where E^i represents the respective bilateral nominal exchange rates, P^i the respective foreign price indexes, and P the equivalent U.S. price index.

The money market is represented by a standard liquidity-preference function (LL):

$$H/P = L(y, i), \tag{2}$$

where H is high-powered money and real money demand (L) is positively related to income and negatively to the nominal interest rate on non-monetary assets (i).

Under floating rates, the two bilateral current account balances are defined as follows:

$$T^*(y, y^*, e^*) + K^*(i, i^*) = 0 \text{ and} \tag{3}$$
$$T^c(y, y^c, e^c) + K^c(i, i^c) = 0, \tag{4}$$

where K^i represents capital flows into the U.S. which rise with i and fall with foreign interest rates.

Price flexibility is represented by a positively sloped "aggregate supply" curve,

$$P = P(y/y^f), \tag{5}$$

where y^f is the natural-rate or NAIRU level of domestic real GDP.

The last equation plays an important role in the cyclical adjustment process. When the output gap is large and/or prices are sticky, as in the short-run Mundell-Fleming model (Arndt, 2011), output responds to aggregate demand and can be increased without serious price repercussions. As the gap between actual and potential (or NAIRU) GDP shrinks, however, additional output can be obtained only at increasing cost. Hence, the trade-off between prices and output (P$_y$) worsens as resource utilization pushes against the limits of the economy's capacity.

Figure 1 presents a pictorial view of the *de jure* U.S. exchange rate regime of floating rates with all trading partners. It is the regime that U.S. policy makers

2

Arndt: Price Moderation and Dual Exchange Rates

prefer, as evidenced by their continuing pressure on China to allow the yuan to float. Equations (1), (2), (3), and (4) are represented in the figure by curves GG, LL, B*B*, and B^cB^c, respectively. The B*B* curve has a relatively flat slope, reflecting the assumption of high capital mobility between the U.S. and the Eurozone. The steeper balance of payments function for China represents low capital mobility.

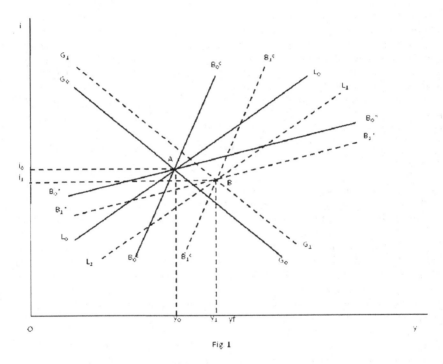

Fig. 1

A monetary expansion shifts the LL curve out in Figure 1. Restoration of "internal" balance requires a rise in income and decline in the interest rate, given at the intersection of the new L_1L_1 curve with the original G_0G_0 curve. As U.S. GDP rises, imports rise and the trade balance deteriorates with respect to both countries. As interest rates fall, capital outflows cause both financial accounts to deteriorate, causing the dollar to depreciate against both currencies. Depreciation shifts the GG, B*B*, and B^cB^c curves out and to the right, giving monetary policy the "turbo" charge celebrated in the open-economy literature.

In this model, inflation is stoked by currency depreciation and by internal cost pressures resulting from a shrinking output gap. An increase in the price

3

Global Economy Journal, Vol. 12 [2012], Iss. 4, Art. 1

level reduces the real money supply and thus would shift the L_1L_1 curve to the left. It would also shift the G_1G_1 curve and the $B_1^*B_1^*$ and $B_1^cB_1^c$ curves to the left. Clearly, domestic inflation reduces the real depreciation associated with a given nominal depreciation. As inflation pushes the relevant curves inward, the effectiveness of a given monetary injection is reduced. The efficacy of monetary policy varies with the economy's position relative to full employment.

Under full floating, therefore, an easy-money policy at the beginning of the period following the short recession of the early nineties would have been very effective in raising economic activity and reducing unemployment, because the policy-induced depreciation of the dollar against all currencies, including the yuan, would have given the policy an extra boost. As the period progressed and the U.S. economy recovered, continued monetary laxity would have started to raise prices as the system approached capacity levels. Rising costs and prices in the U.S. would more and more have negated the benefits of easy-money policy itself and of nominal dollar depreciation. There would also have been some deterioration of the U.S. current account balance.

In the discussion thus far, policy makers have been assumed to target monetary aggregates. In the modern era, however, many central banks have shifted to interest-rate and inflation targeting. Such a policy regime may be represented in Figure 1 by a horizontal LL curve, with the federal funds rate pegged and thus exogenous and money supply endogenous. A monetary expansion then means reduction in the target interest rate, which shifts the LL curve down and causes output and employment to expand. As before, rising prices at high levels of employment diminish the effectiveness of the low-interest policy by reducing the real value of a given nominal quantity of money, but the resulting upward pressure on market interest rates forces the central bank to continually raise the nominal quantity of money.

It may be assumed that the presence of domestic inflation and nominal dollar depreciation would have been taken by policy makers as important signs of an overheating economy. Certainly, a central bank following a Taylor-Rule policy with an inflation target would be compelled to shift to a restrictive policy stance by virtue of both the rising inflation and the shrinking output gap. If such a central bank had nominal exchange-rate stability as an additional target, then the ongoing depreciation of the currency would have raised an additional warning flag.

3. China Fixes; the Euro Floats

The foregoing provides a scenario for the hypothetical case of a U.S. exchange rate regime that matches the IMF's *de jure* classification. In Figure 2, a suitably amended version of the model is used to examine adjustment under the

4

Arndt: Price Moderation and Dual Exchange Rates

arrangements that were actually in place during the period. All previous equations continue to hold, except that equation (4) is now rewritten to take account of Chinese foreign exchange intervention.

$$T^c(y, y^c, e^c) + K^c (i, i^c) + R^c = 0,$$ (4a)

where R^c stands for dollar reserves held by the central bank of China.

As before, a U.S. monetary expansion shifts out the L_0L_0 curve. While internal balance once again moves to the point where the new LL curve intersects the initial G_0G_0 curve, the two balances of payments are once again in deficit there. The dollar again depreciates, but only against the euro, causing the G_0G_0 and $B_0^*B_0^*$ curves to shift to the right and tending to strengthen the effectiveness of the monetary expansion. Note that the right-ward shift of the GG curve is unambiguously smaller than before, indicating that fixing the yuan reduces the

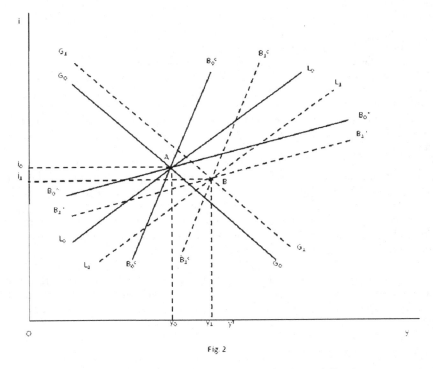

Fig. 2

efficacy of monetary stimulus relative to the case of universal floating.

With the dollar-yuan rate fixed, the bilateral current account deficit between the U.S. and the People's Republic persists and the central bank of China is obliged to intervene and mop up the excess of dollars looking for yuan. The

5

Global Economy Journal, Vol. 12 [2012], Iss. 4, Art. 1

dashed B^cB^c curve represents *overall* equilibrium in the balance of payments with China, that is, balance in the sum of autonomous and official reserve transactions. The Chinese central bank's intervention pulls dollars out of circulation and thus has the effect of taking some liquidity back out of the system and undermining the ability of monetary policy to narrow the output gap.

That, at least, would be the case under a standard fixed-rate system in which the home central bank did the intervening. In the present case, however, the foreign central bank uses intervention dollars to purchase U.S. Treasury securities in the open market and thereby recycles lost liquidity back into the system. In other words, China's intervention prevents the fixed-rate adjustment mechanism from working properly and makes the bilateral payments deficit "permanent."[2]

Up to this point, China's recycling has helped make the Fed's stimulus stick.   As before, however, price pressures will develop as the economy's expansion matures. One source of price inflation is depreciation of the dollar against the euro and the consequent rise in prices of imports from the Eurozone. Another comes from domestic cost pressures as the U.S. output gap declines. A domestic price increase shifts the LL, GG and external-balance curves left, reducing the effectiveness of the easy-money policy.   Note that although the nominal dollar-yuan rate is fixed, price inflation in the U.S. causes the dollar to *appreciate* against the yuan in real terms.

4. Additional Considerations

The argument thus far suggests that Chinese exchange-rate policies made a material difference to economic developments during the period under review. Other factors, however, also played an important role.

Prices in a Globalized Economy

In the early part of the period, overall price pressures in the U.S. were astoundingly moderate. They were an important feature of what became known as the "great moderation."   An important source of price moderation was the yuan-dollar peg. But even with floating rates – such as the euro-dollar rate, the extent of pass-through can be quite low, especially in the United States, where many of the country's imports are priced in dollars. Price moderation was further supported by the ability of China's large economy to supply vast quantities of a broad range of products at stable prices.

---

[2] The causes of global trade imbalances have been a major item on economists' and policy makers' research agendas. For samples from a fairly extensive literature, see Bernanke (2005), Obstfeld and Rogoff (2009), Borio (2011) and Andolfatto (2012).

As the U.S. expansion matured, however, the output gap fell and employment reached and then surpassed natural-rate levels. In our model, wages, other factor prices and costs generally begin to rise as actual output approaches full employment, with the rate of price increase itself rising steadily. Industries producing tradables are limited by foreign competition in their ability to pass cost increases through to higher prices. The current account deteriorates. In industries producing non-tradable goods and services, including health care, education, residential structures, commercial property and construction services, international trade is a less potent source of price moderation. One channel, however, along which trade may provide some cost moderation is through stability in prices of tradable parts and components used in the production of non-tradable goods and services.

In general, however, non-tradables firms are able to pass cost increases through to higher prices. As they seek to attract workers, capital and other productive resources in a high-employment economy, those resources can only come from the tradables sectors. This competition for factors of production spreads wage and cost inflation through the whole economy. Thus, output expansion in non-tradables comes increasingly at the expense of tradables production.

These developments – price inflation in non-tradables, a shrinking tradables sector, rising offshore sourcing and production, and a worsening current account – were not properly understood at the time. The shrinkage of jobs in U.S. manufacturing and in other tradables, for example, was blamed on unfair competition, especially by China. While this accusation was not entirely incorrect, it was too simplistic.

Stock-Flow Adjustment in Asset Markets

Two developments occurred toward the middle and end of the period, which are not typically covered in open-economy macro analysis. They were the asset price booms of the dot.com era in the middle of the period and the real estate boom of the housing bubble toward the end of the period. Rapid increases in the value of financial or real assets create capital gains, which wealth owners may decide to cash in so as to increase consumption expenditures. When they do so, governments collect capital gains taxes, which they often promptly spend on increased outlays. During the dot.com years, for example, many states ran unexpected budget surpluses and ended up committing some of these windfall gains to long-run expenditure programs such as reducing class-room size and hiring teachers.

The model represented in Figure 2, is easily adapted to include wealth effects. A wealth-driven rise in private and public expenditures shifts the GG

Global Economy Journal, Vol. 12 [2012], Iss. 4, Art. 1

curve to the right, thereby adding to the expansionary forces pushing the economy forward. In the dot.com boom, wealth owners cashed in corporate shares; in the housing boom, they cashed in home equity in order to finance additional expenditures on goods and services. With wealth increasing rapidly, there was little need to "save," that is, withhold current income from current consumption. Indeed, by the end of the period, the household saving rate in the U.S. had dropped close to zero. In retrospect it would seem that these developments should have raised eyebrows among policy makers, but there would have been little in the macro policy literature to guide them.

There was a debate about whether so-called asset price bubbles should be of concern to policy makers. In thinking about this question, it is helpful to recall the familiar stock-flow distinction of economic analysis. At any point in time, there exists a stock of assets, be it corporate shares, government bonds or residential property. An increase in demand for *existing* stocks simply raises prices, increasing wealth in the manner discussed above. Over time, however, stocks are increased by new supply flowing into the system. As governments fund new expenditures by issuing debt, or corporations fund new investment by issuing equity, stocks of securities rise. In the case of residential and other types of property, construction of new houses, office buildings and factories adds to the existing real stock.

In these examples, the flow supply of financial instruments funds new expenditures of one type or another, injecting additional demand for productive resources into the system. In a high-employment economy, additions to overall demand for labor and capital cannot fail to raise wages and production costs throughout the economy. For policy makers, therefore, the trick is to distinguish the part that is pure asset inflation from the part that raises aggregate demand for productive resources. In this respect, U.S. policy makers failed rather significantly, although it must be said in fairness that there was not much to guide them in the macro policy literature.

Do Expectations Matter?

Expectations clearly played a powerful role throughout the period, but especially during the go-go years of the dot.com and housing booms. In models of the present type, expectations have received critical attention in the context of Lucas-type expectations-augmented aggregate supply curves and in covered and uncovered interest-arbitrage in foreign exchange markets. In the period in question, however, price expectations were far more complex than is typically assumed in those applications. One degree of complexity arises readily from the separation of tradable and non-tradable goods and services, which allows markets to form distinct expectations about prices in the two respective sectors. In the period under review, a plausible mix of expectations would have been low inflation in tradables and high inflation in non-tradables. While the deflator in equation (2) would probably be some weighted average of the two prices, other decision variables might be deflated by the relevant sectoral price instead.

Consider, for example, one specific possibility in equation (1). For given expected returns on investment, the Fed's easy-money policy moves the system down along the GG curve, as we have seen. A rise in expected returns on investment shifts the curve out. A housing bubble, for instance, in which investors expect higher future prices, raises the demand for existing as well as new housing. The demand for new housing shifts GG out, adding to the overall demand boom. In general, the combination of easy credit and low interest rates, on the one hand, and expectations of rapidly rising equity values or house prices go a long way to explaining the unprecedented degree of leveraging that occurred at all levels of the economy. Of course, when the bubble collapses, and prices fall and are expected to fall further, the GG curve contracts, suggesting again that an asset-price boom can have non-trivial implications for the real economy.

5. Concluding Remarks

In the period of the "great moderation," both tradables and non-tradables prices rose, but inflation in the former was mild for the reasons discussed in the preceding sections. During the high-employment stages of the epoch, the *relative* price of non-tradables would be expected to rise in order to facilitate the inter-sectoral transfer of productive resources.

The combination of inflation in non-tradables prices, steadily worsening current account deficits, increased offshore sourcing and production, and job losses in many tradables industries was widely observed by policy makers, media, and market analysts, but the possible causal linkage to U.S. monetary policy never became a compelling consideration. The housing bubble, widely interpreted as asset inflation, was expected to deflate on its own without significant consequences for the rest of the economy.

Overall, therefore, it seems reasonable to assign some of the blame for those two momentous decades to China's exchange-rate manipulation. But it is clear, as well, that the easy-money policy lasted much too long and that U.S. policy makers made flawed judgments in their interpretation of key economic indicators.

This raises a question reminiscent of the old debate about rules vs. discretion in central bank policy making. If the Fed was following a Taylor Rule, a yellow light would have told it to slow down when actual output reached the consensus full employment level. Perhaps the reality of the great price moderation was enough to allow officials to discount the relevance of the warning signal,

Global Economy Journal, Vol. 12 [2012], Iss. 4, Art. 1

which in itself raises questions about the extent to which the two right-hand-side variables in the Rule are truly independent. A second question arises over the usefulness of an aggregate inflation measure as the primary or sole indicator of overheating. In an open economy with significant links to global markets more attention might have to be paid to inflation in non-tradables and to designing better measures of economy-wide cost pressures.

References

Andolfatto, D. (2012), "Liquidity Shocks, Real Interest Rates, and Global Imbalances, " Federal Reserve Bank of St. Louis <u>Review</u>, 94 (3), (May/June).

Arndt, S. W. (2011), "Adjustment in an Open Economy with Two Exchange-Rate Regimes," <u>Journal of Economic Asymmetries</u>, 8, No. 2 (December).

_____(2012), "Stabilization Policy in an Economy with Two Exchange Rate Regimes," <u>Global Economy Journal</u>, 12, No. 2 (June).

Bernanke, B. (2005), "The Global Saving Glut and the U.S. Current Account Deficit," (March).

Borio, C. (2011), "Rediscovering the macroeconomic roots of financial stability policy: journey, challenges and a way forward," BIS Working Papers, No. 354 (September).

Frankel, J.A. and S.-J. Wei (2007), "Assessing China's Exchange Rate Regime," NBER Working Paper No. 13100.

IMF (2008), "De Facto Classification of Exchange Rate Regimes and Monetary Policy Frameworks," (April).

Levy-Yeyati, E. and F. Sturzenegger (2005), "Classifying Exchange Rate Regimes: Deeds vs. Words," <u>European Economic Review</u>, 49 (6), (August).

Obstfeld, M. and Rogoff, K. (2009), "Global Imbalances and the Financial Crisis: Products of Common Causes," (November).

Index

A

Adjustment speeds 208, 216, 324
Agglomeration 86
Aggregated reciprocal demand curves 62–66
Alternative trade policies 51, 65
Amended macro model 185
ASEAN economic integration 111
Asset market adjustment 324
Assignment principle 216, 217, 237
Association of Southeast Asian Nations (ASEAN)
    and EU and NAFTA 111
    cross-border production sharing 113
    open regionalism 112

B

Balance of payments
    Canada 243
    curve 143, 186, 187, 190
    leads and lags 244
    sustained U.S. imbalance 309
    target 218
Balance of trade — see trade balance

C

Capital flows
    debt and equity 209–211
    trade-related 244
    non-linear estimation 247

Capital mobility 178, 188, 277, 304
    (see chapters 17–21)
China
    competitiveness 96
    exchange-rate policy 282, 310, 324
    (see chapters 17–21)
Control variables 207
Criterion function 208
Cross-border market integration 115
Cross-border production networks — see production networks and production sharing
Customs union 49
    aggregated reciprocal demand curves 62
    effect on non-members 63
    four-country model 60
    rival customs unions 67
    terms-of-trade effects 49, 59

D

Deeper economic integration 87, 98, 103, 112
Direct export-import links 180, 266
Distortions 41, 98
    domestic 71
    free trade 73
    non-tradables sector 72, 78
    specialization in the wrong direction 77
    tradables sector 72, 75
Distributed lag functions 243

Diversity
    OCA criterion 254, 257
Domestic monopoly 37
Dynamic policy model 220

E

Equity capital flows 211, 213
European model 259
Exchange rates 151, 157, 242, 261, 288
    interest arbitrage 247, 248
    fixed and floating 276, 278, 290, 292, 296
    fixed vs. floating 108, 188, 190, 193, 243, 276
    real 302, 305, 311, 313
Exchange-rate protectionism 29
Exchange-rate regime
    de facto 288
    de jure 288
    flexible-price 288, 302, 318
    mixed 278, 290, 296
    sticky-price 276
Expectations
    profit 211
Export promotion 27–28
External balance 208, 210
Externalities 42, 71

F

Factor prices 254
Factor proportions model 84
Fiscal policy 214, 215, 278, 281, 283, 291, 294, 295
Foreign direct investment 85, 106
Fragmentation — see also production sharing and production networks
    export industry 113, 124
    foreign direct investment 85, 106
    import industry 83, 91, 98, 102
    open regionalism 112
    pass-through 184
    rules of origin 125
    scale economies 117
    terms of trade 104

three-country model 130
trade diversion 128
trade regime 123–124

G

General equilibrium model 22, 91
Globalization 91
Gravity model 85

H

Heterogeneous firms 197–203
    firm characteristics 198
    fragmentation 201
    scale economies 199
Horizontal intra-industry trade 30, 31
Housing bubble 303, 313, 326
Hub-and-spoke trade 86

I

Import protection 22
Import industry
    fragmentation 91
    impulse response functions 165
Inflation targeting 321
Interdependence 88
Interest arbitrage 246–247
Internal balance 208, 210
Inter-temporal policy adjustment 222
Intra-firm trade 83
Intra-industry trade 31, 34
    horizontal 84
    vertical 30, 179, 180
Intra-product specialization 91, 102

J

Jobs
    fragmentation 87
Joint production 104–105

L

Lag structure 223
Large country 92
Leads and lags 244
Liquidity recycling 323

M

Maastricht Treaty 259
Marshall-Lerner condition 187
Monetary accommodation 214
Monetary policy 214, 218, 235, 277, 280, 282, 290, 297, 306
Monetary union 227, 233, 237
    Members' internal/external balance 228
    OCA criteria 258
Monopolistic competition 200
Monopoly 71
Multinational companies (MNC) 86, 197–203

N

North American Free Trade Agreement (NAFTA) 154
National fiscal policies 229
Non-linear estimation 247
Non-tariff policies 25
Non-tradables 72, 78, 302–303, 305, 324

O

Open-economy macro modeling — see chapters 18–21
Open regionalism 112
Optimum Currency Areas (OCA) 258
Output 93, 306, 319
Overshooting 224

P

Pareto optimality 71–72
Pass-through 267
Permanent current account deficit 309
Preferential Trade Areas (PTA) 43, 63, 99
Price expectations 325
Product differentiation 30, 32
Production networks 137–143, 186–187
Production sharing 98, 104, 123, 125, 128, 130, 150–162, 184, 187, 190, 298
Profit expectations 211

R

Real exchange rate 311, 313
Real vs. financial integration 254–257
Regional currency arrangements 253–273
Regional integration 87
Relative factor prices 93
Rival customs unions 67
Rules of origin 125

S

Scale economies 32, 86, 117, 199
Service links 83
Specialization
    wrong direction 77
Speculative capital flows 242, 244
State variables 207
Sticky prices 276
Structural asymmetries 254

T

Target weighting function 221
Tariffs
    factor prices 24
Terms of trade 49, 59, 64, 91, 93, 104
Time
    as a target variable 220
    discounting function 220–221
    efficiency units 220
    series analysis 153
Tradables prices 323–324
Trade balance
    econometrics 152
    expectations 182–184
Trade balances
    double in mixed-rate regimes 277, 289, 319
Trade diversion 102
Trade-related capital flows 243
Transmission 297
Trend exchange rate 249

U

Uncovered interest parity (UIP) 304
U.S. current account deficit 284

U.S./Mexico trade
    fragmentation 150f
    heterogeneous firms 202
    motor vehicle trade 162
U.S. policy mistakes 314

V

Value-added chain 83

Value vs. value-added 105
VEC estimation 157
Vertical intra-industry trade 31, 34,
    179–180

W

Wealth effect 233, 236

Printed in the United States
By Bookmasters